Confederate Prisoners
at Fort Delaware

Confederate Prisoners at Fort Delaware

The Legend of Mistreatment Reexamined

Joel D. Citron

McFarland & Company, Inc., Publishers
Jefferson, North Carolina

LIBRARY OF CONGRESS CATALOGUING-IN-PUBLICATION DATA

Names: Citron, Joel D., 1941–2017 author.
Title: Confederate prisoners at Fort Delaware : the legend
of mistreatment reexamined / Joel D. Citron.
Description: Jefferson, North Carolina : McFarland & Company, Inc.,
Publishers, 2018. | Includes bibliographical references and index.
Identifiers: LCCN 2017056468 | ISBN 9781476669229 (softcover : acid free paper) ∞
Subjects: LCSH: Fort Delaware (Del.) | United States—History—Civil War,
1861–1865—Prisoners and prisons. | Prisoners of war—Delaware—Fort
Delaware—History—19th century. | Prisoners of war—Delaware—Fort
Delaware—Social conditions—19th century.
Classification: LCC E616.D3 C56 2018 | DDC 975.1/1—dc23
LC record available at https://lccn.loc.gov/2017056468

BRITISH LIBRARY CATALOGUING DATA ARE AVAILABLE

ISBN (print) 978-1-4766-6922-9
ISBN (ebook) 978-1-4766-2896-7

© 2018 Daniel Citron. All rights reserved

*No part of this book may be reproduced or transmitted in any form
or by any means, electronic or mechanical, including photocopying
or recording, or by any information storage and retrieval system,
without permission in writing from the publisher.*

The front cover image of prisoner barracks and hospital was
drawn by Pvt. Max Neugas, 1st South Carolina Regiment, captured
at Gettysburg, and is dated March 4, 1864 (Fort Delaware Society)

Printed in the United States of America

*McFarland & Company, Inc., Publishers
Box 611, Jefferson, North Carolina 28640
www.mcfarlandpub.com*

Acknowledgments

I have been a volunteer at Fort Delaware State Park for more than a decade. During that time, I have of course spoken with many of the paid staff and volunteers, which has led to many interesting insights and items about the Fort and the people who were present there during the Civil War. In particular I want to thank the late George Contant, who provided me with much pertinent information, such as the Civil War medical staff on the island.

A special thanks to my son, Daniel Citron, who started as a volunteer at Fort Delaware State Park and eventually became the full time Historic Site Manager, for his help and encouragement in this study. He also provided much of the information that the Park had in its files about the Civil War era, and also did some offsite research for me.

The folks at the National Archives were uniformly helpful when I was there, but I especially want to thank (now retired) Archivist John Vandereedt and Ms. Ann Cummings and her staff for helping find and catalog the Commissary records for Fort Delaware (see Chapter 4 for more details), which was a type of prison camp record that had not been known or studied before this time.

The records of the Fort Delaware Society have been collected over the past 60–plus years, and contain many documents not found collectively in any other place. Ms. Martha Bennett, Mr. Hugh Simmons, and Mr. Brendan Mackie were especially helpful in my getting access to, and interpreting, these records and Figures.

Last, but certainly not least, I want to thank my wife Barbara for her support and assistance in this project. Not only did she journey with me to many of the places where the research was done, helping me to document many of the records found, but she also put up with many late dinners, and other inconveniences, in my completing this book.

Table of Contents

Acknowledgments	v
List of Abbreviations	viii
Preface	1
1. Topography and Weather	5
2. Command Structure, Personnel and Administration	11
3. Prison Camp Administration and Security	19
4. The Food Ration	39
5. The Prison Fund	57
6. Shelter and Clothing	72
7. Water Supply and Sanitation	82
8. Outside Help	94
9. Medical Care	105
10. Death Rates: The Final Arbiter	138
11. Life on Pea Patch Island	154
12. Freedom!	175
13. Conclusions	184
Epilogue	198
Appendix: The Shotwell Fort Delaware "Diary"	205
Chapter Notes	213
Bibliography	223
Index	225

List of Abbreviations

AAAG—acting assistant adjutant general
AAQM—acting assistant quartermaster
AAS—acting assistant surgeon
Adj.—adjutant
AG—adjutant general
AGO—adjutant general's office
AL—Alabama
AQM—assistant quartermaster
AR—Arkansas
BGen—Brigadier General
Capt.—captain
CGP—Commissary General of Prisoners
CGS—Commissary General of Subsistence
Col.—colonel
Cpl.—corporal
DE—Delaware
DR—death rate
DRM—death rate, monthly
FL—Florida
GA—Georgia
IN—Indiana
JJ—Julia Jefferson
KS—Kansas
KY—Kentucky
LA—Louisiana
LCol—lieutenant colonel
Lt.—lieutenant
MA—Massachusetts
Maj.—major
MD—Maryland
MGen—major general
MN—Minnesota
MO—Missouri
MS—Mississippi
NC—North Carolina
NJ—New Jersey
NY—New York
OH—Ohio
OK—Oklahoma
OR—*Official Records*
PA—Pennsylvania
POW—prisoner-of-war
Pvt.—private
QM—quartermaster
SC—South Carolina
Sec. War—Secretary of War, Union, Edwin M. Stanton
Sgt.—sergeant
TN—Tennessee
VA—Virginia
VV—Veteran Volunteers

Preface

One of the most contentious subjects about the American Civil War, even today, is how prisoners of war (POWs) were treated by both sides. This is especially true for the last two years of the war, when POWs were held for long periods, after the prisoner exchange cartel had broken down in the spring of 1863.

During the war, each side tended to demonize the other side in various ways, including how the other side mistreated their prisoners of war (POWs),[1] thus starting the controversy. For instance, at various times committees of the U.S. Congress and the Confederate States Congress issued reports on the POW situation, each blaming the other side. Aside from newspaper reports, other types of documents were printed on both sides, each "proving" how the other side was inhumane in its treatment of POWs. For instance, The United States Sanitary Commission, at the behest of the U.S. War Department, undertook an investigation of the treatment of POWs in both Union (which held captured Confederate soldiers) and Confederate (which held captured Union soldiers) prison camps. By interviewing returning Union soldiers who were formerly POWs in Southern prisons, Confederates being held as POWs in Union prison camps, and the officers responsible for running the Union prison camps, they came to the perhaps unsurprising conclusion that POWs in the Union camps were treated much better than POWs in the Confederate prison camps.[2]

This venom between the two sides continued after the war was over, and in a sense was summarized in a single issue of the Southern Historical Society Papers devoted to the subject.[3] This document compiles many of the arguments and issues of the treatment of POWs (from a Southern point of view of course), and argues that the South, especially in the latter part of the war, did not have the resources to appropriately care for Union soldier POWs, while the North, with all of its resources had the wherewithal to properly care for captured Confederates but did not do so. Usually using the arguments raised in this single document, the debate continued unabated and virtually unchanged for about 65 years after the war ended, both sides publishing numerous recollections, memoirs, a few diaries, and other documents, to prove how inhumane the other side was, and how well they treated their POWs.

In 1930 the arguments about this issue were shifted somewhat in a book by Hesseltine[4] in which he described conditions in prisons operated by the Confederate Government, and a "war psychosis" in the North which resulted in the U.S. Government deliberately mistreating captured Confederate soldiers. This war psychosis, which supposedly gripped the people of the North, resulted in irresistible public pressure to retaliate against the

Confederate prisoners held by the Federal Government, and led to bad conditions in Union prison camps.

This type of argument over the treatment of POWs, as well as the more traditional arguments that one or both sides simply were cruel and inhumane, continues today. For example, Sanders[5] in his book *While in the Hands of the Enemy* in a sense carries this discussion to the ultimate conclusions, that both the North and South deliberately mistreated the POWs they held, and this treatment grew progressively worse as the war continued. More recently another line of argument has been advanced by Gillespie over treatment of captured Confederate soldiers in Union prisons.[6] He argues that Union prisons were not as bad as has been generally believed and portrayed, and that much of this misinformation is derived from sources that rely on material (memoirs and recollections, for example) that were written after the war (sometimes long after) which have been colored by the controversy of treatment of Civil War POWs, the "Lost Cause" syndrome, and simply forgotten or not recalled accurately. He points out the great differences in tone and facts reported in documents, especially diaries, written during the war, and those documents written after the war. He also points to much data one can glean from readily available "primary" sources such as the Official Records, and the Medical and Surgical History. Gillespie argues that materials written after the end of the war are not reliable, and that one should rely mostly on documents written during the war, such as contemporaneous diaries and records.[7]

The whole thesis of "war psychosis" or simply deliberate mistreatment of Southern POWs by the North causing inhumane treatment of Confederate POWs, with resulting atrocious living conditions and excessive deaths caused by those conditions, depends of course on there being such inhumane treatment which caused those results. Although Hesseltine, and with more detail Sanders, both mention orders given by the authorities in Washington that they believe were the result of war psychosis or simply being inhumane, they present very little contemporaneous evidence that these orders actually resulted in atrocious living conditions or excess deaths. Both Sanders and Hesseltine prominently mention that the Union authorities engaged in "retaliation," especially starting about mid–1864. Among these orders was the reduction in the prisoners' rations, which took effect on June 1, 1864.[8] As related by Gillespie, retaliation came to mean more than a reduction of rations, but included things such as restrictions on receiving mail (including packages). Indeed, there seems to be a general acceptance by most historians such as Sanders that a "retaliation program" led to excess suffering and deaths of Confederates in Union prisons.[9]

However, there is little good, much less convincing, *published* evidence that the "retaliation policy" actually resulted in excess suffering and/or deaths. Apparently this conclusion is based on anecdotal evidence, much of it based on postwar writings, and some arguments made, such as in the Southern Historical Society Papers. Indeed it seems in many aspects, the general conclusion that Northern prison camps were horrible places to be is based upon such "evidence."

To answer these uncertainties, this study of Fort Delaware, a major Union prison camp, was undertaken as a "model" of Northern Civil War prisons. It was chosen because it became a major northern prison camp about the time the exchange cartel broke down and received a large number of prisoners from May to July 1863 (thousands from Grant's Vicksburg campaign and about 95 percent of the enlisted POWs captured at Gettysburg), and because coincidentally the author is a historical interpreter at Fort Delaware State

Park. The goal of the study was to find as many contemporaneous primary sources of information about what happened there from about April 1863 through June 1865, when almost all of the POWs had been released, and to analyze what these primary sources reveal.

Luckily there are over 20 contemporaneous prisoner diaries in existence, in addition to extensive records in the National Archives and other places. The publication, with various editors, *The War of the Rebellion: A Compilation of the Official Records of the Union and Confederate Armies,* Government Printing Office, Washington, 1880–1900 (often referred to as the *Official Records* or *OR*), a huge work which reproduces many official documents produced during the war, and which has often been used by scholars and writers, is of necessity selective and incomplete.[10] Therefore an extensive search of documents in the National Archives relating to Fort Delaware during the chosen period was done. This resulted in finding many previously unreported items such as routine correspondence between officials at the Fort and in Washington D.C, for example, the Commissary Generals of Subsistence and Prisoners, but also the finding of types of records whose existence had never before been reported.

The numerous contemporaneous prisoner diaries proved useful in providing a "Southern" point of view of what actually happened inside the prison, as well as the attitudes, aspirations, and fears of the prisoners themselves.[11]

The dichotomy concerning what is believed to have happened at the Fort Delaware prison camp is well illustrated in two recent books about Fort Delaware: Brian Temple, *The Union Prison at Fort Delaware: A Perfect Hell on Earth* (McFarland, 2003), and Dale Fetzer and Bruce Mowday, *Unlikely Allies: Fort Delaware's Prison Community in the Civil War* (Stackpole Books, 2000). The former is a typical "old school" description of Fort Delaware as a hell on earth, while the latter has a more sympathetic and benign view of the treatment of POWs by Union authorities.

The present book does not follow the usual pattern of most other books about specific POW camps. These other books are usually arranged chronologically. This book is arranged in chapters by subjects, and then sometimes within the chapters chronologically. This is done so that the subject being discussed, such as the food ration, medical care, prison administration, etc., may be dealt with in a unified fashion and the reader's attention not be interrupted to deal with other topics or happenings which occur in the same time period.

Besides attempting to answer the question whether there was barbaric prisoner treatment at Fort Delaware, the book also attempts to give the reader a palpable idea of what it was to be a prisoner or prison guard, how a prison camp was run, what food was provided and how it was prepared, what medical care consisted of, the effect of orders from higher officials in Washington on prison life, etc.

At the beginning of this narrative, Col. Robert Buchanan has just assumed command of the Post on April 2, 1863.[12] On April 1st there were only 30 prisoners being held on the island.[13] Fort Delaware was built as a coastal defense fortification to protect upstream cities such as Philadelphia, Wilmington and Trenton from naval attack, and, by April 1863, probably few if any in the North believed that there was a serious maritime threat to those cities. Twice previously there had briefly been a few thousand POWs on the island, but they had not stayed long, the Fort being used as a collection and transit station for Confederate POWs being exchanged. Since these men were about to be released there was not much of a security problem, and extensive facilities for POWs were not built earlier than April 1863. In other words, at the beginning of April 1863 Fort Delaware was a relatively unknown and unimportant Army post manned by about 500 artillerists. This was about to change, as within two weeks of Buchanan taking charge, it would have a new commandant, and go on to assume a more important and controversial role in the Civil War.

1

Topography and Weather

If one visits Fort Delaware State Park on Pea Patch Island on a nice summer day, one would probably have the impression that it was not a bad place to live. There are picnic tables under trees, and pleasant walking paths and grassy areas. Is this how it was during the Civil War?

Topography

The topography of the island has changed greatly since the Civil War. During the Civil War the island was about 75 acres (30 ha) in area, surrounded by a seawall. Today the island, including the adjacent marshes, is about 375 acres (151 ha). Just as important, the original 75-acre section there during the Civil War is now about 6–8 feet (2–2.7 m) higher in elevation than it was during the Civil War.[1] How did this come about?

Construction of the Fort started about 1848,[2] on what was essentially a tidal mudflat surrounded by water for at least about a mile (1.6 km) on all sides by the Delaware River opposite Delaware City, Delaware. The mudflat was about equidistant from the Delaware and New Jersey shores. One of the first steps in construction was to build a seawall. The elevation of the seawall top was such that it was higher than high tide except in exceptional circumstances, such as a strong onshore wind from a storm at high tide. However, the interior of the island, except for the Fort and the area immediately surrounding it, was below the normal high tide level. Since the seawall was not impervious to water, water would come into the island slowly at high tide, and recede somewhat at low tide. There was a sluice gate on the island that could be opened at high tide to flood the island, a measure designed to make any land attack on the Fort more difficult. This sluice led to the moat (or wet ditch, as it was called) around the Fort, and the moat could be flushed by the tides twice a day.

All of this meant that the interior of the island was normally fairly wet, especially when there was much rain, since the water did not drain from the island well, even at low tide. In the interior of the island there were channels that were permanently filled with water. Drainage around the various buildings (except the Fort) was difficult, and the ground on the island was often muddy. Because of this boardwalks were built between various areas of the island,[3] and were particularly useful during wet weather. Complaints about the difficulty of keeping mud out of the barracks during wet weather were common.[4]

It is *likely* that the standing water on the island ensured that there was a healthy insect population there during the warmer months, and could have led to outbreaks of insect borne diseases such as Yellow Fever and malaria (see Chapter 9). Another potential problem was that the only source of fresh water on the island was rainwater since the river here is brackish (see Chapter 7 on how this was handled).

Figure 2 is a map of the island in 1864 and includes most of the buildings there at that time, and also shows some of the channels on the island, as well as the boardwalks. Figures 3 and 4 are a couple of general views of the prisoner barracks area. There are a couple of corrections for the Key to Figure 2, the map. Item 2, an open quadrangle, is the officer (and political prisoner) prison yard (sometimes called the "Bull Pen"), and to the top, right and bottom are the barracks for these officer prisoners. To the left of this quadrangle are the enlisted POWs barracks. They are separated by a stockade fence. Building No. 33 is the Convict's Barracks, although its exact placement is uncertain.

Figure 1. Rev. Isaac W. K. Handy, carte-de-visite, unknown date. Handy wrote the most valuable diary giving the Confederate point of view, over the longest period of time, 7/21/63 to 10/12/64 (courtesy Fort Delaware Society).

After the Civil War the topography of the island remained essentially the same for about 40 years, even though in the mid–1880's to 1900 the fort was modernized by addition of the Endicott section and addition of the two 3" gun batteries outside the Fort.[5] However, in the early 1900s the Delaware River channel was deepened to 45 feet, and much of the dredge spoils were dumped onto Pea Patch Island or immediately adjacent to the island. This raised the interior level of the island 6–8 feet (1.8–2.4 m), and also resulted in the formation of the northern part of the island and the marshes currently surrounding most of the island.[6] This raising of the island level meant that all structures present during the Civil War, except the Fort which is at its original level, were razed and/or buried when the island elevation was increased.[7] Today the island is about five times the size it was in the Civil War, currently about 375 acres including the marshes.

Weather

As perhaps one would guess, the climate during the Civil War, was, on average, similar to what it is today. Table 1-1 gives average monthly temperatures for April 1863–July 1865.[8]

Opposite: Figure 2. Map of Pea Patch Island, about mid–1864. Drawn by David Rickman in 1997. See text for some corrections (courtesy Delaware State Parks—Cultural Resources Unit).

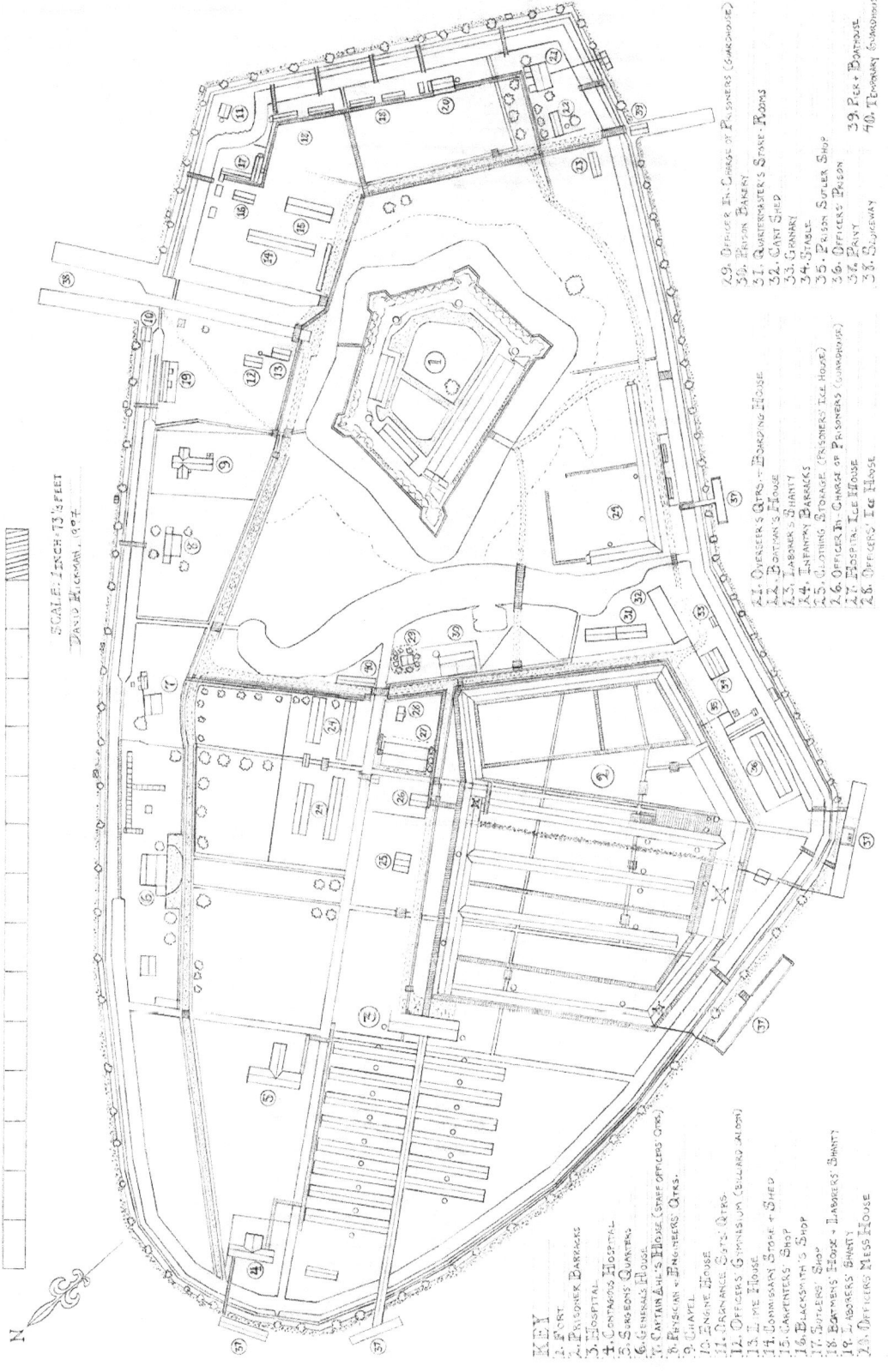

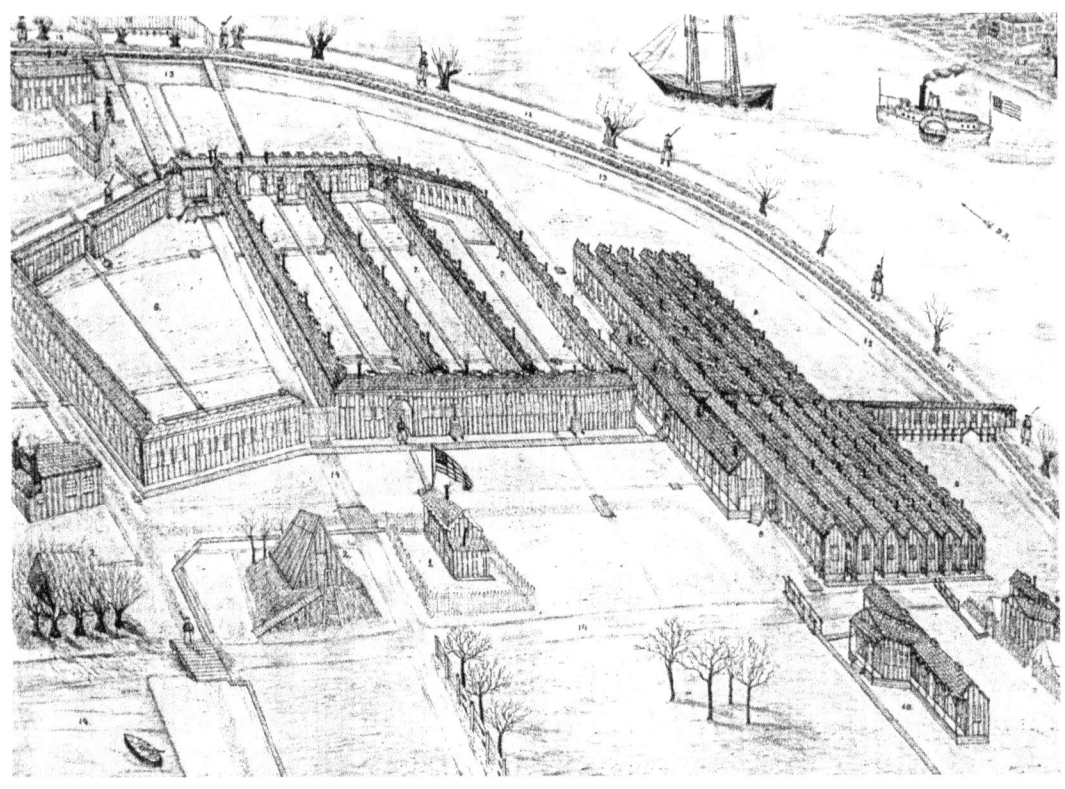

Top: Figure 3. "Prisoner Barracks and Hospital," drawn by Pvt. Max Neugas, 1st SC Regiment, captured at Gettysburg, and dated 3/4/64. The identification of various items may have been added later. The steamship on the right seems to be marked *Osceola*, which was one of the Fort's vessels for going to and from the mainland (courtesy Fort Delaware Society).

Bottom: Figure 4. "POW Officer's Prison Yard," undated and unsigned, from autograph book of 2nd Lt. Andrew J. Leftwich, 22nd Battalion, VA Inf. View, probably from or near the sinks (privies) over the river looking generally eastward towards New Jersey. This area was also called the "Bull Pen" by the POWs. The cylindrical object in the far right corner of the yard is a water tank, the Fort is shown in the top tight-hand corner, and the building in the top center with the large flag is probably the Prison office (Figure 2, item 26). In the background are ships either docked to the Island or in the Delaware River channel (courtesy Mr. John T. Frawner and Mrs. Jean Leftwich Frawner).

Table 1-1. Weather at Fort Delaware, April 1863–July 1865

Month	Monthly Temperatures, °F			Days of		Precipitation, inches
	Maximum	Minimum	Mean	Rain	Snow	
Apr-63	69	31	49.4	5	1	4.6
May-63	85	43	63.7	3	0	4.9
Jun-63	85	51	68.6	5	0	2.6
Jul-63	89	64	71.3	7	0	4.0
Aug-63	95	61	73.8	4	0	0.5
Sep-63	85	49	67.1	4	0	1.2
Oct-63	77	35	56.8	9	0	2.6
Nov-63	69	32	48.0	8	0	0.1
Dec-63	59	19	36.2	11	3	7.0
Jan-64	62	8	34.5	3	4	1.4
Feb-64	56	4	34.6	4	2	0.4
Mar-64	58	20	39.7	9	6	5.4
Apr-64	74	39	50.3	10	0	5.7
May-64	84	50	70.3	6	0	5.7
Jun-64	95	54	71.3	3	0	2.0
Jul-64	95	61	77.1	2	0	2.3
Aug-64	100	67	79.3	4	0	1.4
Sep-64	81	59	66.0	7	0	4.7
Oct-64	75	40	54.2	4	0	1.5
Nov-64	68	31	45.5	4	0	2.5
Dec-64	56	10	36.1	3	2	5.1
Jan-65	56	7	30.0	4	4	3.8
Feb-65	64	5	35.2	4	4	5.2
Mar-65	80	28	49.6	5	0	5.5
Apr-65	85	40	57.4	6	0	3.1
May-65	91	43	66.2	12	0	11.4
Jun-65	97	63	76.8	7	0	4.5
Jul-65	101	61	78.7	5	0	3.9

For comparison, Table 1-2 shows the modern averages for the New Castle County Airport, about 12 miles upstream from the island.[9]

Table 1-2. Modern Monthly Climate Data for Wilmington, Delaware

Month	Monthly Temperatures, °F			Precipitation, inches
	Max	Min.	Mean	
January	39.3	23.7	31.5	3.4
February	42.5	25.8	34.2	2.8
March	51.9	33.4	42.7	4.0
April	62.6	42.1	52.4	3.4
May	72.5	52.4	62.5	4.2
June	81.1	61.8	71.5	3.6
July	86.0	67.3	76.6	4.3
August	84.1	65.8	75.0	3.5
September	77.2	58.1	67.7	4.0
October	65.9	45.6	55.8	3.1
November	55.0	36.9	45.9	3.2
December	44.4	28.4	36.4	3.4

Comparing the Mean Monthly Temperatures in Tables 1-1 and 1-2, one finds that April 1863 and March 1864 were somewhat cooler (3°F or more) than the modern average, while January and August 1864 and May 1865 were somewhat warmer. On the other hand, July 1863 was much cooler (5°F or more) than the modern average, while May 1864 and March, April and June 1865 were much warmer. This is probably not an unusual variation.

However, it is important to note that measurement of weather conditions by the Army during the Civil War, especially temperature and wind speed, was different from modern measurements. Army Regulations required the senior medical officer (surgeon) of each hospital, post, etc., to keep weather records which were recorded on Form 10, actually a register book for weather records.[10] During the Civil War the Army provided a surgeon with thermometers that simply registered the current temperature, and observations were made at 7 a.m., 2 p.m. and 9 p.m., and in Table 1-1 mean, high and low temperatures from these measurements are shown. Wind velocity was highly subjective, being a number scale based on the observer's interpretation of very general instructions.[11] Thus some variation from modern measurements was inevitable.

Cold weather, especially in the December through February period, also resulted in a partial or almost complete freeze up of the Delaware River, which effectively isolated the island until the ice broke up. This is mentioned many times in various diaries and official correspondence. During these periods even Gen. Schoepf was unable to communicate with the outside world, and could not receive or send orders or correspondence. Supplying the island was impossible during these periods.

Finally a personal note. Winds on the island tend to be, or at least feel, much higher than one experiences on the mainland. The island was a small piece of land surrounded by a large expanse of water, and so winds would blow onto the island unimpeded. What seems like a gentle breeze on the mainland may feel like a strong wind on the island. This may be pleasant on a warm day, but in the winter it can make the island seem much colder than the mainland.

2

Command Structure, Personnel and Administration

Command Structure

During the period this book covers, roughly April 1863 through June 1865, except for the first half of April 1863, Brigadier Albin Schoepf was in command of the Fort and everything on the island. When Schoepf came to the fort, the fort was part of the Middle District (later also known as the 8th U.S. Army Corps), headquartered in Baltimore, Maryland, and commanded by MGen Robert C. Schneck. From 5/2/63 to 4/3/64 one can find about 60 messages between Schoepf and the Middle Department headquarters concerning a great deal of things, such as armament of the fort, specific political prisoners, items concerning Union soldiers, various routine reports, orders forwarded from the War Department through the Middle District, etc. Thus, as may be expected, the fort had numerous communications with its governing command.

However, in a sense Schoepf also "reported" to another officer, Col. (later Bvt. BGen and then Bvt. MGen) William Hoffman, the CGP (Commissary General of Prisoners). Hoffman was located in Washington, D.C., and was responsible for the care and security of all Confederate POWs in all Union prison camps, including of course Fort Delaware. As will be seen in the course of this book, his communications with Schoepf were voluminous, and were the most influential external (to the prison camps themselves) factor in how prisoners at Fort Delaware and other Union prison camps were treated. Thus Schoepf had to answer to two "masters" in all matters concerning POWs.

There were no regiment-sized units regularly assigned to the island. Since the Fort itself was an artillery post designed to protect the Delaware River, and cities upstream of the Fort such as Wilmington, Delaware, Philadelphia, Pennsylvania, and Trenton, New Jersey, from attack, there were heavy artillery batteries "permanently" assigned to the fort. Usually there were 3 heavy artillery batteries present, totaling about 400–600 men. Each of these batteries was commanded by a Captain. In fact there were no officers more or less permanently assigned to the island with a rank higher than Captain, except for Schoepf. Independent Battery A, PA Heavy Artillery of the PA Heavy Artillery was commanded by Capt. S. Mlotkowski, while Battery G was commanded by Capt. J.J. Young. The third battery present was known as Capt. Ahl's Battery (officially the 1st DE Heavy Artillery), and was composed of "galvanized" Confederate soldiers, who after arriving at Fort Delaware as POWs switched sides in the summer of 1863.

In addition to these permanent units there usually was a Union infantry regiment present to help guard the POWs. These units were typically not at full strength and had about 400–800 men. These regiments had their own command structure, usually including a Colonel in command who reported to Schoepf.

While some of the officers of the artillery batteries also assumed the duties of staff officers to Schoepf, and/or other additional duties, there were some officers who were not assigned to troop units such as the batteries. There was a Commissary officer, a Quartermaster officer, and a medical staff headed by the surgeon in charge. All of these reported to Schoepf, but none of them was higher in rank than a captain.

On 3/12/64 the War Department issued General Orders 97 War Department, AGO, which stated in part 2. "The commanding officer of Fort Delaware will report directly to the war Department, and his post will not be considered as belongs to any geographical department." This may have come about partially because insofar as POWs were concerned Schoepf was sometimes receiving conflicting orders from the Middle Department and the CGP. It is also believed that Schoepf met with Sec. War Stanton shortly before this order was issued. Perhaps Schoepf convinced Stanton that this was best (Stanton's decision could have been influenced by the fact that Joseph Holt, a powerful politician, backed Schoepf). This meant of course that Schoepf answered directly to the War Department, and especially in the case of POWs would take guidance only from the CGP. To the author's knowledge Fort Delaware was the only Union prison camp reporting directly to the War Department, all others being under the command of a local district (geographical) commander.

Personnel

Some Union officers closely connected with the POWs and other prisoners are listed below.

BGen Albin Francisco Schoepf[1] (Figure 5) was born on March 1, 1822, in Podgorze, in Galicia, then in the Austro-Hungarian Empire, now part of Poland. His father was probably Hungarian and his mother Polish. At the age of 15 he went to a military academy in Vienna, and four years later because a Lieutenant of Artillery in the Austrian Army. Promoted on the field to Captain for bravery, he participated in the Kossuth rebellion against the Austrian empire. After the revolution failed in 1849 it is believed that Schoepf fled to the Ottoman Empire. He may have served in combat around the city of Aleppo (now in Syria), and as an artillery instructor in the Ottoman armed forces with the rank of major. He emigrated to the United Sates in 1851 (or possibly 1852–3) and went to Washington, D.C. Apparently his first job in the U.S. was as a hotel porter. It is believed that at some point he met Joseph Holt, an attorney from Kentucky, who was to become a prominent Washington politician. Possibly through Holt's influence Schoepf obtained a job with the U.S. Coastal Survey. He was married to Julie Bates Kesley, then 18, on May 7, 1855. The Kesley family apparently were also friends with Joseph Holt. In 1859 Schoepf was appointed a second Assistant Examiner in the U.S. Patent Office as a draftsman by Joseph Holt, the Commissioner of the Patent Office. Schoepf then was (temporarily?) transferred to the War Department on January 18, 1861, to conduct a military survey in Virginia. On 9/3/61 Schoepf resigned from the Patent Office and offered his services to the government. At the insistence of Joseph Holt, Schoepf was commissioned as a BGen in the U.S. Volunteers and assigned in Kentucky. In 1861 Schoepf helped win some victories early in the war at a time when victories for the Union were scarce, and gained some fame from them. After the summer campaigns of 1862, on 10/8/62 he was appointed to command the 1st Division of the 3rd Army Corps (12,000 men) which should have meant promotion to MGen. However, two things happened: he became embroiled in the MGen Buell commission investigation, and supposedly became unfit for field duty. His request to resign was refused. At approximately the same time he wrote to Joseph Holt asking Holt to get him a larger command, so Schoepf's actual wishes are a bit unclear. During most of the winter of 1862–1863 and early spring of 1863 he served on the Buell commission, but was not on active field service. He tendered his resignation again around 4/10/63, but it was refused, even though he had been certified on 3/27/63, as "unable to perform duty in the field." On 4/14/63[2] the AGO issued an order appointing Schoepf as commander at Fort Delaware. There is nothing in the record indicating why this was done, but perhaps it was influenced by Joseph Holt, who by now was the Adjutant General of the U.S. Army.

Figure 5. BGen. Albin Francisco Schoepf, unknown date by Ellwood Garrett, Wilmington, Delaware. At some point, this photograph had been given by Schoepf to Lammot DuPont Sr., who commanded Co. B, 5th DE Inf., and were guards at the Fort from 6/20/63 to 8/6/63 (courtesy Hagley Museum and Library [1970.072]).

Capt. George Washington Ahl,[3] who was born in 1834, was a merchant. He enlisted in the Army on 8/22/62 in Independent Battery G, Pennsylvania Heavy Artillery as a 1st Lt. He arrived at Fort Delaware on 9/1/62. From December 1862 through February 1863 he was in charge of new recruits sent to the Post. In March and April 1863 he was in charge of POWs. Starting in May 1863 he was acting Aide-de-Camp to Schoepf and Commissary (General) of Prisoners on the island. On 7/27/63 he was promoted to Captain and assigned to command of Ahl's Battery (1st DE Heavy Artillery) which was made of up "galvanized" Confederates (soldiers who switched sides). On 8/3/63 he was "discharged" from Independent Battery G but retained his captaincy of Ahl's Battery.

Capt. Gilbert Smith Clark[4] (Figure 6) was born in New York City (Manhattan) on October 24, 1817, the son of a sea captain who was later lost at sea. The census of 1860 reports he was residing in Bergen, New Jersey, with his wife and two children, had a servant in his house and owned over $2,500 worth of real estate. He enlisted in the Army as a 2nd Lt. in Battery B, of the 3rd PA Heavy Artillery Regiment on November 16, 1861, for three years for the "unity and integrity" of the nation.[5] He arrived at Fort Delaware in March of 1862. On July 1, 1862, Capt. Gibson, the Post commandant, appointed Clark acting Assistant Commissary Officer and acting Assistant Quartermaster Officer, meaning Clark became responsible for most of the supplies (except arms and ammunition) the Fort needed. On 6/14/63 he was promoted to Captain as a Commissary of Subsistence officer. At that time those wanting to be Commissary officers had to apply and take a test. There is no record of such application or test taking by Clark, so Schoepf may have used his influence in getting the appointment, although there is also no record of this.

Capt. Samuel R. Craig (sometimes spelled Craige) became a Quartermaster Officer in November of 1862, and subsequently assigned on 1/21/63 to the 5th and 6th DE regiments. On 8/8/63, Schoepf issued Special Order 142[6] which stated that Craig had been assigned to Fort Delaware as Assistant Quartermaster, and would take over the duties of quartermaster from Clark. Nothing else is known of Craig.

1st Lt. Charles Hawkins[7] was born in Philadelphia about 1840, and mustered into the 90th PA Infantry as a private on 12/5/61. Wounded at Antietam on 9/17/62 he was mustered out of that regiment on 12/24/62 to join the 3rd PA Heavy Artillery, Battery M as a 1st Lt. From May 1863 to August of 1865 he was on detached service at Fort Delaware serving as an aide-de-camp and/or Provost Marshall on General Schoepf's staff.

Assistant Surgeon Charles E Goddard[8] was trained at the Columbia College School of Physicians and Surgeons in New York, and enlisted as an assistant surgeon on 5/28/61. After various assignments in the Army he was posted to Fort Delaware as Post (Chief) Surgeon on 6/29/64 and served there until 8/12/65.

Assistant Surgeon Henry Ridgway Silliman[9] was born in Pottsville, Pennsylvania, October 29, 1836, and studied medicine at the University of Pennsylvania. He enlisted as an assistant surgeon on 5/27/61 and served in various assignments before coming to Fort Delaware on 6/18/63 as Post (Chief) Surgeon. He was relieved as Post Surgeon by Special Order 221 on 6/28/64, and assigned to the Department of the South.

The Rev. Elon J. Way was born about 1814 in Pennsylvania, and became Post Chaplain in 1863. Before that he was the pastor of the Delaware City Methodist Episcopal Church.

1st Lt Abraham G. Wolf[10] (Figure 7) was born on September 17, 1838, in Harrisburg, Pennsylvania, and was a railroad brakeman before joining the Army. He enlisted as a private in PA Heavy Artillery Independent Battery G on 8/5/62, and was subsequently promoted to Sgt. On

Figure 6. Capt. Gilbert S(mith) Clark, unknown photographer, taken after June 14, 1863 (courtesy Fort Delaware Society).

2. Command Structure, Personnel and Administration

Figure 7. 2nd Lt. Abraham G. Wolf, seated center behind "Bill the Cat," in an undated photograph by J. L. Gihon of Philadelphia. This picture was taken in front of the Prison office (Figure 2, Item 26), and some of the others who are identified are Lt. Charles Hawkins to Wolf's immediate left, Capt. S. Mlotkowski (far left of Wolf, standing with sword), and seated to Wolf's immediate right the rotund civilian is Mr. Welch, the sutler (courtesy Fort Delaware Society).

7/15/63 he was promoted to 1st Lt. in Ahl's Independent Battery. Besides being an artillery officer, he was also an Assistant Commissary of Prisoners starting about March 1864, being in charge of the officer POW compound.

Administration

This section speaks generally of the Administration of the Post and Island, but does not include administration of prisoners. Similar to any Post Commander, Schoepf had many things to "administer," that is items he needed to make sure were being done properly, and reported when needed. Many of these types of items, such as rations, shelter for the troops, security, clothing, and the like are covered in subsequent chapters.

Since Fort Delaware was a heavy artillery post that was built to protect the cities upriver, he had to make sure that the artillerymen were properly trained and equipped. By the time he took command the U.S. Volunteer batteries present were fully trained, and were equipped with a variety of heavy guns. Table 2-1 lists the heavy guns present at various dates.[11]

Table 2-1. The Heavy Guns of Fort Delaware

Gun Type	Carriage	6/30/1862	6/30/1863	6/30/1864	6/30/1865
24 pdr flank howitzer	wood				
First Tier		10	10	10	10
Second Tier		10	10	10	10

Gun Type	Carriage	6/30/1862	6/30/1863	6/30/1864	6/30/1865
32 pdr smoothbore	wood				
First Tier					3
Second Tier				7	4
42 pdr rifle	wood or iron*				
Second Tier					15
8" Columbiad	wood				
Second Tier		8	8	13	13
Third Tier		14	14	14	14
10" Columbiad					
Second Tier	iron			5	
Third Tier	wood	5	25	25	25
8" Rodman	iron				
First Tier					12
Second Tier					1
10" Rodman	iron				
First Tier					7
Second Tier					5
Third Tier					5
Total Guns		47	67	84	124

As can be seen, the number of heavy guns at the Fort nearly doubled during Schoepf's tenure. When Ahl's Battery was formed in July 1863, he also had to ensure that these men were properly trained, guns cared for, ammunition available, etc.

This duty to protect the river from passage of hostile vessels sometimes led to certain communications with civilians. For example, on 11/3/64 Schoepf received a telegram from R. Wesden, Commissioner of Protection in Philadelphia, warning Schoepf a Confederate cruiser was on the loose and to "keep a good lookout for her. She may attempt to come up the river."[12] Hamilton noted in his diary that the CSS Tallahassee had made some excitement and that the Union Navy was looking for it.

Another more amusing anecdote about civilian interaction is also described in the *Philadelphia Press* of 10/28/63, and confirmed by Hamilton on 10/27/63. There was a prize fight on Reedy Island in the Delaware River about 5 miles south of Fort Delaware, and after the fight the group went to Port Penn, a town on the mainland in Delaware about 2 miles south of the Fort, where some of them became violent. Schoepf was notified by the local Sheriff to detain them as the participants were leaving Port Penn mostly by tugboats, and when these tugboats drew abreast of the Fort, the General sent out a steamboat to call on them to surrender. Two of the three did give up (presumably they were aware of the Fort's guns) and brought ashore on Pea Patch Island. The other boat did not stop until the fort fired a shot across its bows. The persons on all three boats were guarded on the island by armed soldiers until some of the "respectable persons," except for the ringleaders and possible participants in the violence at Port Penn, were released. It was reported that about 200 were being held at the Fort until those who actually took part in the violence could be identified.

The Fort was also the place that new recruits from the Philadelphia area were first sent. Many of these new recruits were destined as replacements for older regiments from the Philadelphia area, some were for new regiments, some were for U.S. Colored Troops regiments, and a few were replacements for the batteries at the Fort. There is relatively little correspondence in the files about these men but there are other written documents about them. The *Philadelphia Press* mentions a number of times that recruits have been sent to Fort Delaware, and often mentions they are replacements for the old Philadelphia regiments. On 1/5/64 the *Press* states that in the week of 1/2/64 343 men were sent to the Fort, 177 colored soldiers, 138 recruits for old regiments, and 29 recruits for new regiments, a total of 343. The *Press* reported on 12/30/63 that new recruits averaged about 150 per week (enlistment bounties were being paid). The arrival of new recruits was confirmed in Hamilton's diary. On 6/15/63 he reported 8 recruits were bucked and gagged in the sally port, on 5/31/64 that 9 recruits came in from Camp Copeland, on 9/4/64 that 10 recruits came in for their battery, on 9/29/64 that 21 recruits arrived some of them "hard cases," on 9/3/64 that recruits were sent away, and on 1/8/64 that 10 recruits came from Pittsburg. Crumrine in a letter home on 9/15/64 reports the 32 men he has in the small fort on the Delaware Shore are new recruits, and on 10/26/64 got 6 more recruits.

Although we have only one Post Record Book covering about 5–6 months of April–September 1863, during that time there are 9 mentions of recruits. On 4/20/63 Lt. Ahl was relieved of his responsibility for recruits,[13] and on 4/21/63 Lt. Rodman was given that assignment.[14] On 5/20/63 Lt. Ahl was detailed to take 54 deserters and 45 "recruits for PA regiments" to Washington.[15] On 5/21/63 a Corporal and two privates were detailed to deliver 6 recruits for PA regiments to Harpers Ferry.[16] On 5/31/63 Lt. Addicks was ordered to take 21 recruits to Washington City (DC) with a guard of 7 men.[17] Lt. Hall was ordered to take recruits to 112th PA Regiment in Washington City 6/19/63.[18] With a guard of 7 men Lt. Black was to deliver 20 recruits for PA regiments on 7/30/63,[19] and on 8/7/63 he was also ordered to take 13 recruits and 6 deserters, with a guard of 6, also to Washington City.[20] Similarly on 8/14/63 Lt. Hay and a guard of 5 escorted 11 recruits and 1 deserter to Washington City.[21] On 8/24/63 Lt Roger and 4 guards delivered to Washington City 9 recruits and the rolls and accounts of pay, clothing &c for these recruits.[22]

The above records indicate that in many instances guards were sent with recruits to their next station. Apparently there was concern the recruits may desert, some of them possibly being potential bounty jumpers. The last entry on 8/24/63 indicates that the recruits had uniforms, were on the payroll, and had *possibly* spent some time at the Fort in rudimentary training. This handling of recruits continued, as noted above, in articles in the *Philadelphia Press* and Hamilton's diary, reporting more groups of recruits being sent to the Fort at least through September 1864.

Personnel from Fort Delaware also participated in recruiting in Philadelphia. On 5/4/63[23] and 5/22/63[24] personnel from the Fort were ordered to Philadelphia to assist in recruiting soldiers.

Interpreters on the island often get the question as to how many executions there were during the war. There were no executions on the island of anyone during the war. The closest this came to happening involved Union convicts.

On 6/10/63 the *Philadelphia Press* reported that two soldiers had been sentenced by a court-martial to be shot for desertion and other offenses. The *Press* on 6/18/63 stated that they were to be shot tomorrow. Pvt. Benjamin Hadwin had deserted immediately after collecting a bounty for enlisting and had no intention to actually be a soldier, and Pvt. Samuel D. Crumb was convicted of deserting twice and forging his descriptive list. Also on 6/18/63 Schoepf received a telegram that Crumb was not to be executed.[25] The next day Schoepf received another telegram that the execution of Pvt. Hadwin was suspended.[26] On 6/22/63 the *Press* noted that the 2 soldiers had been reprieved, and that

Hadwin's reprieve was received just in time to save his life. Both men were notified of their reprieves after the time set for their execution had passed.

On 8/14/63 Schoepf wrote[27] to Col. Cheeseborough in Baltimore, the Adjutant General of the Middle District, stating that Hadwin and Crumb had both been sentenced to be shot on June 19th, but the President had commuted Crumb's sentence to imprisonment at Fort Delaware. Schoepf inquires what should be done with Hadwin as he was still being held in close confinement in irons as ordered by Gen. Schneck. The only other mention of Hadwin or Crumb is in a letter written to Col. Cheeseborough by Schoepf on 1/30/64 stating Hadwin was still confined and recommending his dishonorable discharge because his enlistment time was over.[28]

On 12/7/64 Schoepf telegraphed the Middle Department asking whether Pvts. Wm Jones and Jesse Lewis of the 5th MD should be shot.[29] This was also postponed on 12/11/63 when Schoepf received a telegram from Col. Cheeseborough suspending these executions.[30] Nothing further was found in the Fort Delaware records.

3

Prison Camp Administration and Security

Fort Delaware is best known for its prisoner of war (POW) camp during the Civil War, especially from about May 1863 to about June of 1865 when large numbers of POWs were present, some being there for about two years. Except for a short period just after the Battle of Gettysburg, Confederate officers were not held at Fort Delaware until about March or April 1864,[1] when a prison area for them was completed (officer POWs were not allowed to mix with the enlisted POWs).

Classes of Prisoners

There were Union convicts (also sometimes called deserters, and/or members of "Company Q"), and political prisoners on the island. The convicts were mostly Union soldiers who had been convicted at court-martial, most commonly for desertion but also for other crimes such as rape, theft and manslaughter. Generally speaking, Union soldiers sentenced for a short period of time, say less than 6 months, were not sent to Fort Delaware, and men sentenced to more than 5 years were sent to state penitentiaries.

Political prisoners were civilians arrested in the North for all kinds of "disloyal" conduct, such as speech critical of the Federal government. Since President Lincoln had suspended *habeas corpus*, virtually anyone in the government, including the President, cabinet officers, and military officers, especially generals, could order the arrest of civilians without trial and they could be held indefinitely. Typically there were about 30 to about 80 political prisoners held at any time at Fort Delaware. Usually the political prisoners came in individually or in small groups. The largest known group was reported in the *Philadelphia Press* of 7/5/64, "'The Coles County (Ill.) Copperhead rioters, 65 in number, have been removed from Camp Yates, near Springfield, ... and directing him [Col. Oakes] to forward them immediately to Fort Delaware." Many other Union prison camps held political prisoners.

Except for a few high ranking Confederate officers who were held in the Fort, all of the POWs were held in the POW compound. Political prisoners were held in the Fort until May 1864, when they were placed into the POW officer's compound.[2] The convicts were held in a couple of barracks on the Fort parade ground until May 1864, when they were transferred to a separate compound near the POW officers' compound.

POWs consisted of officers and men of the Confederate army, navy and marines. Also considered essentially POWs were captured blockade runners, and these were placed in the officers or enlisted men's POW barracks depending on whether they were officers or seamen of the blockade runner.

In a few instances Union deserters were found among the Confederate POWs. The largest group was 18 deserters sent by Schoepf to Lt. Col. Fry, the Provost Marshall General of Washington 1/16/64.[3] Other such deserters were reported in the *Philadelphia Press*, one on 1/29/64, and two others on 8/1/64. Of the latter two Pvt. Edwin Benton of the 9th New York Artillery "deserted his regiment at Woodbine, on the Baltimore and Ohio Railroad, and went to Gettysburg, where he gave himself up to the Provost Marshall of that place as a rebel deserter and was sent to Fort Delaware." The other of the pair, Duncan McPherson of the 73rd New York, "deserted his regiment at Fredericksburg on the 7th of March and went to Acquia creek, from whence he was forwarded to this city [Washington] as a deserter from the 14th Virginia Cavalry, ... and transferred to Fort Delaware [on June 15th]." These men clearly went to great lengths to desert, as they traveled some distance from their regiments to be "captured."

There were, however, smaller numbers of other types of prisoners on the island. Among these, in at least four instances, were civilian hostages from the South. A group of 60 men from Fredericksburg, Virginia was "held as hostages for the wounded soldiers betrayed into the hands of the enemy by Mayor Slaughter." They arrived at Fort Delaware about 5/27/64, as noted by Hamilton and Alburtis in their diaries.[4] In another instance, according to the 9/12/64 *Philadelphia Press*, "Twenty-four rebel sympathizers arrested in Loudoun county, about a week ago, upon suspicion of being connected with the bushwhacking gangs infesting that neighborhood, have been transferred to Fort Delaware," as noted by both Handy and Mckey on 9/10/64.[5] Handy states, "They were all arrested without a moment's warning, and hurried on to the Old Capitol [Prison], at Washington, as hostages for persons alleged to have been captured by the Confederate army, and now in confinement in Richmond." On 6/15/64 the *Philadelphia Press* reported that eight prisoners "...held as hostages for the Union citizens now in the hands of the rebels..." will be transferred to Fort Delaware. On 8/22/64 Handy reported seven men from Leesburg (Virginia?) arrived "and held as hostages for citizens captured by Moseby." There may of course have been other individuals or groups who were also held as hostages.

Another type of prisoner was a northern civilian who was arrested, and sometimes convicted at court martial, for various "offenses."

Philadelphia Inquirer, August 17, 1864—"George Miller, Quartermaster's employee, found guilty of larceny, was sentenced ... for the term of six months ... will be sent ... to Fort Delaware."

Franklin Repository, June 15, 1864—"Samuel S. Smoot having entered into a contract for army supplies with Col. James A. Ekin, Chief Quartermaster, Cavalry Bureau, and having failed to comply with the agreement, has been tried by General Court Martial on the charge of "willful neglect of duty in violation of the act of Congress of July 17, 1862, found guilty and directed to pay a fine of $10,000, and be confined at Fort Delaware until the fine is paid."

Lebanon Advertiser, June 30, 1864—"A strike occurred at the Cumberland Mines a few days since, and was speedily suppressed by the military authorities and twenty-five of the strikers sent to Fort Delaware. This compelling men to work for such prices as the employers are pleased to pay is one of the blessings of Mr. Lincoln's administration."

It seems as if the military had complete control over civilians it employed (George Miller), its contractors (Samuel S. Smoot), and even striking miners, and could imprison them, with or without a court martial having been conducted. It seems startling to us today that the military would be able to court martial civilians, but that was a result of the suspension of the writ of *habeas corpus* instituted by President Lincoln. The army even interfered with a strike by miners having no apparent direct or indirect connection to the military, although in later years employers were able to convince government officials to use police and/or troops to break union organized strikes. A further aspect of the *Lebanon Advertiser* article is a fairly straightforward criticism of the Lincoln administration.

It is clear that there were many classes of prisoners at Fort Delaware, and that Schoepf and his staff had to keep track of them. For most of these prisoners he also had to deal with two completely separate organizations in Washington, the Adjutant General's Office (AGO) for political prisoners and convicts, and the Commissary General of Prisoners office for POWs and sometimes political prisoners. Correspondence to and from the fort also shows that in many instances other organizations, such as Provost Marshals in different places, and the Middle Military District when the Fort was part of that organization, often ordered or requested actions be taken about prisoners. Indeed, in a few cases Sec. War Stanton personally wrote to inquire or send orders about specific prisoners. This variety of types of prisoners illustrates the sweeping powers that the Lincoln administration amassed during the Civil War concerning imprisonment not only of military personnel of both sides, but also Northern and Southern civilians.

Convicts

One of the larger administrative jobs at the Fort, probably not faced by most other prison camp commanders, were the "convicts" or "deserters," or collectively Company Q (Co. Q), as they were most commonly called. These prisoners were Union soldiers convicted at Court Martial of a crime, such as desertion, rape, murder, failure to obey orders, and many other offensives. Most of them were sentenced to hard labor, many with ball and chain also (see Figure 8).

The Fort had to have procedures in place to deal with the convicts, their needs such as food and shelter, and recordkeeping of them. For example, the Commissary records show that convicts got the usual Union soldier's ration, because the convicts were in fact Union soldiers undergoing punishment. The convicts and their particular "prison" were under the command of the Provost Marshal, who was usually Lt.

Figure 8. "Union Convict with Ball and Chain." From sketchbook of Pvt. Baldwin Coolidge, 6th MA VV, dated 8/26/64 (courtesy Delaware Historical Society).

Hawkins. Besides the paperwork needed at the Fort to administer the convicts there are many communications about them For instance on 8/2/64 Schoepf wrote to the AG in Washington City inquiring about I.B Lewis, who was sentenced to be dishonorably discharged at the end of his term, and whether the term of his regiment had expired[6]; on 8/26/63 wrote to the AGO describing certain difficult cases concerning some convicts[7]; on 2/20/64 wrote to the Middle Department that under orders received from War Department has released C.E. Merrill, Co. K, 1st MS Heavy Artillery who was undergoing sentence of court martial[8]; on 2/23/64 wrote to the Asst. AG that John Shanks, who was a convict (probably not a soldier), was probably not a British subject, even though the British Counsel at Norfolk has inquired about him[9]; wrote to the AGO on 3/25/64 that he had 327 convicts from the U.S. Army and was "full" so requested no more be sent[10]; and on 4/11/64 wrote to the assistant AG in Washington about several matters, including rolls of convicts to be submitted noting that convicts have never been paid at Fort Delaware (Schoepf had asked about this previously), referring to a previous communication from the AGO which basically stated that convicts should not be paid, and finally if convicts should be paid, he will have to make a new roll with Descriptive Lists, which were usually not sent with them men when they arrived here.[11]

Also security had to be provided to make sure the convicts did not escape or otherwise cause a disturbance. Only one such item has been found in the records. On 7/18/63 Schoepf telegraphed the Provost Marshall in Philadelphia that John Ellison a convict from the 72nd PA Volunteers, and Pvt. F. Donnelly of the 152nd PA Volunteers which were assigned to the Fort, "deserted" (escaped) the previous night.[12]

The convicts' presence was noted many times in both Union and Confederate diaries. Hamilton mentions them on 6/3/63 (convicts hung by hands), 7/28/63 (tying up a convict), 10/9/63, 1/16/64, 4/21/64 and 4/23/64 (280 to Fort Jefferson in the Dry Tortugas).

Eames mentions them on 6/12/64 (80 to Dry Tortugas), Crumrine on 7/7/64 (he was in a guard of 1 officer and 43 enlisted men taking 72 convicts to Dry Tortugas starting 6/13/64), and Fletcher 9/1/64. Eames and Fletcher described them as being clothed in obsolete artillery uniforms which had short dark blue coat, hats trimmed with yellow. They also described them as getting no pay, working hard and getting only rations and clothing. They worked hauling timber, stone and gravel around the island in an ordinary cart. One man held the shaft of the cart and about 20 or so would pull the cart using a rope attached to the shaft. The men worked in gangs of 30 or 40.

The convicts were also noticed by the Confederates who could sometimes see them working pulling the carts. Handy records many instances of seeing them as do many others. Handy early on reports that the convicts, of "Company Q," were originally (when he got there) housed in barracks built on the parade ground inside the Fort. On 3/7/64 Handy records that there was a fire set in Q's barracks and shortly thereafter the convicts were moved outside the Fort to a separate prison compound. On average the men of Co. Q were probably the worst treated on the island, being at hard labor most of time, many with both ball and chain. Handy reports that on 6/25/63 two Irishmen of Co. Q were hung by the thumbs and wrists, one of them for returning a blow from the Provost Marshall (probably Lt Hawkins if identification is correct), and the other for cursing one of the galvanized rebels.

Occasionally one of Co. Q was a southerner convicted by a Union court martial of an offense. For example, a (Confederate) Capt. Gordon was removed to the Fort on 7/9/64 (Handy and Mckey diaries) and was convicted of recruiting behind Union lines.

He claimed he was just passing through to his home. He was sentenced to imprisonment at hard labor for the war. Handy saw Gordon at work on 7/11/64 and 7/13/64, and Mckey also saw him on 7/11/64. Eventually Gordon was freed in a special exchange.

In late February 1864 an interesting exchange of correspondence took place between Schoepf and the AGO. On 2/24/64 Schoepf received a message that the Sec. War directed that the cases of 9 convicts be more fully reported to the AGO or Sec. War since Schoepf had recommended executive clemency.[13] Although there does not appear to be a direct reply to this query, Schoepf on 2/28/64 sent the names of 5 members of the 5th MA Vol. The conduct of these men was good during confinement but it was a mistake to recommend them for release.[14] Apparently this was an error for which Schoepf blames his clerk, since these men were convicted of rape or mutiny.[15] Schoepf then goes on to explain he was recommending various convicts whose commendable character, he believed, would be a benefit to the Service. Schoepf then asks the roll of recommended convicts be returned so that he can revise it. It appears Schoepf was asking the sentences of some convicts be remitted and they be allowed to rejoin their units. There is no further discourse on this matter in the next couple of months.

An interesting "convict" story is that of the unfortunate Major Shearer (CSA). Major George Shearer, 1st MD Cav. (CSA) was captured and sent to Fort Delaware about July 1864. On 7/15/64 Schoepf sent a letter to the commanding officer of Ft. McHenry which stated, "I have in my custody a prisoner of war named George M Shearer, captured near Hagerstown, Maryland, during the last rebel raid who was here a prisoner about two years ago as a rebel spy and was sent from here to Washington D.C. and subsequently to Ft. McHenry MD where he was tried by general court martial and sentenced to 15 years hard labor at this Post, but escaped from there before promulgation of his sentence in General Court Martial orders 7/1/64. I have the honor to request that you send some person here who can identify the person George E. Shearer specified in General Court Martial Order 189, so as to enable me to execute the order."[16]

On 8/10/64 Schoepf received a telegram from the CGP asking if the Maj. George M Shearer of the 1st MD Cav. was the same person who transferred in March of 1863 from Fort Delaware to Fort McHenry.[17] In reply on 8/11/64 Schoepf stated that Shearer was at Fort Delaware but Shearer denied being the one referred to.[18] Shearer asked for an order to send him to Fort McHenry or Old Capitol Prison and said if he is the one he is sentenced to 15 years at hard labor. (This last phrase does not make much sense).

Handy reported that on 7/25/64 Maj. Shearer was removed from the barracks and sent to Co. Q. There is no further mention of Shearer in the Fort's correspondence or in diaries.

Political Prisoners

Prisoners of state, or political prisoners as they are more commonly called, were held in many Northern prison camps, and Fort Delaware was no exception.[19] In some ways the administration of these prisoners was similar to that of the convicts, that is Schoepf and his staff had to keep track of their sentences, receive and answer messages about the charges against them, and about their conduct while imprisoned. This involved correspondence with the CGP, AGO, and the War Department directly. It also meant dealing with civilians whose friends, family members or acquaintances were being held, as well as politicians such as governors asking for certain persons to be released.

As noted previously, political prisoners were at first held in the Fort, but in approximately May 1864 were moved to the POW officers' compound, and remained there for the rest of the war. A sampling of correspondence related to political prisoners is: on 5/7/63 Schoepf sends a Roll of the political prisoners to the CGP (this was done every month)[20]; Schoepf issues an order on 5/18/63 that Andrew Siebert will be sent with two guards to Baltimore[21]; in response to an inquiry sends a message to Major LC Taylor, a judge advocate, containing the charges against political prisoner Frank Grady[22]; on 8/18/63 Schoepf receives a request to send a list of political prisoners no longer at Fort Delaware who have been sent to Fort McHenry, together with a list of charges and their date of confinement, and a list of those willing to take the oath of allegiance to the US[23]; on 12/24/63 the CGP directs Schoepf, at the direction of the Sec. War, to release political prisoners HA Ball and AC Belt unconditionally[24]; on 2/7/64 Schoepf replies to an inquiry from the CGP that all political prisoners present at Fort Delaware were arrested within this Department, and sent here by the Department Commander.[25] Thus most of the correspondence between Schoepf and others concerning political prisoners was mostly routine, but it clearly required much administrative work.

Prisoners-of-War

The administration of the POWs, was, in some ways, a bureaucratic nightmare. There was a separate office for administration of the POW prison located near the prison (see item 25 in Figure 2). Every POW that came onto or left the island, by whatever method, had to be accounted for. Rolls of the prisoners were made out when they arrived, and a new POW Form 36, Descriptive List of Prisoner, was filled out in triplicate. One copy was sent to the CGP in Washington and 2 copies were retained at the Fort. When POWs were transferred from the fort one copy of Form 36 went with them, along with a complete roll of all the prisoners being transferred, and a copy of that roll was sent to the CGP. When a batch of POWs was received at the fort from another prison, a roll of those prisoners was sent with them, with a copy to the CGP. The Fort then prepared a roll of those incoming POWs and sent a copy to the CGP. In other words, the CGP's office received copies of rolls of transferred prisoners from both the sending prison and the receiving prison. The CGP then usually compared these rolls. Much of this is revealed in correspondence between the CGP and Schoepf. For example, in the period of approximately May to early September 1863 there were many problems in getting rolls of incoming prisoners to the island to agree with records of these POWs in the CGP's office. Typical correspondence about rolls during this period is: on 5/22/63 POWs sent off for exchange and triplicate rolls sent by mail[26]; Schoepf sends rolls of POW officers and enlisted men at Fort Delaware on 5/10/63[27]; on 7/5/63 Schoepf sent a roll to the CGP of POWs (sent for?) exchange on 7/4/63 in which Schoepf stated the numerous alterations were needed because the rolls were ordered to be made out a month in advance[28]; on 7/27/63 Schoepf sends a roll of all POWs received since the last rolls were forwarded to the CGP[29]; on 9/2/63 the CGP writes to Schoepf that "A number of petitions from POWs at Fort Delaware have recently been received whose names are not on the rolls of this office and I have to request that you will direct that whenever over 20 prisoners are present whose names have not been furnished a roll may be forwarded without waiting until the end of the month."[30]; on 9/5/63 the CGP again wrote stating that every 5th day of the month rolls of newly arrived prisoners be sent to the CGP's office or an explanation why it cannot be done on that day and an estimate of when it will be done, and when prisoners are transferred to another station the CGP be notified by telegram of the numbers being transferred together with a roll to follow with as little delay as possible.[31] It is clear from the above correspondence that the CGP was unhappy with the accuracy and timing of the sending of rolls, although the CGP had set up the timetable for routine submission of rolls.

Some of the reasons for this seem to be that POWs changed their names when they reported to a new prison, or while they were at a prison, that (naturally) there were clerical errors, and other similar things. POWs could change their names relatively easily because in those days soldiers did not carry personal identification such as the "dog tags" carried by 20th century U.S. soldiers, and there was no other way of identifying the POWs such as photographs or fingerprints. This is probably at least part of the reason that about 39,000 names of POWs appear in the Fort Delaware Society roster of POWs, but it is believed that only about 32,000 or 33,000 actual POWs were present during the war. Although some of this "excess" is due to clerical errors such as name misspellings, a lot of them are probably also due to the POWs changing their names. For these reasons it is likely we will never be able to know the exact number of individual POWs present over the war, but the actual number of POWs present at any one time is known from the morning reports. Thus simply knowing who was a POW was a serious problem for the CGP and those keeping the POW records at the Fort, while knowing the actual number of POWs present at any given time was much more precise. These problems were reported to the CGP in a letter from Schoepf on 9/9/63[32] and paraphrased in the records as "Reports that in consequence of the misrepresentations of many of the prisoners sent there & the incorrectness of the rolls accompanying them it is impossible to have all their names correctly recorded," and hence the absence from his records of the correct names of some of the prisoners concerning when enquiries have been made by CGP Gives example of Lt BH Philpot, 7th VA Cav. alias WT Cooper, Pvt. Co. B, 1st MD Cav., Stephen Glancey[?] alias Thos Pots, Pvt. Co. D, 5th FL, LT JC Lee 15th AR. Three had assumed the rank of Sergt. Says many similar ones are known and unknown to him. Says all care and attention is exercised in the preparation of the rolls but that he finds it impossible to prevent some discrepancies. Desires if any mistake occurs in the future that he will be notified by the CGP before making his endorsement and he will find the proper person and notify the CGP" (some of the above names may be incorrect because of copying handwriting).

Requests for release from various POWs were also the source of much administrative time and correspondence. POWs could request release for various reasons. Most commonly it would have been because they were "impressed" (drafted) into the Confederate Army. This meant officers in the Confederate Army were not eligible because none were drafted. Schoepf then usually reported to the CGP his opinion of whether the prisoner was sincere and telling the truth, and whether he recommended the POW should be released. However, the War Department had the final say on whether a man was to be released.

Particularly from about July to about November 1863 there were many petitions by prisoners, and from the correspondence it seems that Schoepf had spoken personally to many if not all of these men. Correspondence on 11/3/63 sent from Schoepf to the CGP is typical of these requests.[33]

- Forwards letter from John O'Leary and Patrick Kelly requesting to be admitted to return to their allegiance. Their families residing in Boston. Both were

conscripted. Forwarded with recommendation the oath be given to both and both be released.
- Forwards letter from NW Reynolds enclosing a petition. Sets forth that he has a mother and small brother depending on him.
- Transmits letter from Andrew J O'mear, Co. F, 35th AL desiring to take the oath of allegiance, claiming that he voted against secession also that he is a conscript that he has a wife and 2 children in Huntsville, Alabama, and desirous of taking them to Illinois and residing there permanently with them.
- Forwards a letter from RS Heath desiring to know whether he will be permitted to take the oath of allegiance and go north as he is the only support of his family.
- Forwards letter from CM Morrill, Co. K, 20th GA saying he was forced into the rebel service to save his bother-in-law and sister's property. Desires to take the oath of allegiance and stay north.
- Forwards an application for the release of Simon Davis.

As noted in the first item in the list above, Schoepf often remarked in these types of communications that he believed the man to be sincere and the request should be granted.

In some instances, men were granted release but in many instances they were denied or the decision was put off. This is illustrated by correspondence from the CGP to Schoepf on 11/3/63.[34]

- Petitions for release from a number of POWs [list of names and units] have been submitted to Sec. War and were returned to this office with no decision for now.
- By Sec. War release Enoch Bayes, a POW, on taking the oath. The cases of Charles Lisey, Co. E, 36th VA, Carman Nathan, 61st MS, Co. C and RE RUSSell, Co. E, 9th VA have been submitted to the Sec. War and no decision has been made.

In fact, this kind of correspondence continued for at least one more year at a reduced rate, not counting the flurry of requests sent when the Confederacy was collapsing after the surrenders at Appomattox and other places.

Another source of administrative work was the volunteering of POWs to join the Union Army, another way of escaping being a POW. Again the POW had to be drafted into Confederate service. Generally speaking, it appears that such volunteers were not assigned to units that had frontline duty against Confederate forces (they may have been shot as traitors if captured and identified). Rather they were assigned to places such as Fort Delaware, or to units in the West which were "keeping the peace" with the Indians (natives).

On 6/20/63 Schoepf received a telegram from Sec. War which stated that "POWs who have been impressed into the rebel service who wish to take the oath of allegiance and join our army be permitted to do so.[35] You will satisfy yourself that accuracy of the applicant's statement and his good faith." Thus it was left up to Schoepf to decide if a man could join the U.S. Army. Men who did so were often called "galvanized" or "galvanized rebels." There was no shortage of POWs volunteering to join the Union Army. Schoepf apparently wasted little time in recruiting POWs for the Union Army. On 8/5/63[36] Schoepf issued GO 12 which stated "By special authority of the Sec. War Capt. Ahl has raised a battery of artillery for the state of Delaware. This battery is designated 1st DE

Heavy Artillery." The order goes on to state the officers of the battery who were all promoted Union soldiers. This battery was more commonly called "Ahl's Battery" and served faithfully at the Fort throughout the remainder of the war.

An example of some of the confusion about recruiting captured Rebels for the Union Army is the recruiting the 3rd MD Cavalry. The first indication in the records of NARA of recruiting being done for this regiment at Fort Delaware is a telegram sent by Schoepf on 8/10/63[37] to Capt. Jeffries, the AAQM at 8th Army (Middle District) Headquarters, requesting that he order the Quartermaster of the 3rd MD Cavalry to send 400 sets of cavalry jackets, pants, caps and boots for Col. Tevis' regiment. Col Tevis was recruiting to form this regiment, which he would command. Next Schoepf receives a telegram on 8/21/63[38] stating "The Sec. War countermands any authority which may have been given any one to recruit rebels for the US service and directs you to allow no one to recruit from them and discharge any one of them except on orders from this Dept. Order LCol Tevis to return forthwith to his Regiment. You will take possession of any cavalry clothing or property has at Fort Delaware. Direct Col. Tevis to report his arrival at his station with his regiment." A telegram was also sent to Col. Tevis ordering him to report immediately to his station and to report his arrival to the AGO, and to turn over all cavalry clothing in his possession to Capt. Craig, AQM. The next day, 8/22/63, Schoepf,[39] reported that Col. Tevis did not report to him as ordered but simply left Fort Delaware for Philadelphia, without turning in any cavalry clothing, which he had already distributed to his "recruits."

On 8/25/63[40] Schoepf received a telegram signed by Sec. War Stanton stating that they had just received word that there was recruiting among the rebel prisoners, and ordering it to be stopped, except for that already done to recruit a battery for the Fort. He further ordered that if any clothing, weapons, etc., had been given to the new "recruits" it was to be recovered from them, and further ordering that no further recruiting of POWs was to take place without express written orders from the War Department. In his reply by telegram (8/25/63)[41] Schoepf stated that he recovered the jackets, which were in very good condition, and that he had not collected the shoes or pants as the men wearing them needed them. He also stated no man had been discharged from the Post without the approval of the Sec. War. In another telegram on the same day to the Sec. War,[42] Schoepf also wrote saying no one had been recruiting at the Fort for the State of Delaware and that Schoepf had obeyed orders from Gen Schneck to permit Col. Tevis to recruit. Tevis had left the Fort last Saturday and had distributed the clothing before he left without Schoepf's knowledge.

On 8/26/63[43] the Sec. War replied to Schoepf that no blame attached to Schoepf for this incident, and that Schoepf had the Sec. War's full confidence. Also stated that if in Schoepf's opinion it was better to leave the pants and shoes with the POWs, he could do so (and which was done).

On 9/19/63 the Sec. War (or CGP) sent a telegram asking how many recruits had been taken from the POWs, where and by whom.[44] Schoepf replied on 9/19/63[45] to the CGP (or Sec. War) that 147 men were taken to fill Ahl's battery and another 108 to fill up 2 other batteries at Fort Delaware. In addition, Col. Tevis recruited 120 men, 1 man was ordered to report to the Provost Marshall in Boston, and one ordered to Springfield, and 5 men were enlisted for navy service.

This was the end of recruiting for the Army, but on 1/11/64[46] the CGP wrote to Schoepf that the Sec. War directed Schoepf to turn over to the Navy any POWs who would take the oath of allegiance and join the Navy. On 3/8/64 Schoepf wrote to the

Commanding Officer of the Philadelphia Navy Yard[47] that "I have at this Post among the prisoners two men, John Joist and Geo Thompson, the former a Norwegian by birth and is a good sail maker, the latter from Steubenville, Ohio, and an excellent finisher and educated engineer. I have the authority to transfer them to you should you signify the willingness to given them employment. I can recommend them as exemplary good men." A few days later he telegraphed that same Navy Officer, CH Stribling,[48] "if the two men are not willing to enlist in the Navy I will send for them on Wednesday." Then on 3/17/64, Schoepf transmitted a roll of POWs transferred to the U.S. Navy at Philedelphia.[49]

From the totality of the records, it appears that Schoepf was constantly attempting to free POWs, within his orders, using various "methods." For example, on 3/15/64 he wrote to the CGP[50] a message paraphrased in vol. 12 as "Reports that in accordance with General Order No. 64 AGO, February 18, 1864, he has released 3 POWs of whose desertion from the rebel army he has positive proof and whose names will be reported. He has a number of similar cases as per enclosed roll which he wished returned with information whether the order does not apply to their cases," and in a similar vein Schoepf wrote to the CGP on 3/31/64,[51] enclosing two packages of oaths of allegiance, the one marked "A": containing those oaths taken by deserters who delivered themselves to the Union Army, and other marked "B" who claim to be deserters. Schoepf states he is appealed to daily by them to get justice done for them.

There were many other miscellaneous items Schoepf had to deal with. Prisoners could have visitors, but only with the permission of someone of higher authority than Schoepf, for example the Sec. War or CGP. Schoepf issued Special Order 91 on 6/17/63 that stated in part, "No person will be permitted to visit prisoners except by higher authority than the Commanding Officer at this Post having business inside the Post barracks. In no case will Lt. Ahl, commanding the prisoners, permit prisoners to leave the barracks for the purpose of having private interviews with friends."[52] There were many requests for prisoner visits, in some cases because the POW was very ill. For instance, on 10/6/63[53] the CGP wrote twice concerning two prisoners, "Mrs. Ann McElroy wishes to visit her son Pvt. A. McElroy, a prisoner of war at Fort Delaware who is ill. Please allow her to visit him for a few days when you deem it proper." The usual condition attached to these visits was that the visitor had to sign the oath of allegiance to the U.S. In cases where Schoepf found that the visit was on account of illness, and the POW was not ill, the visit was denied. However, apparently there were many such visitors who did get to "interview" their relatives.

Another item that Schoepf had to handle was relations with civilians. Some of them, including ladies, would come to the island on excursions (there was regular steamboat service to Philadelphia, including stops in between). As Handy noted in his day on 7/23/63, "They seemed to enjoy themselves, much, in promenading the ramparts, perambulating the enclosures, and in gazing upon our poor ragged Confederates, as they marched in crowds to the cisterns to fill their canteens." These civilians, besides embarrassing the Confederates, also interfered with the smooth running of the island and to some extent were a security problem. Other civilians also showed up on the island without prior permission, and/or wrote to or sent packages to the POWs in defiance or ignorance of regulations. Thus eventually Schoepf banned casual visitors from the island, and went so far as to sponsor newspaper advertisements which read,[54] "May 23, 1864, Special Orders No. 148-I. Visiting this post out of curiosity is strictly forbidden. II. Relatives of prisoners *seriously ill* will be permitted to make them *short visits* with satisfactory proof of their loyalty to the Unites States Government to Brigadier General A. Schoepf, commanding this post. Under no circumstances will any person be allowed to visit the prisoners without special permission from the President, Sec. War, or Commissary General of Prisoners. III. All contributions to prisoners must be forwarded by express, plainly direct giving name, rank, and regiment in care of Captain George W Ahl, AAAG. Uniform clothing military equipments and intoxicating liquors are among the contraband articles. IV. Prisoners will be permitted to write and receive letters of a *strictly personal nature*, which must be invariably limited to *one page of common letter paper.* By command of BGen A. Schoepf. George W. Ahl, Captain AAAG" (emphasis in original). Note that this later published order is in accord with Special Order 90 in the previous paragraph, and represents how outside contacts with the POWs were handled in May 1864.

As a consequence of being able to send the prisoners money or packages, the CGP on 8/5/64[55] ordered that records be kept of all parcels received for prisoners, together with the disposition of those parcels. The CGP made this order because he received many complaints about parcels not delivered or missing items and in this instance a parcel of clothing had allegedly not been received. On 8/18/64[56] Schoepf sent a receipt for the parcel, indicating the addressee had received his parcel. The result of this is that we have records available at NARA of the packages and money received by the POWs (see Chapter 8).[57]

Prison Security, Shootings and Escapes

As one can plainly conclude, if one visits the island, the fact that the prison was on an island, about 1 mile or more from the mainland, was the best security against escape. In addition, the tidal currents in the Delaware River are very strong, reaching about 4.5 knots (2.3 m/sec). Only during intertidal periods are the currents weak, and these periods are relatively short, making swimming to the shore difficult under the best of conditions.[58] Moreover, during the colder months, such an escape was impossible, since hypothermia would kill anyone who tried such a swim. Of course tunneling (to where?) was useless, especially since most of the island was below the high tide line. Thus one of the reasons for choosing Fort Delaware as a prison camp, the difficulty of escaping, was validated.

Another reason for choosing it was it was an Army base that already existed, and the Fort itself provided security against prisoner uprisings. At any one time there were very few POWs allowed in the Fort. The heavy guns of the Fort could be trained on the POW barracks, and when firing canister shot, could rapidly reduce the barracks to kindling, and kill or wound many of the people who happened to be in the area. Even if the POWs got free of the prison area, they had no chance to capture the Fort, assuming the guards could secure the sally port entrance before the POWs arrived there.

Thus in April through July of 1863, when large numbers of POWs were beginning to be held, the "prison" eventually consisted of the barracks buildings, kitchens, dining rooms, and sinks (privies over the river). Guards were posted in and near these areas, as well as generally about the island.

There were no dead lines, places beyond which a POW would be shot on sight, nor were any orders ever issued (that there are any records of) that guards could shoot POWs anywhere on the island on sight, in other words without warning. The first order we have concerning possible shooting of POWs was issued on 6/29/63, and Special Order 96[59] stated "Prisoners who disobey the Guards are to be shot on the spot." Thus on 8/14/63 Special Order 148[60] stated, "Several prisoners of war have made the attempt to desert from this post is of which now confined. The General Commanding warns prisoners of war at this Post to desist from all such attempts or plots to desert. The good behavior of the prisoners will secure good treatment but at the slightest attempt to create disturbance the guns of the Fort will open fire on the barracks. The Sentinels are instructed to instantly shoot any prisoners refusing to obey this order." Later orders were more explicit about what a sentry could do or not; Special Orders 157, 6/1/64[61] stated, in part, "II. It is the duty of the sentinel to prevent prisoners from escaping, or cutting or defacing, or in any way damaging any of the Government property, or from committing any nuisance in or about their barracks, or from using any abusive or insolent language toward them, and from any violation of good order. Should the sentinel detect any prisoner in violating these instructions, he must order him three distinct time to halt, and if the prisoner obeys the order the sentinel must call for the corporal of the guard and have the prisoner placed in arrest. But should the prisoner fail to halt when so ordered, the sentinel must enforce his orders by bayonet or ball."

The idea of not shooting a prisoner without warning seems to be what actually happened. For example, Handy reports on 7/28/63 that on 7/27/63, a sentry discovered three men trying to escape by wading out into the river after they had gone through the privy holes. The guard ordered them to return and two did so and were not fired on, but the third escapee persisted and was shot and killed. Similarly on 7/7/64 Mckey described the capture of 3 officers who were attempting to escape by crawling through ditches in the camp. They were recaptured without a shot being fired. A list of shootings and (attempted) escapes compiled from Diaries and some official correspondence appear in Table 3-1.

Table 3-1. Escapes and Shootings

Date	Source	Reason	Description
6/19/63	Peters	Man refused to stop when challenged.	Bullet went into barracks, no one hurt.
6/24/63	Peters, also RG393, Pt. 4, E346, OB522, p. 71	None by Peters, but Schoepf on 10/26/63 reports to Middle Dept.	Schoepf—Geo Geck(?), Co. A, 25th AL, accident, when one of the POWs attempted to escape and the bullet went into a barracks killing Geck.
7/26/63	Handy	Guard thought he was trying to escape.	Victim was standing in line for the privy, killed
7/27/63	Handy, See also RG393, Pt. 4, E352, p. 77, and Hamilton	Attempted escape through privy holes.	3 POWs wading out challenged. Two returned. One who did not return shot and killed by buckshot.
7/28/63	Peters, Franklin, Purvis	Attempt to escape by swimming	Killed.
8/13/63	Handy, Peters, Hamilton		Said 9 men escaped last night. Purvis—30 tried but some recaptured. Hamilton—3 men found drowned.

3. Prison Camp Administration and Security

Date	Source	Reason	Description
8/14/63	Hamilton		Last night 2 Lt.s escaped from hospital
8/15/63	Handy		Two escapees found drowned 8 miles from fort. Several others caught in escape attempts.
8/30/63	Handy	Rumor of shooting	Said to be man trying to escape.
9/20/63	Handy		One drowned trying to escape, several days ago.
10/22/63	Handy		A convict named Johnson escaped on a coal boat.
11/4/63	Hamilton		Rebels left on raft, 3 drowned and 2 alive.
2/18/64	Nugent		Several prisoners escaped last weekend. but recaptured.
3/10/64	Hamilton		Caught 10 rebels trying to escape. Put in cell
3/13/64	Hamilton		Foil plan by rebels to take steamer and escape.
4/10/64	Handy & Allen	Two men going to privy shot.	Stormy night. Apparently men did not hear guard's challenge. Both wounded, but one dies later.
4/10/64	Allen & Handy	Unknown.	Lt. Halliburton(?) shot while playing ball.
4/12/64	RG249, E10, vol. 12, #465		Schoepf forwards investigation of shooting of S.B. David, Co. B, 8th TN Cav. to CGP
5/10/64	Handy, McCrorey, Mckey, Allen, Boyle	Refused to follow guard's orders.	Col Jones shot (later dies)
6/5/64	Nugent	Shot heard	Unknown
7/2/64	Mckey	Several officers & privates escaped last night	One officer lost way and went back to island and recaptured. Several privates picked up this morning, one carried 16 miles downstream.
7/6/64	Hamilton		Five rebel officers captured on beach trying to escape.
7/7/64	Mckey, McCrorey, Handy		Mckey—3 officers attempted to escape by crawling through ditch which ran through camp. Were spotted by outside sentry, and a squad of 1 Lt. and soldiers went there. Lt. stopped soldiers from shooting. POWs taken to Fort.
7/9/64	Hamilton		Five rebels captured trying to escape.

Date	Source	Reason	Description
7/10/64	RG393, Pt. 4, E346, OB522, p. 122	Schoepf reports on shooting of Col. Jones	Schoepf states an inquiry was held and the shooting was found justified because Col. Jones did not obey an order from Sentinel.
7/15/64	Eames		Rebs are trying to get away almost every night. Use "life preservers.
7/29/64	Handy	Body found in water, drowned.	Apparently man trying to escape.
8/3/64	Handy	Unknown.	Handy heard a shot. Result unknown.
8/7/64	Handy	Gun(s) fired. Unknown reason.	One killed and one arm amputation
8/8/64	Cox	Man shot near privy.	Reason unknown.
8/18/64	Handy		Rumor. 50 men escaped last Sunday and another 44 last Monday. Only 4 caught.
8/27/64	Fletcher		Man shot for using insulting language to sentinel and refusing to desist. Wounded slightly in leg.
8/28/64	Handy	Two men escaping fired on, No known hits.	Thought the guards deliberately missed.
9/3/64	Mckey, Handy (on Aug. 30)	Sentry claimed man stopped to urinate	Mckey—he stopped to give friends chew of tobacco. Leg broken and had to be amputated. Died.
10/6/64	Handy		Two men on burial detail escaped.
12/20/64	Mckey, Alburtis	One private disobeyed order not to throw water out from barracks	Sentry fired at man, missing him. Innocent man in barracks hit and killed.
5/27/65	Alburtis	Accidental	Member of 11th MD regt. was shot by one of his own men.

It is very *likely* that not all shootings, escapes and escape attempts are listed in Table 3-1. Also *probably* not listed are escapees who were caught after getting off the island, for example by provost guards in various cities such as Baltimore.

A complete survey of escapes from other records, including perusing the register of POWs in M598, as well as other records including newspaper (North and South) accounts, memoirs, etc., was made by Mackie.[62] According to his compilation, in 1863 there were a total of 27 POWs and one convict who escaped. Of these apparently 13 POWs apparently survived and made it back South; the fate of the other 14 POWs is unknown. In 1864 13 men attempted to escape, of which 8 made it successfully, one whose fate is unknown, 2 who were recaptured and two who drowned. In 1865 12 men allegedly escaped, but there is no documentation for 11 of them, and the other one was successful. In addition there are listed in the records 29 other escapees without dates. Of these the fate of 23 is unknown and six were successful. All of these numbers must be taken as approximate, as recordkeeping was difficult, and sometimes haphazard, at best, particularly for those whose fate is unknown. For those whose fate is unknown, it is quite *likely*

3. Prison Camp Administration and Security

that of those who did actually try to escape, a goodly percentage of them died probably by drowning.

There were some interesting methods used to escape as detailed by Mackie. Many used boards and/or canteens as flotation devices.

- On 8/6/63 an unknown POW apparently shouldered a knapsack and marched off with the 5th DE Regiment which was leaving.
- On 8/15/63 Joseph G. Marable and William D. Reid walked out the gate without being stopped, found a ladder, reentered and boiled their clothes in the prison (to free them of lice), walked out again and then used the ladder as a boat as they paddled to New Jersey. They found a farmer's boat there and paddled to Delaware.
- James Johnson, a convict, after three unsuccessful escape attempts, hid on a coal boat, and was not discovered when it was searched.
- In July 1863 Charles W. Rivenbark bribed a guard and successfully escaped.
- On an unknown date an unknown prisoner who was at the hospital removed a body from a coffin, and then hid in the coffin. When the coffin landed in New Jersey (for burial), the man jumped out and escaped through an apple orchard.
- One of the more interesting escapes was described in later years by a guard at the Fort.[63] In the winter of 1863–1864 the Union soldiers spent some of their spare time ice skating on the frozen river. At one point some of the guards asked a couple of POWs, who were from Florida and who had shown great interest in the skating, whether they would like to try it. They strapped skates on the Floridians and then the guards laughed as they watched the POWs repeatedly falling. One of the POWs kept getting further and further away, taking hilarious pratfalls. However, when he was out of musket range, he "set off down the river like a professional skater" and was never seen again.

The OR also gives data for escapes from various prisons.[64] Fort Delaware's escapes from this source are listed in Table 3-2.

Table 3-2. Escapes from Fort Delaware

Month	1863	1864	1865
January		0	0
February		1	0
March		1	0
April	0	0	0
May	0	0	11
June	1	0	0
July	0	10	
August	8	8	
September	10	0	
October	4	2	
November	1	1	
December	1	0	

One may ask what happened to a prisoner who tried to escape and was recaptured. Schoepf wondered this also and on 7/8/64 asked the CGP whether attempted escape should be punished.[65] The CGP replied on 7/13/64[66] that "The simple attempt to escape by a prisoner is not an offence for which he should be punished, but he may with great propriety be placed in more strict confinement where he will have no opportunity to make the attempt." The CGP went on to say that if crimes such as forgery, bribery and wearing a Federal uniform are involved the confinement may be so vigorous as to be a punishment, and for violating prison discipline they may also be punished. It appears that many of the prisoners caught while trying to escape were first sent to the guard house or fort, but there is no record, in diaries or NARA records, that these men were held outside the general prison population for more than a few days.[67]

Another factor to be considered was the ratio of Union soldiers to POWs on the island. Typically this was about 5 to about 12 to each Union soldier. The "permanent" garrison of artillerymen numbered much less than 1,000, so other units, infantry regiments or parts of infantry regiments were usually present on the island. Table 3-3 is a list of such units which were present.[68]

Table 3-3. Union Infantry Regiments Present on Pea Patch Island

Arrival Date	Departure Date	Unit	Notes
6/20/63	8/6/63	5th DE Infantry	Mustered in Oct./Nov. 1862
8/7/63	8/22/63	6th DE Infantry	Mustered in Dec. 1862
8/22/63	10/30/63	Purnell Legion Infantry (MD)	3 year regiment—combat veterans
11/1/63	6/6/64	5th MD Infantry	3 year regiment—combat veterans
1/30/64	3/10/64	1st Eastern Shore Regt. (MD)	combat veterans
6/6/64	8/24/64	157th OH Infantry	100 days regiment
8/14/64	10/19/64	6th MA Veteran Vol.	100 days state militia—some combat veterans
10/19/64	1/20/65	9th DE Infantry	100 days regiment
11/5/64	11/15/64	196th PA Infantry	100 days regiment
1/20/65	5/30/65	11th MD Infantry	100 days regiment—combat veterans
4/16/65	6/1/65	165th NY Infantry	3 year regiment—combat veterans
5/26/65	6/15/65	201st PA Infantry	1 year regiment
5/31/65	7/31/65	215th PA Infantry	100 days militia regiment

These units ranged from inexperienced such as the 157th OH, to combat veterans such as the Purnell Legion and 165th NY. In some instances veteran units were probably assigned to Fort Delaware to recuperate and rebuild their numbers.

As time went on, security, and methods for improving security, were changed. On 2/16/64 Schoepf recommended to the CGP that an enclosure be built around the POW camp as this would be of "more effectually securing the prisoners with less guards."[69] On 3/5/64 the CGP replied[70] that the Sec. War approved the construction of a fence. As it turned out, this fence was seven feet (2.1 m) high,[71] topped in some portions with walkways for guards. This fence encircled the entirety of the POW barracks, the prison bakery, the paths to the sinks (privies), and the kitchens and dining rooms, so virtually all the activities of the prison camp were within these walls.

On 6/29/64 Handy recorded that "cupolas" (guard towers?) were being erected on the adjoining barracks, in which were to be placed large lamps in the charge of the guards. He commented this would, together with the Drummond light, light up a large part of the island.

On 4/10/64 Handy noted that "A magnificent Drummond light has been erected on the west bank of the island, in front of the barracks, and in the direction of the Delaware shore. It is capable of illuminating the water, and bank, for a space of 100 yards [91 m] in circumference [radius?]—another precautionary measure adopted since the arrival of the Confederate officers."

The Drummond light was the most powerful illumination device for most of the 19th century.[72] It is the device that caused the coining of the term "limelight," since it works by heating a piece of lime to a very high temperature using an oxygen/hydrogen torch (other fuels, such as illuminating gas, may be substituted for hydrogen, but hydrogen gives the brightest light), which causes the lime to glow with an intense white light. These lights are most famous for being used in theaters to illuminate the players, hence the phrase "being in the limelight." Their use required a supply of oxygen and hydrogen (or other fuel). Operating the light required a skilled operator, otherwise fires or explosions were more likely to happen.

Nothing more is stated about this light in any record that was found. This advanced technology was used at Fort Delaware to prevent escapes, especially since it overlooked the privies which were commonly used to get into the river. Interestingly enough, although Drummond lights were used in the theater, for lighthouses, and for large outdoor gatherings, a short internet search did not find any mention of them being used as searchlights in prisons, except for Fort Delaware.

The things available to the POWs which could be of use in an escape did not avoid "regulation." Schoepf sent a roll of prisoners who had escaped in the last month to the CGP on 8/10/64,[73] and mentions that many of them used canteens as buoys (flotation devices) and case knives were used as saws to saw through the sinks (privies) which were over the river. He mentions he has confiscated all canteens and case knives from the POWs. This was largely confirmed in prisoners' diaries. Handy reported on 7/28/63 that some Confederates who were trying to escape were discovered and they had used canteens as floats. Handy also mentions that the body of a drowned POW washed ashore on 9/20/63, and canteens were attached to the body. Handy reported a drowned man with canteens attached was discovered on 8/3/64. On 7/3/64 perhaps 3,000 canteens were removed from the enlisted men's quarters (Handy and Mckey), and on 7/5/64 canteens were confiscated from the officer POWs (Mckey and Handy). There was another search on 7/8/64 in the officer's quarters and more canteens seized (Mauck).

On 7/29/64 both Mckey and Handy reported that the prisoners were not furnished knives, forks or spoons for eating with. This apparently continued for the remainder of the war. On 8/25/64 Handy quotes a note thrown over the fence from the enlisted men's barracks stating, "We are not even allowed a knife, or spoon, because one of our officers got drunk, and threatened that he could take the Fort with knives." The truth of this cannot be confirmed. Prisoners were apparently allowed to keep small knives for they continued to make bone jewelry and other items for sale, and carry on occupations such as cobbler and tailor. On 7/2/64 some pocket knives were confiscated from the officer POWs.

On 7/4/64, with Independence Day celebrations taking place on the island, Handy reported that "Several of our officers have availed themselves of the festive occasion by donning the costume of 'Uncle Sam' and walking out of 'the pen' (Item 2, Figure 2).

How they managed to prepare for this feat has not been revealed." There is no mention of their trying to escape, but just enjoying the day on the island. Schoepf's response to this was to confiscate all dark (blue) clothing from the POWs, as well as valuables that could be used to bribe guards such as paper money, gold, and pocket watches on 7/5/64 and 7/6/64 as reported by Mauck, Mckey, Handy, and Allen. Confiscated clothing was replaced with grey clothing, and sutler's coupons were given in exchange for the gold and money taken.

Clearly Schoepf was angered (and *probably* embarrassed) by the events of 7/4/64, and the large number of escapes attempted around that date. Handy reported that on 7/8/64, Schoepf visited the POW officer pen and said he would put a stop to escape attempts, and that "They [guards] shall shoot any man the tries to get away." *Probably* as a result of all this POW activity McCrorey reported on 7/9/64 that "The guns of the fort have been turned on the Barracks."

Another security measure was the USS *Moccasin*.[74] This ship was originally built as the wooden screw tug *Hero*, purchased by the Navy on 7/11/64 and commissioned on 7/11/64 as the gunboat *Moccasin*, Acting Ensign James Brown in command. As there were fears at the time that there may have been a plot afoot to help POWs escape from Fort Delaware, she was assigned as a guard boat off Fort Delaware from 7/25/64 to 8/13/64, and again from 8/19/64 until early 1865.

The gunboat was essentially unarmed except for personal weapons until 9/3/64, when she was equipped with 3 12–pounder cannons. Nevertheless she may have been responsible for recapturing, or recovering some of the bodies of POW escapees as reported in Table 3-2.

Detectives were also used by Schoepf to gather intelligence about the POWs and their intentions, and for other purposes. On 1/16/64 Schoepf wrote to the Provost Marshall General[75] that with the aid of Detectives (*apparently* in the prisoner pens) he was able to find 18 Union deserters among the POWs. Schoepf suggests they be used in a similar fashion in other POW camps to detect Union deserters. On 8/24/64[76] Schoepf reports a Detective has found that Dr. Edward P. Worrell of Delaware City helped a POW to escape and has been arrested. On 2/25/64 Schoepf sent the report of a detective to the CGP[77] who had been sent to Philadelphia to get information on certain rebel sympathizers and abettors who are conniving at the escape of prisoners from Fort Delaware and other depots. Schoepf goes on to state if the CGP has similar views he will try to implicate further persons in the plot(s). Finally, on 9/29/64[78] the CGP telegraphs Schoepf that the Sec. War has ordered that all the detectives employed at Fort Delaware be discharged.

Apparently the POWs were not unaware that there were spies among them. Handy reports on 7/11/64 that "spies" were in the pen. On 6/7/64 Handy stated that Lt. Wolf (Union) was in the quarters after Taps and overheard how letters were smuggled out (without censorship), and again on 9/26/64 Wolf, in disguise, was detected.

There do not appear to be any further major changes in security precautions at the prison camp until the end of the war.

Punishment

Aside from imprisonment, the most severe form of sanctioned punishment in the U.S. Army was "Corporeal Punishemnt."[79] However, the Regulations did not specify what corporeal punishments could be used.

There is not much mention of routine punishment of prisoners of various sorts in the official records (excluding convicts) or diaries. Hanging by the thumbs was probably considered the most severe punishment (see Figure 9). It is mentioned twice by Handy as having been applied to convicts in Company Q, on 10/5/64 and 10/21/64. He also reports that on 10/1/64 a galvanized (now Union) soldier was hung by the thumbs for selling his uniform, that a deserter from the Union army was punished similarly on 8/19/64, and a POW was hung "*a la Sepoy*" on 11/3/64 for stealing a pair of boots while drunk. Handy reports this POW was a New Yorker, and a generally "bad boy" and probably deserved punishment. Handy also reports the punishment was not rigidly applied. Park describes how on 4/20/65 a POW adjutant bribed a guard to mail a letter to his sweetheart, the letter was discovered, and the adjutant was then hung by his thumbs when he refused to divulge the name of the person who helped him. Park described how the man finally fainted after this "cruel torture." Hamilton also reports that a Union soldier was hung by his thumbs on 5/26/63 for inducing a guard to get drunk while on duty.

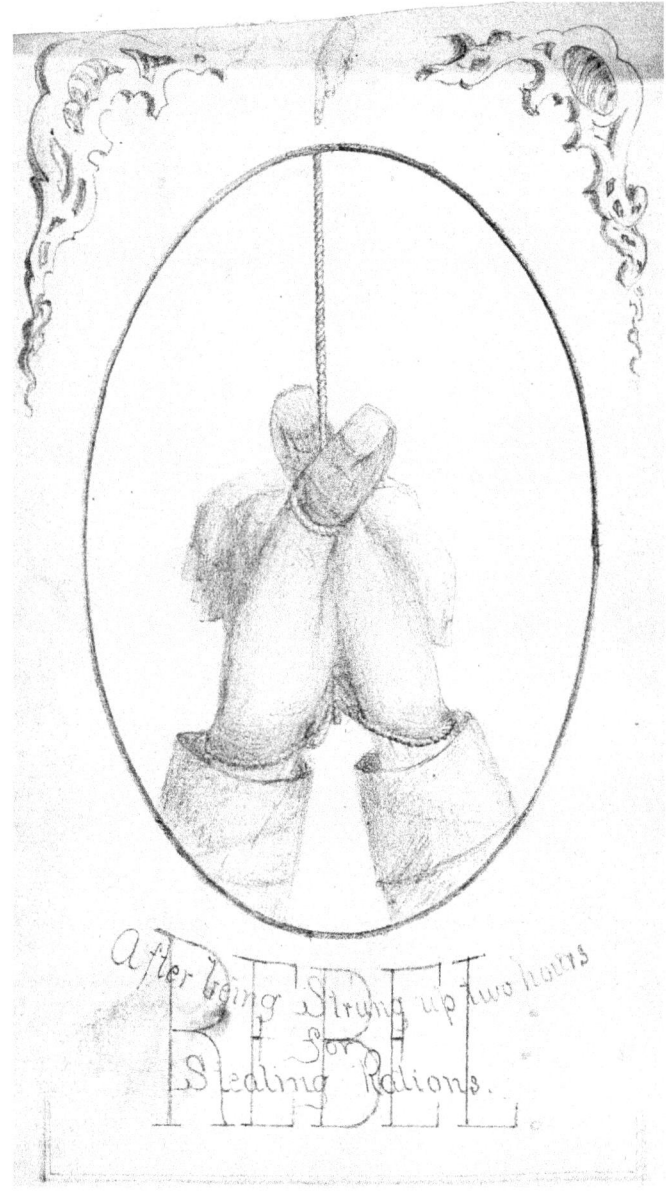

Figure 9. "Rebel Hands After Being Strung Up Two Hours." Undated from the sketchbook of Pvt. Baldwin Coolidge, 6th MA VV. States the rebel was punished for stealing rations (courtesy Delaware Historical Society).

A less severe punishment was "wearing the barrel" (see Figure 10). The miscreant would be forced to put on his shoulders a barrel, one of whose ends was taken out, and the other end had a circular hole cut in it so it would slip over his head. There were two holes cut in the side of the barrel near the end that had the hole for his head, so that he could slip his arms through those side holes. Perhaps an appropriate sign would be hung around his neck saying something such as "Thief," "Drunkard," etc. He would then be

Left: Figure 10. Punishment—Wearing the Barrel, dated 9/17/64, from the sketchbook of Pvt. Baldwin Coolidge, 6th MA VV. This punishment was designed to embarrass the miscreant, in this case for being drunk. Note the drummer accompanying the group, to bring attention to the drunkard. Unknown if the drunkard is a Union or Confederate soldier (courtesy Delaware Historical Society).

Right: Figure 11. Punishment—Walking the Beat, undated drawing from the sketchbook of Pvt. Baldwin Coolidge, 6th MA VV. The man is carrying a log as if carrying a musket on guard duty, in this instance for the third day. This was done to punish Union soldiers, in this case for fighting (courtesy Delaware Historical Society).

forced to parade around an area where he was known, such as the prisoner's barracks or the Fort parade ground, accompanied by a drummer and (usually) an armed guard. Although wearing the barrel was probably uncomfortable, the main point of this punishment seems to be humiliation and embarrassment. See Figure 10 for how this was done. It is mentioned only once, by Handy, and that on 10/14/63 it was applied to a convict.

Another punishment, apparently meted out only to Union solders for slight offenses, was reported by Fletcher on 9/17/64 to be walking a "beat" (similar to a guard post) carrying a log instead of a musket (see Figure 11). The length of time this had to be done depended on the severity of the offense.

4

The Food Ration

I missed getting my supper and feel very hungry, but expect to be hungry as long as I stay here.—Sgt. Joseph E. Purvis, 19th Virginia Infantry, July 9, 1863

If you want to know what the government did, follow the money.—John Vandereedt, NARA Archivist (Retired)

One of the most controversial aspects of treatment of POWs by both sides during the Civil War was whether prisoners were seriously underfed, sometimes to the point of starvation. Was Sgt. Purvis' expectation about going hungry met, or were he and the other prisoners given adequate rations? How did the POW rations compare to Union Army rations? Up until now the only sources we have had for the actual amount and quality of food given to the prisoners have been accounts from the prisoners themselves, sometimes in contemporaneous diaries such as Sgt. Purvis,' but mostly in postwar accounts. As noted in the Preface, postwar accounts are very often unreliable, and so there has been almost no "hard" information available as to what the POWs actually got to eat. The detailed Commissary records for Fort Delaware in the National Archives have been found, and these are the key to answering the questions "What did the prisoners get to eat?," and "How did the prisoner rations compare to Union Soldiers' rations?"

The Commissary Records

The tale of the Commissary records in the National Archives is fascinating. According to Mr. John Vandereedt, retired archivist, these records were believed lost or destroyed, until, when Archives II was completed in the 1990's, and huge numbers of records were being moved from warehouses in Suitland, Maryland, to the new building, hundreds of old wooden record boxes with these records were discovered. Before transferring these boxes to Archives II, the records were haphazardly dumped into nonarchival cardboard cartons and were classified as RG 217, UD (undocumented) 1001.

These records, which appear to contain reports from all army Commissary officers from 1861 to 1894, are part of Record Group 217, records of the Treasury Department. Commissary officers sent their monthly reports to the Commissary General of Subsistence in Washington for auditing. After approval they were then sent to the 3rd Auditor of the Treasury for reauditing and reapproval. They then were classified as part of the Treasury Department records.

When I tried to start finding Fort Delaware's records (under the names of

Commissary officers such as Lt. Steck and Lt. or Capt. Clark) with Mr. Vandereedt by literally going through the cardboard boxes in the stacks, we happened to find Lt. Steck's records from April to June 1862. This convinced me that the Fort Delaware records were most likely among the approximately 1,200 boxes of records. I then started to retrieve the boxes and go through them, but due to the fragile nature of the records, the Archives personnel decided they had to be reboxed before I could do that. Ms. Ann Cummings, a supervisor there, was true to her word. After about 6 months I was able, with Mr. Vandereedt's help, even though he was then retired, to get back into the stacks and find the 5 boxes among the now over 3,200 archival record boxes which contained the Fort Delaware records. For the record, although there is a rough index of all the boxes' contents (by Commissary officer last name and year), it is not always accurate. The Fort Delaware records from Capt. Clark, which cover the time period of this book, are in new box numbers 594 (1863), 909 (1864), and 1739 (1865). It is likely that data from most if not all other Union prison camps are also in this set of records, as well as information on other U.S. Army units in general from 1861 to 1894.

Nominal Rations

Rations for Union soldiers were originally set forth in the Army Regulations of 1861, and stated what those rations would be in section 1194.[1] In addition, section 745 stated "They [POWs] receive for subsistence one ration each, without regard to rank." The Union soldier's and prisoner's rations stayed the same until April 20, 1864, when prisoners rations were reduced, fresh beef to 14 oz./day and soft bread to 16 oz./day.[2] On June 1, 1864, both prisoner and Union soldier rations were reduced.[3] The Union soldier's ration was reduced somewhat in quantity because the War Department felt too much food was being wasted,[4] but the prisoner's ration was reduced more drastically to what the War Department believed the nominal ration for Union prisoners in Confederate prisons was. These rations are summarized in Table 4-1.[5]

Table 4-1. Nominal Rations, POW and Union Soldiers

	All		POW		Union Soldier	
	Before x/64	*After 4/20/64*	*After 5/64*	*After 1/65*	*After 6/1/64*	*After 7/8/64*
Fresh Beef	20 oz	14 oz	14 oz	14 oz	20 oz	20 oz
Soft Bread	22 oz	18 oz	16 oz	16 oz	18 oz	18 oz
Per 100 Rations						
Beans or Peas	15 lbs	6 qts	12.5 lbs	12.5 lbs	15 lbs	15 lbs
Green Coffee	10 lbs	7 lbs	-	-	10 lbs	10 lbs
Sugar	15 lbs	14 lbs	-	-	15 lbs	15 lbs
Vinegar	4 qts	-	3 qts	2 qts	4 qts	4 qts
Candles	20 oz	6 candles	-	-	20 oz	20 oz
Soap	4 lbs	4 lbs	4 lbs	2 lbs	4 lbs	4 lbs
Salt	3 lbs, 12 oz	2 qts	3 lbs, 12 oz	2 lbs	3 lbs, 12 oz	3 lbs, 12 oz
Pepper	4 oz	-	-	-	4 oz	4 oz
Potatoes	30 lbs	30 lbs	15 lbs	-	30 lbs	-
Rice or Hominy	-	8 lbs	-	8 lbs	-	10 lbs

As can be seen from Table 4-1, the main ingredients in the ration were bread, soft (freshly baked) or hard (hardtack), and meat. The meat was not necessarily fresh beef but could be a preserved meat such as salt pork or salt beef. These preserved meats were also reduced proportionately. At Fort Delaware fresh beef and soft bread were served the majority of the time to both the Union soldiers and prisoners.

Many who argue that the POWs were "starved" argue that they did not get the full ration, especially after May 1864.[6] In support of this they point to the very large amounts of money left in Union prisons' "Prison Funds," which they state largely came from withholding additional food from prisoners. The accuracy of this type of statement is dealt with in more detail in Chapter 5, "The Prison Fund." Clearly this argument is not necessarily rendered false by a simple listing of prisoner rations in Army regulations or orders, or an order issued by the CGP, but using the detailed records contemporaneously created by Capt. Clark, we can determine what the prisoners were actually fed.

Actual Prisoner Rations

In Clark's reports to the CGS each month were his accounts of how much food he got, what happened to that food, accounting for the cash he spent, etc. Many of these forms are found in Article XLIII of the Revised Army Regulations of 1863.[7] Of particular interest in finding the actual prisoner provisions issued is Form 2, on pages 262–263 of the Regulations. Form 2 was meant to record issues to U.S. troops, but Capt. Clark adapted it to his own use by crossing out and replacing various words, such as crossing out "troops" and substituting for it "prisoners." Besides detailing what food the prisoners received, Form 2 also had the accounting for the amount of money spent on the rations, and the running account of the Prison Fund. A complete summary of all food issued to POWs (in this chapter POWs include political prisoners, who were fed with the POWs) from April 1863 through July 1865 (when essentially all prisoners had been released) is shown in Table 4-2.

All of the quantities in Table 4-2 are in pounds, except for vinegar which is in gallons. If one cares to divide the quantities of any particular item in the ration by the number of rations for that month one finds that for most of this time period full rations, as shown in Table 4-1, were given to the prisoners. There are some "shortages" of various items in April–October 1863 and February 1864, but no shortages of any food item, except salt, after May of 1864. These "shortages" are detailed in Tables 5-2, 5-3 and 5-4, the chapter on the Prison Fund. It is believed that, before June 1864, this food was withheld to build the Prison Fund so that certain facilities that the prisoners used or shared, such as the Hospital, could be built. Again details of how much money was saved, and by the withholding of these items, is detailed in Tables 5-2 and 5-3. How the money was spent is also detailed in Chapter 5.

In some ways the prisoners were better off than both Union and Confederate soldiers in the field. On average the prisoners' meat ration was about 60 percent (4 days per week) fresh beef, and their bread ration was soft (freshly baked) bread about 60–80 percent (5–6 days per week) of the time. These were considered luxuries by soldiers in the field, especially those on the march.[8] If one glances at Table 4-2 one finds corn meal listed, and corn meal was not part of the U.S. Army ration. According to Capt. Clark, "The bread as now issued, is made of one-fifth of corn meal and four-fifths of flour. This change was made at the request of the prisoners."[9] Thus, at least to some extent, the prisoners taste in food was being accommodated.

Table 4-2. Prisoners'

Month		Total Rations	Pork	Bacon	Salt Beef	Fresh Beef	Flour	Hard Bread	Beans	Corn Meal
Apr-63	Rations	11314	2395		2357	6433	7273	4041	4752	
	Quantity		1796		2428	8041	10000	4041	660	
May-63	Rations	21482	4930		8979	7573	12653	8829	10432	
	Quantity		3697		9151	7573	17397	8829	1560	
Jun-63	Rations	68223	15437		21411	31325	41716	26507	25230	
	Quantity		11615		22168	39156	46930	26507	3780	
Jul-63	Rations	245009	85559		53137	106313	132741	112268	105407	
	Quantity		64169		54137	132891	149333	112268	15780	
Aug-63	Rations	269792	69538		43576	156678	155292	114500	113114	
	Quantity		52153		44406	195807	213526	114500	16967	
Sep-63	Rations	231180	53154		46236	131790	76784	146562	99390	7834
	Quantity		39865		47139	164737	105578	146562	14908	9792
Oct-63	Rations	137561	35609		31126	76818	72889	49740	60743	20924
	Quantity		26706		31729	96022	100222	49740	9111	26155
Nov-63	Rations	71615	14057	11866	11990	33702	57708		37913	13907
	Quantity		10542	8899	12249	42127	79348		5686	17383
Dec-63	Rations	69658	8766	11354	9100	40438	56484		29220	13174
	Quantity		6574	8515	9303	50547	77665		4383	16467
Jan-64	Rations	67046	17053	4420	6633	38940	54352		28106	12694
	Quantity		12789	3315	8291	48675	74734		4215	15867
Feb-64	Rations	65569	13562		13652	38445	54469	2197	27124	8903
	Quantity		16952		16952	48056	79894	2197	4068	11128
Mar-64	Rations	147742	30797		39546	77399	81843	51087	70343	10812
	Quantity		23097		49432	96748	112534	51087	10551	13515
Apr-64	Rations	163597	32588		33617	97392	87912	59562	66205	16123
	Quantity		24441		42031	121740	120879	59562	9930	24153
May-64	Rations	209546	34946	19839	35119	119622	163556	26131	19924	19859
	Quantity		21841	12411	43898	144669	184000	2284	4341	22341
Jun-64	Rations	230679	46859	46521		137299	138570	68862	92906	23247
	Quantity		29286	29075		120136	138570	60254	11613	23247
Jul-64	Rations	260203	50145	25560	33400	157095	243502	16701	100634	
	Quantity		31340	15975	29225	132214	243502	14613	12579	
Aug-64	Rations	283215	47625	52235	8206	145149	172434	25954	96227	54827
	Quantity		29765	32646	7180	127005	172434	22709	12028	54827
Sep-64	Rations	231451	46031	31085	15534	138801	231451		93165	
	Quantity		28764	19428	13592	121450	231451		11645	
Oct-64	Rations	224773	36369	36394		152010	210446		84998	14327
	Quantity		22730	22746		133008	210446		10624	14327
Nov-64	Rations	209123	34746	20937		152439	146494	41750	66250	20878
	Quantity		21716	13085		134259	146494	36531	8281	20878
Dec-64	Rations	212971	54958	20552		137461	170627	13758	66837	28586
	Quantity		34348	12845		120278	170827	12038	8354	28586
Jan-65	Rations	210900	54348	27308	27316	101928	170172		52318	40728
	Quantity		33987	17067	23901	89187	170172		6602	40728
Feb-65	Rations	194134	48714	48623	20634	76168	194134		52263	
	Quantity		30446	30389	18054	66642	194134		6532	
Mar-65	Rations	202893	71644	54816		76433	178795	24095	76318	
	Quantity		44777	34260		66878	178795	15061	9539	
Apr-65	Rations	214990	58803	49810	20930	85447	127388	87602	88441	
	Quantity		36751	31131	18313	74766	127388	54751	11055	
May-65	Rations	207803	46655	53142	27437	80568	66019	141784	53148	
	Quantity		29159	33214	24007	74497	66019	88605	6643	
Jun-65	Rations	107248	28341	28348	6200	41926	89305	17943	49173	
	Quantity		17713	17717	5425	36685	89305	11214	6147	
Jul-65	Rations	1782			676	390	716		1782	1386
	Quantity				423	341	627		1114	173

4. The Food Ration

Rations, Complete Listing

Rice	Ground Coffee	Coffee	Tea	Sugar	Vinegar	Candles	Salt	Pepper	Molasses	Potatoes	Soap
6562		11314		11314	11314	11314	11314				11314
656		1131		1697	113	141	420				452
7572	3477	18005		21482	21482	21482	21482		3673	4948	21482
757	278	1800		3222	268	268	780		36	4948	850
34051	4508	63715		68223	68223	68223	68223		13682	572	68223
3405	345	5734		9537	632	852	2520		136	572	2728
139602	3220	241789		245009	245009	245009	245009				245009
13960	225	21761		34301	2450	3062	9180				9800
156678		269792		269792	269792	269792	269792				269792
15667		24281		37770	2697	3372	10117				10791
131790	69180	162000		231180	231180	231180	231180			69860	231180
13179	4842	14580		32365	2383	2889	8669			20958	9247
76818		135374	2187	137561	137561	137561	137561	13122	15356	137561	137561
7681		12183	32	19258	1375	1719	5158	32	38	44268	5502
33702	6960	64665		71615	71615	71615	71615	23730	1330	70865	71615
3370	487	5818		10026	716	895	2685	59	3	21259	2864
40438	68077	1581		69658	69658	69658	69658	69658	1581	69658	69658
4043	4765	142		9752	696	870	2612	174	3 Galls	20897	2612
38940	66066	980		67046	67046	67046	67046	67046	67046	67046	67046
3894	4624	88		9386	670	838	2514	167	167	20113	2681
38445	64283	1286		65569	65569	65569	65569	65569	65569	65569	65569
3844	4499	115		9179	655	819	2458	163	163	19670	2622
77399	146836	906		147742	147742	147742	147742	147742	147742	147742	147742
7739	10278	81		20682	1477	1846	5540	369	369	44322	5909
97392	162507	1090		163597	163597	163597	163597	163597	163597	163597	13597
9739	11375	98		22903	1635	2044	6134	405	405	49079	6593
119622	208743	550		209546	209546	209546	209546	209546	209546	209546	209546
9569	10437	32		29336	1571	873	7851	523	523	62863	522
137773					230664		230664			148280	230664
11021					1729		8644			22242	9226
67808					260203		260203			258662	260203
5424					1457		9757			38799	10405
120498					249549		249549			248949	
9639					9981		9358			37343	
138286					231451		231451			163451	
11062					1735		9288			24517	
139775					224773		224773			224707	224773
11182					1685		8428			33706	8990
90327					209184		209122			209122	209123
7266					1563		7842			31368	8364
53238					212971		212971			212971	212971
4259					1597		7986			31945	8518
52714					210900		210900			210900	210900
4317					1581		7908			31635	3436
48467					194134		194134				194134
3277					970		3882				3882
50656					202893		202893				202893
4052					1014		4057				4057
51475					214990		214990				214990
4118					4299		4299				4299
42134					207803		207803				207803
3380					4156		4156				4156
17293					104815		104815				104815
1384					524		2096				2096
136					1782		1782				1782
11					9		36				36

One question is whether the food was distributed equally among the prisoners. This, as well as other matters, was covered in a report by Capt. Penrose,[10] a Commissary officer, written on 11/28/64, and the main body of this report is given below. Besides reporting on food distribution, the report gives details about food and its preparation found nowhere else.

In accordance with Special Orders from the war Department No. 379 of November 2nd 1864 I have the honor to report the following as the result of my inspection of the Commissariat at Fort Delaware.

The total number to whom rations are issued is 9127 of these 7637 are Prisoner of War, the balance being a garrison of 1192 and 308 convicts. The Officer in charge Captain G.S. Clark is an energetic and efficient officer but lacking in experience and but poorly supported by his assistants all of whom with the exception of one clerk being detailed men. The facilities for storing supplies are poor and the storerooms badly located consisting of one warehouse capable of holding by crowding 200,000 rations built on the lowest point of the island four feet below the level of the dyke one old building once used as a stable at a distant part of the island and entirely unfit for the purpose, besides being in danger of fire from the presence of straw in the same room.

In addition to these, two casemates in the Fort are used for storing flour. Even were these storerooms properly located their storage capacity would not be sufficient. At present the barrels being piled so high, six and more tiers, that stores are lost by the heating of the packages. The amount of stores on hand had not however been carefully looked to and while of some articles there was six weeks supply of, others there was but ten days. The quality of the stores issued is most excellent. The fresh beef in an inspection of which I have been most careful looking at both the condition of the cattle to be slaughtered and meat when ready for issue was of a superior quality.

I should here mention as tending to show healthiness of the food provided that in a garrison of nearly 8000 Prisoners, only twenty-four deaths have occurred since the 1st of October.

The issues to the garrison are made every ten days on a consolidated return. The issues to Prisoners are also every ten days and are made to an officer in charge.

The bread is baked at two different bakeries, the one called the Post Bakery in the casemates of the Fort, at which the bread for all of the US troops is baked.

This bakery contains three ovens capable of baking 600 rations at a time and under the superintendence of one detailed man. The bake house is small, necessarily dark, and is kept dirty and in a confused state. The bread however is good.

The bakery for prisoners is outside the Fort on the Island. This contains five ovens capable of 6000 bread rations at each baking.

This is also under the charge of a detailed man.

The bread is baked by detailed prisoners [who] mess and sleep in the bakery and in consequence the bakery is also in a dirty condition though not so much as the Fort bakery. In making bread for the prisoners one tenth part corn meal is used. This makes a good sweet bread and said to be better liked by the prisoners than all wheat. The savings of flour from this bakery are purchased by the Commissary and constitute what is called the Prison Bakery Fund and is disbursed separately from the Prison Fund. Why this should be done there seems no good reason.

Feeding Prisoners: This is done under the charge of an officer detailed for the purpose. The system of feeding is similar to that adopted at Soldiers Posts, all food being cooked in the kitchens—one for rebel officers the other for privates. The work in these kitchens is done by the prisoners themselves, superintended by detailed men. Kitchens and mess rooms were clean, the cups however were not. Two meals are given per day. The first consists of bread and meat, the second of bread meat and soup. Five days in the week fresh beef is served, the other two pork or bacon. The soup I found was made of bacon, beans and mixed vegetables and was a greasy unpalatable compound. The amount of meat furnished was unequally distributed, being cut without any judgment, some pieces being twice the size of others. The pieces cut for the officers was [sic] much larger, the excess of their allowance coming from the rations of the privates. The officer in charge of these kitchens during my inspection was not to be found. His chief assistant however was present. This man seemed either ignorant or else unwilling to answer questions put to him, telling me there was little refuse from the kitchens and no grease, not more than the men could use in greasing their boots. Even with the little care apparently taken, I found one mess of some 300 had saved in six weeks one barrel of grease worth no less than thirty dollars. I strongly suspect that bacon is used for soup as yielding more grease than pork the skin on the bacon preventing the fat being absorbed by the soup.

The prisoner ration of both salt and soap is found to be much larger than can be used and at present there is a large quantity in the prison storehouse.

What is done with this I could ascertain now however has been returned to the Commissary.

Why the management of feeding the prisoners should be taken from the Commissary, who is evidently the proper officer to have such a charge, and should be given to an officer entirely unacquainted with the duties and who entrusts the management to detailed subordinates I cannot understand. The evil is a serious one and calls for immediate action.

Having thus stated the condition of the Commissariat I have the honor to make the following recommendations. First. That a new storehouse capable of holding 500,000 rations be built on the highest portion of island so to guard against an overflow by the breaking of the dyke also as adverse winds and tides in the spring of the year might cause an overflow of the whole island storage would be prepared in the casemates of the Fort for a reserve of 300,000 rations to be stored there during the winter and spring. 2nd After these storerooms are prepared Captain Clark be instructed to keep during the winter not less than three months supply of rations on hand. This is deemed highly important in order to provide against the contingency of a long interruption of navigation by ice.

Third—That an immediate change be made in the feeding of prisoners and Captain Clark put in charge: but care should be taken to distribute the food equitably. That any savings from the rations be turned into the Subsistence Department and the amount credited to the Prison Fund. Also that care should be taken of the refuse from the Kitchens and the proceeds of this also be credited to the Fund. That during the winter pork and bacon be issued at least three times in the week. That the soup be made from the pork while the bacon is kept for the morning meal.

Fourth—That the bakery in the Fort be abandoned but the ovens be left to be used in case of emergency. The bread for the garrison and the Prisoners be then all baked in the same bakery; the savings of Flour to belong to the Subsistence Department if should this suggestion not meet the views of the Department it is recommended that Captain Clark be relieved of the Post bakery and Post fund in considerations of his having charge of the Kitchens, and that instead of a separate fund being kept of the savings of the Prisoners bakery the savings be credited to the general Prison Fund.

Fifthly—To carry out the above it is recommended that Captain Clark be authorized to employ one citizen as clerk, one as superintendent of bakery, and two as superintendents of kitchens to be paid from the Prisoners fund.

Believing the above suggestions to be entirely necessary and indispensable in order to properly conduct the Subsistence Department at Fort Delaware.

Capt. Penrose's report confirms several items in Capt. Clark's records. Some corn meal was used in the soft bread, although Capt. Penrose got the proportion wrong: it was actually one-fifth corn meal. Mixed vegetables (desiccated vegetables) were served to the prisoners to alleviate scurvy, and the prisoners were not using their full rations of salt and soap during this period.

Endorsements on the outside of the main report indicate it was sent to Brig. Gen. Eaton, the CGS, who in turn sent it on to the CGP. The CGP wrote that new storehouses could be constructed only with approval of Sec. of War, and then stated in the endorsement returning it to the CGS that "The attention of the Comdg Officer has been called to the inequality in amount of component parts of the ration on hand; and also to the condition of the bakeries and the Savings arising there from the distribution of food to the prisoners and the manner of making Soup." On 12/21/64 The CGP sent Gen. Schoepf a letter indicating these problems. One can *presume* that some action was taken on the mentioned problems, but there is no record of it. Another endorsement from the CGS indicates Penrose's report was sent on to Maj. Gen. Halleck on 12/22/64 "for information of the proper authorities."

On the same date, 11/28/64, Capt. Penrose also wrote a second letter[11] to the CGS recommending that salt beef be issued to the POWs and convicts, so that large stores of this item could be used up before they spoiled. Such an order was issued by the CGP to all prison camps on 1/13/65.[12]

In regards to the bakeries on the island, on 1/26/65 Capt. Clark wrote to the CGS[13] that he was not in charge of the garrison bakery in the Fort but would take charge of it on February 1. In reply on 1/31/65[14] the CGS ordered that the garrison bakery in the Fort be abandoned, but kept ready for an "emergency," and that all bread be made in the prison bakery.

Another question is whether the prisoners received the food listed by Capt. Clark as having been provided to them. There is no indication of any kind in the official records, or prisoners' diaries, that food was being diverted to other places, for the profit of anyone such as Capt. Clark, or for the benefit of others such as increased rations for the Union soldiers. Indeed, the only official record of this is an anonymous "complaint" in a letter to Sec. War Stanton claiming that Capt. Clark and the fresh beef supplier (Holz & Barnhart) were in collusion to somehow cheat the government. An investigation was made by a Board of Inquiry and no irregularities were found.[15]

Indeed, if one thinks about the situation for a moment, the diversion of significant amounts of food from Pea Patch Island seems very unlikely. All food was "checked in" when it arrived on the island. Except for fresh beef and other fresh items obtained locally, other items such as flour were shipped from a Commissary warehouse in Philadelphia (receipts in Capt. Clark's records show the origin of this food). If for instance only 10 percent of the prisoner's flour was being diverted, it would have meant that in November 1864, for example, about 68 barrels, each holding 195 pounds of flour, would have had to be surreptitiously shipped off the island. This is most unlikely, because everyone and everything going on or off the island had to be accounted for. Also it was not "discarded" as spoilage (a favorite way to cheat the government), because Capt. Clark's records show no food accounted for as spoilage during his tenure.

Prisoners' Food Supply and Preparation

From the Commissary records there is no indication that the food was any different for the Union soldiers and the POWs on the island. Nonperishable staples such as flour, salt, soap, dried beans, vinegar, coffee, sugar, etc., were ordered and obtained, usually from the Subsistence Department in Philadelphia.[16] We do not know if these were delivered directly by steamboat (there was once or twice daily service to and from Philadelphia) or were sent overland to New Castle or Delaware City and then delivered by boat to the island. There are descriptions of prisoners rolling barrels and other food items from the wharves, and around the island in general to distribute the food.

Perishable items, especially fresh beef, were obtained locally. In the case of fresh beef, Capt. Clark as a Commissary officer was authorized to sign contracts for the government, and he would advertise for bids for supplying the island with fresh beef for 3 months.[17] The slaughterhouse was *probably* in or near Delaware City, and one *presumes* that Capt. Clark would make known his needs some period in advance and the fresh beef would be brought out to the island less than 24 hours before it was to be used.

The amount of food handled in a single day just to feed the prisoners was immense.

4. The Food Ration

Assuming fresh beef and soft bread were being served on a particular day, the amount of food needed for 8,000 prisoners (after May 1864) would be:

Fresh Beef—7,000 pounds (3,125 kg)
Flour—8,000 pounds (3,571 kg) (about 41 barrels)
Beans or Peas—1,000 pounds (446 kg)
Soap—320 pounds (143 kg)
Vinegar—60 gallons (264 liters)
Salt—300 pounds (134 kg)
Potatoes—1,200 pounds (536 kg)

This is a total of about 18,000 pounds (about 8,000 kg) of food per day to be moved around and cooked. POWs were employed to move and cook the food (for employment of POWs, see Chapter 11). As noted above, there are several accounts of prisoners being seen moving various kinds of food, especially barrels, around the island.[18]

When the prison population swelled in the summer of 1863 there was clearly a need for a food storehouse. Capt. Clark requested that one be built, not just because of the large amount of food being used, but also because of the possibility that the island would be cut off from the mainland by ice during the winter. Capt. Clark's recommendation was relayed by Gen. Schoepf to the CGP on 9/15/63[19] and the CGP replied on 9/21/63[20] that the storehouse should be built (Item 14, Figure 2). The CGP stated that if possible the cost of the storehouse should come out of the Prison Fund. This building was built and measured 127 ft. (39 m) long by 23 ft. (7 m) wide by 11 ft. (3 m) high.[21] Form 1 was filled out monthly by Capt. Clark, and it enumerates the food on hand at the beginning of the month, the amount of food acquired, the amount issued, and the amount left at the end of the month. These forms clearly show that in both 1863 and 1864 Capt. Clark built up supplies of nonperishable items such as preserved meats, flour and hard bread in October and November, in preparation for the winter and possible isolation of the island because of ice in the Delaware River. This was prescient, especially during the winter of 1864–65, which was especially cold, and during which the island was cut off from the mainland by ice for several weeks. This stockpile was gradually reduced when warmer weather came.

The prisoners described what they got for their two meals each day, and the general consensus is for breakfast it was usually meat and bread (Capt. Penrose, above, confirms this), and for supper (or "dinner" in mid-afternoon) it was meat, bread, and "soup."[22] The prisoners also reported that the fresh beef or other meat was boiled.[23] Large amounts of food could be easily prepared by boiling, it was a simple and common way for soldiers to prepare food,[24] and its use was even described in Army Regulations. Indeed Army Regulations section 117[25] states in part, "The soup must be boiled at least five hours, and the vegetables always cooked sufficiently to be perfectly soft and digestible." In other words, by current standards, "overcooked." While such long cooking was more likely to destroy disease-causing pathogens (unknown to them at the time), it also of course destroyed nutritive value.

There is some evidence in the cooking equipment used in the Prisoners' kitchens as to how the food, other than bread, was prepared (see Figure 12). In Table 5-6, in March 1865 Voucher No. 5 for the Prison Fund lists cooking implements, *presumably* for the prisoner's cookhouse. It lists cauldrons or parts for cauldrons of 60 gallons and 120 gallons. Since a cauldron is a container is which liquids such as water are boiled, it would

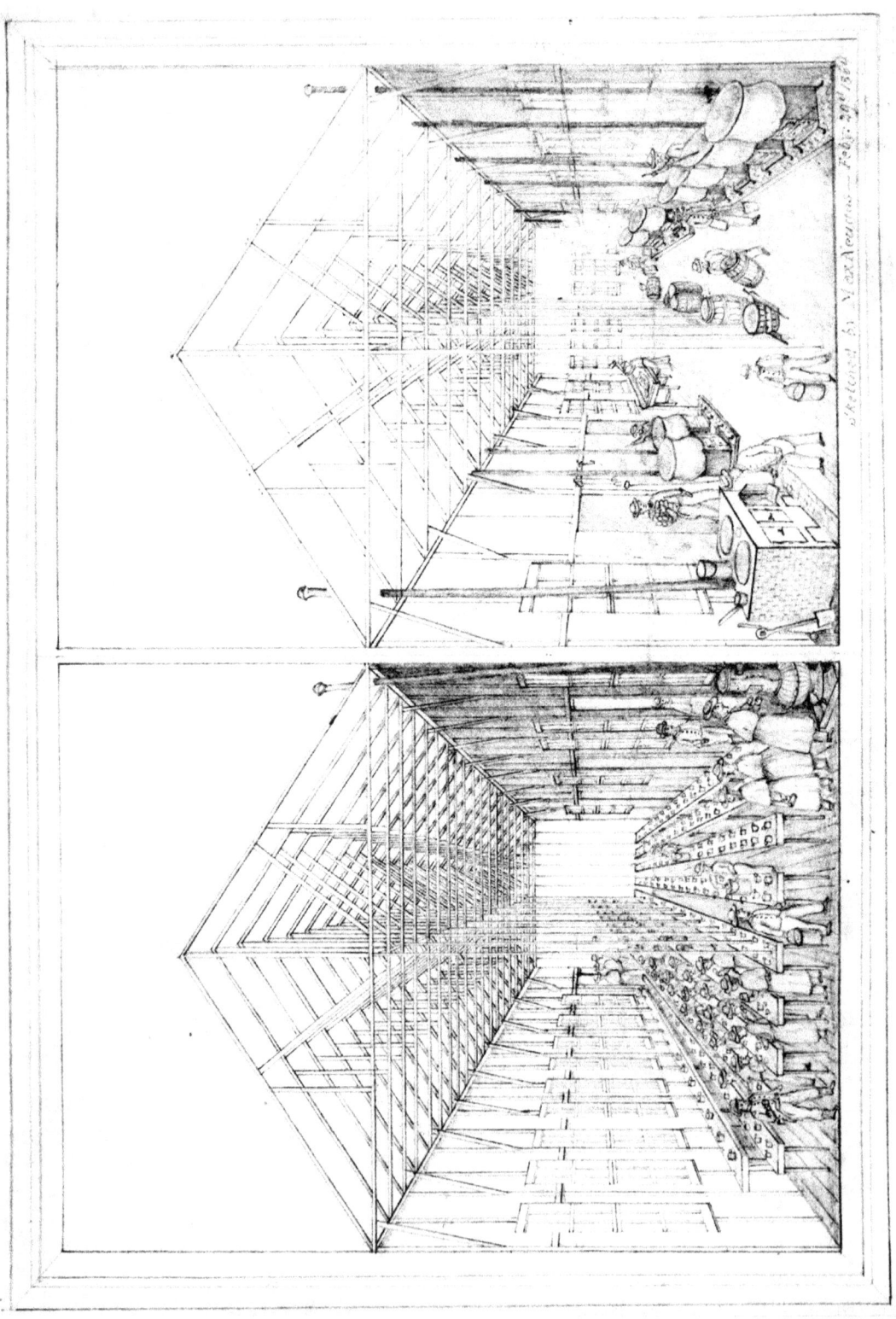

make sense that most of the cooked items were boiled. These cauldrons apparently had their own stands and grates, and perhaps their own heaters. It is pointed out that 100 gallons of water weighs about 850 pounds (380 kg) and the cauldron itself had to weigh 100, perhaps 200, pounds (45–90 kg) so they were not portable when full. We do not know the details of how the food was transferred from the cooking vessels to the prisoners.

The combined kitchen and "dining hall" for the officers was 162 × 113 feet (49 × 34 m), while that for the enlisted men was 232 × 47 feet (70 × 14 m).[26] Clearly these would be insufficient for all of the officers, which at times numbered almost 2,000, or all of the enlisted men, which at times numbers over 8,000, to eat simultaneously in their dining halls. The kitchens also had to be quite small for the number of men fed. This is *presumably* why the men usually just picked up their food and took it to their barracks or ate it outside, and why only two meals a day were served after 5/10/64 [Allen].

The bread was probably baked using "standard" recipes of the time for army soft bread,[27] except for the substitution of corn meal for some of the wheat flour. The bread was baked in the prison bakery (see Penrose report above). The bakers were prisoners who were issued clothing for doing the baking, although what exactly they were issued and how often (if ever) it was cleaned is not known.[28] Eighteen POWs are listed as bakers. As for the quality of the soft bread the only complaints recorded were by Handy, who on 4/19/64 and 6/17/64 stated the bread was "very coarse."

Prisoners' Comments on Their Rations

Of course there are many comments on the prisoners' rations in their diaries, and some of them are given below.

Our fare here is only tolerably good. Bread meat & coffee. Soup for dinner.—Mckey, 3/28/64

Bread was very coarse and meat boiled without salt. They have rice and beans occasionally but no other vegetables.—Handy, 4/19/64

The Yankees have stopped giving us any coffee for breakfast now it is nothing but hard tack for breakfast do for dinner with half an Irish Potato and the water the meat is boiled in.—Alburtis, 6/2/64

Rations growing worse, coarse bread, mean gruel and bad meat.—Handy, 6/17/64

I am very hungry breakfast over, one slice of bread and a piece of salt pork cup of water. Dinner over it was very light neither plate, spoon or knife on the table.—McCrorey, 6/29/64

We had no meat for dinner—only bean soup and I had eaten all my bread up. They give us a loaf, full small every other day...—Bingham, 7/14/64

Soup served in cups without spoons. We are not allowed knives or forks. Salt is deposited in piles at regular distances on the rough greasy tables.—Handy, 9/10/64.

Fare is very hard and growing smaller almost daily we get about fours ozs of meat and about nine ozs of bread per day and about ½ or ¾ of a pint of rice or been supe.—Cox, 10/19/64.

Opposite: Figure 12. Prison Kitchen and Mess (Dining Hall), drawn by Max Neugas, 1st SC Regiment, and dated 2/29/64. The men appear to be wearing winter dress appropriate for the time, and eating in the mess hall. There may have been enough room in the mess hall for all the men to eat, at least in shifts, since there were "only" 2,600 POWs present. In the lower left of the kitchen is the only stove shown, while in the upper left a man seems to be chopping meat with an ax(?). On the left and right hand sides of the kitchen are 8 large cauldrons, which indicate boiling was probably the most common method of cooking POW food (courtesy Fort Delaware Society).

The rice [soup] usually contains a rather unpalatable mixture of small bugs and flies; the bean soup usually has neither.—Mckey, 10/21/64.

Short rations. Six small crackers, 2 oz meat, and [?]—Berkeley, 4/2/65

However, the most complete "reporting" about meals appears in the diary of Allen. Almost every day of the period of the diary, 3/28/64 to 8/20/64, he reports what was fed to him. He reports that there were three meals per day until 5/10/64. When three meals per day was started we don't know, but they usually consisted of breakfast coffee, bread and meat, dinner soup, bread and sometimes potatoes, and supper coffee, bread and meat. When the change was made to two meals a day breakfast remained the same but meat was added to dinner. Coffee was then served only at breakfast until 6/2/64, when it was discontinued. He reports other items being served that do not appear on Clark's records. He ate pickles 4/5/64, 4/18/64, 7/19/64 and 7/25/64, but pickles may have been bought from the Sutler. Corn soup was served on 7/9/64 and 7/12/64, while cabbage soup was served 7/11/64 and the next day (cabbage was not part of the regular ration). Complaints about the food were spoiled beef for breakfast on 6/2/64, 6/7/64, 7/10/64 and 7/11/64, no meat for breakfast on 7/28/64, 8/5/64, 8/8/64, 8/10/64 and 8/11/64, and a "poor dinner" on 8/7/64 and a half ration for breakfast on 4/22/64. On the other hand, on 7/10/64 dinner was very good, and apparently on 8/14/64, 8/16/64 and 8/17/64 rations were particularly good. Except for the comments listed above, Allen did not state he was hungry, or worse starving, or otherwise particularly comment on the rations.

Given the mostly negative prisoner comments about the size and quality of the rations, how or can this be reconciled with Capt. Clark's commissary records? The comments above do indicate that the records are correct in one respect, that items such as meat, bread, beans, rice, and potatoes were served on a regular basis.

There is probably no doubt that on some days items were omitted. Meat was apparently omitted to some or all men on July 14th, August 8th, and December 1st 1864. However, the very fact that this seemed noteworthy seems to indicate that it may have been the exception rather than the rule.

As for quantities of food, there are some positive and mostly negative comments. Dr. Handy notes that on 8/13/64 and 9/10/64 rations were unusually abundant. It is human nature that most people (especially soldiers?) are more likely to complain than praise, so the dearth of compliments is understandable. Some of the negative comments, such as Rufous Barringer's of 4/20/65, seem to imply an exceptional circumstance. However, none of this overcomes the large litany of negative comments about the quantity of food issued. Are there any other explanations? Well, these are a few *potential* ones.

There was a problem with the amount of food supplied, either constantly or intermittently, not reflected in Capt. Clark's records.

Cooking, and especially overcooking (boiling), of meat, shrinks the size of the meat and reduces its weight. This effect is well known to cooks.

The prisoners did not have scales with which to weigh their food. They may be simply underestimating the weight of various items, especially if they were hungry.

Cooks, who were Confederate prisoners, and/or the detailed (Union) men in charge of the kitchens, were bribed to supply some individuals with more and/or better food, short weighting others.

Bread containing corn meal is denser than all wheat flour bread, so the "small loaves" may actually have been of the proper weight.

There was, according to Capt. Penrose, a variation, day to day, in the amount of food served to the individual prisoners, with the total still being correct.

4. The Food Ration

Admittedly these are rationalizations for the "short quantities" of food issued but all are possible, and it is *probable* that some combination of the above account for at least some of the prisoner comments. As for bribery of the cooks, this is mentioned by Handy on 6/22/64 when he states, "Best food reserved for those who can pay cooks." These were pieces which were fried or in a stew, but most of it was boiled.

Another factor may also be at work here in explaining these comments. The prisoners were fed only two meals a day, breakfast about 9 a.m. and dinner about 3 p.m. This *probably* was at least partially because of the inability to cook three meals in the relatively restricted kitchens, and also lack of dining space. The prisoners picked up their food and took it out of the "Dining Hall" (see Figure 12), which was not big enough to accommodate all of them, and then either took it back to their barracks or ate it outside. Eating only two meals a day, and having the last meal served about 3 p.m. in the afternoon meant that the prisoners had to go about 18 hours between supper and breakfast the next day, a long time without a meal, and most persons would have been quite hungry by the time breakfast was served the next day. This may explain in part why the men so often stated they were hungry.

As for the quality of the food, most of the comments concern the meat. Army preserved (salted) meat was notorious for often being of poor quality, even that issued to Union troops. However, Capt. Penrose's report indicates the food (by Army standards) was of high quality before cooking. He also reported that the cooking process was below par, and could have accounted for many of the negative prisoner comments. Many of these negative comments were about the "soup," which Capt. Penrose agreed was relatively unpalatable after preparation. Allen's diary notes (only) five instances of spoiled meat in almost five months, and only at breakfast.

Union Soldiers' Rations

Union enlisted men's rations were the nominal rations as listed in Table 4-1. They received fresh beef an average of 5 days per week and soft bread 5–6 days per week. We know from an unnumbered form for "Company Savings" that some of the ration was not eaten or used (for candles and/or soap) by the Union soldiers and the value of that unused part of the ration was credited to the Company Fund, which was used for the benefit of the enlisted men in the Company. How those funds were spent are detailed in Chapter 8, "Outside Help."

As noted above, the Union soldiers' rations came from the same sources as the Confederate prisoners' rations. However, we know very little about how the Union rations were prepared and served. There were four mess halls in the Fort, and plans for the Fort show that each had an attached kitchen. Each kitchen had a hand pump for water, which came from cisterns underneath the Fort (see Chapter 7). We have no description of the cooking equipment or utensils in these kitchens. We also know that at least some of the wooden Union soldiers' barracks outside the Fort had kitchens also.[29] Apparently coal was used as the fuel in these kitchens, as reported by Hamilton in his diary on 4/28/64, when he was on cooking duty. Surgeon Eames, on 7/27/64, wrote home that he was eating regular army rations with the post band, and described them as, "We commenced yesterday noon & had some boiled rice & beef & bread—For supper we had bread & beef & tea—For breakfast we had hash of onions & potatoes & bread and coffee—the latter very weak—The hash had no meat about it & was not cooked very delicately or hashed very much I tried to eat a little of it but was sorry for it..."

We do not know where the band was quartered or where the meals were cooked or eaten, but it would *seem* that at least some of the food was not boiled, but may have been fried, potted or roasted. This is supported by the description of the Thanksgiving meal of 1863 by Sgt. Crumrine on 12/3/63, which included turkey and cranberries, unlikely to have been boiled. It would *seem* that, depending on the skill of the cooks, reasonably attractive meals could have been prepared for the Union enlisted men, although the actual types of food in those meals would have been monotonous.

Union officers were responsible for providing their own food, although if needed they could buy food at cost from the Commissary.[30] Officers were provided with an allowance for servants,[31] the number of such servants depending on the officer's rank. *Probably* some of the officers permanently assigned to the Fort had such servants who cooked for them. However, others found other places to eat on the island. Surgeon Eames, besides eating with the Band, reported in a letter 6/10/64 that he was living in a "Boarding House" which from his description was the Surgeon's quarters, while Surgeon Nugent wrote home on 3/9/64 that he was eating at the "Hotel." It seems that the officers utilized many possible sources for their meals. Since the officers bought their food, either directly or indirectly, it *seems* likely that on average their meals had more variety and were better prepared than enlisted men's meals.

Nutritional Value of the Ration

The author is a volunteer historical interpreter at Fort Delaware interpreting Capt. Clark, the Commissary Officer, and when discussing the ration one of the common questions asked is "Weren't there any fresh fruits or vegetables in the ration?," and of course the answer is no. Most people today realize that a so-called balanced diet is needed to avoid certain diseases caused by lack of certain nutrients such as vitamins, but also needed for good general health. This was not understood at that time, either by physicians or laymen (see Chapter 9), and of course by modern standards the U.S. and Confederate Army rations without supplementation were bound to cause dietary deficiencies if not malnutrition. Table 4-3 gives selected nutrients for January 1864 and January 1865, based on the actual average daily ration served in those months to each prisoner and to each Union soldier, which was calculated by dividing the total number of pounds of each food provided by the total number of rations for the month provided to the men.

Table 4-3. Nutritional Value of Rations

Food	kcal		Vitamin C, mg		Vitamin A, IU		Folate, mcg		Niacin, mg	
	1/64	1/65	1/64	1/65	1/64	1/65	1/64	1/65	1/64	1/65
Confederate POW's Ration										
Pork	550	233	0	0	82	35	0.0	0.4	2.8	1.2
Bacon	121	327	0	0	8	49	0.5	0.5	2.5	1.7
Salt Beef	140	622	0	0	0	0	5.1	15.4	1.4	8.2
Fresh Beef	802	310	0	0	0	0	19.8	7.6	10.6	4.0
Flour	1827	1322	0	0	10	7	167.0	120.8	5.1	3.7
Corn meal	387	317	0	0	229	188	26.8	21.9	3.9	3.2

4. The Food Ration

Food	kcal		Vitamin C, mg		Vitamin A, IU		Folate, mcg		Niacin, mg	
	1/64	1/65	1/64	1/65	1/64	1/65	1/64	1/65	1/64	1/65
Beans	36	18	0	0	0	0	37.1	18.5	0.2	0.1
Peas	0	17	0	0.1	0	1	0.0	9.2	0.0	0.2
Rice	34	12	0	0	0	0	15.3	0.0	0.5	5.3
Sugar	264	0	0	0	0	0	0.0	0.0	0.0	0.0
Hominy	0	7	0	0	0	10	0.0	0.0	0.0	0.1
Potatoes	106	53	7.1	3.5	0	0	13.6	6.8	1.7	0.8
POW Total	4267	3238	7.1	3.6	329	290	285.2	201.1	28.7	28.5
Recommended daily intake			35		1000		320.0		16.0	
Union Total	4184	3945	7.1	0	46	123	362.7	246.0	26.6	27.8
Union Soldier's Ration										
Pork	244	579	0	0	36	87	0.0	0.0	1.2	3.0
Bacon	150	435	0	0	10	29	0.6	1.8	3.1	9.0
Salt Beef	218	10	0	0	0	0	7.9	0.4	2.2	0.1
Fresh Beef	804	751	0	0	0	0	19.9	18.5	10.2	10.0
Flour	2252	1841	0	0	0	0	205.9	168.3	6.3	5.2
Corn meal	0	0	0	0	0	0	0.0	0.0	0.0	0.0
Beans	86	53	0	0	0	0	88.5	54.0	0.5	0.3
Peas	0	0	0	0	0	0	0.0	0.0	0.0	0.0
Rice	59	7	0	0	0	0	26.3	3.0	0.9	0.1
Sugar	264	264	0	0	0	0	0.0	0.0	0.0	0.0
Hominy	0	5	0	0	0	7	0.0	0.0	0.0	0.1
Potatoes	107	0	7.1	0	0	0	13.6	0.0	2.2	0.0

The number of calories in the original POW and Union ration in January 1864 was about 4,200, a very high total even though 14 percent of the meat ration and 8 percent of the bread ration were withheld from the prisoners that month (see Table 5-3). The number of calories in the ration in January 1865 was lower for both the POWs and Union soldiers, although the prisoners' rations were smaller. This is a result of the reductions in the rations in 1864 (see Table 4-1). The recommended calorie intake for a man with a lightly active lifestyle is about 2525 kcal, while for a very active person (hard work) it is about 3,700 kcal.[32] Since most of the prisoners did not work, the rations in January 1864 or 1865 were more than adequate calorie wise. If a prisoner volunteered to work, he received the full ration of a Union soldier in January 1865.

The other nutrients listed in Table 4-3 were considered important or possibly deficient by Alfred J. Bollet.[33] It is fortunate that the Union personnel at Fort Delaware decided to substitute corn meal for some of the wheat in the bread, since the corn was the major source of Vitamin A for the prisoners, lack of which causes night blindness. Although the amount received at Fort Delaware was well below the modern recommended amount,[34] there were no reported cases of night blindness among the prisoners.

Probably the most infamous disease caused by malnutrition in the Civil War, both among prisoners and soldiers in the field, was scurvy, caused by a lack of Vitamin C (ascorbic acid). In the ration of January 1864, potatoes were critical in providing 16 percent of the modern recommended daily requirement.[35] The halving of the prisoner's potato ration after May 1864 was important not for the calories it cut from the ration, but for the halving of the amount of Vitamin C the POWs got. On the other hand, after July 8, 1864, no potatoes were issued to Union soldiers, and so there was no source of

Vitamin C in their diet! It was known at the time that potatoes helped prevent or at least helped cure scurvy.[36]

Given the potato's importance in preventing scurvy, or at least lessening its severity, it is interesting to see the distribution of potatoes to the POWs over the April 1863–July 1865 time period. The average potato ration for April 1863 was 105 gm (grams); May 1863 4 gm; June–August 1863 0 gm; September 1863, 41 gm; October 1863–May 1864, 136 gm, June 1864–January 1865, 68 gm; February 1865, 28 gm; and March–July 1865, 0 gm. It is noteworthy that even now the potato harvest starts in late August or September in Delaware, so Capt. Clark probably could not obtain significant quantities of locally grown potatoes to feed the island's greatly increased population until September 1863. The POWs got the full ration of potatoes, including the full reduced ration, until February of 1865, when this part of the ration was eliminated. Lack of vitamin C also affected Union soldiers in early 1865, since Hamilton states in his diary for 4/3/65 that many of the boys in his battery were getting scurvy because their supply of vegetables was very limited the preceding winter. For a more detailed discussion of scurvy, see Chapter 9.

Surprisingly, one could make the argument that the POW ration at Fort Delaware was more nutritious than the Union Soldier's ration. The fortuitous inclusion of corn meal in the soft bread provided a relatively good source of Vitamin A for most of the period April 1863–June 1865 that the Union soldiers did not have. From July 1864 to the end of January 1865 POWs still got the "half ration" of potatoes which provided some Vitamin C. This difference in the potato ration of the Union soldiers and POWs was *probably* a clerical oversight, since the last reduction of prisoner's rations occurred on June 1, 1864, while the elimination of the Union soldier's potato ration did not occur until July 8, 1864. This last change in the Union soldier's ration *apparently* was not taken into account until noticed by Brig. Gen. Wessells (the CGP for a short period of time) in January 1865, when he ordered the elimination of the POW potato ration starting February 1, 1865.[37]

The values for the nutrients shown in Table 4-3 are derived from U.S. Department of Agriculture data.[38] However, these data do not take into account that many of the items eaten by the POWs, except the bread, were *probably* overcooked, and so these numbers may be high because of nutrient degradation. Nevertheless, at least for the nutrients listed above, with a bit of luck (adding corn meal for instance), most of the time the prisoners received at least a significant portion of the most important nutrients as outlined by Bollet.

One item that could be substituted into Union soldiers' rations were desiccated (or "mixed") vegetables. They apparently tasted and/or felt so bad that the Union soldiers termed them "Desecrated Vegetables," and often refused to eat them. They were thought to be antiscourbetics, so when General Schoepf asked permission to buy vegetables (no record of this exists) the CGP replied on 7/2/64[39] and 7/3/64[40] (telegram and letter, respectively) that desiccated vegetables were to be used, as furnished by the Commissary Department. Thus during August 1864 7,100 pounds (3170 kg) of them were received by Capt. Clark. This may not sound like much but vegetables are about 90 percent water, so they represented about 10 times as much fresh vegetables. Of this 1,136 lb. (507 kg) were distributed in October 1864, 3,977 lbs. (1517 kg) in December 1864, 1,704 lbs. (761 kg) in January 1865, and the remaining 284 lbs. (127 kg) in February 1865. Gen. Schoepf was cautioned by the CGP to consult with his surgeon on how to cook these to make them palatable. This method was simply boiling them for hours. The nutritional value of these vegetables is dubious, except perhaps for roughage (fiber). The heating step in

4. The Food Ration

the dehydration of the vegetables, the long storage time, and then the long cooking (boiling) time, probably destroyed a great deal of the nutritional value such as the Vitamin C.

Prisoner Rations' Cost

From the accounts reported by Capt. Clark on Form 2, we can calculate the total amount of money spent by the Federal Government on prisoner rations. From March 1863 through July 1865, a total of 5,089,231 prisoner rations were provided. This includes rations issued to prisoners in the hospital, and prisoners on working details (working prisoners received a full Union soldier's ration after June 1, 1864, not the reduced prisoner's ration). The total cost of these rations was $1,047,303.57, giving an average cost per ration of 20.6 cents for food actually issued. During this time the cost per full ration issued to Union troops was 17.5 to about 35 cents, there being a large increase in food costs in 1864. More detail is shown in Table 4-4.

Table 4-4. Cost of Prisoners' Rations

Month	Total Rations	Avg. Rations/Day	Cost per Ration, $	Total Cost of Rations, $
Mar-63	671	22	0.1750	117.43
Apr-63	11,314	377	0.1750	1,979.95
May-63	21,957	708	0.2000	4,391.40
Jun-63	72,376	2413	0.1950	14,113.32
Jul-63	253,894	8190	0.1950	49,509.33
Aug-63	277,433	8949	0.1875	52,018.69
Sep-63	250,636	8355	0.1875	46,994.25
Oct-63	160,414	5175	0.1875	30,077.63
Nov-63	93,955	3031	0.1875	17,616.56
Dec-63	91,255	2944	0.1875	17,110.31
Jan-64	87,537	2824	0.1875	16,413.19
Feb-64	81,623	2815	0.2150	17,548.95
Mar-64	166,679	5377	0.2138	35,635.97
Apr-64	183,877	6129	0.2938	54,023.06
May-64	231,412	7465	0.3025	70,002.13
Jun-64	251,839	8395	0.3025	76,181.30
Jul-64	285,010	9194	0.3700	105,453.70
Aug-64	309,566	9986	0.3700	114,539.42
Sep-64	255,931	8531	0.3700	94,694.47
Oct-64	243,873	7867	0.4653	113,474.11
Nov-64	228,463	7615	0.3205	73,222.39
Dec-64	236,256	7621	0.3530	83,398.37
Jan-65	238,154	7682	0.3531	84,092.18
Feb-65	219,913	7854	0.3475	76,419.77
Mar-65	230,712	7442	0.3313	76,434.89
Apr-65	242,735	8091	0.3200	77,675.20
May-65	235,621	7601	0.3075	72,453.46
Jun-65	123,883	4129	0.3075	38,094.02
Jul-65	2,242	72	0.2538	569.02
Totals	5,089,231			1,514,254.44
			Less	
			Prison Fund Remainder	316,674.10
			Spent from Prison Fund	75,560.80
			Prison Fund Correction	74,715.97
			Subtotal	466,950.87
			Total Actually Spent	1,047,303.57
			avg./ration	0.206

Of course Capt. Clark had to account for all of the food and other items he ordered, and pay for items he bought from private citizens or firms. This he did in his monthly submissions to the CGS in Washington. When they were received in Washington they were audited, and there is much correspondence between Capt. Clark and the CGS concerning his accounts. After the CGS was satisfied with his returns, they were sent to the Third Auditor of the Treasury Department where they were reaudited, and corrections made if needed. There are numerous check marks and other notations on the forms, often in red, made by the auditors.

Capt. Clark also had to pay in "cash," actually *probably* mostly drafts on the U.S. Treasury, for items he bought from civilians. The biggest item in this category was fresh beef. As a Commissary officer he had an account at the Treasury Department he could draw on. Every month he would fill out a form with an estimate of funds he would need to have the next month in his account. If there were not sufficient funds in the account already, he would make an estimate of additional funds needed and sent this to the CGS. In turn the CGS would pass along the request to the Treasury Department, which would credit his account with this amount. This cash also had to be accounted for with receipts in his monthly returns.

For those who claim the prisoners were starved, for whatever reason, it is clear that from March 1863 through July 1865 the federal government spent over one million dollars in feeding them. Using a typical inflation multiplier of about 20 from Civil War times to the present, in modern dollars this amounts to over $20,000,000, a considerable sum even by today's standards!

One can very roughly compare the cost of the Civil War Prisoner ration with the cost of modern Federal civilian prisoner's "rations." This is somewhat complicated by the fact that food price inflation during the Civil War was severe, especially in the last two years of the war, when food prices generally increased about 46 percent between 1863 and 1865.[41]

Nevertheless, using older historical data[42] and more recent data (after about 1950) in the Bureau of Labor Statistics price index data (available online), one can roughly calculate that the general increase in prices between the second half of the Civil War is about 20 to 30 times. The price of wheat flour was about 6 to 8 times, and the increase in beef prices was about 20 to 30 times.

The average cost to feed a prisoner in a civilian penitentiary in 2013 was approximately $3.84 in 2013. Multiply the average cost of the POW ration at Fort Delaware (20.6¢) by 20–30 and one gets a "modern" price range for this ration of $4.12 to $6.18, more than what is actually being spent on food for Federal (civilian) prisoners in 2013.[43] Admittedly, these calculations are very rough, but show that what was spent on POW rations at Fort Delaware in 1863–1865 are comparable to what is being used to feed Federal prisoners now.

5

The Prison Fund

> *General Hoffman, ..., finally returned to the United States Treasury the then enormous sum of over $1.8 million, representing more than half the total of the prison funds accumulated by deduction from rations. It represented the unacknowledged price of many prisoners' lives.* —Frank L. Byrne[1]

The above statement about the prison funds is a current widely held view that the large sum of money "returned" to the Treasury after the war was over proved that Confederate prisoners were "starved" and often, perhaps never, received their complete rations, even the reduced rations of June 1, 1864. The discovery of the complete Commissary records for Fort Delaware allows us to investigate this allegation in detail.[2]

Origin of the Prison Fund

The Prison Fund had its roots in the Company Fund and Hospital Fund in the Army before (and after) 1860.[3] The Company Fund was a fund which was to be used for the benefit of the soldiers of a company, and was administered by the Company Commander, in cooperation with the Company Council, which was all of the Company officers. The main sources of the fund were the unused rations of the company, and distributions from the Post or Regimental fund. Soldiers sometimes did not eat all of their rations, or their full rations could not be provided, and the value of these unused rations was credited by the Commissary Officer to the Company Fund. The Fund could be used to provide luxuries, such as foods outside the regular ration, to the soldiers. For instance, Pvt. Hamilton reports in his diary on 8/9/64 that the Captain bought bushels of peaches for the company out of the Company Fund, and similarly extra bread on 1/9/65. The Hospital Fund was funded in an analogous manner by unconsumed rations of patients (Union soldiers or prisoners) in the Hospital, and was typically used to buy foods for the patients that were not part of the regular ration that the surgeons believed would help cure them.

A "Prison Fund" is first officially established by a circular issued July 7, 1862, by Col. Hoffman, the CGP, and the pertinent part is as follows[4]:

> 5. A general fund for the benefit of the prisoners will be made by withholding from their rations all that can be spared without inconvenience to them, and selling this surplus under existing regulations to the commissary, who will hold the funds in his hands and be accountable for them subject to the commanding officer's order to cover purchases. The purchases with the fund will be made by or through the quartermaster with the approval or order of the commanding officer, the bills being paid by the commissary, who will keep an account book in which will be carefully entered all receipts and

payments with the vouchers; and he will keep the commanding officer advised from time to time of the amount of this fund. At the end of the month he will furnish the commanding officer with an account of the fund for the month showing the receipts and disbursements, which account will be forwarded to the commissary-general of prisoners with the remarks of the commanding officer. With this fund will be purchased all such articles as may be necessary for the health and comfort of the prisoners and which would otherwise have to be purchased by the Government. Among these articles are all table furniture and cooking utensils, articles for policing purposes, bedticks and straw, the means of improving or enlarging the barrack accommodations, extra pay to clerks who have charge of the camp post-office, and who keep the accounts of moneys deposited with the commanding officer, &c., &c.

The existing regulations referred to were probably Articles 205–208 of the Army Regulations of 1861, which dealt with Company funds, and perhaps also Articles 1195–1197, which dealt with the Hospital Fund. Since there was no "Company Commander," and the Commissary officer kept the records for the Hospital Fund, it fell to the Commissary Officer to keep the records of the Prison Fund, which is why they appear in Capt. Clark's records. Money was spent from the Prison Fund with the approval of the Prison Commandant, in the case of Fort Delaware, Gen. Schoepf.

The Prison Fund, April 1863–May 1864

For discussion purposes, the Prison Fund at Fort Delaware is most conveniently divided into two periods, April 1863–May 1864, and June 1864–July 1865. Table 5-1 shows the Prison Fund accumulation for the first period, while Graph 5-1 shows this graphically.[5]

Table 5-1. Prison Fund Additions, March 1863–May 1864

Month	Monthly Savings	Cumulative Total
Mar-63	0.00	0.00
Apr-63	125.44	125.44
May-63	1148.95	1274.39
Jun-63	3332.34	4606.73
Jul-63	10997.12	15603.85
Aug-63	11539.34	27143.19
Sep-63	6440.16	33583.35
Oct-63	3704.05	37287.40
Nov-63	0.00	37287.40
Dec-63	3673.56	40960.96
Jan-64	3275.05	44236.01
Feb-64	3063.84	47299.85
Mar-64	4718.52	52018.37
Apr-64	6188.16	58206.53
May-64	0.00	58206.53

As can be seen, the amount collected for the Prison Fund increased rapidly through the summer of 1863, leveled off somewhat in the winter of 63–64, and then increased again in the spring of 1864. This may be due in part to the fact that the prison population decreased markedly during the fall of 1863, and then increased again in the spring of 1864. However, it was *probably* due more to the fact that funds were needed in the summer of 1863 to construct facilities for the prisoners, such as the Hospital, that this need was minimal in the winter, and then increased again in the early spring as the prisoners' barracks and other facilities had to be reconstructed and expanded.

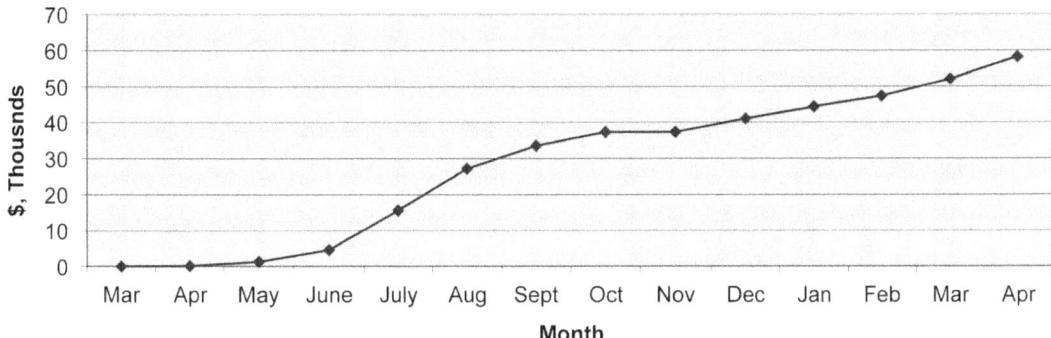

Graph 5-1. Prison Fund Cumulative Additions, 1863–1864

The most important question for many will be, "How much food was withheld from the prisoners to fund the cumulative $58,206 through May 1864?" As described in the previous chapter, until April 20, 1864, the prisoners received the standard Union troop ration (see Table 4-1), which was ample as far as calories supplied (Table 4-3). Table 5-2 (see next page) shows what was withheld from the prisoners by month, from March 1863–May 1864.[6]

Table 5-2 does not show ration items that were not withheld in this period, such as fresh beef, hard bread and corn meal. It is interesting that in months where relatively large sums were saved for the Prison fund, such as July–September 1863 and April 1864, and in other months as well, much of the saving came from a reduction in coffee and/or sugar. Although these would have been sorely missed by the prisoners, their only dietary contribution would have been the calories from the sugar, which were not needed in this calorically ample ration. Withholding of these items generated relatively large amounts of money for the Prison Fund, since they were relatively expensive. Nevertheless, it is interesting to calculate the percentages of the two main ration constituents withheld, meat and bread, and this is shown in Table 5-3.[7]

Table 5-3. Percentages of Bread and Meat Withheld, March 1863–May 1864

Month	Total Meat	Meat Withheld	% Meat Withheld	Total "Bread"	"Bread" Withheld	% "Bread" Withheld
Mar-63			0			0
Apr-63			0			0
May-63	20421	4060	17	28226	3136	10
Jun-63	72939	5490	7	73437	7840	10
Jul-63	251197	10851	4	261601	32926	11
Aug-63			0	269792	38808	13
Sep-63			0	231180	19012	8
Oct-63			0			0
Nov-63			0			0
Dec-63	69658	19400	22			0
Jan-64	67046	10805	14	67046	5880	8
Feb-64	65569	8200	11	65569	6272	9
Mar-64	147742	11000	7	143742	9800	6
Apr-64	163597	9000	5	163597	10780	6
May-64			0			0

Table 5-2. Rations Withheld from Prisoners, March 1863–May 1864

Month		Total Rations	Pork	Bacon	Salt Beef	Flour	Beans	Rice	Ground Coffee	Sugar	Vinegar	Candles	Salt	Soap	Total Savings
Mar-63	Amount	671			Nothing Withheld										0.00
Apr-63	Amount	11314					360	325		285	88		150	19	125.44
	Price						0.048	0.076		0.124	0.120		0.010	0.075	
	Total						17.40	24.70		35.19	10.56		1.57	1.92	
May-63	Amount	21482	800			3136	960	214		1887	100	150	420	239	1148.95
	Price		0.061			0.040	0.048	0.076		0.124	0.120	0.240	0.010	0.075	
	Total		48.96			123.84	46.40	16.26		233.05	12.00	36.00	4.48	17.92	
Jun-63	Amount	68223	600			7840	1200	2000		6000	400	700	1440	2000	3332.34
	Price		0.061			0.040	0.048	0.076		0.113	0.120	0.240	0.010	0.075	
	Total		36.72			309.60	58.00	152.00		678.00	48.00	168.00	15.12	150.00	
Jul-63	Amount	245009	6400		4451	32926	6000			15000	1500	1750	3600	5000	10997.12
	Price		0.080		0.088	0.034	0.064			0.113	0.109	0.250	0.010	0.070	
	Total		511.36		389.40	1122.24	385.00			1695.00	163.12	437.50	42.00	350.00	
Aug-63	Amount	269792				38808	10000	10000		25000	1900	2500		6000	11539.34
	Price					0.032	0.063	0.095		0.118	0.107	0.250		0.070	
	Total					1237.50	603.33	1175.20		2937.50	198.31	625.00		420.00	
Sep-63	Amount	231180				19012	9000	9000	2500	20000	1300	2000		4500	6440.16
	Price					0.032	0.060	0.081	0.335	0.118	0.107	0.232		0.069	
	Total					610.13	542.70	728.10	837.50	2350.00	135.68	463.00		312.30	
Oct-63	Amount	137561					4000	4500		12000	200	1400		3000	3704.05
	Price						0.600	0.080		0.118	0.104	0.232		0.070	
	Total						241.20	340.00		1410.00	20.75	324.00		210.00	
Nov-63	Amount	71615			Nothing Withheld										0.00
Dec-63	Amount	69658	7400	800	11200		2053	2883	2730	6698	485	750	563	2306	3673.56
	Price		0.07	0.064	0.077		0.050	0.080	0.335	0.112	0.104	0.232	0.012	0.070	
	Total		378.00	50.88	857.92		102.65	230.64	941.55	746.82	50.31	173.62	6.75	161.42	
Jan-64	Amount	67046	4000	805	6000	5880	2800	2300	2600	4800	500	738	772	2441	3275.05
	Price		0.070	0.064	0.077	0.043	0.050	0.080	0.335	0.132	0.140	0.232	0.012	0.070	
	Total		280.00	51.19	459.60	237.00	140.00	184.00	871.00	633.60	70.00	168.53	9.26	170.84	
Feb-64	Amount	65569	4200		4000	6272	3216	2242	2474	4000		739	1400	2400	3063.84
	Price		0.070		0.077	0.043	0.050	0.080	0.335	0.158		0.232	0.013	0.070	
	Total		294.00		360.40	252.80	160.80	179.36	828.79	630.00		171.07	18.62	168.00	
Mar-64	Amount	147742	5000		6000	9800	7000		4020	6500		1000	2407	3349	4718.52
	Price		0.070		0.077	0.040	0.050		0.335	0.134		0.232	0.014	0.085	
	Total		350.00		459.60	395.00	350.00		1346.70	869.05		231.50	32.01	284.66	
Apr-64	Amount	163597	4000		5000	10780	2054	4892	6000	1020		2000	3043	4020	6188.16
	Price		0.070		0.077	0.041	0.045	0.910	0.450	0.141		0.232	0.018	0.085	
	Total		280.00		383.00	434.50	93.42	446.63	2700.00	991.22		463.00	55.68	341.70	
May-64	Amount	209546			Nothing Withheld										0.00

Table 5-3 shows the total meat "served," total meat withheld, and the percentage of meat withheld as a percent of the total meat served plus total meat withheld, as well as similar figures for "bread" ingredients (flour, hard bread and corn meal). High percentages of meat or bread were never withheld from the prisoners. In January 1864 in which 14 percent of the meat ration and 8 percent of the bread ration were withheld, the prisoners still got an average of 4249 kcal/day (see Table 4-3), a more than adequate amount. Thus in the period of March 1863–May 1864 the prisoners were not starved to generate money for the Prison Fund.

The Prison Fund, June 1864–July 1865

To one casually studying the Prison Fund, this period appears to be very different from the period preceding June 1864. Accounting for the Prison Fund in the Commissary records was now much more detailed, because in a circular dated 4/20/64, Col. Hoffman, the CGP, appears to have required more detailed accounts of the Prison Fund be sent to him every month. Prison Fund accounting is shown in Table 5-4, and graphically in Graph 5-2.[8]

In Table 5-4 notes are (see columns I and L) are: (a) Savings from Working Details of POWs; (b) includes $6188.16 credit for April 1864 savings; (c) includes credit for transfer from Post Bakery of $1139.16, savings of salt & soap from 12/64, $1181.66 and correction for errors in 7, 8, 9 and 10/64 of ($75,560,80); (d) includes credits for auction of deceased prisoner's effects of $53.42 and value of savings of soap & salt 12/64 of $1325.97; (e) includes $198.58 due prison fund, savings of Prison bakery for month of 9 & 10/64 of 3629.74, & 12/64 of $918.12 & savings of soap in 1/65 of $947.64; (f) includes $424.98 from savings of soap & salt 3/65 and $9.88 cash of deceased POWs in hands of Commanding Officer; (g) includes $261.45 from savings on soap; (h) includes $98.96 from sale of lumber.

By far the most obvious difference from the previous period is the much larger amount of money accumulated in the Prison Fund, both monthly and cumulatively. This is very clear from Graph 5-2, and at the end of the war the Prison Fund totaled over $300,000, which was returned, along with prison fund money from other camps, by Gen. Hoffman to the U.S. Treasury (see quote at beginning of this chapter).

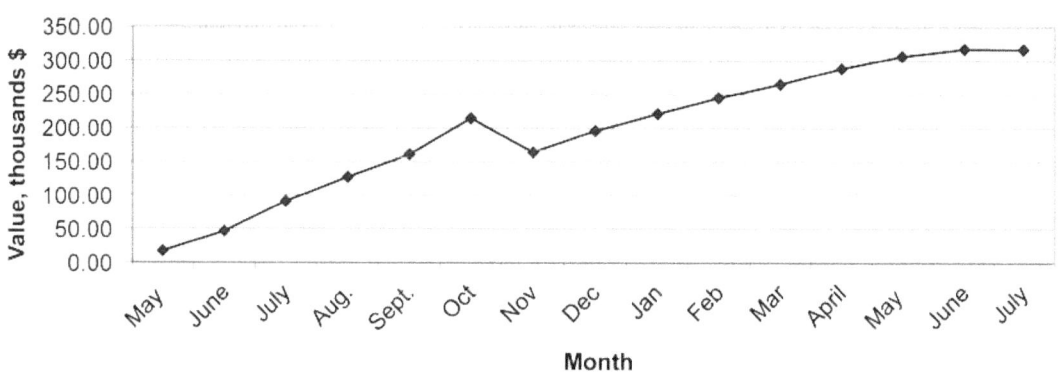

Graph 5-2. Prison Fund Cumulative Additions, May 1864–July 1865

Table 5-4. Prison Fund Account,

Month	A Bal Carried Forward	B # Rations	C Cost Per Ration	D Total Cost	E Total Credit	F Actual Ration Cost
Jun-64	17,087.12	230679	0.3025	69,780.40	86,867.57	37,789.76
Jul-64	46,764.62	260243	0.3700	96,275.11	149,227.89	49,698.51
Aug-64	91,440.65	253215	0.3700	93,689.55	185,130.21	48,439.80
Sep-64	127,415.38	231451	0.3700	85,636.87	213,052.24	46,147.96
Oct-64	160,725.91	224773	0.4653	104,586.87	265,312.78	44,898.41
Nov-64	214,611.26	209122	0.3205	67,023.60	281,634.86	42,064.86
Dec-64	164,399.53	213971	0.3530	75,200.06	239,599.59	44,142.50
Jan-65	196,194.77	210900	0.3531	74,468.79	370,663.56	45,831.23
Feb-65	221,015.44	194134	0.3475	67,461.51	288,477.00	41,851.88
Mar-65	245,076.08	202893	0.3313	67,208.30	312,284.38	41,872.32
Apr-65	264,560.82	214990	0.3200	68,796.80	333,357.62	42,646.25
May-65	288,268.11	207803	0.3075	63,899.42	352,167.53	41,542.27
Jun-65	307,036.56	107248	0.3075	32,973.76	340,015.32	20,825.01
Jul-65	317,722.26	1782	0.2538	452.18	318,174.44	323.16
Aug-65	316,909.11	93	0.2538	23.60	316,932.71	16.72

Details of the accounting are shown in Table 5-4, and it would be well to review how this Table is calculated. Column A is the balance forward from the previous month of the Prison Fund, Col. B is the number of rations that month, Col. C is the cost of the ration *for Union soldiers* that month, Col. D is the total credited for rations (Co. B times Col. C), Col. E is the total credit (Col. A plus Col. D), Col. F is the actual cost of the reduced prisoner ration, Col. G is purchases from the Prison Fund, Col. H is total actual expenditures (Col. F plus Col. G), Col. I is savings from prisoner work details (the prisoners did not eat all of their full ration), and Col. J is the Prison Fund balance at the end of the month (Col. E plus Col. I minus Col. H). Finally Col. K is the increase in the Prison Fund for that month (Col. J minus Col. A). During this period there was one major accounting error: Capt. Clark overestimated the average ration cost from July to October 1864 (footnote c), and this correction is reflected in the November 1864 accounting, and shows up as the "dip" in the Prison Fund in November 1864 in Graph 5-2.

One can ask "Where did all this money for the Prison Fund come from?" Were the prisoners starved in retaliation for supposed ill treatment of Union soldiers in Confederate prisons? Actually, at Fort Delaware there was nothing withheld from the ration during this time period. The savings noted for salt and soap in some of the footnotes are not because these items were withheld, but because the prisoners simply did not take all that was provided. This is explicitly noted on the Commissary returns for those months. Note that these savings of salt and soap were in the wintertime, and it is *likely* the prisoners could not use that much soap because of the freezing temperatures, and perhaps did not use that much salt in the cold weather.

So one asks again, "Where did all this money come from?" To try to answer that question we must first look to the circular of April 20, 1864[9] from the CGP, which further defined the reduced rations for the prisoners and other matters, especially those related to the Prison Fund. It stated in part:

> "V. A fund, to be called "The Prison Fund," and to be applied in procuring such articles as may be necessary for the health and convenience of the prisoners, not expressly provided for by General

5. The Prison Fund

June 1864–August 1865

Month	G Purchases	H Total Expenditures	I a	J Balance End of Month	K Increase	L
Jun-64	2,313.13	40,102.00		46,764.62	–	
Jul-64	8,357.52	58,056.83	268.79	91,440.65	44,676.03	b
Aug-64	9,667.35	58,107.15	392.32	127,415.38	35,974.73	
Sep-64	6,605.77	52,753.73	427.40	160,725.91	33,310.53	
Oct-64	6,781.80	51,680.21	478.64	214,611.26	53,885.35	
Nov-64	2,718.56	44,780.43	158.07	164,399.53	-50,212.00	c
Dec-64	854.84	44,997.34	213.13	196,194.77	31,795.24	d
Jan-65	9,532.24	55,363.47	198.58	221,015.44	24,820.67	e
Feb-65	3,069.23	44,921.21		245,076.08	24,060.64	
Mar-65	6,463.80	48,336.12	177.70	264,560.82	19,484.74	f
Apr-65	5,101.65	47,747.90		288,269.21	23,708.39	g
May-65	3,956.85	45,499.12		307,036.56	18,767.35	
Jun-65	1,553.29	22,378.30	35.24	317,722.26	10,685.70	
Jul-65	1,039.13	1,362.29		316,909.11	-813.15	h
Aug-65	248.90	264.72		316,667.99	-241.12	

Army Regulations, 1863, will be made by withholding from their rations such parts thereof which can be conveniently dispensed with."

This part then goes on to list a somewhat reduced ration for the prisoners. Part V, in combination with the large amounts of money turned back in the Prison Funds at the end of the war, has been cited as the proof that Confederate prisoners were starved in a retaliatory policy starting about mid-1864. As we have seen, however, at Fort Delaware nothing was withheld from the reduced prisoners' rations after May 1864, so the question "Where did the Prison Fund money come from?" is still unanswered.

The answer lies in a second circular issued June 1, 1864[10] by the CGP concerning the ration. The first part of the circular sets out the ration as shown in Table 4-1, and the second part reads:

> II. The difference between the ration as above established and the ration allowed by law to the soldiers of the United States army, constitutes the "savings" from which is formed the prison fund.

Could this "difference" account for the funds accrued in the Prison Fund during this period? In his accounting to the Commissary General of Subsistence in November 1864, Clark included a sheet of paper on which he gave the costs of the various components of the ration. Using these costs, one can calculate the total cost of a Union soldier's ration and a Confederate prisoner's ration, and this is shown in Table 5-5.

Table 5-5. Costs of Daily Rations

	Cost/ration, cents		Savings/Ration
	Union	POW	
Meat	15.09	10.56	4.53
Flour	7.22	6.42	0.80
Beans, etc.	0.90	0.75	0.15
Coffee	3.67	0.00	3.67
Sugar	3.58	0.00	3.58
Vinegar	0.32	0.24	0.08
Candles	0.56	0.00	0.56

	Cost/ration, cents		Savings/Ration
	Union	POW	
Soap	0.49	0.49	0.00
Salt	0.09	0.09	0.00
Pepper	0.13	0.00	0.13
Total	32.05	18.55	13.50

As can be seen in Table 5-5 a Union soldier's ration cost 13.5¢ more than a prisoner's ration. This was compared with the actual cost of the prisoner's ration for November 1864. In that month there were 209,122 prisoner's rations issued at a cost of $42,064.86 for an average cost of 20.1¢/ration, for a difference in cost of 11.95¢ between a prisoner's and a Union soldier's ration, in reasonable agreement with the calculated difference. This difference may have come about because prisoners were still receiving potatoes instead of hominy and rice. Most of the savings is in three parts of the ration, meat, coffee and sugar. The meat ration was reduced by about a third, while coffee and sugar were eliminated. Coffee and sugar were among the most expensive parts of the ration on a cost per pound basis.

If one has 8,000 prisoners, about what Fort Delaware had during most of this period, one "saves" about $28,680 to about $32,400 in a 30-day month. This is in basic agreement with the "surplus" that is added to the Prison Fund each month; see the difference between Column D and Column F in Table 5-4. So the origin of the huge surpluses in the Fort Delaware Prison Fund and most likely other northern Prison Funds is solved. These large amounts of money in the Prison Fund arise not from starvation of the prisoners because of additional withholding of food from the reduced prisoner ration, but because of the difference in cost between a Union soldier's ration and the reduced prisoner's ration. This derives directly from the apparently little noticed second section of the Circular of June 1, 1864.

Prison Fund Accounting

One author states,[11] in part, about Prison Funds: "This account was supposed to be used for the benefit and relief of prisoners, such as building additional barracks, improving sanitation systems, or purchasing vegetables to prevent scurvy. Instead at many institutions the accounts became almost sacred and never used, while at others they were embezzled, pilfered, or badly mishandled." In order to ascertain whether mismanagement of the Prison Fund at Fort Delaware occurred, it is helpful to know how it was audited and controlled.

In his Circular of July 7, 1862, the CGP required that the Commanding Officer at each prison be kept informed of the status of the Prison Fund, and that the commissary would keep the accounts of the Prison Fund and report them to the Commissary General of Subsistence. The Circular of April 20, 1864, from the CGP ordered essentially the same thing, except Section VII ordered that the accounts sent to the CGP were to be more detailed. At Fort Delaware, the first report to the CGP on the Prison Fund was actually sent on 7/10/63, and essentially monthly thereafter. The Prison Fund account was detailed by Capt. Clark on Subsistence Department Form 2[12] that Capt. Clark modified slightly (or had his clerk make by hand) so that he could use it for prisoners. In the "Remarks" column he put the overall account of the Prison Fund, including savings from the ration that went into the Prison Fund, how much was spent from the Prison Fund, and how much was in the fund at the end of the month.

Capt. Clark did not detail what was bought using the Prison Fund on Form 2, but merely gave the total with a notation such as "Amount of expenditures for prisoners of war as per abstract." Unfortunately, this "abstract" is absent in all of the months except March and May 1865. The reports sent to the CGP also apparently do not survive, although the CGP's registry of letters reporting the receipt of the transmission letters notes that the accounts themselves were placed in the prison fund files.

In the March and May 1865 accounts submitted to the Commissary General of Subsistence, and now in RG 217, there are multiple copies of a form which is described as follows.

On one side are printed the following lines so that they would appear on the outside of the sheet when it was folded for filing. They read as follows: (O. C. G. P. No. 16); M. P. F.; Voucher No. _____; ABSTRACT OF DISBURSEMENT; _____, 18,; $_____.

The other side of the form is headlined "THE UNITED STATES" and the line stating "To _____" which is meant to be the person or organization which was paid. There is a table, with a space for the date in the left-hand column, a wide middle column for a description of the item(s), and a right-hand column for cost ($). At the bottom there are three sections:

> (1) I certify, on honor, that the specified articles were purchased and services rendered on the requisition of the Commandant of _____, and that the expenditure was necessary for the public service. (Then a line for the officer to sign)
> (2) _____, C.S. and Treasurer of the Military Prison Fund will pay the above amount. (Then a line for the Commandant to sign.)
> (3) Received at _____, this _____ day of _____ 186_ from _____, C.S. and Treasurer of the Military Prison Fund _____, in full of the above account. (Then a line for the supplier to sign.)

The author has never seen this form anywhere else, and it was obviously designed to help account for the "Military Prison Fund." There is no indication when it came into use. On the Form 16s from Fort Delaware, Capt. Craig signed section (1), Gen. Schoepf signed section (2), and the money for the items which was received from the disbursing officer, Capt. Clark, was signed for in section (3).

Table 5-6 shows the detail that was reported on OCGP Form 16 for March and May 1865. It is clear that the accounts of the Prison Funds were monitored as closely as the Subsistence accounts. Totals on Form 16 were checked out, as evidenced by notations or check marks in red ink (typical for auditors) on some of the forms. In addition, on 3/17/65[13] the CGP questioned an outlay for a civilian coxswain for the "dead boat" (see Figure 13) which carried the dead to New Jersey asking why a soldier couldn't be employed, on 6/9/65[14] questioned a large outlay for lumber in April 1865 without asking permission for new construction per the Circular of April 20, 1864, on 7/18/65[15] points out that the Prison Fund statement for June lists 1446–5/8 lb. of rice at 16¢/lb. should be $244.96 instead of $344.96, and on 8/8/65[16] authorizes payment for whiskey for the Hospital from the Prison Fund. These clearly indicate that the CGP was keeping a close watch on the expenditures from the Prison Fund.

It is noteworthy that in Table 5-6 the outlays for which Forms 16 are submitted closely match the total expenditures reported on Form 2 by Clark. Why they don't match

Figure 13. The Yacht *Dead Rebel,* dated 8/24/64, from the sketchbook of Pvt. Baldwin Coolidge, 6th MA VV. This is probably the boat usually called the "dead boat," that transported both Union and Confederate dead to New Jersey for burial (courtesy Delaware Historical Society).

exactly is unknown, but it could have been a transcription error, or a Form 16 or other expenditure on another form is simply missing. It seems apparent that for the Prison Fund of Fort Delaware the chances of misappropriation of funds was low, and the accounts were sound. Given Col. Hoffman's (the CGP) propensity for detail it is difficult to envision widespread mismanagement of the prison funds in general, but of course a group of dishonest officers and civilians could have done it.

The Prison Fund was a bookkeeping device, and the funds existed only on paper as a charge against the Commissary Department. When funds (cash) were needed for disbursements Clark could withdraw money from his account at the Treasury Department, which was in turn charged against the Commissary Department. With the departure of the prisoners, on 8/15/65 the CGP ordered the Fort Delaware Prison Fund be closed.[17] On 11/11/65 the CGP ordered that "money" in the Prison fund be "returned," credited to, the Commissary Department, and ultimately to the Treasury Department. Of course no actual money changed hands.

What Did Prison Fund Money Buy?

As noted above, for the most part we don't have the accounting records for most of this period for what was bought with the Prison Fund, but they do exist for March and May 1865. There are also a few vouchers for July 1865, but they don't add much to the discussion. The March and May vouchers are listed below in Table 5-6.[18]

Table 5-6. Expenditures from the Prison Fund

Date	Voucher Item	Cost	Date	Voucher Item	Cost
March			May		
1	1 bbl. Dubbing, 43 gills	61.92	1	Storing prisoners' clothing	3.00
1	Repairing 23 sections hose putting on screws, patches & splicing	56.50	2	1 hand stamp	2.50
1	18 feet seal(?) belting, 2.5"	6.30	2	2 stamp pads	2.00
1	5 sections suction hose, 33-8/12"	336.67	2	1 bot. Ink	0.50
2	5142 ft NP Lumber	231.39	2	1 eyelet punch	2.50
2	802 ft NP Flooring	38.09	2	5 boxes eyelets	2.50
2	300 ft NP Posts	15.66	2	11 boxes pens	6.00
2	111 ft NP Plank(?)	6.27	2	20 sheets blotter	4.00
3	6 doz brooms	31.50	2	4 doz green bands	2.50
4	1 Record of prisoners, 300 pp	22.50	2	1 reel red tape	4.50
4	40 4? Roll Books 100 pp	50.00	2	1 letter file	2.00
4	6 3 gr Blank Books	9.00	2	2 baskets	3.00
5	3 120 gal cauldrons	360.00	2	3 files	1.20
5	18 120 gal cauldron grates	144.00	2	1 Ribbon stamp	8.00
5	4 60 gall Cauldron furnace bottom	36.00	2	2 cups & sponge	1.50
5	6 120 gal cauldron rests	18.00	2	2 copying books oil sheet & blotter	7.00
5	5 120 gal cauldron furnace bottoms	60.00	2	4 paper cutters	1.00
5	1 12 inch heating stove	18.00	2	1 Rm cap paper	7.00
5	6 14 inch heating stove	150.00	2	5 grs Ex blotter	12.50
5	2 grates & sets fire brick for cook stove	12.00	2	1 stamp with changes	10.00
5	6 ??? For stoves	42.00	3	40 doz corn brooms	242.00
5	387 lbs stove pip & elbows	85.14	3	6 doz wall brushes	54.00
5	79 lbs zinc	27.65	3	1 doz hard scrubs	4.00
5	21 shaking grates	52.50	3	1 doz hard scrub handles	5.00
5	2 sets range bricks	9.00	4	6 gross Lippincott Cont Pens	7.50
5	2 sets range grates	12.00	4	4 doz Arnold's Fluid ½ pts	18.00
5	24 range bars	24.00	4	10 Rms 1st class Letter Smith	65.00
5	24 range brick	7.20	4	8 Copying books 700 pages	40.00
6	Postage for prisoners' letters for month of February	18.67	4	500 Buff legal env	4.50
7	20 doz corn brooms + drayage	121.00	4	1000 Buff Legal Env	5.00
8	400 bus lime	200.00	4	10 Rms 1st class letter Irving	65.00
9	5 bbl coal oil 220 gill	209.00	4	1 Gross 303 pens	2.00
9	3 bbl W Sperm oil, 70 gills	202.80	4	5 Rms Comb Note Paper	22.50
9	6000 ft NP lumber	2040.00	5	Repairing 4 Head Lights	10.00
9	20000 feet newlock scantling	480.00	5	2 doz CH light chimneys	10.50
10	2.5 doz spades	55.00	5	6 doz station light chimneys	13.50
10	30 kegs nails	262.50	6	3 bbls coal oil 727 gills	101.60
10	1 putty knife	0.35	7	6 Barrel yellow ochre	32.10
10	1 riveting hammer	0.50	7	1 cask chloride lime	44.39
10	1 glazier diamond	8.00	7	300 lbs pure grd w lead	25.00
10	1 Hack knife	0.50	7	21 galls linseed oil	27.40
10	1 Carpenters saw	1.60	7	90 lbs putty	5.40
10	2 Carpenters saws	4.00	7	5 gall benzine	4.00
10	2 chisels	1.50	7	2 ltf boxes glass 12/15	7.80
10	2 chisels	3.20	7	2 ltf Boxes glass 12/14	7.80

Date	Voucher Item	Cost	Date	Voucher Item	Cost
March			*May*		
10	1 doz carpenters pencils	0.65	8	Repairing 9 section hose 5 splices and 11 patches	37.00
10	4 doz hatchets	40.00	8	Repairing 9 sections hose 22 patches, 3 splices &c	133.00
10	165 lbs zinc	36.30	8	Repairing 7 sections hose 8 patches, 1 splice & screws	40.00
10	6 CS Picks	9.50	8	1 bbl dubbing 42 galls	73.50
10	6 hoes	5.75	8	Repairing 10 sections hose 4 splices, 6 patches & 2 screws	30.00
10	1 doz short handle shovels	19.00	8	Repairing 2 sections hose 2 patches & 1 splice	9.00
10	6 long handle shovels	9.50	8	24 sections leading hose	2108.75
10	6 store door padlocks	18.00	8	24 sets couplings	192.00
11	12 Wheelbarrows	96.00	8	Attaching couplings	24.00
12	Sending & Receiving telegrams	48.53	9	2 1in St Nipple	0.70
13	Rat killing services 3/4 to 3/30	270.00	9	1.5 ft 1 in st tube	0.53
14	4 casks yellow ochre	58.42	9	3 1 in nipples	0.57
14	1 Cask chloride lime	98.30	9	1 1 in elbow	0.27
14	100 lbs white lead	18.00	9	2 hours time 2 men	1.00
14	10 lbs patent dryer	2.50	9	1 syphon for st gauge	1.25
14	40 lbs chlorate potash	36.40	10	2 spring chest locks	2.20
			10	1 pr flush chest hdles	0.30
			10	1 pr table hinges	0.18
			10	10 kegs 13 nails	62.50
			11	Sending & Receiving telegrams	54.27
			12	13 lbs rope	4.15
			12	25 lbs Lead	6.00
			12	1 keg black paint	3.25
			12	10 lbs R lead	2.50
			12	5 lbs green paint	2.00
			12	8.5 lbs rope	2.48
			12	40.5 yds muslin	15.60
			12	1 keg tar	1.25
			12	1.75 lb B Wax	1.31
			13	Clerks	220.10
	Total	6298.76		Total	3936.85

In the following discussion March vouchers are designated 3-X and May vouchers are designated 5-X, X being the voucher number. Many of the vouchers for one or both months seem to fall into certain categories and these are discussed below.

Vouchers 3-1 and 5-8 are for hoses and the material for maintaining and/or repairing hoses. For instance, "dubbing," on both vouchers, is "a dressing of oil and tallow for leather."[19] The only extensive use of hose, especially large hose, on the island that we are aware of was for the water distribution system. Thus it *appears* that maintenance and repair of this system accounted for a significant amount of the prison funds spent, about 30 percent in total combined for the months of March and May 1865.

Another type of expenditure in both months is for office supplies, vouchers 3-4, 5-2, and 5-4. *Presumably* these were for maintaining records of the prisoners. A related expense was the cost of sending and receiving telegrams, vouchers 3-12 and 5-11. Again *presumably* these telegrams were related to running the POW camp. Cleaning implements and materials also were bought both months; see vouchers 3-3, 3-7, and 5-3. Maintenance items, such as paints and ingredients for paints (3-14 and 5-7), and other supplies and implements (3-10, 5-9, 5-10 and 5-12) are another class of item bought. Vouchers 3-9, 5-5 and 5-6 list oil for lamps, lamp supplies and repairs. *Presumably* these lamps were used for the prison camp, providing light for the guards to see on their posts at night, perhaps to illuminate certain areas so escapees could be seen, and also for the prison camp offices. The wheelbarrows (3-11) bought in March *could have been* used for moving food and/or items related to maintenance. There is a large voucher (3-5) for various items for the kitchen.

Voucher 3-6 is for "Postage for prisoner's letters for the month of February." We don't know whether this is postage for official letters dealing with the prison camp, or whether the prison fund actually paid for stamps for indigent prisoners. It of course literally means that the prisoner's postage was paid out of the prison fund. At 3¢ per letter this would have paid for about 622 letters, *presumably* a small percentage of those sent.

Another item bought in March was lumber (3-2). As noted above, on 6/9/65 the CGP requested information about lumber bought in April 1865. We can't find a reply to this inquiry but given the fact that there is no information about additional structures, such as barracks, being built on the island at this point, one *suspects* that this lumber is for repair of existing structures. It is well to remember the approximately 1 mile (1.6 km) of barracks (if laid end to end), the fencing around the prison camp, the boardwalks in and near the prison camp, and other structures related to the prison camp. Given that most of the time the ground of the prison camp was marshy, it is not surprising that wooden structures would have to be repaired, and even replaced, frequently.

Voucher 5-13 is for clerks. Section IX of the circular of April 20, 1864, states that the Prison Fund will be "…used to pay clerks and other employees engaged in labors connected with the prisoners," as does General Orders No. 1 issued by the CGP on 1/13/65.[20] The voucher shows that 14 soldiers worked for 31 days for 40¢/day and 6 soldiers worked for 31 days for 25¢/day. Since the circular of April 20, 1864, allowed 40¢ per day for clerks and 25¢/day for laborers, we assume the former group was clerks and the latter laborers. Why so many clerks? Most of them were *probably* employed as mail clerks to read or inspect the prisoner's incoming and outgoing letters and (mostly) incoming packages (see Chapter 8), and some were *probably* employed in keeping the Prison records.

These vouchers also provide valuable information about what was happening on the island and how the prison operated. For example, the cooking ware listed in Voucher 3-5 gives us some idea how the food was prepared, and details of the water supply system can be inferred from Vouchers 3-1 and 5-8. These details are not available anywhere else.

From correspondence between the CGP and Schoepf we can also glean other uses or potential uses for the Prison Fund. On 9/1/63[21] CGP sent Schoepf a report by a medical inspector, telling Schoepf that "sanitary" problems noted in the report can be fixed by paying for them from the Prison Fund, and on 9/21/63[22] the CGP writes that a Commissary warehouse may be built using the Prison fund and that clothing and blankets for the prisoners may also be bought using the Prison Fund. Similarly, on 11/26/63[23] the CGP suggests that a trial amount of two barrels of "Ridgewood Disinfectant Powder" recommended by the Medical Inspector be tried and paid for out of the Prison Fund (no mention in any other correspondence about the "trial"). On 11/30/63[24] the CGP writes to Schoepf that the Sec. War approves building a "smallpox hospital" on the New Jersey shore away from the island, and says it can be paid for out of the Prison Fund (this hospital was never built), and on 12/2/63[25] the CGP writes the "fund" (*presumably* the

Prison Fund) will allow purchase of articles for the sick as needed. In the same letter purchases of vegetables are authorized but the specific resource for paying for them is not stated.

Items to benefit the prisoners were not the only items to be bought with the Prison Fund. On 3/5/64[26] the CGP writes that the Sec. War has approved the erection of a fence to enclose the prison barracks, and it is to be paid for out of the Prison Fund. This is at the time when the Prison Fund was not too large (before reduction of the prisoner rations), so it probably used a good percentage of the fund. However, approval continued to be obtained for items that benefited the prisoners. On 7/2/64[27] the CGP telegraphs Schoepf that [anti]scourbetics may be purchased using the Prison Fund or Hospital Fund and that tea and sugar for the sick may also be bought. However these may only be done on recommendation of the Surgeon. This was followed up by a letter on the next day (7/3/64)[28] which states "…that on the certificate of the Surgeon as to the necessity of tea & sugar for the sick when the ration allowed is not sufficient may be purchased from the Prison Hospital Fund. Antiscourbetics may be purchased with the Prisoner's Fund for the prisoners generally on the surgeon's certificate they are necessary. These purchases must have your approval…. The Comm. Gen'l. of Subsistence will order a small supply of desiccated vegetables to be sent to Commander Fort Delaware and I wish them to be purchased as antiscourbetics in place of other vegetables which are more difficult to obtain."

One of the more interesting uses of the Prison Fund was to hire rat catchers (Voucher 3-13 from Table 5-6). On 3/5/65[29] the CGP received a letter from Schoepf which was summarized as "Reports that he has authorized a contract at $5 per day for two men, for one month, or six weeks, to kill rats, which are a great and damaging nuisance." On 3/9/65[30] the CGP replied that the Secretary of War had approved the hiring of the rat catchers, and instructs that the charges be paid from the Prison Fund. In 1879 apparently the *Philadelphia Times* newspaper published an article which was reproduced at least in part by two other publications.[31] In this article a professional rat catcher from the Kensington section of Philadelphia, John Gregory, who used ferrets to kill rats, is described as saying he was a rat catcher at Fort Delaware. The article states, "During the war he took his ferrets down to Fort Delaware to clean the prisoners' pens and warehouses of rats. It was the largest job he ever had. 'I killed over 16,000 rats in three months down there.'" It is not stated whether this included muskrats and/or rats as we usually think of them such as the Norway rat (*rattus norvegicus*) or the black rat (*rattus rattus*). One would *suspect* it was probably both.

The final authorization is somewhat amusing. On 8/8/65[32] the CGP wrote, "On the recommendation of the Acting Surgeon General the bill of G. Adams for 144 gills of whiskey asking $648 purchased for the prison hospital presented by Asst. Surgeon Goddard and forwarded by you on the 20th ult will be paid from the Prison Fund on a bill properly certified by Dr. Goddard and approved by yourself." This payment is accounted for in Voucher 6 for July 1865.

One last item not actually found in the official accounts but mentioned in several communications is about fire engines. On 2/17/65[33] the CGP wrote to Gen. Schoepf asking what precautions had been taken in regard to fire occurring in the soldiers or prison barracks. There had not been a fire at Fort Delaware, so why this was written at that particular time is not known. The CGP stated, "It is desirable that a sufficient supply of ladders, fire hooks, axes and water buckets should always be in readiness in charge of the guard, and if these articles have not already been purchased please direct these purchases from the Prison Fund and report to this office." On 2/20/65[34] Schoepf replied recommending the purchase of one or two fire engines to pump drinking water and extinguish fires. On 2/28/65[35] the CGP replied that the use of steam fire engines was not advisable because of their cost, the need for training crews, and the need to maintain them. Instead he suggested the use of a hand engine called the Carys patent premium sold by Cary and Branard, Brockport, New York. He recommended ordering the "largish" size, and suggested that Schoepf have a discussion about the pumps with the manufacturer. He requested that Schoepf report the results to him (the CGP) and if they are found suitable the CGP wished to introduce them into other camps. Schoepf replied on 3/24/65[36] that he authorized the Quartermaster to procure 5 C and B fire engines, and Schoepf also enclosed a catalogue. No further correspondence can be found, so we don't know whether the fire engines were actually received or not, and apparently no further report was made to the CGP.

6

Shelter and Clothing

> *I have the honor to report in my judgment it would seem advisable to prepare barracks at Fort Delaware to accommodate in all 10,000 prisoners of war.—*
> Col. W. Hoffman, Commissary General of Prisoners, April 9, 1863[1]

With this letter, events were set in motion to construct a "permanent" POW camp on Pea Patch Island. Hoffman was responding to a request of some sort from the War Department, possibly about whether Pea Patch Island was suitable for a POW camp, since on April 2 QM General Meigs reported Pea Patch Island was suitable for prisoners.[2] Thus the first impulse after Union authorities decided to place a POW camp on Pea Patch island was to provide shelter for the prisoners.

Hoffman explained in his April 9th letter that the barracks would be prepared even though they may not have to shelter so many prisoners, but it would be better "to be prepared permanently for any number that may be thrown into our hands at any one time." At this point no one expressed in writing the possibility that the prisoner exchange system could break down and POWs would have to be held indefinitely.

The Barracks

The main enlisted POW barracks on Pea Patch Island were built in two stages, one section in (approximately) May 1862, and the second section in May–June 1863. In the spring of 1862 the POW population was rising rapidly at Fort Delaware, especially after the first Battle of Kernstown, which happened on March 23, 1862. The POWs sent to Fort Delaware filled every available space and when Capt. Gibson, the commandant of the Fort, was asked if he could accommodate more prisoners said he could not.[3] As a result, Col. Hoffman, the CGP, requested that Gen. Meigs, the QM General, authorize construction of POW barracks at Pea Patch Island. On 4/22/62 Meigs wrote to Col. Crossman, the QM in Philadelphia, and stated, "Prepare shanties to shelter 2,000 prisoners of war at Fort Delaware on the island outside the fort but under its guns."[4] These barracks subsequently became known as the "old barracks."

This was the only barracks built for POWS on the island before Hoffman's letter of 4/9/63. This was because the Dix-Hill Cartel agreement for exchanging POWs was agreed to on 7/22/62. On 7/27/62 Sec. War Stanton directed that (a) Adjutant General Thomas be the agent for the exchange of POWs, and (b) that QM General Meigs provide transports to take the prisoners at Fort Delaware to Aiken's Landing on the James River for exchange.[5]

6. Shelter and Clothing

The POW population at Fort Delaware decreased rapidly, and thereafter (until May 1863) the POW population was mostly very low. POWs stopped at Fort Delaware, mainly as a way station for being exchanged. Thus there was no need for additional barracks and the "old barracks" were largely unused.

On April 11, 1863, Bvt. Col. E.S. Sibley, Deputy QM General, wrote to Col. G.H. Crossman, AQM Philadelphia that the Sec. War directed that barracks for 5,000 POWs were to be built on Pea Patch Island.[6] Col. Hoffman visited Pea Patch Island on April 15–16, 1863 and immediately wrote to Col. Crossman asking that the contracts not be signed until Hoffman suggested some changes to the barracks that Hoffman felt in the long run would save money.[7] Hoffman wrote again to Crossman on April 18th stating he had sent his proposed changes to the QM General but had not yet received a reply,[8] and on April 21st Hoffman again wrote to Crossman detailing the modifications that had been approved by the QM General.[9] On April 29th Hoffman wrote to Schoepf to look over previously proposed alterations to the existing barracks and approve or change them, and also estimate their cost.[10] Finally on 5/11/63, it appears that the final plans for the new barracks are about to be approved.[11] Unfortunately there is no indication in the records when the new barracks were partially or completely finished.

These activates were mirrored in the outside world. On 4/15/63 an advertisement appeared in the *Philadelphia Inquirer* and *Philadelphia Press* soliciting bids for the construction of barracks for 5,000 prisoners at Fort Delaware. On 5/4/63 a brief note appeared in the *Philadelphia Inquirer* stating barracks for 5,000 prisoners would be erected at Fort Delaware, and on 5/13/63 an ad appeared in the *Philadelphia Press* stating "Wanted vessels to load lumber for Fort Delaware."

Meanwhile, Gen Schoepf had not been idle regarding the "old barracks." On 5/5/63[12] he wrote the CGP including plans for remodeling those barracks, and on 5/7/63[13] wrote that he was "in a fair way" of remodeling the old barracks and hoped to have it done in a few days. On 5/8/63 Schoepf wrote that repairs to the old barracks were nearly done (by the Post's carpenters), only the roof still needing repair. In a few days they would be able to accommodate about (total) 6000 prisoners.[14]

The Barracks that resulted are listed in Table 6-1, this Table including both Union and Confederate barracks outside the Fort on Pea Patch Island.[15] The "Date Built" in Table 6-1 is approximate.

Table 6-1. Barracks Buildings at Fort Delaware

Designation	Date Built	Use	Length	Width	Height	Description
A	May 1862	POW Barracks	177	24	12	Frame, stripped, shingle roof
B	May 1862	POW Barracks	372	24	12	Frame, stripped, shingle roof
C	May 1862	POW Barracks	185	24	12	Frame, stripped, shingle roof
D	June 1863	POW Barracks	519	24	14	Frame, stripped, shingle roof
E	June 1863	POW Barracks	378	24	14	Frame, stripped, shingle roof
F	June 1863	POW Barracks	478	24	14	Frame, stripped, shingle roof

Designation	Date Built	Use	Length	Width	Height	Description
G	June 1863	POW Barracks	455	24	14	Frame, stripped, shingle roof
H	June 1863	POW Barracks	435	24	14	Frame, stripped, shingle roof
I	June 1863	POW Barracks	211	24	14	Frame, stripped, shingle roof
J	July 1863, July 1864	Union enlisted quarters	140	24	14	Frame, stripped, shingle roof
K	July 1863, July 1864	Union enlisted quarters	322	24	14	Frame, stripped, shingle roof
L	?	Convicts' Barracks	133	24	12	Frame, stripped, felt roof
M	July 1864	Union officers' quarters	80	20	20	Frame, 2 story, stripped, shingle roof
N	July 1864	Union enlisted quarters	125	24	20	Frame, 2 story, stripped, shingle roof
O	July 1864	Union enlisted quarters	125	24	20	Frame, 2 story, stripped, shingle roof
P	July 1864	Union officers' quarters	80	20	20	Frame, 2 story, stripped, shingle roof
Q	?	Union officers' quarters	103	29	14	Frame, stripped, lined with tongued boards, shingle roof

Barracks A–C are the "old barracks," and D–I are the "new Barracks, and were the main place POWs were held.

Barracks J and K combined were an "L" shaped building originally built in front of the Fort in approximately July 1863 to house the infantry regiment which provided guards for the POWs.[16] In July 1864, at the same time barracks M–P were built, K and L were dismantled and moved further away from the Fort because of the perceived danger of a fire in K and L spreading to the Fort. K and L were indeed used as Union infantry barracks until sometime in 1864.

K and L apparently have a further interesting history. At least no later than 9/1/64, K and L were diverted from their original use of housing Union infantry to housing "galvanized" Rebels, men who took the oath of allegiance to the U.S.[17] It is reasonable to *assume* that the Union authorities believed it would not be safe for these men to remain in the regular POW barracks. Apparently this was planned in June or July 1864, when Schoepf requested permission to build new Union barracks M–P.[18] Schoepf reported on 8/23/64 that these barracks were completed for less than $7000.[19] Private William Fletcher of the 6th MA VV, (infantry) on guard on the island, described these enlisted men's barracks:

> They are 2 stories high, and water tight, with a large number of windows opening at either top or bottom. The buildings were erected with a view to accommodation of artillery, each one to contain 2

companies, but we have to go into them at the rate of 3 companies to a building. The upper story is for bunks and the lower for mess-rooms (i.e. eating rooms) and sergeant's rooms. Co's G, H and I occupy the same building. The bunks in the upper rooms contain all the men, but the sergeants and corporals and 4 privates from each company, who occupy the sergeant's rooms. The 2 kitchens are used by Co's G and I while we have a small cook-house outside. The 2 mess-rooms accommodate a Co. and a half each, Co. H being divided between the 2.

We also have descriptions of the POW barracks as well as pictures drawn by the POWs (see Figure 14). It clearly shows that the prisoners slept in three tiers of pallets, the lowest one apparently being the floor, and also shows the construction of the building. The floor shown probably is just above the earth, since as far as we know these building had minimal if any foundations. We also have several descriptions of these barracks; for example in an undated entry near the beginning of his diary Gibson states:

> The Barracks are laid off in Divisions 40 or 50 feet long by 25 wide and 15 feet high constructed of frame work (planks laid?) up and down in [illegible] was there[?]. [?] in of bunks the first bunk only about 2 feet from the [g]round it is the coldest in winter [missing] next is about 4 feet above that fixed with uprights of [scan]tling 3 by 4 inches from [missing] [r]oof down and about 7 [missing] from the outer wall and two scantling of about the same size reaching from the outer wall to 3 uprights and inch planks nailed to the cross ties the next [missing] & top bunk is about 4 feet above the middle one and is the warmest in the cold weather There is one stove in each Division to heat and warm all hands but it is hardly sufficient in very cold weather although it has been very pleasant up to this time (Nov. 29, 1864). There are cross pieces about 12 or 15 inches long nailed to the uprights to enable the men of the upper [illegible] to get up to roost.

Towards the end of his diary in an undated entry he also states, "The divisions are lighted by a globe lamp hung to a wire in the centre of the division an[d] is kept burning all night…" In Cox's diary on 7/25/64 he notes, "the camp the building in which we quarter is about 24 feet wide and cut up in rooms from 40 to 60 feet long termed Divisions there are 15 of these in the camp each division contains from 100 to 120 men with a few exceptions there are 3 tiers of Bunks in each Div they are each furnished with 2 tables 4 benches 2 water buckets 2 brooms and one globe lamp which burns all night is the furniture complete"

Park notes in his diary on 2/5/65 that "The bunks or berths in each division are six feet long and about four feet apart, extending entirely across the room. Each division is heated by one large upright stove, which the prisoners keep very hot when sufficient coal can be obtained. The room is so open and cold, however, that a half dozen or more stoves would be required to heat it. Several poor fellows, who have no bunk mates and a scarcity of covering, sit up around the stoves and nod all night." Thus with the exception of the lowest pallet being elevated above the floor, these three descriptions agree with Shotwell's drawing.

Stoves were present in the cooler months and taken out for the warmer months. Mckey reported in his diary on 4/8/64 that the stoves had been removed, then on 4/9/64 they had been returned, and finally on 5/2/64 the stoves were removed again. Mckey then reports on 10/19/64 that the stoves were brought back but prepared for use. Boyle in his diary makes the same report on 10/18/64. Mckey states on 10/28/64 that no fuel has been received yet, and Boyle confirms this on 11/6/64. On 11/15/64 Boyle reports the stove is keeping the room warm. On 4/20/65 PAMcMichael states in his diary that the stoves have been removed. So it appears that the stoves were present in the barracks from about October or November to late April or early May.

Unfortunately, the QM records for Fort Delaware cannot be found, so we do not

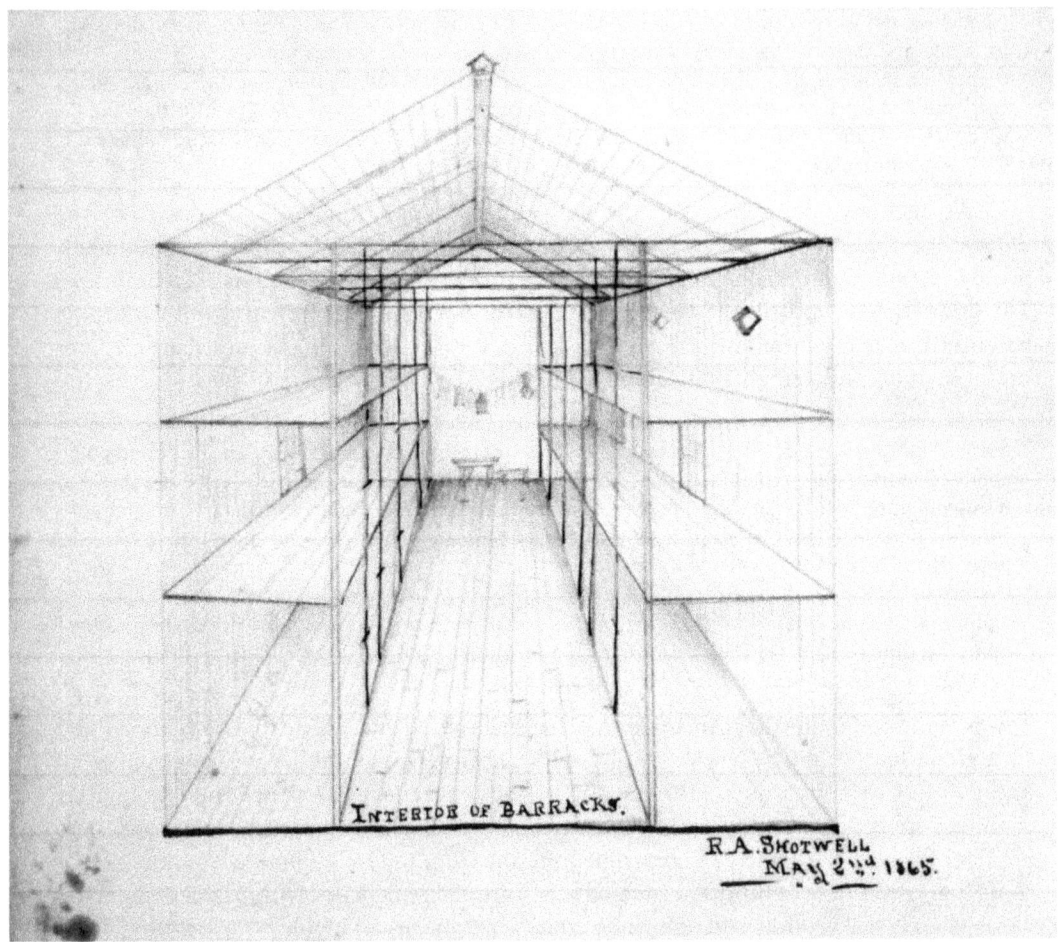

Figure 14. Interior of POW Barracks, drawn by Lt. R(andolph) A(bbott) Shotwell, 8th VA Inf., and dated 5/2/65, in the autograph book of 2nd Lt. Andrew J. Leftwich, 22nd Battalion, VA Inf. Notice the wooden floors, the crosspieces on the vertical beams to allow men to climb to the upper pallets, furniture and the hanging wash (courtesy Mr. John T. Frawner and Mrs. Jean Leftwich Frawner).

know from these records how much coal was used on the island, especially for heating the prisoner's barracks. We do have two clues, however. In a deposition taken on June 21, 1864, Capt. Clark averred that he had provided about 1,000 tons (2,000,000 pounds/ 893.000 kg) of coal to heat the prisoners' barracks in the winter of 1863–1864, and Capt. Craig averred he had supplied 300 tons (600,000 pounds/268,000 kg) of coal to heat the prisoners' barracks during the same winter.[20] On 11/28/64 Gen. Schoepf wrote a communication to Capt. Craig, the Fort's QM officer, stating, "Judging from last winter's experience in regard to the number of prisoners and the quantity of coal then purchased it will be necessary for you to purchase without delay 2000 additional tons of coal. In view of the approaching winter season and the probability of being ice bound for the same length of time as last year it will be too late to purchase by advertising for it and you must buy it at the lowest market price and if possible contract for it as furnished for the Government at Phila PA."[21] How much of this was used for the prisoners we do not know. However, the totality of the prisoners' reports in their diaries and reported in this paragraph indicate that at least some heat was provided to the prisoner's barracks in the colder months.

From the information we have it appears that the quality of construction of the prisoners' barracks was similar to the Union infantry barracks J and K which were constructed around the same time as the "new barracks" (buildings D–I) for POWs. We know this because of the information prepared for the sale of the barracks in December 1865, which gave the number of linear feet of "hemlock scantling" and "rough board" for each building. [Scantling was a word used for relatively small structural timbers, for example 2 × 3 or 2 × 4 inches (4.5 × 6.7 or 4.5 × 9.0 cm).] For the POW barracks A–I there were 51.9 linear feet (15.8m) of scantling and 125.6 linear feet (38.3m) of rough board, while for the Union barracks J–K there were 49.8 linear feet of (15.2m) of scantling and 117.5 linear feet (35.8m) of rough board; all of these number are per linear foot (0.31m) of the length of the respective barracks. There is actually slightly more timber in the POW barracks, and this could be due to the timber used to build the pallets that the POWs slept on. It is believed that the Union soldiers had "double bunks" (one on top of another) to sleep in. Therefore it seems that the construction of the POW and Union barracks discussed above were of the same design.

POW barracks A–I had a total length of 3210 feet (979m). The highest number of POWs plus political prisoners at any one time was about 9491about 8/20/64.[22] Since there were 6 tiers of sleeping pallets there were about 19260 linear feet (5874m) of sleeping space, which for 9,491 men (assuming about 300 were hospitalized) about 2.0 feet (24 inches, 61 cm) of space on average for each prisoner. While crowded it was still enough room for each man; for instance, an American modern standard double bed is 54 inches wide (1.4m), or 27 inches (0.7m) on average for each person. As noted above in Cox's diary, men mostly slept in pairs ("bunk mates") in cold weather to conserve heat, so together they probably occupied less than 48" of space. Most of the time, however, there were fewer 8000 POWs and political prisoners in the barracks (the hospital held about 600 patients), so each man had an average of at least 2.5 linear feet (30 inches, 0.76m) of sleeping space.

As generally described by Handy in his diary, when he got there in June 1863, enlisted men were housed in the old and new prisoners' barracks (Buildings A–I). Political prisoners and POW officers were housed in the Fort, in the general area above the sally port. Union convicts were housed in a barracks that was inside the Fort on the Parade ground (which was not used for reviews because of the building thereon) until about 5/1/64, when they were moved to the convicts' barracks.[23] Except for a few, all of the Confederate officers were sent to the Johnson's Island POW camp until about April 1864, when the old barracks (Buildings A–C) started to be used to house officer POWs. At this time a stockade fence with a guard walk was built between the square encompassed by building A–C and the remainder of the POW barracks, so the officer POWs were separated from the enlisted POWs. At about the same time, the political prisoners were moved from the Fort to the officer POW buildings. This was the configuration of the prison camp for the remainder of the war, except as explained above, galvanized rebels were moved to the (former) infantry barracks, J and K.

Union enlisted soldiers were housed in the Fort or in barracks outside the Fort. A description of some of the barracks outside the Fort is given above in Pvt. Fletcher's letter. We have almost no description of the Union enlisted men's barracks inside the Fort. They still exist (in part) and are on the second and third floors on the west side of the Fort.

There are some smaller rooms also in this section and perhaps they were for noncommissioned officers. We *assume* they had double bunks in them. The larger rooms had fireplaces, although there are openings for stovepipes, so perhaps iron stoves were used, as they were in the prisoner barracks. Given the fact that the Fort was a permanent structure, built to withstand bombardment, it is likely the Fort's enlisted men's barracks were the best accommodations on the island, except for Union Officer quarters. However, these barracks had problems apparently common to most living quarters on the island. Hamilton reports on 4/3/63 that they just received new straw, *presumably* to put into their "tickings" (mattress covers). In turn this (and probably other factors) led to bugs being present, as Hamilton reports killing bugs on 4/6/64.

Not surprisingly, Union officers had the best quarters on the island. In a letter to his wife on 6/10/64 Surgeon Eames stated, "Our quarters consist of a building of some 20 rooms and each one is occupied by one doctor or a Chaplain. This was the surgeons' quarters near the hospital and contained 2 chaplains so most of the occupants were surgeons." Eames goes on to write, "There is a good side walk from here to the other end of the island and in going there we pass on the left hand—first the guard quarters, next a bridge over a wide ditch next the General's premises, consisting of a barn and out building, garden-dwelling house (very pretty one indeed), then another house with fine grounds occupied by a doctor [believed to be Dr. Arrott's home] then one occupied by some Captain [Captain Ahl?] then the Chapel (a new one & very large & tasty),…." It is also believed there were a few other homes beside this walk. This area may have been referred to as "officer's row." On 8/28/64 Pvt. Fletcher wrote in a letter "The street on which the chapel stands present(s) a very neat appearance there being two very pretty cottage houses on the same side, occupied by officers and surrounded by flower and vegetable gardens." However, apparently not all officers had "good" quarters, since in a 6/29/64 letter Surgeon Eames of the 157th OH wrote, "We have in this tent 3 Surgeons and this Reg't and all have good bed and a good chair apiece and one good writing & medicine table."

Another place Union officers were housed was in the Fort; in particular, the two buildings which had offices in them also had officers' quarters on the second and third floors. On a particular floor there was one row of rooms for these quarters (on the side of the building facing the Fort's parade ground) and all of these were interconnected by doors. Each also had a door to the outside hallway. Thus these rooms could be divided into apartments of varying size for the officers and, if present, their families. Army Regulations[24] stated the number of rooms an officer was entitled to. The higher his rank the more rooms he got: for example, a Lieutenant got one room, a Captain 2 rooms, a Major 3, etc. It is believed that most of the Union officers housed in the Fort were members of the "permanent" garrison, that is, not members of the infantry regiment temporarily assigned to the island.

Clothing

Supply of clothing, for both prisoners and Union soldiers, was the responsibility of the QM Department. Unfortunately, the QM records from Fort Delaware (Captain Clark and then in August 1863 and later Capt. Craig) have not apparently survived. The QM records from Philadelphia, which supplied most QM supplies to Fort Delaware, also have apparently not survived.[25]

6. Shelter and Clothing

Prisoners often arrived with an incomplete set of clothing and/or clothing that was in bad condition. For the purposes of this section, clothing includes shoes and blankets. With time, of course, the clothing of prisoners which had arrived in good condition started to wear out. Prisoners (including political prisoners) generally then had three methods of getting new or at least better clothing. They could request that the prison administration (U.S. Army) provide clothes, ask someone such as a relative or a friend to send clothes, or if someone sent them money they could buy clothes from the Sutler. In some cases, although apparently against camp rules, if they had money or other items they could buy or trade clothes with other prisoners. Rules and availability of clothing for these types of acquisitions varied somewhat from April 1863 through June of 1865.

Getting clothing from prison officials apparently did not occur until about October 1863. It is not clear why it was not available before then; perhaps the U.S. Army had not made provisions [for whatever reason(s)] to provide clothes to the prisoners, perhaps they were deliberately withheld, or some other reason(s). Handy comments on 8/3/63 that the prisoners have "just enough clothing to hide their nakedness" and also reports on 9/12/63 of the "scarcity of clothing" for the prisoners. Then on 10/8/63 and 10/9/63 Hamilton (a Union soldier) reports in his diary that large amounts of clothing have arrived for the prisoners. On 10/3/63 Handy reports men from North Carolina got a shirt, drawers, shoes and perhaps other things, and on 10/9/63 men from Virginia, Mississippi and Alabama regiments got 2 shirts, 2 drawers, one pair of pant and 1 pair of shoes, if needed. This is somewhat confirmed in a sworn statement of Capt. S.R. Craig, the QM officer at Fort Delaware, who averred[26] that between 9/10/63 and 5/1/64 the prisoners had received:

- 7175 Pair Drawers (Canton flannel.)
- 6260 shirt (flannel)
- 8807 Pairs Woolen Stockings
- 1094 Jackets and Coats
- 3480 Pairs Bootees
- 1310 Pairs Trowsers
- 4378 Woolen Blankets
- 2680 Great Coats

Craig also stated that most of these items were "issued in October and November, 1863," and "every prisoner not having an overcoat and blanket of his own, was provided with one." It should be noted that by the end of October 1863 the prisoner population at Fort Delaware was under 3000 men.[27] This is confirmed by medical inspector Clark on 11/13/63 and Lt. Col. Irvine on 12/5/63.[28]

After the fall of 1863 there is little mention of the prisoners receiving clothing from the U.S. Army. However, on 7/5/64 Handy reports that blue clothing was confiscated (see Chapter 3), which Mckey also confirms on 7/5/64, and that grey clothing was given in its place.[29] However, it seems clothing may have still been issued to the prisoners in the fall of 1864 since Pvt. C.N. Clark of the 6th MA VV reported in a letter home he was assigned to work in the prisoners' clothing room (see Figure 2, item No. 25).[30] Capt. Craig wrote to the CGP on 9/26/64[31] enclosing an estimate of clothing needed for the prisoners (unfortunately the actual list is not in the file). Figures 15 and 16 show some not-too-well-clad prisoners about this time.

Early on, some of the political prisoners seemed to have plenty of blankets, probably

Left: Figure 15. Young POW, undated, from the sketchbook of Pvt. Baldwin Coolidge, 6th MA VV. The text states he is 12 or 14 years old. No shoes (by choice?) and needs better pants (courtesy Delaware Historical Society).

Right: Figure 16. Two POWs in "Warm Weather" (?) Dress, undated, from the sketchbook of Pvt. Baldwin Coolidge, 6th MA VV. Coolidge was present in late summer 1864 (courtesy Delaware Historical Society).

which they brought with them or were sent to them. For instance, Handy reported on 7/22/63 that he had slept with three blankets, and on 11/18/63 Tibbits had more than one blanket. Purvis reported on 8/27/63 that nearly all the men were without blankets, but three days later wrote that the Yankees were giving them blankets. As noted above there was a distribution of blankets in October and November of 1863. However, by the spring of 1864 the POW population was rising again. Mauck received a blanket from Lt. Wolf on 5/21/64. On 9/1/64 Morton noted it was nice to sleep under a pair of blankets and on 10/18/64 Boyle had plenty of blankets. About 11/2/64 McKey, Cox and Boyle all noted that all the men were allowed to keep only one blanket supplied by the U.S. Army. Then on 1/12/65 Gibson reported the Yankees counted the blankets in each division. This was a prelude to the next day when blankets were removed, so each man had only one blanket (Cox, Gibson). On 1/30/65 Boyle noted that blankets had been received for the "needy." Finally, on 2/7/65 Cox noted that a large quantity of blankets had been received, probably as part of the Cotton for Clothes Exchange.

6. Shelter and Clothing

During this period, we also have some references to blankets in the Union records. On 5/13/63 the CGP telegraphed Schoepf[32] that blankets distributed to the prisoners should be taken away from Fort Delaware. On 9/21/63 the CGP wrote,[33] "It [prison fund] may be used also in the purchase of store for the use of the prisoners or anything else that may be necessary to promote their comfort, blankets, clothing, etc." On 9/25/64 Schoepf wrote to the CGP[34]

> I have the honor to report that 210 prisoners' blankets were delivered by Capt. Prentice Comdg detachment of 600 rebel officers sent to Hilton Head SC to Capt. Lamb PM at Hilton Head SC for which he was to forward receipts to me but has not done so. I would therefore respectfully request that you require Capt. Lamb to immediately forward the necessary receipts. I usually send blankets with the prisoners during disagreeable weather with instructions to the officer in charge to turn them over to a US QM and take receipts for them or when possible return them to this Post. Please inform me whether it is proper to do so.

From this it is reasonable to *conclude* that at least many of the prisoners had blankets supplied by the U.S. Army. On 11/15/64 Schoepf again wrote[35] to the CGP stating he had ordered blankets for the prisoners but they had not arrived, and that the CGP expedite delivery of the blankets. Finally, on 8/23/65 the CGP wrote[36] to Schoepf stating he did not think it advisable to wash the prisoners' blankets as the cost and trouble would be more than could be obtained in the sale of these blankets.

7

Water Supply and Sanitation

The prevention of disease is the highest object of medical science. —Jonathan Letterman, MD[1]

Water, water, every where,
Nor any drop to drink.
—Samuel Taylor Coleridge, *The Rime of the Ancient Mariner*

Water supply and sanitation are inextricably linked in most Civil War POW prisons, both North and South. There are numerous instances of prison camps which had, virtually all now concede, contaminated water supplies, often being contaminated, sometimes unavoidably, by the POWs themselves.[2] There is also general agreement that this lack of sanitation, not just of the water but often more generally, led to increased death rates from diseases such as diarrhea, dysentery, typhus, typhoid fever, and others. Thus these were critical factors determining death rates in the prison camps.

Water Supply

The quotation from Coleridge above is extremely apt for Fort Delaware, since it was on Pea Patch Island in the middle of the Delaware River. However, the water at this point of the river is brackish, and for the most part not potable except perhaps in the spring when runoff made it less salty for a short period of time.[3] Thus in practical terms the only fresh water available on the island was rainwater. Since most of the time between April 1863 and June 1865 the island had 4,000–13,000 residents, rain would not supply sufficient potable water, especially in drier periods.

The first mention of drinking water found in any of the records is by Sgt. Edward Purvis of the 19th VA Infantry on 7/8/63 where he noted, "It has been raining nearly every day, but that is good for our side as we have to drink rain water." Rainwater was collected in barrels from the roofs of the prisoners' barracks, and also from the top surfaces of the fort, where the rain was collected and sent into underground cisterns to be pumped out as needed. On 7/17/63 Purvis noted it had rained and that was good because they were nearly out of water. On 7/22/63 JRMcMichael stated the water tanks were nearly empty, while Handy in the Fort reported that the cisterns on the fort roof were empty and he had to wash with brownish filthy water. On 7/23/63 Franklin reported the water tanks dry and that they had to drink river water, while Handy reported the water is much improved, and they (in the Fort) can obtain clear and good bathing water by turning a cock at the head of the stairway.

This shortage of water occurred even though the rainfall for that month was 4.0 inches (see Table 1-1), about average for the month (see Table 1-2). Undoubtedly the large increase in the prison population from 45 to over 9,000 POWs between May and mid–July caused this shortage of water. Unknown to the POWs, General Schoepf recognized the problem, and 7/13/63 directly telegraphed the Sec. War asking that a "water boat" be assigned to supply the island with water.[4] On 8/19/63, as part of a more general report,[5] Schoepf informed the Sec. War that "In regard to water I would state that the steam water tank employed here is supplying a sufficient quantity of good fresh water from a creek in the neighborhood noted for its pure water. The water is pumped by a steam pump into tanks in close proximity to the Barracks and is used for cooking and drinking by the soldiers of the Garrison as well as the prisoners."

This was confirmed in prisoners' diaries in late July. On 7/23/63 Handy reported that in the Fort he could get tolerably good water, even for a bath. In the prison on 7/24/63 Purvis stated they now get plenty of water from the other side of the river, on the 7/26/63 Franklin declared that water was now supplied by steamer once a day from Delaware City (the location was wrong), and on 7/30/63 Peters reported correctly that water from the river Brandywine at Wilmington, Delaware, was very good when they got it.

There are others sources confirming this. An article in the *New York Times* of 8/31/63 states that "Government supplies the barracks with thirty thousand gallons of pure water daily from the Brandywine River. This is conveyed to large tanks, accessible to all the prisoners at a minutes' walk." The *Times* also reported on 9/28/64 that water was also supplied from a steam condenser (distillation apparatus) that was recently introduced. An article in the *Philadelphia Inquirer* of 6/22/65 confirmed that these water supply options were still operating at the end of the war. Finally, Surgeon A.M. Clark, Medical Inspector in his inspection report stated,[6] "Water, source and supply—partly by rain in tanks, partly by boat from Brandywine Creek, partly by condenser, capacity 10,000 gallons. Water, quality and effect—generally good."

A "preview" of what was being planned for a water supply system is contained in Surgeon Alden's inspection report of 7/11/63.[7] The inspection states in part that

> The water on the island is chiefly rain-water of good quality. At intervals along the outside of the barracks are tanks fin' [sic] the collection and storage of rain-water.... There are also tanks connected with the hospitals and other buildings around the fort. Under the casemates of the main work are a series of large cistern which are designed to be filled by the rain-fall on the parapets percolating through the earth, sand and gravel (forming a filtering arrangement), down into them. They are of large capacity, but at present have a small supply in them. When rain-water is scarce it has been the practice to send for water by vessel to the Brandywine; ... The latter [prisoners] use the river water in part, if not entirely, for cooking purposes.... Measures are, however, being taken, by bringing water from the Brandywine and by pumping up (by steam apparatus) water from the river, throwing it overs the parapets, and allowing it to filter through into the cisterns beneath, to obtain a good supply. A condensing apparatus [distillation plant] has also been ordered.

If this report is completely accurate, at least brackish river water was being supplied to the fort, where most of the inhabitants were Union soldiers.

From a map of the vicinity of the prisoners' barracks, which includes other structures such as fences, Union soldier barracks, etc., when these barracks were sold for scrap, we can identify at least 31 water tanks (the sale included 32 water tanks). Of these 3 were in the POW officer's pen, and 15 in the enlisted men's pen. The others were scattered about near Union barracks, outside the walls of the prison, (perhaps for guards), and other places. The description of the sale stated that the tanks were 2,000 to 6,000 gallons each, but does not identify what size each tank is.[8]

Thus a complete water supply system was created on Pea Patch Island for both the Union soldiers and POWs, and perhaps also the civilians on the island. We have no indication whether civilians had access to the water provided by the Army. This water supply system required much thought and effort to construct and keep running. For example, in order to bring water to the island by boat, the boat had to have equipment to pump the water on board the boat, and also fuel for the propulsion engine, that fuel *probably* being coal.

For the "condenser" (distillation apparatus) large amounts of fuel (coal) would have been needed to distill 10,000 gallons of water a day. If we assume the distillation apparatus had a 20 percent thermal efficiency in boiling the water, approximately 25 tons (23 tonnes) of coal each day would be needed to produce 10,000 gallons of distilled water.

Once the water was available on the island it had to be distributed. If arriving by water boat, it was pumped through hoses and pipes, the pump on the wharf being powered by a steam engine *probably* fired with coal. In addition, the hoses and pipes that distributed the water about the island had to be maintained. This was not necessarily a minor task, since the whole system was not built to last a long period of time. Indeed, for the only two full months which we have complete records of spending from the Prison Fund, which includes maintenance of the water system, 30 percent of the funds spent were for maintenance and repair of the water distribution system (see Table 5-6).

The water system was complicated and had many parts, which made it subject to breaking down. Some of these breakdowns appear to have been documented in prisoners' diaries. The first of these instances is when Handy recorded on 7/2/64 that the water house at the rear was closed up, by McCrorey on 7/15/64 that water was scarce, and by Cox on 7/31/64 that water was very scarce. Note that the number of prisoners at the end of July 1864 was over 9000. On 8/18/64 Handy noted that the *Osceola*, a boat owned by the Fort usually used to transport passengers and freight, is now being used to transport water, and on 8/22/64 Handy stated the *Osceola* is now towing the water boat. Obviously there was a problem with the water boat. In November or December 1864 Gibson affirmed that water was still being obtained from Brandywine Creek.

A couple of problems occur in the water system in the winter of 1864–65. McKey reported on 12/13/64 that the water tanks were frozen, and they had to melt ice for cooking water. On 2/12/65 Boyle stated they were almost out of water, possibly because of a mechanical breakdown. Both of these may have been caused by the exceptionally cold weather the winter of 1864–65, which was considered by many to be the coldest in 30 years. The river was blocked with ice for considerable periods, so it is likely that the water boat could not get water during those periods. Thus the island would have been relying on rain and the condenser for water, a greatly restricted supply, which could also have accounted for some of the water scarcity.

Thus the water supply at Fort Delaware seems superior to what was available at many, if not most, prison camps. However, that superiority would only be effective if the handling and use of the water was done using good sanitary practices. It is also noted that the POWs and the Union soldiers used water from the same sources.

Sanitation

Sanitation in this section is given a very general meaning, and encompasses personal hygiene such as bathing and clothes washing, cleanliness of barracks, handling and serving of food, and other items that affect sanitation.

The POWs as well as Union soldiers received throughout this period their full allowance of soap in the ration, 4 pounds per 100 men per day, except after December 1864 POWs received 2 pounds per hundred men per day (Table 4-1). Four pounds of soap per day per 100 men works out to about 0.64 ounces (18.3 gm) per day per man. Although not a lot it would have been sufficient to wash hands and face, bathe every few days, and wash a limited amount of clothing.

The biggest problem with personal hygiene seems to be mostly the water that was used for bathing and washing clothes and dishes. It is likely that in mid–July 1863 when Purvis and Park reported water was in short supply that little bathing or washing was done. The first specific mention of bathing is by Handy (he was housed in the Fort) on 7/23/63, when he stated the water was good and he was able to take a bath. He also wrote that on 7/25/63 the men from his rooms were allowed to go to the riverbank and take a bath. This may or may not have been a good idea, since the sinks (privies) may have been nearby. Dr. S. Weir Mitchell visited the island in late July on behalf of the United States Sanitary Commission and wrote two letters,[9] one of which stated that the POWs in the barracks would wash themselves and their clothes from the banks and dikes (seawall?), which means they were using river water and perhaps water in the ditches on the island, none of it being too sanitary. Purvis noted on 8/20/63 that they were not allowed to go to the river to bathe anymore, so they would have been confined to using the ditches for this purpose. At some point, *perhaps* when the POW population decreased in the fall of 1863, the POWs must have been allowed to use the cleaner water in the tanks, since on 6/28/64 Handy (who was now in the officer POW's barracks) noted they must now use the water in the ditches to wash themselves and their clothing. Perhaps this is because the population of the island was up again with the increase in the number of POWs. Handy affirms this condition on 9/10/64 when he described the vile appearance of the water in the ditches. It appears that after 6/28/63 until final release, bathing and clothes washing was apparently allowed only using ditch water. The following mention bathing, and where noted in the ditches: Bingham (7/11/64), JRMcMichael (8/1/64), Park (2/17/65 and 3/7/65, ditch), and Berkeley (3/25/65, also washed clothes). These clearly were not good sanitary conditions for washing clothes or people, and may have been caused by the high population on the island requiring a restriction of how fresh water was used.

The penalty for using "good" water for other than drinking or cooking could be serious. In his diary entry for 9/10/64, as noted above, Handy described how all washing of clothes, people and dishes had to be done in ditch water. Handy further reported that on the same day one officer POW was taken to the guard house for drawing a basin of water, while another was ordered to empty his basin into the ditch.

By contrast, Union enlisted men's clothing was washed by laundresses hired by the Army for that purpose.[10] Laundresses were authorized one ration per day, and were paid by the piece or by the month, as determined by the Council of Administration for the command. At Fort Delaware the laundress's quarters were located on the second floor of the Fort, and their laundry room was downstairs. Thus they *probably* would have used whatever water was available inside the Fort. Union officers could have hired these laundresses, or had their servants do their clothes washing.

Another type of personal hygiene is taking care of one's teeth, and this is mentioned in several prisoner diaries. On 9/28/64 Handy mentions that one of the political prisoners has a toothbrush, Mauck reports on 6/10/64 that his toothbrush was taken (although it is not clear whether this was before or after he reached Fort Delaware), and Alburtis (July 24, 1864) and McCrorey (August 2, 1864) both receive toothbrushes in packages. It is perhaps likely that many other men had toothbrushes and simply did not mention it. In a list provided by Gen Schoepf[11] on 8/5/64 of what the Sutler can sell to the prisoners, "brushes" are included, but whether this included toothbrushes is not known. However, one study[12] reports sutlers in the Civil War did not usually sell toothbrushes. Nevertheless, "authentic" period toothbrushes from the Civil War are commonly offered for sale on the internet. Which type of water the men used to brush their teeth was not stated but it would have been easy enough to use a cup of drinking water within their barracks.

The POWs lived in wood shingle barracks, which they policed (cleaned) themselves (see Chapter 11). These barracks were difficult to keep clean, especially in rainy weather. Since the island was low lying, beneath the high tide, when it rained it did not drain well, and as a result became very muddy. This mud in turn was tracked into the barracks, and made it impossible to keep the floors clean until the ground dried. There are many reports in diaries about the mud problem: Handy (2/1/64, 4/3/64, 4/13/64, 5/20/64, 5/26/64, 6/6/64, 8/27/64, 9/5/64, 10/2/64, and 10/6/64), McKey (10/2/64, 12/11/64), Morton (10/4/64), Cox (11/29/64, 12/17–19/64), Park (2/4/65), Alburtis (3/23/65), Mauck (3/31/65) and Berkeley (5/2/65). This occurred even though there were boardwalks between certain points, even within the prisoners' pens. Handy reports on 9/12/64 that men were stealing wood from the boardwalks for cooking fires, and on 10/5/64 that it is so muddy it would be almost impossible to get around except for the boardwalks.

Who, if anyone, besides the prisoners themselves, was making sure that the POW barracks were being kept clean? Handy reported that while he is held in the Fort, they had an inspection by Schoepf, Ahl and Silliman (11/7/63), Ahl (2/7/64) and Silliman (3/20/64). He further reported on 5/10/64, after he has been transferred to the officers' barracks, that they will have a regular inspection. On 6/1/64 Mauck stated there was an inspection by a surgeon, while on 8/10/64 Handy said there was an inspection by Schoepf, Ahl, and another officer. Thereafter there are reports of barracks inspections by McKey (10/31/64), Cox (11/1/64, 1/8/65, 1/16/65, and Berkeley (3/18–19/65, 4/16/65). In addition, Berkeley reported that on 3/19/65 and 4/16/65 they did not pass inspection, so they had to reclean their barracks.

What prompted this apparent intensification of inspections from mid–1864 on? On 8/14/64 the CGP sent General Schoepf a letter (and all other Union prison camps) which states,[13] "I have the honor to request a weekly report be made to this office showing the condition of the prisoners and camp under your charge in every particular personal cleanliness, clothing, bedding quarters, kitchen, messing, sink, policing of grounds, drainage, etc. and the Hospital and all connected with it. Let nothing pass unnoticed. For this service please select a suitable officer as an Inspector of the Camp." For this task Schoepf picked Capt. Ahl, a logical choice since he is in charge of all POWs and political prisoners on the island. Ahl then carried out these weekly inspections, gave the reports to Schoepf, who in turn sent them to the CGP. The correspondence to the CGP with these weekly reports is recorded in the files of the CGP, but the reports are not there. However, some of the reports are repeated verbatim in the OR. While many believe these were just self-serving statements by Ahl to whitewash conditions in the prison camp, there are many notations and somewhat negative comments in these reports that are interesting and lend them credibility[14]:

    August 21, 1864—Gen. Schoepf in an endorsement stated that the clothing was not as good as desired and requested 4,000 suits of gray clothing. He also stated he inspected the barracks and hospital in person. (Confirmed by Handy on 8/10/64, see above).

> September 4, 1864—Prisoners were required to bathe regularly. Drainage being improved.
> September 17, 1864—…clothing, comfortable, and sufficient with very few exceptions.
> October 9, 1864—…sinks, are kept clean by tide and force pumps.
> December 19, 1864—"Clothing—requisition made by prisoners on General Beall for such clothing as is needed. Bedding—receive allowance, which is kept clean. State of quarters –being renovated by whitewashing and improvement of bunks…. Police of grounds—the grounds are kept clean and are being improved with stone walks…. The recent cold weather has greatly retarded the progress of improvements and at time the work has been altogether suspended. With favorable weather it would require but a short time to complete the same, and the work will be resumed as soon as possible.
> December 27, 1864—Clothing—some of the prisoners are needy, and the weather is very cold, the deficiencies should be promptly supplied by General Beall…. I have inspected the barracks in person and found them all in good condition.
> January 22, 1865—Clothing—good, with a few exceptions, but insufficient.
> January 29, 1865—Clothing—some are too thinly clad for such exceedingly cold weather…. Many of the prisoners apply for permission to purchase bedsacks. I have the honor to inquire whether their application can be granted.

A bedsack was a cloth bag in the shape of a mattress that could be filled, as with straw. This made sleeping not only more comfortable but warmer, as one would be lying on what amounted to an insulated surface.

    Almost all of the other ratings in these reports are favorable. This can be seen as self-serving, but the above comments in these reports, and the reports by Berkeley (see above) that they had twice failed inspection, seem to give at least some credibility to them. The remarks concerning improvements to the prison seem to indicate that there was a more or less constant effort to better the conditions in the prison.

    The fact that "stone walks" (see December 19th above) were being installed indicates that the prison administrators were well aware of the mud problem, and the consequent difficulty in keeping the barracks clean. In fact, they could hardly have been unaware of the mud problem if they walked around the island during wet periods, but the significant thing is they were trying to do something about the mud's effect on sanitation.

    However, what were probably the most influential inspections as far as the authorities in Washington were concerned were probably those of Medical Inspectors usually sent by the CGP. These Medical Inspectors were surgeons assigned to that task, and typically while they were medical inspectors of prisons, inspected many prisons. A perusal of their reports in the OR, Series II, volumes VI to VIII shows that they seemed to be unstinting in their criticism of conditions in various prisons when this was warranted. They could be considered more "neutral" in their reports, since they did not report to the prison camp commandants, but to the CGP. The CGP in turn usually "requested" that camp commandants "fix" most problems that these inspectors found.

    There are six full or partial reports by medical inspectors in the record,[15] each done by a different inspector: Alden on 7/11/63, Cuyler on 8/28/63, Crane on 9/3/63, Clark on 11/13/63, Johnson on 2/29/64, and Alexander on 6/28/64. In addition, there is a report[16] by LCol. Irvine of the 10th NY Cavalry on 12/5/63 to MGen Hitchcock, Commissioner for Exchange of Prisoners. Briefly summarized below are items related to sanitation in these inspection reports.

The date of Cuyler's report is uncertain since he was ordered on 7/6/63 to do the inspection, but the partial report in the OR is dated 8/28/63. It states in its entirety

> Improving ventilation by making openings flush with the floor of barracks at intervals of fifteen feet; additional windows at ends of buildings; reducing the number of bunks by removing one tier; constructing wooden troughs in or near the buildings for washing faces and hands; urinals at convenient distances, with movable soil tubs or latrines, for use of sick in quarters at night, the distance to the sinks being considerable; ditches and drains to be kept free, and the interior of barracks whitewashed at least every six weeks. The prisoners have no bedding, and so little clothing that it is almost impossible to enforce cleanliness of person.

Except for the last two items, we have no record that these things were carried out, at least in the late summer of 1863.

The first full medical inspection report we have is by Surgeon C.H. Alden on 7/11/63, and the MSH states prison conditions were probably the worst at this time (large number of POWs from Gettysburg were arriving). The ventilation of the barracks was very poor, the barracks were very crowded, barracks, mess-halls and prisoners themselves were very dirty. There were several ditches and inlets, and drainage was imperfect. At that time the moat around the fort was drained for construction purposes and the human effluent from inside the Fort was lying decomposing and stinking in the moat. The police in the five hospitals was poor, especially the grounds around the hospitals. Alden was told officer POWs could not bathe, and it appeared from their appearance the enlisted POWs had not either. One can conclude from Alden's report that sanitary conditions on the island at that time were poor.

The next inspection was by Surgeon C.H. Crane on 9/3/63, and was quite brief. He states the sick and well POWs were often in the same barracks, so it was impossible to keep these barracks clean. Rigid policing in the areas of the kitchen, mess-rooms and barracks was needed. He believed the opening of the new hospital would greatly improve the condition of the sick.

Surgeon A.M. Clark made the next medical inspection on 11/13/63, and his report is quite extensive. He records the following observations related to sanitation. Drainage very imperfect due to topography, the police of the camp generally good, sinks (privies) two platforms built out over the river covered in by sheds and the tide effectively removes the "excretia." The police of the sinks was good, they were kept well whitewashed. The kitchens were considered to be well appointed and policed. However, the cleanliness of the men was not as good as it should have been. Laundry (for clothes) facilities were deficient, since clothes were washed in the outer ditch, and two boilers were provided to help wash clothes. Blankets and bedding in the barracks were in tolerable order. Surgeon Clark summarizes with the following remarks: "The barracks are clean and kept well whitewashed.... Blankets and bedding are duly aired. The kitchen and mess-room are well appointed and well policed. The ground within the line of barracks is being gradually raised by depositing thereon ashes from the various fires.... The present laundry facilities for the prisoners in barracks are very poor, they being obliged to wash their clothes in the outer ditch. This will do very well when the tide keeps the water constantly changing, but at present the washing does not much to improve the articles washed." He also commented on the stench from the moat around the Fort which was then partially dry, construction being performed on the moat and Fort. The comparison of Clark's report with that of Alden indicates that sanitary conditions had improved greatly between mid–July and early November of 1863. Except for washing of the POWs clothing, the sanitary conditions on the island were tolerably good in November 1863.

The next reported inspection is by LCol. Wm. Irvine of the 10th NY Cav., not a medical inspector. He finds on inspection, and interrogation of the POWs, that conditions on the island for the prisoners were quite good. According to Irvine no prisoner complained about anything except for a single man who complained he did not get enough bread. Perhaps this report is a bit too rosy, as Irvine made the inspection at the request of MGen Hitchcock, the Commissioner for Exchange of Prisoners, because Mr. Ould, the Confederate agent for exchange, had complained of the treatment of prisoners at Fort Delaware. Irvine's report was forwarded to Ould. In return Irvine got a report about treatment of Union soldiers who were POWs in Richmond. Irvine, based on his own experiences in prison as a POW in Richmond, and other Union personnel who had been prisoners there, said the Confederate report was delusion. One *suspects* the Confederates probably thought the same about Irvine's report about Fort Delaware.

The remaining medical inspectors' reports (Johnson and Alexander) have the same tone as Clark's inspection report. Among the interesting sanitation related items in Johnson's report are that the police of the grounds was at a moderate level, and most of the men showed a marked neglect of personal cleanliness, while Alexander's report states, "The quarters of the prisoners are fairly policed and could be kept in good condition if the inmates were not too lazy to consult self-interest and comfort," the privies were a nuisance and source of complaint, and were set back too far to have the "excrescence" removed by the tide, and the men were quite clean in appearance, as they are forced to bathe once a week (not specified where).

There are other sources besides inspection reports as to what actions, if any, were taken to improve the sanitation on the island. The following do not include sanitation of medical facilities.

Keeping the barracks clean and in some cases "disinfected" was a never-ending challenge, for example, because of the above mentioned mud problem and the everyday living of many men in somewhat crowded conditions. Routine cleaning of the barracks was carried out by men appointed by each Division Chief (see Chapter 11 for details). It is clear from the descriptions of prisoners when weekly inspections were to take place, that many if not all of the men helped clean and straighten up (see above). Whitewashing was considered a form of disinfection and the whitewashing of the barracks is mentioned numerous times: Franklin 7/23/63; Handy (in the Fort) 10/13/63, 1/29/64, 2/9/64, 3/28/64, 5/5/64, (in the officer barracks) 8/27/64, 9/17/64, and 10/1/64; Mauck 6/11/64, 4/4/65, and 5/16/65; Cox 8/26/64, 10/29/64, and 3/13/65; McKey 8/26/64, 10/29/64, 11/16/64, and 1/4/65; Morton 9/16/64; PAMcMichael 1/6/65, 3/21/65, 4/20/65, and 5/20/65; Gibson 1/6/65 and 5/20/65; Boyle 3/20/65; Berkeley 4/7/65 and 5/18/65; and Barringer 5/20/65. Spreading lime was also another method of disinfection, and Franklin reported this being done on 7/24/63. In order to hold down the dust in a presumably drier period, McCrorey reported on 8/1/64 that the Yankees were spraying water from a hose onto the grounds of the pen.

A letter from the CGP to General Schoepf on 11/26/63[17] asks if "Ridgewood Disinfectant Powder" had been recommended by Acting Medical Inspector Cuyler and asks Schoepf to order 2 barrels of it (to be paid from the Prison Fund), use it, and report on its efficacy, especially compared to other disinfectants that may have been used on the island. As it turns out, this powder contained carbolic acid (5–8 percent), iron sesquichloride, charcoal or pumice, lime, and Fuller's Earth (70–80 percent).[18] Carbolic acid (phenol) is a disinfectant; in fact, it was the disinfectant Dr. Lister used in his first operations under aseptic conditions. Although perhaps it was an effective disinfectant, no further references to it were found in correspondence to or from Fort Delaware.

The sanitary conditions of serving (as opposed to cooking) the food is also of interest. The best descriptions of how the food was served were given by Handy on 9/9/64, who stated, "The soup is always served in tin cups, without spoons, we are not allowed knives and forks." Park on 2/5/65 wrote, "The mess room is next to '22' and near 'the rear.' It is a long, dark room, having a long pine table, on which the food is placed in separate piles, either on a tin plate or on the uncovered, greasy table, at meal hours, twice a day. No knives nor forks, nor spoons are furnished. Captain Browne kindly brought my meals to me." Others describe a series of long narrow tables on which the food is placed to be picked up by the POWs. They filed down between these tables to pick up their food (see Figure 12). Usually they take the food to their barracks or other places to be eaten. It would appear that the process of picking up food was not too good from a sanitation viewpoint. However, since virtually all the food was cooked by boiling well in water (see Chapter 4), the food itself when first put out was probably reasonably aseptic. Lack of eating utensils[19] may have also contributed to unsanitary conditions. The POWs did have tin plates and cups.

In addition it appears that men who were cooks or bakers also got clothing, at least if they needed it. A few pages on a microfilm roll[20] show that 18 cooks got clothing on 6/2?/64 which included a shirt and/or pants, and/or shoes. Interestingly enough from the names shown, most of these appear to be of Irish descent. The same page shows 16 cooks got similar items on September 10th or 15th, but although names are partly illegible, it appears that these were different men. On another page of the same microfilm, it shows that 18 bakers got the same items as the cooks on September 10 or 15, 1864.

Finally, we come to a portion of sanitation that proved very troublesome to many army camps and prison camps, Union and Confederate, during the war: getting rid of human waste. As has been related in bits and pieces above, the sinks (privies) on the island for the prisoners were out over the river, so that the POWs had to walk to the sinks, sometimes a distance of a few hundred feet. Not much is said about these privies by the prisoners, except for one remark by Park on 2/13/65, who stated, "The seats are very filthy, and cannot be occupied without being defiled. The sea water proves no disinfectant, and the constant frequenters of the place are sickened by the offensive odors which are wafted to their sensitive olafactories. Diarrhea and dysentery are so prevalent, and the pen is so crowded, that parties are very often compelled to wait an hour or longer before they can be relieved. The door and seats are too filthy and nauseating for description; yet very many who suffer from the diseases mentioned visit the foul place dozens of times, day and night, in rain, wind, hail, sleet and snow, and in spite of the most intense cold and blackest, most impenetrable darkness, pollution is scarcely avoidable on such occasions." This description is not surprising, given the fact, as Park notes, that men often suffered from diarrhea. We have no record of the sinks themselves being washed. However, the fact that the sinks were out over the river, or at least the effluent was washed into the river periodically by hoses, meant that, in theory, human waste from the POWs was not a problem on the island itself.

However, putting human waste into the river may have caused other problems (aside from those from our modern environmental views), since POWs and probably their clothes were washed in a ditch, and the ditches at best were flushed by the tides through one or more gates. It is quite possible that as river water eddied around the island when the tide was running, and/or between the tides when the river was not flowing much, some of the human waste got into the outer ditch and the POW and/or their clothes were contaminated with the human waste.

Park, on 2/5/65, is also the only person to note that "Tubs, made of barrels, are placed at night in front of the doors, and used as urinals. These are emptied by details of prisoners early every morning." This had been suggested by Surgeon Cuyler in the summer of 1863, but this is the only mention that it had ever been done.

General Schoepf was also aware that keeping human excrement away from the POW area was important, since on 6/1/64 he had an order issued, Special Orders No. 157, which read in part[21]:

> II. It is the duty of the sentinel to prevent the prisoners from escaping, or cutting, defacing, or in any way damaging any of the Government property, or from committing any nuisance in or about their barracks, or from using any abusive or insolent language toward them, and from any violation of good order.
>
> Should the sentinel detect any prisoner in violating these instructions, he must order him three distinct times to halt, and if the prisoner obeys the order the sentinel must call for the corporal of the guard and have the prisoner placed in arrest; but should the prisoner fail to halt when so ordered, the sentinel must enforce his orders by bayonet or ball.

By a nuisance was meant, in part, urinating or defecating in or around the barracks or throwing urine or feces from the barracks. This eventually resulted, on 12/20/64, in Private John H. Bibb being killed when someone threw from his barracks what was believed to be a bowl of urine, and that Pvt. Bibb was shot and killed by mistake by a guard. Pvt. Bibb was an innocent party, but a court of inquiry cleared the guard of wrongdoing, since other POWs testified that someone had thrown something from the barracks.

The sanitary conditions for Union soldiers were similar to that of the POWs, with some exceptions, which were perhaps important. As mentioned above Union soldiers clothing was washed by laundresses, whose workroom was in the Fort, so one can *assume* the water they used was from the Fort's supply, which was drinking water of reasonably good quality. The Union soldiers in the Fort, and also those in barracks outside the Fort, also possibly washed themselves with the drinking water. Soldiers in the Fort would have used the flush toilets the Fort had. We don't know where Union soldiers housed outside the Fort would have urinated or defecated, but presumably they used a sink (privy) over the river.

Conclusion

It is very easy for present-day readers to criticize much about the water and sanitary conditions on the island, but it must be remembered this is being done from a modern perspective, for example, knowledge of the germ (bacteria and viruses) theory of disease, which was not accepted or known to most people during the Civil War. It is difficult to put oneself in a mindset of the period to understand why certain things related to water supply and sanitation were and were not done.

During the Civil War the most accepted theory among Doctors about how diseases spread was the "miasmatic" theory (see also Chapter 9). A modern definition of this theory from Wikipedia states, "Miasma was considered to be poisonous vapor or mist filled with particles of decomposed matter (miasmata) that caused illness. The Miasmatic position was that diseases were the product of environmental factors such as contaminated water, foul air, and poor hygienic conditions. Such infection was not passed between individuals but would affect individuals who resided within the particular locale that gave rise to such vapors. It was identifiable by its foul smell." Thus it was not bad water itself, or a poor hygienic condition, but the mist or vapor from these conditions that caused disease.

One can clearly see this thread of reasoning in two medical tracts written during the Civil War by surgeons in the Union army.[22] Chapter 1 of Hammond, the Surgeon General, states, "If military necessity should require an encampment in the neighborhood of an extensive marsh, the ground should always, if possible, be selected on the windward side, so that the prevailing winds should carry away the noxious emanations from the soil." "The Disposition of Excrements and Offal. Pits should be dug on· the leeward side of the camp, and ordinarily at a distance of not less than two hundred yards.", and "No pit should be dug for such purposes near any source from which water is supplied to the camp." Chapter 2 of Hammond by Surgeon Harris states: "It is manifest, therefore, that hygienic measures for the control and the prevention of infectious contamination will mainly consist in sanitary works for the preservation of atmospheric purity, and for the special restoration of such purity to the places, things, and persons contaminated" (emphasis added). Chapter 1 of Woodward gives a list of diseases which are considered "miasmatic" by the army, and these are typhoid fever, typhus fever, typhomalarial fever, yellow fever, remittent fever, intermittent fever, diarrhea, dysentery, cholera, erysipelas, hospital gangrene, pysemia, smallpox, measles, scarlet fever, diphtheria, mumps and epidemic catarrh (for definitions of some of these terms and more details, see Chapter 9). Except for scurvy, these include almost all of the serious diseases encountered at Fort Delaware.

Thus the medical system of the U.S. Army was geared to minimizing the generation of miasmata wherever Union soldiers were, and by implication where POWs were being held. Surgeon Harris writes in Chapter 2 of Hammond that certain diseases such as smallpox or measles could also be transmitted by contacting persons or their belongings that had these diseases. Both of these sanitary measures were carried out at Fort Delaware. Persons who had smallpox or measles were placed in a separate hospital, the Contagious Hospital, or as it was more popularly called the smallpox hospital. As for minimizing the presence of miasmata, clean water, in the form of rainwater, water from the Brandywine Creek, or distilled water was used on the island for drinking and cooking purposes. Other water on the island, except for the water in the ditches on the interior of the island, was supposedly regularly changed by the tides. This included the water in the Fort moat and in the outer ditch. Barracks were regularly cleaned and inspected, and occasionally whitewashed to keep them clean. At some point the POWs were required to bathe once a week and keep their clothes washed, to aid in keeping odors in check. All of these actions resulted in minimizing odors and the resulting miasmata which caused disease. Nevertheless, especially in warmer weather, the odor around the island was foul and sometimes could be smelled a couple of miles downind.[23] There was simply no way to eliminate the odor from a small Island having 5,000–14,000 people living on it, using sanitary methods available at the time.

One aspect of preventing diseases under the miasma theory was that the Army insisted that buildings such as hospitals and barracks have a minimum volume of air per resident, and also good ventilation.[24] This probably did help prevent the spread of disease from person to person through the air, and coincidentally is in agreement with disease prevention under the germ theory of disease. The level of airborne gems would be reduced by large volumes of air and good ventilation.

As noted above the germ theory of disease was not yet discovered, so the ideas that diseases could be transmitted by drinking contaminated water, or by eating contaminated food, or that insects were vectors for spreading some diseases were not considered. This meant, for instance, that water was good for use if it tasted all right, and did not have an objectionable odor. The drinking water supply on the island probably met these criteria, since there are no complaints of this type in any contemporaneous writings. As noted above, throughout this period there were attempts to improve drainage around the POW barracks, probably at least in part to hold down odor from water collected in these areas.

Poor sanitation during the period April to about October 1863 probably was a result of lack of experience of the island administration, lack of proper physical facilities of various kinds, and lack of properly trained persons, such as surgeons. There is much evidence outlined above that great improvements were made during this early period, and improvement continued at a lesser pace almost to the final release of the POWs. There is also some evidence that some of the lack of sanitation of the POWs was due to the POWs themselves, as noted by some of the Medical Inspectors.[25] However, overall it *seems* that by the medical standards of the day, eventually, overall water supply and sanitation on the island was reasonably good.

8

Outside Help

For all of the men on Pea Patch Island, not everything they desired or needed was necessarily available to them on the island. Since Union soldiers, POWs and political prisoners could send and receive mail and packages (the POWs sometimes with restrictions), one method of obtaining these items, or the resources for obtaining these items (money) was to write to relatives, friends, or even strangers to send them the items or money to buy the items. This chapter is concerned with this "outside help," who provided it, who got it, and what it consisted of.

Union Soldiers

Union soldiers were probably the least needy of the men on the island, since they could freely buy anything the sutler had for sale, and were provided clothing (uniforms), food and other needed items by the government. They could use their salary ($13–16/month for a private) to buy the items they desired from the sutler. For the men of the "permanent" garrison they could also get off the island occasionally either on a short leave or on a detail such as a guard escort for POWs being transferred. During these absences from the island they could of course use their money to buy items from civilians such as shopkeepers. Some of the items they may have wanted to obtain include alcoholic beverages, tobacco, extra clothing, and personal items such as toothbrushes, etc.

Hamilton's diary lists several instances in which he got these kinds of items in various ways. On 6/12/63 while on a detail in New Jersey, he bought and had some milk and pie. On many other occasions when off the island, Hamilton bought meals and other items; see Chapter 9. On 1/7/64 Hamilton received a box of various eatables (name of person sending illegible), including butter cookies.

Crumrine was more active requesting items from home. On 6/10/63 he wrote home and asked for two woolen shirts, complaining he had to pay $5.00 a piece on the island, and they were of poor quality. He promised to send home the money for the shirts. On 6/23/63 he asked that the shirts be sent soon. On 7/2/63 he wrote to ask them to send him some linen handkerchiefs and linen collars, and again asks for the woolen shirts. In a letter home on 8/30/63 he asked to be sent some (postage) stamps and some magazines and books, and said he has no money to buy any. On 9/10/63 he wrote to say he received the stamps, and sent home rings he got from one of the Rebs. On 10/12/63 he acknowledged receipt of a novel. On 11/12/63 he says he got the dime novel, and asks for "good novels.," and a couple of more shirts as his are pretty well worn. On 1/28/64 he asked for a copy of "Horace," and stated he would like to read history also. On 2/12/64 he acknowledged books that were sent to him, while on 3/5/64 requested two more shirts with the sleeves a little longer. Said he will send money on receipt of the shirts. Also asked for a couple of pair of socks, as the Government issued ones are "poor things," and a Latin grammar.

On 12/30/64 Lank wrote home that he had received the bundle from them. The bundle apparently contained food, including turkey and sauce. On 1/4/65 he wrote home that he received the 3 bundles sent in John Hall's box, which apparently contained food. He wrote that a good many boxes were sent to the men in his regiment for Christmas. Foods he has eaten this week (presumably from their boxes) include hog, biscuits and sweet potatoes. Note—Lank's regiment, the 9th DE Volunteers, was from Sussex County, Delaware, and so the packages did not have far to travel.

It is obvious from the brief description above that the items the Union soldiers got from home and friends were not "essential," but were merely to make their life more comfortable and convenient. The Union soldiers' salary and their ability to buy things both on and off the island was a great advantage to them.

POWs and Political Prisoners

In contrast to the Union soldiers, prisoners did not have the opportunity to buy things off the island, and they did not receive a salary with which to buy things. What they could buy at the sutler was restricted to certain items. The approved list for items the sutler could sell were[1] tobacco, cigars, pipes, snuff, steel pens, paper, envelopes, lead pencils, pen knives, postage stamps, buttons, tape, thread, sewing cotton, pins and needles, handkerchiefs, suspenders, socks, underclothes, caps, shoes, towels, looking glasses, brushes, combs, clothes brooms, pocket knives, scissors, *groceries,* crushed sugar, syrup, family soap, butter, lard, smoked beef, beef tongues, bologna sausage, corn meal, nutmegs, pepper, mustard, table salt, salt fish, crackers, cheese, pickles, sauces, meat and fish in cans, *vegetables,* dried fruit, syrups, *lemons,* nuts, *apples,* matches, yeast powder, table furniture, crockery, glassware and tin ware (underlining in original). In addition, both the prisoners and the Union soldiers complained of high prices at the sutler. For example, Handy reported (10/5/64) molasses $2.40/gall, cheese 60 cts/lb., butter 80 cts., coffee, $1.00, tea $2.25, tobacco $1.25/bar, sugar 60 cts. per lb., sweet potatoes 90 cts. per lb., writing paper 5 cts, and envelopes 2 cts. each. Others noted the high prices: Boyle on 9/14/64 noted sugar at 60 cents/lb. (20 cents in newspapers), and paper at $1.00/quire, while Mckey wrote on 10/21/64 that coffee was $1.00/lb. and butter was 70 cents/lb., potatoes 90 cent/peck, apples 2–1/2 cents apiece, and paper $1.00/quire.

For those with money we know that the sutler sold, or at least attempted to sell, many other items. Handy reports clothing could be bought from other merchants through the sutler (9/24/63), and the sutler also sold liquor (5/20/64), eggs (5/16/64), ice cream (6/11/64, but this did not last long), coffee (6/13/64), ice (6/27/64), and beer by the barrel (6/27/64). Wood for burning, at least for a time, was also sold by the sutler (Mckey 02114).

Most of the period between May 1863 and June 1865 (and later) the sutler was open. This seems a bit strange since supposedly an order was sent to Schoepf on 12/1/63 from the CGP that the Sec. War ordered that the sutler shop at Fort Delaware be closed to the prisoners.[2] Although this was supposedly sent to all prison camps, correspondence in the OR in December 1863, which mentions a sutler, makes no acknowledgment that this order seemed to go into effect. Handy mentions on 12/4/63 that Schoepf said he got the order, but an entry in Handy's diary on 12/9/63 is ambiguous as to whether the sutler was closed. On 3/30/64, an entry in Handy's diary clearly indicates the sutler was open.

There apparently was a rumor among the prisoners around 8/21/64 (Handy) that the sutler was about to be ordered to close; this was apparently false. The sutler may have been closed from about 8/19/64 (Allen, JRMcMichael, Mckey) to about 8/25/64, when Cox noted that the sutler was open. Apparently what was being offered for sale was limited from about 8/25/64 to about 8/30/64 (Mckey, 8/26/64 and 8/29/64, Boyle 8/29/64, and Cox 8/30/64). By 9/14/64 the sutler was again selling "eatables" (Boyle).

Initially prisoners could apparently pay for things at the sutler with greenbacks, U.S. money. On 10/29/63 Handy noted that there were also sutler tickets available. On 7/5/64 Mckey reports that all greenbacks were taken and sutler's tickets of equal value were given.[3]

The Prisoner's "Bank"

The above discussion brings us to the question of how prisoners got the money to buy things at the sutler. According to Section XIV of the CGP's Circular of 4/20/64,[4] an officer must receive all money sent to prisoners. Section XIV also details how accounts are to be kept of all monies received for the prisoners and spent at the sutler.

What actually happened at Fort Delaware appears to be the following, based on the prisoner account record books.[5] When money, cash (greenbacks), or a check came for a prisoner, it is believed it was sent, after opening, to the Provost Marshall, who was usually Lt. Charles Hawkins. If the amount of money sent was $10 or less, it was immediately given to the prisoner in the form of sutler's tickets, at the face value of the money sent; see for instance Mckey (8/26/64). If it was more than $10, it is obvious from the account books that only a portion of the money was given as sutler tickets, and an account was opened for the prisoner. The money was doled out in the form of sutler tickets as the prisoner used the sutler tickets he already had, so that no prisoner was in possession of a large face value amount of these tickets. These tickets could be used to bribe Union guards, since the guards could also use these tickets on the island. These transactions are clearly described by the "deposits" and "withdrawals" in the account books.

It appears that Hawkins truly carried out some of the functions of a bank. It is noted in the account books in what form the monies for the prisoners were received, cash, postal checks, express checks, or just checks (presumably drawn on a bank). All of these were eventually credited to the prisoner. Whether Hawkins waited for the checks to clear before issuing a credit, and the sutler tickets, on an account is unknown.

There is only one complaint of record to Schoepf or the CGP concerning lost or stolen money, including cash.[6] This one complaint was reported by the CGP to Schoepf on 2/25/65. On 2/28/65 Schoepf replied with a receipt enclosed signed by the POW that he had received all of the missing items.[7] This seems quite remarkable since the amounts of money handled were large, and the number of packages or envelopes containing cash (and checks) was large.

As a sample of how much money was sent to the prisoners, the month of January 1865 was chosen, since the prisoner population was relatively stable at that time, the campaigning season for 1864 being over because of the cold weather. Thus most prisoners' friends and relatives would have known that they were at Fort Delaware. In the compilations below, only amounts of $10 or more are included because amounts of less than $10 were not entered in the account book. From the account books the following is deduced[8]:

- Officers and citizens received a total of approximately $4045 in 171 contributions in January. This is an average of about $24 per contribution.
- Enlisted men received a total of approximately $5220 in 319 contributions in January. This is an average of about $16 per contribution.
- Since there were approximately 1277 officers and citizens present in January 1865, this is an average of $3.17 per officer and civilian.
- There were approximately 6245 enlisted prisoners in January 1865, so this is an average of $0.89 per enlisted man.

These numbers show a variety of facts. As noted above, many packages and letters with some form of "money" in them arrived for the prisoners in January 1865, and, if one glances through the account books, this month does not seem to be abnormal. The total amount of money (which does not count contributions of less than $10) was very large, about $9300, especially considering that a private in the U.S. Army made about $16/month at that time.

The differences between what the officers and citizens on one hand and the enlisted men got per capita is also striking. Officers received over three times as much, per capita, on average, as enlisted men. Since the officer and enlisted barracks were separate, we can in a sense consider them separate economies. Aside from what the prisoners in both of these economies earned from selling trinkets, the "Gross National Product" of these economies was these contributions (and packages received, see below). In other words, in January 1864 the per capita income of the officers' economy was three time that of the enlisted men's economy. Although not every officer got contributions, and the contributions were certainly not the same for each officer that got one or more contributions, all officers and enlisted men would have benefitted from these contributions. We have more information about the officers, and there are numerous references to officers buying food from the sutler and sharing some of this bought food.[9] In addition, anyone receiving money (in the form of sutler's tickets) could use it to buy services from other prisoners, such as (see Chapter 9) washing laundry, making shoes, tailoring, etc. Thus while much of the money (in the form of sutler's tickets) went directly to the sutler, some of it was bartered to other prisoners before ending up in the sutler's hands. The overall economies of both the officers and enlisted men thus benefitted from these contributions.

Pvt. William B Alburtis of Richardson's Cavalry Battery (possibly part of the 1st Regiment, VA Artillery) kept a diary from 5/3/64 to 6/9/65. Although he did record some of what was happening at the prison camp, much of the diary is taken up with his and his friend's "business," recording letters that he and other prisoners wrote to various people they presumably knew, asking for money or other items to be sent to them. Although most of the other prisoners are only identified by their initials, three of them were Jos B. Lumpkin, IT Smith, and WH Lookabill (spellings are problematical). Replies from the various people contacted were carefully recorded, especially if they sent money. Acknowledgments were also sent if money was sent. It is not indicated whether the men involved shared the money or each kept what he solicited. It appears as if Alburtis and his compatriots were essentially running a "business" soliciting money and other items from anyone they knew. They were keeping careful records of who they wrote to and when the replies were received, and which one of the prisoners wrote to them. This "business" was highly successful.

How did the prisoners spend the money they had received? There are several mentions of some of the officers buying clothes, in some cases what seemed to be expensive clothes. However, most of the mentions of spending this money are for items such as bread, cheese, meat, beer, and tobacco. To a person in the early 21st century who is familiar with modern ideas of nutrition, one would think that items such as vegetables and fruits would be bought often. However, this does appear to be the case. The most commonly named items purchased in this category were apples and peaches (peaches were widely grown in Delaware at this time). On 9/8/64 McCrorey reported he had some fine peaches, Barringer had peaches and cream on 5/14/65, on 9/22/64 Handy reports the sutler got apples, was selling apples on 10/5/64, and that many apples were sold out quickly by the sutler on 10/11/64, and finally Gibson bought 3 apples for 10 cents on 12/21/64.

Allen's diary has detailed lists of what he bought, the cost, and the money he received from April to mid–August 1864, and these details are given in Table 8-1.

Table 8-1. Cash Receipts and Expenditures of Lt. John C. Allen, 1864

Date	Received	Spent	Remarks
10-Apr	2.50		From Lt. Bushell
		0.20	For paper & en(velopes)
		0.20	tobbacco
		0.15	stamps
		0.20	milk
		0.35	for a file
		0.10	for buttons
		0.15	for tobacco
		0.25	crackers
		0.03	Apples
		0.15	ink & pens
		0.10	newspaper
		0.50	for washing
		2.50	Total
5-May	10.00		From Rosa
5-May		4.00	For a hat
5-May		0.25	Tobacco
6-May		0.10	collars
6-May		0.20	stamps
6-May		0.25	milk
6-May		2.00	Pictures
		1.00	Lt. Tarku(?)
7-May		0.05	milk
7-May		0.10	3 large envelopes
7-May		0.05	milk
7-May		0.25	Tobacco
8-May		0.05	milk
9-May		0.05	milk
10-May		0.15	Tobacco & Milk
10-May		0.10	Capt Isreal
10-May		0.05	Lt. McCristian

8. Outside Help

Date	Received	Spent	Remarks
11-May		0.05	milk
12-May		0.10	Paper & Milk
13-May		0.30	Milk, crackers & cheese
14-May		0.10	Milk
15-May		0.05	Milk
16-May		0.15	Tobacco & Milk
17-May		0.05	Milk
18-May		0.20	Cheese & crackers
19-May		0.10	milk
20-May		0.10	Milk
21-May		0.25	Buttons & Milk
		10.00	Total (actually 10.10)
9-Jun	4.95		From Rosa
9-Jun		0.85	stamps, pens, bread, tobacco & buttons
10-Jun		0.85	ice cream & cakes, tobacco, milk & candles for church
11-Jun		0.55	bread, milk & cheese
12-Jun	4.95		From Rosa
13-Jun		1.05	Tobacco, milk, Ice cream (&) cakes, & Bread
14-Jun		0.45	Molasses Bread cheese & Milk
14-Jun		0.45	Tobacco, buttons, bread, cakes & Raisens
16-Jun		0.30	Bread 20-17, Bread 10-
16-Jun		0.50	Washing
22-Jun	0.50		From Lt. Baushall
22-Jun		0.50	tobacco, & stamps
25-Jun	0.50		From Lt O'Neill in trade of hats
29-Jun	1.50		from Lt. O'Neill
29-Jun		0.80	Tobacco, Bread & onions, cheese
27-Jun		0.35	ice cream & cakes, tobacco
28-Jun		3.50	Sundries
	12.40	10.15	Totals
6-Jul	1.00		Borrow of Lt. O'Neill
9-Jul	0.50		of H. Stephans
15-Jul	7.00		by express from bank(?) to
15-Jul		1.00	to Lt. O'Neill
15-Jul		0.50	to H Steffins
15-Jul		0.65	Bread, cheese. sugar & Molasses
15-Jul		0.40	for washing
15-Jul		0.10	??? shoes
16-Jul		0.40	Bread .10 stamps .30
16-Jul		1.00	Coand(?) & Leffert
18-Jul		0.30	Bread, Tobacco, & pepper
19-Jul		0.50	Bread, paper & beer
19-Jul	3.00		Recd of BCH
19-Jul		2.00	Loaned to Dunn
20-Jul		0.40	Lemon, paper & Tobacco
21-Jul		0.55	Envelopes candle pens photgraph bread
22-Jul		0.15	cakes & Beer
22-Jul		0.30	Bread
23-Jul		0.30	Bread & Berr cheese
23-Jul		0.60	Tobacco, Bread & milk Buttons
26-Jul	4.95		Recd from sister sent to me 6/28
26-Jul		0.75	for Autograph Book
26-Jul		0.30	Bread, cheese & Beer
27-Jul		0.60	bread 20 cheese 10 Beer 10 Tobacco
28-Jul		2.30	for Gold pen, Bread & Beer

Date	Received	Spent	Remarks
29-Jul		0.40	Bread Beer & Tobacco
30-Jul		0.55	Bread, cheese, stamps, & Beer
31-Jul		0.10	Beer
	16.45	14.15	Totals
1-Aug	2.80		on hand
1-Aug	0.65		of Dunn
1-Aug		0.75	Molasses Bread & cheese, Beer
2-Aug		0.50	Tobacco, cakes & Beer
2-Aug		0.50	Lt. Hughes loaned
2-Aug		0.10	for church
3-Aug		0.20	Sundries
3-Aug		0.25	for specks for Dr. Handy
3-Aug		0.60	Bread & stamps 10 Tobacco 20 Beer 10
4-Aug		0.30	Tobacco 20 Beer 10
6-Aug	2.00		of Lt Stephen
6-Aug		0.50	Bread & Molasses
6-Aug		0.60	condensed milk
6-Aug		0.25	cheese & cakes
6-Aug		0.20	Tobacco smoking
	5.45	4.75	Totals

On a separate diary page, Allen reports he got and spent $40.55 during the time period covered by Table 8-1. As can be seen, Allen reports buying fruits or vegetables only twice, an apple on April 10th, and a lemon on May 12th. Meanwhile he expended much money on bread, cheese, tobacco, beer, photographs, milk, ice cream & cakes, and washing (laundry). Somewhat incredibly, Allen also spent about $2 for a "gold pen" on 7/28/64! The washing, presumably performed by one of the other officers, is an example of how monies received as contributions by the prisoners could contribute to the prison economy. Most of Allen's expenditures went to the sutler, although not all. Pay for the washing was distributed, as were his church contributions, his contribution for "specks" for Dr. Handy, and perhaps beer, which could have been home brew made by the prisoners.

Prisoner Packages

Aside from sending money, packages containing items needed by the prisoners could also be sent. As the war went on more restrictions were placed on such shipments, but they were rarely completely stopped.

These packages typically contained food and/or clothing. In the summer of 1863 there were apparently few restrictions on such packages, although one can reasonably *assume* that the packages were inspected for obvious contraband such as weapons. Handy, who was quartered in the Fort at the time with other political prisoners, and the few Confederate officers present, received a number of packages (packages is used as a general term and include bundle, box, etc.) On 7/26/63 Handy received two baskets, a box and bundle, which may have contained baked chicken, pickled beets, bread, and apple pie which Handy shared with all quartered in his room, saving the lemons and "confectionary" for the next day. On 2/16/64 Handy reports that he and another prisoner received packages, and the men in his room rarely draw anything but bread from their rations, yet they live very well. They have tea, coffee, sweetmeats, beef, poultry, milk and "other luxuries." On 7/28/64 and 8/23/64 Handy states, Mrs. Emley has been sending him much clothing, which he passed on to those in need. He complains about some of the clothing being misappropriated. On 8/17/64 Handy gets a box containing books, tea, sugar and tobacco. Not included in the listed of Handy's packages are those containing religious books and pamphlets for distribution to others, of which he received several.

However, this easy access of prisoners to packages sent to them ended in the period August–October 1864. Before that period, packages containing clothing, provisions (food), tobacco, and other items were commonly reported by the prisoners in their diaries as being delivered to them.[10] However, on 8/22/64 both Boyle and Alburtis report that suddenly no more boxes are being allowed.

There is nothing in the record that bears directly on this issue, but on 8/5/64 Schoepf wrote to C.A. Dana the following[11]: "In compliance with your instructions in the within telegram I have the honor to enclose herewith a circular dated April 20, 1864 and an order from Col. Hoffman both of which appearing to have been approved by the Sec. War I was compelled to obey. I would respectfully state, that in view of these orders, I could not ascertain who were the contributors to the prisoners, but when anything in excess of the allowance was received here, I would always send it to the hospital, for the sick, or if it was clothing, would keep it for distribution among such men as are discharged by order of the Sec. War, upon their taking the oath. No person is permitted to visit prisoners without a pass from the President, Sec. War or Col. Hoffman." Among the enclosures was a list of items sold to prisoners by Sutler. We do not have the text of the telegram from Dana to Schoepf so it is a bit speculative as to why Schoepf replied as he did, but one can *hypothesize* that at the time there was a good deal of public pressure to retaliate against Confederate POWs because of the public's perception of mistreatment of Union POWs in Confederate prisons.[12] This resulted in pressure from the Northern public not to allow POWs in Northern prisons to have "luxuries," such as being allowed to receive packages of clothing or provisions. *Perhaps* Dana's telegram alarmed Schoepf and on further reflection he decided to stop the delivery of packages. However, there is no record of any further correspondence with Dana on this subject.

On 9/25/64 Handy reports that new orders will be issued concerning the delivery of boxes to the POWs, and then on 9/27/64 Handy and Boyle on 9/29/64 report that permits are being issued for the men to receive clothing. As Handy writes, "Several officers, who asked permission to be allowed supplies of clothing, have been permitted to write to what they need. Printed cards or bills are to be given to them, which they are to forward to parties furnishing the clothing; and are to be returned, pasted on the outside of the boxes, as authority for the Express agents."

This system apparently stayed in place until at least May 1865, when Berkeley reported on 6/5/65 that he had applied for a permit. However, on 10/5/564 Handy reported that they had a "box call" in which boxes of tobacco of tobacco from Dixie were distributed along with some containing provisions or clothing. Apparently the order concerning permits had not yet gone into effect, but he reported on 10/11/64 that permits were being granted, and Cox reported the same thing on 10/2/64. Also there was one interruption in granting of permits. On 10/15/64 Cox reports that clothing permits are being given out, but on the next day, 10/16/64, he states they have been stopped until they can determine what officers are to leave here. On 11/5/64 Cox stated permits were being granted again.

What was the reason for clothing permits? It is not explicitly stated anywhere, but one could *hypothesize* that a permit became needed by the POWs because of Section XV of the Circular of 4/20/64 which stated "Any excess of clothing over what is required for immediate use is contraband." This may have been a method of controlling the amount of clothing coming to the prisoners. This, *possibly* combined with the public pressure to retaliate against Confederate POWs for the supposed mistreatment of Union soldier POWs, may have contributed to the imposition of the permit system.

Additionally, Handy on 12/19/63 reports that boxes could only be sent by "immediate relatives." This was easily gotten around by the prisoners and donors by simply addressing letters to "Dear Cousin" or "Dear Sister." As Boyle described this type of restriction on 8/22/64 in regard to sending and received letters, it was easily evaded by using this subterfuge. In fact, it was used for those who were well known to be sending many packages to different prisoners, such as Mrs. Emley and Miss Jefferson (see below). Apparently no one at the Fort either realized that this was going on, or *more likely,* simply ignored it.

How many packages did the prisoners receive? In January 1865 prisoners, enlisted, officer POWs, and civilians received a total of 336 packages. We know this because on 8/5/64 the CGP wrote to Schoepf that a Mrs. Balter of Philadelphia had sent a package to a POW containing "clothing and valuables" and it had never been received. The CGP ordered that all parcels received should be reported and a notation made of how they were "disposed of."[13] Schoepf reported that the package sent by Mrs. Balter was delivered to the POW.[14] The records of articles received actually indicate that if a prisoner has been transferred to a new location (prison camp), the package was forwarded to him.

Of the 336 packages received in January 1865, 120 were for officers, 6 were for civilians (housed with the officers), 201 were for the enlisted men, and 3 were to unknown persons. The records do not indicate what types of things were in these packages. Based on the prison population in January 1865, this was an average of 0.10 packages per capita for the officer and civilian prisoners and 0.032 packages per capita for the enlisted POWs. Again, as with money received, on a per capita basis, the officers and civilians received about 3 times as many packages as the enlisted men.

Besides receiving packages and money from friends and relatives, the prisoners also received such items from persons in the North who were strangers before the war, who may have been Southern sympathizers, and/or persons who just were charitable souls who felt sorry for the plight of the prisoners. Among them was Mrs. Ann W. Emley of Philadelphia and Miss Julia Jefferson of New Castle, Delaware and her friends and family.

Mrs. A.W. Emley, 608 Spruce Street, Philadelphia, a member of the Religious Society of Friends (Quakers), apparently helped Southern POWs at other prison camps also. A letter[15] from C.A. Verser (a sgt of the 18th VA) Co., B, 7th Division, at the Point Lookout prison camp dated 12/3/63, thanks her for her package containing a hat, pants, shirt, shoes and four blankets (for other prisoners). She is mentioned numerous times in this book. Mrs. Emley first came to the attention of Union authorities on 7/30/62 when a U.S. Marshall in Philadelphia wrote to the Sec. War stating, "I have just searched the house of a lady named Emley, who has four women at work making clothing for secesh prisoners. She does not deny it. Says all her sympathies are with them. There are other parties connected with her. I found two letters from Capt. Gibson, commander at Fort Delaware, thanking her for her kindness. What shall I do with the parties? Strong feeling here against such parties. It operates against recruiting." The reply by telegram the same day from P.H. Watson, an Assistant Sec. War, stated, "Send the two letters to this Department. Mistress Emley must be permitted to exercise her charity by supplying clothing or other necessaries or comforts to those who are sick or in prison."[16]

Miss Julia Jefferson lived in New Castle, Delaware, not far from Fort Delaware. Letters to her and her friends and family from Fort Delaware, including those from prisoners and a Union officer, survive.[17] Three of the earliest letters to JJ (Julia Jefferson or one of her circle) after April 1863 are from a Union Officer, Lt. MacConnell, who, when they were written was the Adjutant of the island. On 7/11/63 MacConnell wrote to JJ accepting and thanking her for her offer to furnish pillows for the Hospital. He also requested that she send any delicacies (food) that she could. Near the end of the letter he states, "The General directs me to say that you have permission to visit the island at pleasure." JJ is the only civilian we know of during the war that had such blanket permission to visit the island.

The next letter sent by MacConnell on 7/17/63 thanks her for sending the pillow cases, eatables, and delicacies for the Hospital, and also declines her offer to have ladies from New Castle help in the Hospital. On 8/4/633 MacConnell again wrote to JJ thanking her for the (custom) smoking cap made for him, and other kindnesses.

Most of the other letters from prisoners at Fort Delaware to JJ—3 in 1863, 3 in 1864 and 8 in 1865—are thanking her for many kindnesses, or more specifically for items sent such as clothing, or asking for items such as clothing and/or food. Wm. C. Lenny of the 11th NC Inf. wrote on 2/27/65 asking for a size 8 coat, pants size 32, 33, No. 6 shoes, and a 7/8 Hat, and he enclosed a permit for them to be sent to him. Several letters asked for her photograph. On 2/25/65 and 2/27/65 George Herrick, a Ward master (in the Hospital?), wrote to JJ informing her of the death of Lt. WA Dunn from pneumonia, including something about moving his remains.

There are three letters from prisoners at Point Lookout. Apparently JJ provided help to prisoners there, much as Mrs. Emley did (see above). One of these letters from Charles Ebert offered to sell her fans made by the prisoners for $6/dozen, and asked her to send money for ribbons or the ribbon itself to him so the fan could be decorated. We don't know if JJ bought the fans.

Strangely none of the prisoners except Handy mentions JJ. On 8/28/63 and 10/4/63 he mentions that he received boxes of clothing, the clothing to be distributed to those in need. On 9/12/63 he states that JJ is a true friend of the South.

Thus prisoners could obtain help in the form of packages, not only from friends and family, but sometimes also from citizens who were sympathetic to them.

Cotton for Clothing[18]

In October–November 1864 Union and Confederate authorities negotiated an agreement whereby each side could ship to its soldiers who were POWs items such as food and clothing. Since the South was destitute of funds to provide these items, and also had no stores of these items to send North, part of the agreement was that the Confederacy would be allowed to send 1000 bales of cotton to New York to be sold at auction, with proceeds to be spent in the North on things such as clothing and food to be distributed to POWs in northern prisons. Brig. Gen. Beall, CSA was paroled from Johnson's Island prison camp and set up his "headquarters" at 75 Murray Street in New York City (Manhattan) to lead the effort. He chose General Vance, who was imprisoned at Fort Delaware, to assist him, and General Vance was ordered paroled on 1/15/65.

This took quite a while to come to fruition, but in the meantime Beall sent, with the cooperation of Union authorities, a circular to each prison camp on 12/9/64 that asked the POWs in each camp to determine the supplies needed—blankets, clothing or provisions—together with the amount of each needed. He also requested information on the number of enlisted men, officers and southern citizens in the camp, and to name a committee of officers who would administer and distribute the supplies.

It wasn't until early February that the first shipment arrived at Fort Delaware. A detailed listing of these shipments is given in Table 8-2.

Table 8-2. Shipments to Fort Delaware Under the Clothing for Cotton Program

Date, 1865	Blankets	Coats	Pants	Shirts	Drawers	Socks	Shoes
8-Feb	984		209			840	
11-Feb	202	186	563		848	156	475
14-Feb	500	900	1004	1340	600	500	1000
15-Mar	500	500	500	300	300		650
17-Mar	500	288	505	620	500	1200	180
28-Mar	164		360		700	1296	180
Totals	2850	1874	3141	2260	2948	3992	2485

After this clothing was received, the head of the committee reported back to Beall several times, furnishing him with receipts for the clothing and confirming its distribution among the men. The first head of the committee at Fort Delaware was LCol Jno. M. Maury, who was apparently succeeded by Col. R.C. Morgan.

Schoepf was not totally uninvolved. On 2/4/65 he received a telegram[19] ordering him to select 3 field officers, not generals, to distribute the clothing that was to be sent by Beall. On 2/22/65, he was directed to send for exchange prisoners who had not been provided clothing by Beall.[20] Also, Schoepf was cognizant of the need for blankets, especially due to the cold weather, as on 1/23/65 he wrote to the CGP[21] with a requisition for 2000 blankets for prisoners ordered to the island, as he believed blankets that were being arranged for by Beall would not arrive soon, and Schoepf did not want the POWs to suffer.

This "program" was also recognized by the POWs themselves. On 2/20/65 Boyle reported that 2 officers had been paroled to attend to the distribution of clothing, on 3/7/65 Cox reported a lot of clothing for distribution for the most needy had arrived, on 3/21/65 Berkeley briefly described the program and that Gen. Page and Lt. Anderson had been placed on a committee to oversee the distribution, and finally on 3/22/65 Mauck got a jacket and pair of pants.

9

Medical Care

The Hospital is a very good one, the best I ever saw, I think. —Inslee Deaderick, Private, 2nd Tennessee (Ashby's) Cav.[1]

Prisoner of war Inslee Deaderick was "only" a cavalry private, but he apparently had a very high opinion of the post hospital in February 1865. Was this high opinion justified by procedures and treatment in the hospital? Perhaps most important, how successful was the hospital and the medical care system on Pea Patch Island in preventing and curing disease?

At the beginning of April 1863 there were very few POWs on Pea Patch Island, and the entire population of the island was probably less than 2,000, including military and civilian.[2] By the end of July 1863 there were 9835 POWs (this includes political prisoners but not convicts) on the island,[3] many of whom needed medical care. While the island had previously "hosted" Confederate POWs, all of these men were present on the island for only short periods of time, awaiting exchange, so there had been no need for an extensive medical establishment. How did the medical system on the island develop between March 1863 and the time of Pvt. Deaderick's remark, and how effective was it?

Medical Personnel

One critical component of any medical care system is the number of competent physicians, or surgeons as the Army called them. The number of Surgeons at Fort Delaware by month is given in Table 9-1.[4] These numbers do not include surgeons attached to Union infantry regiments who were responsible only for the men in their regiment.

Table 9-1. Number of Surgeons by Month

Month	1863	1864	1865
January		9	9
February		9	6
March		8	6
April		8	6
May	3	8	6
June	4	8	5
July	5	8	4
August	5	8	
September	5	9	

Month	1863	1864	1865
October	5	9	
November	8	10	
December	9	9	

As can be seen from Table 4-1, there were relatively few surgeons present in the May to October 1863 period, especially given that by the end of June there were 3,764 POWs, climbing to over 9,000 during July, and then falling starting in August to 3,156 by the end of October.[5] Many of these men required medical care.

The Post Surgeon in March 1863 was Colin Arrott, AAS (Acting Assistant Surgeon), and on June 18, 1863, H.R. Silliman, AAS U.S. Army, took over as Post Surgeon. He in turn was relieved as Post Surgeon on 7/29/64 by C.E. Goddard, AAS, U.S. Army.[6] Surgeon Nugent reports in his letter of 6/2/64 that Silliman is well-liked by the surgeons, and on 9/17/64 that "We all like Dr. Goddard very much he is very clever but has not dignity of Dr. Silliman." The other surgeons present at Fort Delaware during this time period were a combination of AASs and contract surgeons, the latter usually being employed for a few months or so.[7]

The early shortage of surgeons was cured in November 1863 when at the end of the month there were 8 on the island. Ironically by this time the POW population had dropped to about 3,000. A letter from Schoepf of 10/31/63 to LCol. Cheeseborough in Baltimore indicates that at least 3 additional surgeons had been requested but not yet assigned to the island as of that date.

Even though the POW population had dropped by November the higher number of surgeons on the island was maintained into early 1865. This was fortunate, since the POW population climbed again in the spring of 1864, and this population was maintained at a relatively high number until June 1865 (see Table 10-1). The reduction of surgeons in early 1865 probably was not as serious as it may sound, since by that time the medical system on the island was well established and the level of serious illness had apparently declined, as measured by mortality rates (see Table 10-1).

We know less about other medical personnel who were present on the island. On November 13, 1863, Nugent writes in a letter that they have "good [Hospital] Stewards" at the hospital, so things work well. However, later on in letters of 1/31/64 and 12/2/64 he describes some problems with Stewards.

Facilities and Supplies

The conditions, shortly after the POW population exploded, of other parts of the medical establishment on Pea Patch Island are reported by Medical Inspector and Assistant Surgeon C.H. Alden on 7/11/63,[8] and some of the parts dealing with this establishment are as follows:

> There are five hospitals on the island, one for the garrison and four for the prisoners of war, all outside the fort. They are frame buildings. Two are old, badly ventilated and poorly adapted for the purpose; the three others are merely sheds, which have, however, the advantage of being tolerably ventilated through chinks of the rough boarding. One of the wards of the post-hospital was particularly small, and though it had but 17 men in it, they had an allowance of less than 300 cubic feet of air per man; it was besides badly ventilated. Two hospital tents are also occupied by such prisoners of war. All the hospitals but more particularly those of the prisoners, were in poor police; the grounds

9. Medical Care

around them particularly so. There was great deficiency, or almost an entire want of stores, clothing and medical supplies of all kinds; bedding was also very insufficient. There were no bedsteads for most of the sick prisoners of war. A sufficiency of stimulants for immediate use is, I was informed obtained through the Quartermaster's Department. [Surgeon Silliman has just arrived and ordered supplies] The books and records of the hospital were in much confusion, or rather none were, I believe, kept except a register of the sick of the garrison and a morning report.

This want of correct records makes it difficult to obtain exactly the number of sick, deaths, etc., but the following data are believed to be tolerably accurate: There are 210 sick prisoners of war, among whom are included a few wounded just received from the battlefields in Pennsylvania. The morning report shows that there are 69 of the garrison sick, 24 being in the hospital and 45 in quarters. The chief, and I may say almost exclusive, disease is chronic diarrhea.

This report paints a rather dire picture of the medical department on the island in early July 1863, just after the Battle of Gettysburg and while POWs from that battle were arriving on the island.

Other observers are also good sources for information about medical personnel, facilities and supplies. For instance, Handy made the following observations in his diary: July 24; "Harwood was ordered to the hospital, and after wandering all about the island under guard, in search of the place, he had to return, ..." (shows confusion about locating proper hospital) August 12; "passed by ... a dirty looking hospital, ...," August 27; "The physicians have their hands full; and are, perhaps, doing the best they can." August 31; Found Mr. Paddock [a Union chaplain] at the hospital this morning peaches ... the poor fellows received one apiece." September 3; "The few persons who still remained at the old hospitals were removed, at about noon, to the new buildings at the other end of the island ... the food furnished at the hospitals is utterly repulsive." September 7; Handy was able to gather this information because Schoepf had given him a pass to minister to hospital patients. His observations indicate that there were a number of hospital locations on the island before the new main hospital was built and then fully occupied on 9/7/63. It is interesting that Handy made many of the same observation as Surgeon Alden did in his inspection of 7/11/63 (above).

At the behest of the United States Sanitary Commission, Dr. S. Weir Mitchell of Philadelphia visited the island in late July 1863, and in one of the two letters[9] he wrote said in part:

My letter only points at evils. I thought I added to these a statement as to the efficiency of the medical corps, which by hint and request has done its best to keep things right on the island. Gen. Schoepf, the Commandant is himself disposed to follow our suggestions & is personally most devoted in his efforts but there is an engineer corps wh. somehow is a little jealous & insists on its rights & takes its time to remedy evils. The general told me that he had made urgent representations as to the state of things now existent. [Thus far these reports] of his went, as against the site as a prison depot, I cannot say. Neither the general nor the doctor have neglected their duties as to sanitary efforts, but the real evil is one which no one can do much to alter. Dr. Silliman, Med. Director will make requisitions for his sick & afoot & if need be I will go down again & avoid this if possible as I am over busy.

In sum, Dr. Mitchell seems to think that while the Medical Staff and Schoepf were trying to do their best, various circumstances mostly related to the unpreparedness of the island to receive large numbers of prisoners were responsible for the medical care at the time.

Another set of observers were four Confederate Surgeons who were prisoners of war (it was later decided by North and South that surgeons were noncombatants and they were simply released, not exchanged), and they wrote a letter[10] as follows:

Having been prisoners at this fort for nearly one month, and being in attendance upon the sick Confederate prisoners every morning, thereby enable to judge upon their situation, we, the undersigned, surgeons of the C.S. Army, would respectfully ask to make the following statement in regard to the health of the prison of this place:

On careful examination of the official lists of deaths we find from July 1, 1863 to August 19, 1863, 180 deaths, making an average of less than 4 per day, which taking into consideration the large amount of prisoners confined here, being nearly 10,000, is exceedingly small.

In justice to the officer commanding this post we would beg leave to state that everything in his power to add to the comfort of these prisoners is being done. The sick are cared for as well as possible and new hospitals [are being] built for the accommodation of more. They are not compelled to drink water from the ditches, as reported: but water sufficient to supply the island is brought here by the boat twice daily from a distance, besides the supply of rain water constantly on hand.

The barracks are being kept as comfortable as can be expected under the circumstances.

The factual parts of this letter, *i.e.*, death rate, population, building of new hospitals, and getting water by a water boat (but only once a day according to other records), are confirmed by other records. The other parts of the letter are opinions of these surgeons.

In contradiction to this letter from the four confederate surgeons, Handy in his diary entry for 8/26/63 reported that Dr. Marshall—another prisoner, and Medical Director and Chief of Physicians of Morgan's command—said that the surgeons who signed the letter "did so to secure personal comfort to themselves, whilst in confinement." Handy reports that the four surgeons have not visited the hospitals, nor that the statistics they quote are from personal observation. Dr. Marshall states "that there is a great deal of sickness, great scarcity of medicines, very little attention to the patients, and the daily number of deaths far exceeds the statement in the paper." In fact, both "sides" here are factually correct! Deaths early in the period quoted by the four surgeons were relatively low, while they increased rapidly in the second half of August (see Chapter 9). It is *possible* that both sides in this argument are correct, that is, the medical situation on the island about August 20th was not good but the Commandant and others were trying to do the best they could.

Handy goes on to state that he has had confirmation of the scarcity of medicines from others on the island, but that after some delay patients did get their medicines. He also states that surgeons sometimes did not promptly see their patients, and gives several examples. Perhaps one should not be surprised at this given the scarcity of Union surgeons on the island. Dr. Marshall implies that Confederate surgeons were also tending to the sick, but why the twenty or so other Confederate Surgeons on the island were not relieving the "suffering" is not explained. Given the circumstance that neither side is explicitly lying, this seems to be more of a propaganda battle than an objective discussion. As often happens, the "truth" probably lies somewhere in between both sides' positions.

Given the shortcomings in the medical system on the island, how did the authorities react? On 5/5/63 Schoepf forwarded to the CGP a letter from the Assistant Surgeon "urging" the construction of a hospital for 300 men.[11] On 7/11/63 General Schoepf sent a telegram to Col. Crossman, the Quartermaster in Philadelphia, asking for the delivery of 6 hospital tents that day, as he had no more room for sick prisoners.[12] It was during this time period that the prisoner population was rising rapidly, as almost all of the enlisted prisoners from the Battle of Gettysburg eventually went to Fort Delaware.

In the 6/30/63 issue of the *Philadelphia Bulletin* the Quartermaster's Office in Philadelphia ran a request for bids for "A Hospital to accommodate six hundred men," and other items. The 7/8/63 issue of the *Bulletin* reported that a contract to build a

"Hospital" at Fort Delaware for $35,481 had been awarded to Richard Sharp of Philadelphia. The hospital on the island was occupied and being used within 2 months of the awarding of the building contract (see Handy above, and Crane below)! This *presumably* also included not only completion of the building itself, but also at least partial if not complete outfitting of the building with beds, linens, lamps, kitchens, and the myriad other things needed in a hospital. Given what we know about costs for other buildings on the island, it was probably by far the most expensive building on the island other than the Fort itself.

On 7/16/63 Schoepf telegraphed MGen Schneck in Baltimore, the commander of the Middle Military Department of which Fort Delaware was a part, that he had been ordered to send "sick" to Philadelphia.[13] On 7/20/63 Schoepf sent a telegram to the CGP[14] informing him he had sent 175 sick POWs to the Chester, Pennsylvania Army Hospital, and on 7/23/63 the CGP[15] replied by telegram that the Sec. War wanted to know by what authority they had been sent. Schoepf replied by telegram on the 23rd to the Sec. War stating, "On Saturday last the Surg. Gen. directed me send 500 sick to the Chester Hospital for treatment. I did so and they were all returned save 160. I now have 1500 very ill and only accommodation for 500. What shall I do?" This is a remarkable communication, since Schoepf is asking (appealing to?) the Sec. War directly what he should do about the medical situation on this Island. Also on July 23rd a telegram was sent to the CGP describing essentially the same circumstances. A note on that telegram said, "Shown to Sec. War July 24 1863." Thus no later than July 24th, the highest echelon of Union command knew about the medical situation on Pea Patch Island.[16]

On 8/19/63 Schoepf sent to the Sec. War a letter[17] describing conditions on the island, including a report from Surgeon Silliman and a letter from Surgeons of the "Rebel Army" (see above) concerning conditions at Fort Delaware. Schoepf stated, "From my own observations I consider the POWs at this post mas[?] Good condition as it would possible to keep them at any other places. The mortality is less at the present time the no. of prisoners (about 10,000) than in any city of the same population. Taking into consideration that the months of July and August are most fatal to exhausted men, as was the case especially with those from Vicksburgh." Thus Schoepf informed Stanton that he believed that the situation at Pea Patch Island was under control and that much of the illness and death was due to the poor condition of the Confederate troops when they arrived, especially those from Vicksburg.

Medical Inspector Crane reported[18] that on 9/3/63, patients were being moved into the new hospital, which he thought would improve the condition of the sick very much, and the "separation" of the sick (into general hospital and contagious hospital?) would improve their condition greatly.

The September 3rd correspondence is the last correspondence on medical affairs to and from Fort Delaware found until 10/31/63, when Schoepf wrote to LCol Cheeseborough (Adjutant in Baltimore)[19] in which the surgeon for the Purnell Legion, a "regiment" assigned temporarily to the island as part of the guard, is to be retained on the island until the 3 assistant surgeons for whom "application had been made to the Medical Director should have arrived." There were apparently only 2 other surgeons on the island at the time. This surgeon, Dr. Rippard, according to Schoepf, "deserted his post without giving notice to any one leaving the sick to the mercy of the nurses only." Schoepf then goes on to recommend dismissal of Rippard from the service without trial. It is clear from this letter that the medical staff at Fort Delaware is still short of surgeons.

On 11/13/63, Surgeon A.M. Clark, acting medical inspector of prisoners of war, inspected facilities on the island, and reported as follows on the hospital[20]:

> Condition of men—good as can be looked for under the circumstances; in hospital, comfortable. Hospital building—twelve barracks on upper end of island raised two to six feet from surface. Hospital tents—eight, connected with smallpox hospital; overcrowded, six patients in a tent. Hospital police—very good in every respect. Hospital discipline—generally good, but not so strict as it should be. Hospital diet and cooking—U.S. Army general hospital diet table; cooking facilities ample and food well prepared. Hospital heat and ventilation—well heated by stoves, but not properly ventilated, especially with windows closed. Hospital capacity—150 beds in smallpox hospital, 596 in general hospital, total 746; overcrowded, proper capacity about 600. Number sick—smallpox 150, other diseases 557, total 707 (federal smallpox 8, other diseases 23, total 31; prisoners, smallpox 142, other diseases 534, total 676). State of medical supplies—well kept up, dispensary in very good order. State of surgical instruments—sufficient and well kept. State of hospital records-books well kept and in good order. State of hospital fund—October 31 $1,396.07; purchases, articles of diet, table furniture, policing utensils, washing &c., invoiced for account. Medical attendance—sufficient and apparently good. Nursing—by convalescents and detail of prisoners. Interments—by detail in grave-yard on Jersey shore opposite fort. Diseases, local-miasmatic. Diseases, prevalent-variola, miasmatic. Diseases, zymotic—variola. Diseases, mitigation of—the location of the hospital is very unfavorable. Diseases, prevention of every man is vaccinated on entrance into hospital, and many in barracks. Mortality from diseases—October 12 5/31 percent of all diseases; smallpox, daily average sick 6 14/31, daily average deaths 2 16/31.
> Medical officers—Asst. Surg. H.R. Silliman, U.S. Army in charge. Judging from the general condition of the hospital and sick the surgeon in charge is evidently an energetic and competent officer. [*list of other surgeons follows*] Nine rebel surgeons are also assigned by surgeon in charge to duty in barracks and smallpox hospital. Prison fund due November 1—$1,700. Articles purchased—water condenser, stoves, lumber, table furniture, policing utensils, vegetables, &c., accounted for by retaining original bills as vouchers, and keeping invoices for all articles purchased.
> The hospital is in excellent condition and the patients look clean and comfortable. The smallpox hospital is overcrowded at present but this will soon be obviated, for the disease is rapidly on the decrease. Each ward is provided with a bath-room for the patients and containing all the necessary appliances. The smallpox hospital is located too near the general hospital, nearly adjoining it, but this the limits of the island render necessary. Additional material for vaccination should be obtained and every man on the [island] vaccinated. This is the only sure means of eradicating the disease.

If Inspector Clark's report of 11/13/63 (immediately above) is compared with that of Surgeon Alden's 7/11/63 (beginning of this section), one finds an apparent complete turnaround in the quality of the medical facilities and supplies. By early November both hospitals are in good order, with the exception that the smallpox (contagious) hospital is somewhat overcrowded. Sanitation, medical attendance on the sick, food and food preparation, and many other factors are now good to excellent. There are a few problems but they seem relatively small compared to those listed in the July 11th inspection. From early November 1863 forward, there seems to have been little change noted by anyone in the facilities or supplies of the medical department on the island, until release of most of the prisoners in June 1865.

Medical Records

As noted in the two inspection reports of Surgeons Alden and Clark, the general level of care by the medical establishment on the island improved markedly between August and November of 1863. A case in point are the commissary records, at least those that survive in the National Archives, and much of this discussion about medical care depends on them. Microfilm 598, Roll 47, contains a Register of Deaths at Fort Delaware from April 1862 to July 1865, and does not list the cause of death until about mid–September 1863. RG94, E544, contains a number of medical registers from Delaware, including some from Fort Delaware. Register 36 lists all prisoner hospital admissions from August 1, 1863, to May 1864, while Register 49 lists these admissions from June 1, 1864, until the end of the war. These records are for the most part fairly complete, listing the patient's name, rank, unit, diagnosis, date admitted, date discharged or died, and when and where captured. Register 35 lists similar information for Union soldiers from November 1863 to September 1865. There are other registers from the hospital, such as Register 26 listing Union soldiers from 1861 to 1863, Register 47 listing sick call for prisoners for January of 1864 (see below), and Registers 49, 50, 52, 53 which have lists of prisoner patient names, and also some additional information in some instances such as what ward they were in. Register 54 (see below) is apparently a listing of sick calls for Confederate officers from June 21, 1864, to January 28, 1865, listing diagnosis and medicine prescribed, if applicable. It is also clear that there are items missing from the archives that were at least cataloged initially. It is obvious from these surviving documents that careful medical records were being kept by the beginning of November 1863, as described by Surgeon Clark.

Aside from medical records dealing with patient treatment, the personnel records of virtually all the surgeons (including Dr. Lee, see below) that served at Fort Delaware are found in RG 94, E561.

"Routine" Medical Care

For the average Union enlisted man or Confederate prisoner, unless it was an emergency such as an injury or a gunshot wound, care would start at sick call. Surgeon Nugent in several letters mentions sick calls: "…and in all probability have to take charge of the rebel barracks…" (12/15/63); "…and make someone else attend to Sick Call" (1/31/64); "I had nearly 200 at sick call this morning…" [probably Confederate enlisted from the number] (4/14/64); "My morning calls have increased in number both in officers and men…" (5/30/64); and finally "The garrison sick call is at half past six in the morning…" "I have three different calls—garrison, Reb officers and the other rebs who are brought up in separate squads so that I am pretty busily engaged until about one o'clock" (6/4/64). From this recitation it would seem that sick call for Union soldiers was at 6:30 a.m. and that for Confederate prisoners around midday, with officers and enlisted men having separate sick calls.

A couple of prisoners had a somewhat different view of sick call. On 2/4/64 Pvt. Inslee Deaderick wrote[21]: "You ask why we don't play off sick. That is an old game here. Besides there is such a crowd at the gate while examination is going on that it is difficult to get near the examiners. Those who do are punched and beat on the heads with bayonets by the guards." [Note—Standard civil war bayonets were stabbing weapons and using the sides of the bayonets would usually, at worst, just inflict a bruise.] Park wrote on 4/16/65 in his diary: "I attend surgeon's call every morning. The doctor is a drunken sot, and seldom attends his nine o'clock morning sick call, but sends his detailed Rebel clerk, a young Mississippi lawyer, from the privates' pen, who sits on the outside of the fence and listens to the grievances of the sick officers through a "pigeon hole," size eight by twelve inches, which the sick approach, one by one, in his turn, and, peeping through, make known their wants. This little "hole in the wall" is crowded for hours frequently, and the young, inexperienced, but accommodating Rebel substitute for the Yankee surgeon does his best to serve his patients. He tries to supply such medicines as are called for."

There are a couple of journals (registers) from the medical department that survive in the National Archives that record sick calls. RG94, E544, Register 47 list enlisted POWs sick call for the month of January 1864 only. It shows sick call was held every day except January 1st, and possibly January 31st (there are one or more pages missing). During January 838 men were seen. The second register RG92, is E544, Register 54, which appears to be Confederate Officers sick call from 6/21/64 to 1/28/65. This register was written by Surgeon William D. Lee. For a more detailed analysis of these registers see below.

Dr. Lee, in a sense, illustrates the extent that Schoepf would go to to assure care of the POWs, and Schoepf's overall use of all resources at his disposal. Dr. Lee, who was from Memphis, Tennessee, reported for duty as a surgeon at Camp Douglas on November 30, 1863. He was arrested on 1/28/64 on a charge of conniving in the escape of prisoners. He had given a prisoner some money and had taken out some letters. His defense was that he had known the prisoner before the war and was merely trying to be charitable. He was convicted in May 1864 and sent to Fort Delaware with a sentence of two years.[22]

No later than 6/21/64 Dr. Lee was attending to the Confederate officers at Fort Delaware, even though technically he was a "convict." At the request of Schoepf he was released in September 1864. On 11/7/64 Schoepf requested that he be allowed to attend the Confederate officers (he was already doing this) and on 11/8/64 Schoepf forwarded a contract he had made with Lee. This contract was rejected by the Surgeon General, but Schoepf persisted in a letter on 11/15/64, and the Lee contract was then approved.

Lee attempted to join the army as a surgeon and Schoepf, Dr. Goddard and Chaplain Paddock wrote letters of recommendation in June 1865. He was not successful in his application to become a regular army surgeon, but did serve as a contract surgeon in New Orleans, Louisiana, for about 18 months from September 1865 on.

It is evident from Registers 47 and 54 that men who were deemed seriously sick or injured were sent to one of the hospitals, either the general hospital or the contagious hospital. We have two accounts from POWs who were sent to the general hospital, both officers. Boyle wrote in his diary for 1/25/5:

> I have just been three days to the hospital, and have had enough of that institution. A feast on what under other circumstances would have been a very harmless dish, *vis* fried potatoes, brought on a violent fit of indigestion on Friday last and on Sunday I was obliged to go to the Hosp, a timely course of medicine prevented any further ill effects, and after a few days dieting I today returned to my quarters, very glad to get back to them though in a prison. Everything it seems, is only bad or good by comparison. The Hospital arrangements on this Island are in many respects good, but the supply of food is entirely insufficient for many patients. Convalescents and men with wounds that rapidly exhaust the system are, in common with those who require less, fed upon 3/7 of a pound loaf per day, or 3 slices of said loaf, very light, spongy, innutritious and dry, and a few mouthfuls of unsweetened coffee at breakfast, a cup of thin, very thin soup at dinner, and at night a cup of gruel. During my three days stay this was all the patients on full diet received, except once a small piece of cold beef, & twice a very small quantity of mush (one time with about a spoonful of molasses upon it.)

9. Medical Care

The patients must stay in bed from 9 p.m. till six a.m. although on my narrow iron bedstead I was nearly frozen. The wards are kept very clean and under rigid discipline. Each ward is warmed by 4 stoves (enough in ordinarily cold weather) and contain about 30 or 40 beds. On entering each patient is required to strip off his clothing (wh. is bundled up, labeled, and put away) and after bathing to put on clean cotton underclothing, and under no circumstances is he allowed to resume any part of his outer clothing till he leaves the Hospital. This is not convenient to those who sit up, but perhaps for general health, desirable.... While at Hospital I read an interesting book from the Library there, "Science a Witness for the Bible" by the Rev'd (Gen.) W.K. Pendleton."

The other description appears in the Handy diary as a letter from Lt. G.W. Finley written on 8/3/65, and which states in part:

We were directed to Ward No. 1, and on reaching it Dr. A____, the surgeon in charge, gave us a rapid, careless examination, and then left us, to complete preparations for the beds our aching limbs so much needed. The regulations of the hospital require each patient, on entering, to take off every article of clothing, and if his condition will admit it, he must take a bath. There seems to be a great want of care about ascertaining the condition of patients, and cases occur of injury while improperly bathing. After the bath a thin cotton shirt is furnished, with cotton drawers; which is all the patient is-except in special cases-permitted to wear until he is discharged.... On representing my condition, being then under the influence of mercury, I was excused from the bath, and on earnest application was permitted to retain my flannel. It was with feeling of relief I was at length permitted to stretch myself upon the bed assigned me. The room was well ventilated, cool, neat, and quiet, presenting a strong contrast with the crowded barracks I had just left. Indeed the pains taken to secure these results would be very commendable, were it not made, as I soon observed, a prime object, while close attention to the sick was but a secondary consideration.... As I needed rest and quiet more than anything else, having got my system under the influence of medicine before entering the hospital, but little more was given me, and I improved rapidly. About the fourth day, my mouth became quite sore, ulcers formed around and the tongue and lips, and in the throat. I at last got the surgeon to pay attention to this matter, and he gave me some solution with which to wash the mouth, and touched the ulcers with caustic. Being still feeble, and not being permitted to have my clothing so as to sit up and regain strength, and finding the diet too low to build me up, on the eighth day, when the call for *volunteers* to return to the barracks was made. I determined to go back, I do not regret doing so, for my improvement here has been much more rapid than I had any reason to expect it to be there.

There were a few points which came under my observation to which I will briefly refer. The surgeon in charge of the hospital, while doubtless fully competent, did not take time and care enough to ascertain the real condition of his patients. [details follow] The nurses were willing and generally desirous to do what they could at alleviate the condition of the patients by prompt attention to their wants. But they lacked experience, and in one or two instances failed to control their temper, exhibiting a culpable negligence and irritability, very discouraging to a sick, low-spirited sufferer.

I was somewhat surprised to see how recklessly the patients in that ward were exposed to smallpox, ... Cases about which there was little doubt at first, were brought into the war, scattered among us and allowed to remain until the disease was fully developed....

...As you will perceive, there are some things pertaining to the hospital highly commendable; and more *attention* to the *patients* by the surgeon and nurses would make it all the exacting could require.

Both the Boyle diary entry and the Finley letter agree on many things, particularly the routine for admitting a new patient, the cleanliness of the wards, and the inadequacy of the diet. The latter may be partially due to the fact that in mid-nineteenth century medicine, diet was considered particularly important in helping cure a patient. For example, Dunglison's *Dictionary of Medical Science*[23] has almost five pages devoted to the word "diet." Sample diets from many different medical facilities are given, among them being common (or full or high) diet, middle (or medium) diet, low diet, milk diet, fever diet, broth diet, etc. Surgeon General Hammond also issued a diet table for the U.S. Army on 10/28/62.[24] It had a full diet, half diet and low diet, as well as some other diets such as

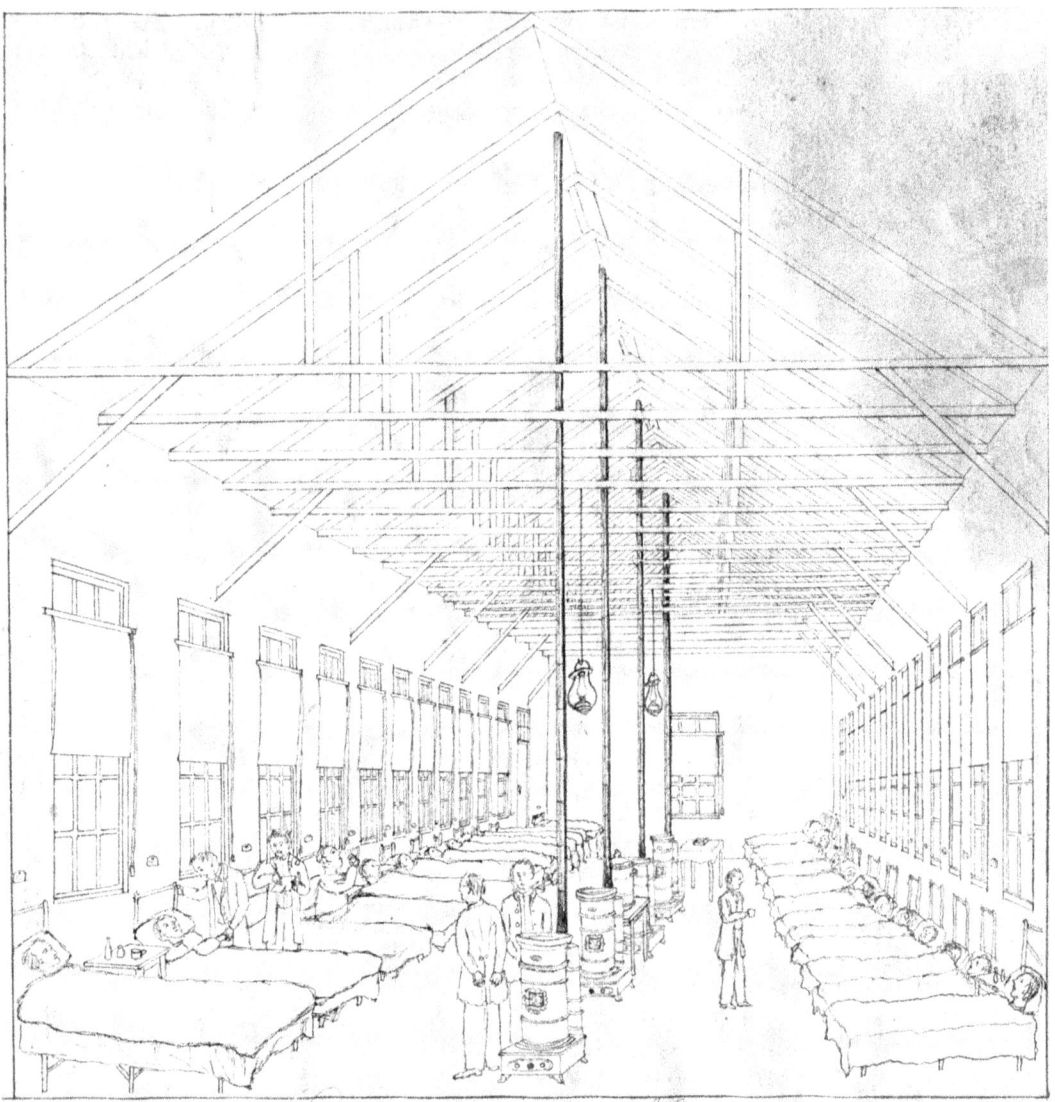

Figure 17. Ward No. 9, Post General Hospital, undated drawing by unknown artist. Outside the margins of the drawing it indicates that among those depicted are Assistant Surgeon A.C. Taylor M.D. in charge of the ward, C.H. Parker, Ward master, and Harrison Head Nurse. Interestingly only about 23 beds (patients) are shown. As related by Boyle (see above), 4 iron stoves are shown, and on 3/20/65 Park reported that the cards shown on the wall at the head of each bed contained information such as the name and rank of the patient, character of his disease, and number of his bed. Taylor was a contract Surgeon at Fort Delaware from 1/13/65 to about 5/13/65 (RG 94, E544, Registers 36 and 40) (courtesy Fort Delaware Society).

chicken diet, milk diet and beef-tea diet. The order listing these diets was detailed enough to offer suggested daily menus (for each weekday) for the full and half diets, and daily meal diets for the other diets. Low diets could consist of one or more of bread, milk, tea, beef tea, gruel, sugar, etc., and sometimes meat such as beef, all in relatively small quantities. Thus the use of diets containing relatively little food, especially solid food, was often considered efficacious in treating certain diseases. As Dunglison's states in part of the definition of "dietetics," "A well regulated system of diet has great power in checking disease, and likewise in preventing it."

Some of the other items complained about by Boyle and Finley, such as the hospital clothing they were forced to wear and the cleanliness of the hospital, would be considered commendable today from a sanitary point of view. Such things as bacteria and viruses were not known during the Civil War, nor was the reason for sepsis. However there seemed to be a general "feeling" among many medical men at the time that cleanliness (sanitation) was important, especially in a hospital.

Getting another viewpoint, Surgeon Nugent in his letter of 11/13/63 stated, "The duties in general are not arduous, I visit my ward of fifty patients at 8½ in the mornings, at four in the after noon, and as often between times as I feel disposed. I prescribe for them, fix the diet table, and order whatever I please in regard to arrangement of my patients, the Surg. In Charge gives entire control to each one in his own ward. When you are Officer of the Day your business is to visit every ward twice daily, once at 12 o'clock at night, inspect all food when it is ready to be taken to the wards, and in the absence of the Surg. in Charge the Officer of the Day stands in his boots." As Nugent's later letters describe, sometimes he had 2 or 3 wards he was in charge of and/or did one or more sick calls. This of course seems somewhat at odds with what Finley relates above, but there probably was a difference in the quality of the Surgeons there, as well as their level of care for their patients.

We have no description of how Union enlisted men were treated, but we *presume* it was similar to how the POWs were treated. Union officers (and their families) were treated at home or in their quarters, at the request of the officer.

The Hospital Fund

Very similar to the Prison Fund (see Chapter 5), the hospital fund was funded by the unused rations of the patients in the hospital. At Fort Delaware, separate hospital fund records were kept for the prisoners and Union soldiers (the convicts were considered Union soldiers for this purpose). Since many patients were given much less than a full ration, the average amount per man collected daily was relatively high. Clark, as Commissary Officer, was required to keep the account of the Hospital Fund for both the Union soldiers and prisoners, as well as record what money in these funds was used to buy. The items bought from the prisoner Hospital Fund in the period May 1863 to June 1865, and their total monthly cost, are presented in Chart 9-1.

Chart 9-1. Prisoner Hospital Fund Supplies by Month

May 1863
Total Number of Rations Supplied: 475
Average number of men/day: 15
4 cans prunes
Total Cost: $9.45

June 1863
Total Number of Rations Supplied: 4153
Average number of men/day: 138
6 bushels potatoes
12 corn brooms
2 lanterns
1.5 doz chamber pots
1 pitcher
0.5 doz tumblers
2 pounds ground pepper
21 pounds ham
15 pounds white sugar
164 quarts milk
1 bottle ink
1 ball lampwick
3 buckets
Total cost: $32.04

July 1863

Total Number of Rations Supplied: 8885
Average number of men/day: 287
11.5 bushels onions
33 bushels potatoes
45 pounds flour
25 pounds loaf sugar
2 pounds pepper
5 pounds butter
10 pounds lard
9.25 bushels corn meal
1.67 doz water buckets
4 dozen chamber pots
0.67 dozen corn brooms
1.5 dozen wash basins
0.33 dozen scrub brushes
2 dozen candle sticks
5/6 dozen dippers
1 dozen tumblers
1 tin bucket
3 sauce pans
2 sauce pans
1 coffee pot
1 wash boiler
1 tea kettle
3 dripping pans
3 tin boilers
2 dish pans
1 coffee mill
1 cooking pot
4 carving knives
3 pairs shears
6 pad locks
0.25 gross matches
178 gallons milk
Total cost: $163.41

August 1863

Total Number of Rations Supplied: 7641
Average number of men/day: 246
1 pound black pepper
2 pounds tea
75 pounds corn meal
1 bucket
2 corn brooms
45 tin plates
45 tin cups
4 doz tablespoons
4 dozen knives & forks
2 tin wash pans
2 tin sauce pans
2 tin ladles
Total cost: $45.97

September 1863

Total Number of Rations Supplied: 19456
Average number of men/day: 649
361 dozen eggs
442 pounds codfish
900 pounds mutton
637 pounds chicken
700 pounds butter
6–2/60 bushels onions
7 barrels cabbage
49 bushels ice
597 gallons milk
42.5 gallons refined oil
Total cost: $726.84

October 1863

Total Number of Rations Supplied: 21597
Average number of men/day: 697
1650 lbs butter
10 barrels turnips
19 barrels cabbage
1000 lbs chicken
40 gals soft soap
520 doz eggs
1921 lbs mutton
475 lbs dried fruit
80 gals coal oil
3 barrels onions
709.5 gals milk
15 gals coal oil
4 doz tin cups
3 lanterns
2 balls lamp wick
washing ($120.00)
Total cost: $1517.58

November 1863

Total Number of Rations Supplied: 22340
Average number of men/day: 721
1986 pounds butter
576 doz eggs
4 doz [?]
24 bbls cabbage
5 bbls apples
4 bbls turnips
1963 pounds mutton
1175 pounds chicken
39 gall coal oil
485 pounds dried meat[?]
57 bbls onions
2 bbls carrots
2675 qts milk
Washing ($120)
Total cost—1742.86

December 1863

Total Number of Rations Supplied: 21597
Average number of men/day: 697
1650 lbs butter
10 barrels turnips
19 barrels cabbage
1000 lbs chicken
40 gals soft soap
520 doz eggs
1921 lbs mutton
475 lbs dried fruit
80 gall coal oil
3 barrels onions
709.5 galls milk
15 galls coal oil
3 lanterns
2 balls lamp wick
washing ($120.00)
Total cost: $1517.58

January 1864

Total Number of Rations Supplied 20491
Average number of men/day: 661
1101 pounds butter
500 doz eggs
5 barrels onions
3 barrels cabbage
660 pounds chickens
970 pounds mutton
5 barrels turnips
350 pounds cod fish
4 barrels carrots
65.6 gallons whiskey
420 pounds dried fruit
80 gallons kerosene oil
2964 quarts milk
washing for prisoners ($96.00)
Total cost: $1267.90

February 1864

Total Number of Rations Supplied: 16054
Average number of men/day: 554
976.5 pounds butter
1156.5 pounds chicken
870.5 pounds mutton
300 pounds cod fish
100 pounds barley

9. Medical Care

369 doz eggs
13.5 barrels cabbage
5.5 barrels turnips
3 barrels onions
3 barrels carrots
4 barrels soft soap
1 barrel parsnips
282 pounds dried apples
1 box lemons
5 barrels beets
121 galls coal oil
706 galls milk
6 doz plates
6800 pieces washing
Total cost: $1248.25

March 1864

Total Number of Rations Supplied: 18937
Average number of men/day: 611
1086 pounds butter
966 pounds chicken
570.5 doz eggs
296 pounds dried apples
784 pounds mutton
3.5 barrels carrots
6.5 barrels cabbage
8.5 barrels turnips
11 barrels onions
1 barrel parsnips
2 barrels soft soap
285 pounds cod fish
81 pounds barley
1 box lemons
3.75 doz lamp chimneys
53 pounds lard
35.5 gallons coal oil
3 dozen stove blacking
washing 6000 pieces
Total cost: $1135.97

April 1864

Total Number of Rations Supplied: 20280
Average number of men/day: 676
6 bbls soft soap
677.5 doz eggs
2 boxes lemons
354 pounds dried apples
973.5 pounds butter
1184 pounds mutton
761 pounds chicken
580 pounds codfish
9 bbls carrots
14.5 bbls turnips
3.5 bbls onions

6 bbls cabbage
37 gall coal oil
37 pounds lard
6 tin scoops
1 tin oil can
11 doz brooms
1 doz mops
4 yds oil cloth
1 doz paper tacks
0.5 doz wash boards
3 doz lamp wicks
1 doz stove polish
250 iron spoons
250 iron knives
250 iron forks
5 gallons sperm oil
1 block for hospital flag
3.5 gallons whiskey
4008 quarts milk
8200 pieces washing
Total cost: $1930.16

May 1864

Total Number of Rations Supplied: 21866
Average number of men/day: 705
1276 pounds butter
780 pounds chicken
467 pounds dried apples
50 pounds lard
845 pounds mutton
260 pounds cod fish
739 doz eggs
18 barrels turnips
6 barrel soft soap
1 barrel onions
1 doz spools cotton
3 garden hoes
3 boxes lemons
3 doz stove polish
3.5 doz lamp chimneys
1 box clothes pins
35 gallons coal oil
1 coffee mill
6 butcher knives
12 plates
1085 gallons milk
1 doz bread pans
1 doz pudding pans
1 doz coffee pails (7 gal)
10000 pieces washing
Total cost: $1671.49

June 1864

Total Number of Rations Supplied: 21160

Average number of men/day: 705
859.5 pounds chicken
977.25 pounds mutton
1379 pounds butter
938 doz eggs
6 doz wash basin
329 pounds dried fruit
4 boxes lemons
1 box oranges
1 barrel coal oil, 36,5 gallons
4.5 barrels onions
6 arm chairs
105 pounds corn starch
14 water coolers
7 barrels soft soap
175.5 pounds lard
304 pounds cod fish
43 gallons whiskey
2 barrels cabbage
3 gross matches
2 doz buckets
2 doz brooms
1 doz white wash brushes
6 doz shirt [?] R(B)?
2 doz spittoons
12 papers tacks
12.5 gross screws
1 large refrigerator
1120 gallons milk
10114 pieces washing
300 window curtains
Total cost $2874.00

July 1864

Total Number of Rations Supplied: 22017
Average Number of Men/Day: 710
1537.25 doz. eggs
1267 lbs. mutton
1349.5 lbs. chicken
945 lbs. butter
300 lbs. dried apples
300 lbs cod fish
4 boxes lemons
12 bbls. cabbage
8.5 bbls onions
6 bbls soft soap
1 bbl whiskey (42 gal)
1 bbl coal oil (25.5 gal)
2 scythes with handles
4.5 doz brooms
6 lamp chimneys
1 blank book
1 tap borer
11400 pieces washing

3000 bed cards
50 pounds mixed tea
750 pounds brown sugar
1395 gallons milk
Total cost $2644.60

August 1864

Total Number of Rations Supplied: 21944
Average number of men/day: 708
1411 pounds butter
1553.5 doz eggs
800 pounds chicken
22 barrels cabbage
5 boxes lemons
720 pounds dried apples
152 pounds lard
5 barrels soft soap
6 doz stove polish
8 doz lamp wicks
5 barrels onions
3 doz mops
1 doz paper sacks
1400 yards cocoa matting
2S[?] B[?]
13 doz buckets
215.5 pounds zinc
7 pounds copper rivets
4 doz brooms
2 doz work boards
65 baskets peaches
37.5 gallons coal oil
40 gallons sperm oil
998 pound mutton
2 doz chairs
2 gross matches
3 doz knives & forks
47 gals whiskey
200 pounds brown sugar
5580 quarts milk
15867 pieces washing
Total cost: $5170.83

September 1864

Total Number of Rations Supplied: 19440
Average number of men/day: 648
112 pounds lard
111 doz lamp wicks
1 lamp
1 lamp chimney
30 lbs black pepper
1 box (Gillotts) pens
6 botts carmine ink
2 doz Cayarre brushes
2 doz brooms
6 doz brooms (is storing)
86 pounds tea
6 doz tin pans
2 steamers
3 sauce pans
2 dish pans
2 wood saws
6—3 gall coffee pots
6 wash boilers
3 tin boilers
1 wrench
2 bbls apples
561 pounds dried apples
2 bbls potatoes
10 pounds copper rivets
7 bbls onions
1 clock
14 pounds soft soap
50 pounds chicken
1269 pounds mutton
1215.5 doz eggs
1392 pounds butter
3 doz spoons
6 chairs
33 bbls cabbage
560 lbs codfish
12 doz chamber pots
3 boxes lemons
124 Galls whiskey
50 pounds green paint
1 coffee mill
3 doz coal scuttles
1 bottle whiskey
4.25 gallons whiskey
Total cost: $4214.49

October 1864

Total Number of Rations Supplied: 13732
Average number of men/day: 443
1 oz Ext Canab Indicae Squires Gumone
8 oz aongl[?] bals poner[?]
3 oz morphia acetus
1 oz acid hydrocyan
3 oz chloride propylannou
40 gals ?al Brandy
41.5 gals ?al Port
1 gal ?al Angelica
2 gal ?al Muscatel
1 sail needle & palm
12 doz pkg stove polish
1 tap be[?]ll
10 window shades
40 window curtains
1 dark lantern
12 gross buttons
12 lamp brackets
50 chairs
6 arm chairs
322 yds coca matting
3 office desk
1682 pounds chicken
5 boxes lemons
695 doz eggs
1292 lbs butter
17 bbls cabbage
831 lbs mutton
16.7 bush potatoes
1bbl apples
5 bbl green apples
5 bbl onions
240 lbs cod fish
42 gall molasses
9 bbl soft soap
78 galls coal oil
88 galls whiskey
167 lbs glue
5665 lbs ice
137 lbs paint
20 lbs sole leather
5 scouring brushes
1 grind stone
2 doz white wash brushes
1 doz stove brushes
113300 pieces washing
233 pounds sugar
150 pounds Rio coffee
5085 qts milk
Total cost: $4740.94

November 1864

Total Number of Rations Supplied: 14000
Average number of men/day: 467
155 pounds butter
246 pounds chicken
82.5 doz eggs
221.3 pounds mutton
224 pounds dried apples
1174.75 galls milk
Total cost: $685.66

December 1864

Total Number of Rations Supplied: 17663
Average number men/day: 570
13 barrels onions
1127 pounds butter
1162 pounds chicken
200 doz eggs

15 barrels soft soap
868 pounds mutton
32.5 barrels turnips
5 boxes of lemons
464 pounds of dried apples
85 gallons molasses
200 gallon coal oil
43 gallons sperm oil
2 barrels cabbage
79 pounds sand
2 1 doz elastics
3 1doz stove brushes
4 1 doz spittoons
5 large globe lanterns
1 doz lamps & brackets
2 1 doz erasers
2 1 doz mops
6 1doz brooms
1 box clothes pins
1 large wash tub
7 doz large lamp chimneys
2 doz lamps
4732 quarts milk
10,400 pieces of washing
Total cost—$3155.30

January 1865

Total Number of Rations Supplied: 21612
Average number of men/day: 697
790 doz eggs
2200 pounds butter
900 pounds mutton
600 lbs dried apples
1220 pounds chicken
680 pounds codfish
12 bbls onions
170 galls molasses
1 desk
3 [?] stove polish
6 doz stove brushes
48 lamps (for coal oil) & brackets
200 pounds paint
7 dozen lamp chimney
1800 feet lumber
1070 Galls milk
11200 pieces washing
Total cost: $3827.80

February 1865

Total Number of Rations Supplied: 20647
Average number of men/day: 737
287 pounds lard

7.5 barrels soft soap
12 barrels onions
84 gallons coal oil
1752 pounds butter
885 pounds chicken
788 dozen eggs
993 lbs mutton
6 barrels turnips
665 pounds cod fish
92 gallons molasses
346 pounds dried apples
6 barrels carrots
1.5 doz papers of tacks
3 butcher knives
1 varnish brush
1 gallon linseed oil
0.5 gallon varnish
6 tumblers
3 bottles sherry wine
85 gallons whiskey
969.5 gallons milk
13200 pieces washing
1550 pounds potatoes
2 barrels flour
120 gallons whiskey
175 pounds white sugar
Total cost: $3774.56

March 1865

Total Number of Rations Supplied: 21905
Average number of men/day: 707
4 barrels flour
311 pounds white sugar
1500 pounds potatoes
30 gallon syrup
87.5 gallons whiskey
1255.5 doz eggs
1523 lbs chicken
2388 lbs butter
1715 lbs mutton
11 barrels soft soap
16 barrels onions
500 pounds cod fish
17 barrels carrots
19 barrels turnips
1 barrel parsnips
3 barrels green apples
10 barrels cabbage
12 arm chairs
1 doz lamps
2 doz lamp chimneys
3 doz lamp wicks
56 lbs zinc
12 doz stone spittoons
12 doz strong brooms

2 gross buttons
1 Lt[?] patent thread
1 castor
1 cast iron sink
2 doz medicine bottles
1 gross stove polish
1275.5 gallons milk
11200 pieces washing
Total cost: $4016.18

April 1865

Total Number of Rations Supplied: 21925
Average number of men/day: 730
64 pounds butter
734 doz eggs
790.75 pounds chicken
694.5 pounds mutton
4 barrels pickles
7 barrels onions
10 barrels soft soap
225 pounds lard
6 barrels carrots or parsnips
901 pounds dried apples
166 galls coal oil
3 doz Cay[?] Broom
6 doz mops
3 doz wooden buckets
420 doz eggs
7 barrels onions
6 barrels turnips
785 pounds mutton
266 pounds dried apples
3 barrels pickles
422 galls molasses
41.5 galls coal oil
431.25 pounds chicken
312 pounds cod fish
1 molasses gate
2 boxes farina
67 lbs zinc
1 joint of R[?] labor
6574 quarts milk
11867 pieces washing
8 barrels potatoes
3 barrels ale
1 bottle sherry wine
10 bushels carrots
39.5 gallons whiskey
48.5 [?] alpaca spools call on & side
3 barrels flour
42.5 gallons whiskey
Total cost: $3298.09

May 1865
Total Number of Rations Supplied: 21804
Average number of men/day, 703
2 boxes lemons
24 mess kettles
2 scythes
2 tin cans
2 gross corks
2 gallons turpentine
2 gallons linseed oil
300 pounds dried apples
39 bushels potatoes
4 barrels potatoes
2 barrels pickels
4 barrels turnips
2 barrels carrotts
10 barrels onions
6 barrels onions
651 doz eggs
252 pounds mutton
173.5 pounds chicken
328 pounds beef liver
626 2/3 doz eggs
4.5 galls cod oil
3 doz lamp chimneys
12 dripping pans
189 pounds butter
188 pounds butter
1 barrel turnips
1 meat sais[?]
21 pounds sole leather
10 barrels soft soap
45 bushels potatoes
7172 quarts milk
9600 pieces of washing
1 barrel of pork[?]
5 barrels of flour
161 pound of white sugar
1500 pounds of potatoes
71 gallons whiskey
Total cost: $3047.32

June 1865
Total Number of Rations Supplied: 12755
Average number of men/day, 425
502 pounds butter
514 pounds butter
946 pounds mutton
752.5 pounds butter
100 pounds cod fish
378 doz eggs
20 barrels soft soap
3 l barrels pickels
10 gallons syrup
78 gallons molasses
120 pounds farina
6 barrels cabbage
2 barrels onions
12 covers for barrels
5 paint brushes
2 gross buttons
12 stone ware spittoons
2 barrels cod oil 82 gals
3 barrels cabbage
113 pounds white sugar
32 galls syrup
3628 galls milk
14400 pieces of washing
Total cost: $1928.61

July 1865
Total Number of Rations Supplied: 460
Average number of men/day, 15
1110 quarts milk
Total cost: $111.00

As can be seen from Chart 9-1, the hospital fund was used to buy for the prisoner patients large amounts of foods that were not part of the normal army or prisoner ration. Among the types of food bought were fruits, vegetables, fresh meats, eggs, fish, and dairy products. Some of the amounts of these are quite astonishing. For instance, choosing four months at random after the general hospital opened (11/63, 7/64, 12/64 and 5/65), the average amount of milk given to each patient each day was 7.7 ounces (229 mL), while each patient received an average of 0.46 eggs/day. It is likely the actual amount of milk and/or eggs or other foods a patient received would depend on the diet prescribed for him. For example, it was believed by some surgeons that milk was important for the treatment of several diseases, especially typho-malarial fever, acute dysentery and chronic diarrhea.

In those same months 0.47 pieces of washing/day was done for each patient. This would presumably include their hospital clothing and bedding. This is very low by modern standards, but considering men not in the hospital may have not washed their shirt or drawers more than once every 2–4 weeks, probably good for that time.

Other things bought with the hospital fund gives some insight into the hospital operation. Maintenance items such as paint, paint brushes, linseed oil, lamps, lamp oil, lamp chimneys, stove polish, sinks, and various tools were ordered, as well as many items needed for the operation of the hospital, such as spoons, chamber pots, spittoons, pens, ink, bed cards, water coolers, clothes pins, spoons, knives, forks, plates and lanterns among others. Clearly the hospital in many ways was a self-contained unit, in which food was cooked and served, clerical tasks performed, as well as direct care of the patients.

Diseases Treated

In this section will be discussed the prevalent diseases on the island and how they were, in general, diagnosed and treated by surgeons of the Civil War era. As Surgeon Nugent noted in his letter of 11/13/63, "It is a first rate place here to see every character and type of disease."

Sick call was the first time a disease would be diagnosed by a surgeon. A single sick call register, which happens to be for the month of January 1864, exists for Confederate enlisted men (see above). In it are listed the man's name, rank, unit, his complaint (diagnosis), and whether sent to hospital (if he was sent his diagnosis was not noted), and sometimes when and where captured. These data, along with diagnoses for the men sent to the hospital, are shown in Table 9-2.[25]

In order to better understand the following information it would be well to review what some diseases were called in the Civil War. Below are listed some disease names that are not familiar or what changed since then.

Catarrh—A cold (upper respiratory infection).
Cholera Morbus—Cholera and various gastrointestinal conditions.
Colic—Same as modern meaning but refers specifically to the colon.
Erysipelas—An inflammation of the skin with general fever and swelling, extending gradually to neighboring parts. In modern terms it is a type of skin infection (cellulitis) usually caused by Group A Streptococcus bacteria.
Inflammation of the lungs—pneumonia.
Malaria—The modern term for various conditions which usually signified malaria. Included in malaria are remittent fever, intermittent fever, malarial fever, typho-malarial fever, remittent tertian, tertian fever, and intermittent quotidian.
Odentalgia—A toothache.
Rheumatism, acute—Joint pain in major joints which often switches joints rapidly, usually accompanied by fever.

Table 9-2. Prisoner Sick Call, January 1864

Condition	Diagnosis			% to	% of
	Sick Call	Hospital	Total	Hospital	Total
Abscess	26	1	27	4	3.3
Bronchitis Acute	23	11	34	32	4.2
Bronchitis Chronic	2	3	5	60	0.6
Catarrh	126	5	131	4	16.2
Constipation	11	0	11	0	1.4
Diarrhea Acute	28	3	31	10	3.8
Diarrhea Chronic	12	4	16	25	2.0
Ear Ache	24	0	24	0	3.0
Erysipelas	4	3	7	43	0.9
Inflammation of Pleura	4	1	5	20	0.6
Inflammation of Lungs	1	13	14	93	1.7
Inflammation of Tonsils	6	1	7	14	0.9
Itch	15	1	16	6	2.0
Malaria	71	10	81	12	10.0
Neuralgia	66	6	72	8	8.9
Rheumatism Acute	35	9	44	20	5.4
Rheumatism Chronic	13	4	17	24	2.1

Condition	Diagnosis			% to Hospital	% of Total
	Sick Call	Hospital	Total		
Scurvy	158	26	184	14	22.8
Smallpox & Variola	0	7	7	100	0.9
Ulcer	6	0	6	0	0.7
Vaccine Complications	22	0	22	0	2.7
Other (less than 5 each)	39	8	47	17	5.8
Total	692	116	808	14	
Not Listed		13			
Unknown	5				

The top 3 conditions found at sick call were scurvy (22.8 percent), catarrh (16.2 percent), and intermittent fever (9.0 percent). Since there were no vegetables in the army ration, and the only source of Vitamin C was potatoes, it is not surprising that scurvy tops the list. In the winter catarrh (a "cold") is common even today, so it is to be expected that it too would be near the top of the list. As far as being sent to the hospital is concerned, not surprisingly all smallpox cases were sent to the hospital, and very high percentages of inflammation of the lungs and typho-malarial fever were also sent to the hospital. Smallpox was very contagious, and all cases were sent to the contagious hospital, while the death rates from typho-malarial fever and inflammation of the lungs were very high (see next chapter).

While compiling Table 9-2, it was found that there were approximately 150 other admissions to the Hospital of patients that are not noted in the sick call register. Why this is we can only speculate. Perhaps men who were obviously seriously sick were sent directly to the hospital without being noted in the book, or perhaps there was more than one sick call. In any event these unnoted (in the sick call register) hospital admissions and those shown in Table 9-2 are combined below in Table 9-4, for January 1864.

Confederate officers are not included in Table 9-2, simply because officers were not being held prisoner at Fort Delaware at that time. However, sick call for Confederate officers from June 1864 to January 1865 was recorded and is extant, and those for the months of July 1864 and January 1865 are summarized in Table 9-3.[26]

Table 9-3. Confederate Officers Sick Call for July 1864 and January 1865

Condition	July 1864				
	Diagnosis			% to Hospital	% of Total
	Sick Call	Hospital	Totals		
Anemia	19		19	0	1.3
Bowels, Inflamed	19		19	0	1.3
Bronchitis, Chronic	1		1	0	0.1
Catarrh & Cough	119	2	121	2	8.1
Cholera Morbus	7	4	11	36	0.7
Constipation	204		204	0	13.6
Debility, General	25		25	0	1.7
Diarrhea, Acute	382	22	404	5	26.9
Diarrhea, Chronic	52		52	0	3.5
Dysentery, Acute	35	9	44	20	2.9
Fever	11		11	0	0.7
Itch	63		63	0	4.2
Kidney, Inflamed	16		16	0	1.1

Condition	July 1864				
	Diagnosis			% to	% of
	Sick Call	Hospital	Totals	Hospital	Total
Inebriation	5		5	0	0.3
Laryngitis	12		12	0	0.8
Liver, Inflammation	6		6	0	0.4
"Malaria"	171		171	0	11.4
Neuralgia	26	1	27	4	1.8
Odentalgia	16		16	0	1.1
Pneumonia	5		5	0	0.3
Rheumatism, Acute	17		17	0	1.1
Scurvy	7		7	0	0.5
Smallpox & Variola	0		0	NA	0.0
Syphilis	12		12	0	0.8
Tetter	20		20	0	1.3
Typhoid Fever	4	12	16	75	1.1
Typhus	20		20	0	1.3
Ulcer	18		18	0	1.2
Unknown	40		40	0	2.7
Urine, Retention of	0		0	NA	0.0
Vaccine Complications	21		21	0	1.4
Wound	17	4	21	19	1.4
Other (less than 10 each)	73	4	77	5	5.1
Totals	1443	58	1501	4	
	January 1865				
Anemia	0		0	NA	0.0
Bowels, Inflamed	0		0	NA	0.0
Bronchitis, Chronic	1	10	11	91	1.1
Catarrh & Cough	345	2	347	1	34.9
Cholera Morbus	0		0	NA	0.0
Constipation	109		109	0	11.0
Debility, General	31		31	0	3.1
Diarrhea, Acute	83	2	85	2	8.6
Diarrhea, Chronic	11	6	17	35	1.7
Dysentery, Acute	3		3	0	0.3
Fever	0		0	NA	0.0
Itch	0		0	NA	0.0
Kidney, Inflamed	0		0	NA	0.0
Inebriation	0		0	NA	0.0
Laryngitis	1	1	2	50	0.2
Liver, Inflammation	0		0	NA	0.0
"Malaria"	74	2	76	3	7.6
Neuralgia	48	5	53	9	5.3
Odentalgia	0		0	NA	0.0
Pneumonia	0	4	4	100	0.4
Rheumatism, Acute	33	1	34	3	3.4
Scurvy	93	2	95	2	9.6
Smallpox & Variola	0		0	NA	0.0
Syphilis	8	1	9	11	0.9
Tetter	11		11	0	1.1
Typhoid Fever	0	1	1	100	0.1
Typhus	0		0	NA	0.0
Ulcer	14	1	15	7	1.5
Unknown	7		7	0	0.7
Urine, Retention of	10		10	0	1.0

Condition	January 1865				
	Diagnosis			% to	% of
	Sick Call	Hospital	Totals	Hospital	Total
Vaccine Complications	0		0	NA	0.0
Wound	5	29	34	85	3.4
Other (less than 10 each)	18	22	40	55	4.0
Totals	905	89	994	9	

Here again we see trends that are somewhat expected in which types of diseases are most common in summer vs. winter. Comparing January to June, catarrh increased greatly in January, while pneumonia cases in January seemed more severe, with all occurring in January being sent to the hospital. Scurvy also increased greatly in January, perhaps because vegetables and fruits were not as readily available from the Sutler in the winter. Wounds also increased, but see below. Diseases, such as dysentery, diarrhea, and cholera Morbus that are caused by contaminated water and/or food, decreased in January, as did vaccine complications and typhus. Perhaps diseases contracted by contact or by ingestion decreased because the microorganisms that cause them did not multiply as readily in the cold winter weather. This may have been especially true of the winter of 1864–65 because it was the coldest on record for at least 30 years (see Chapter 1).

Many of the "wounds" listed are clearly old wounds, probably incurred before coming to the island. For example, several of the wounds listed are incised wounds (cuts), while some are listed as shell wounds. There is no record of any artillery piece on the island ever being fired at the prisoners. In Table 9-3 most of the wounds in the hospital are almost certainly officers who were wounded, *presumably* treated in a field hospital and/or a general army hospital and then transferred to Fort Delaware while still needing hospital treatment. For example, (see Table 9-4, below) 48 men were admitted to the hospital in January 1865 with wounds, mostly "gunshot" wounds. Of these 39 were officers captured mostly in 3 recent battles: 14 at Winchester, Virginia (9/19/64), 5 at Cedar Creek, Virginia (10/19/64), and 18 at Franklin, Tennessee (11/30/64). The timing of these battles is reasonable in the sense that these officers could have been hospitalized for 1.5 to 3.5 months before being sent to Fort Delaware. None of these officers died from their wounds.

Once having passed through sick call, if the condition was serious enough, the man was sent to the hospital, and the hospital records are fairly complete, listing the man's name, rank, unit, date of admission to the hospital, diagnosis, and date of discharge from the hospital or date of death, and in many instances when and where captured.[27] Similar registers exist for Union soldiers.[28] A summary of hospital admissions of POWs for four months is shown in Table 9-4.

Table 9-4. All POW Hospitalizations by Selected Month

Condition	October 1863					January 1864				
	A	B	C	D	E	A	B	C	D	E
Anemia	19	2	2	11	0.7					
Bronchitis, Acute						13	3	1	23	1.0
Bronchitis, Chronic										
Catarrh & Cough	1	0	0	0	0.0	10	2	1	20	0.7
Cholera Morbus										
Colic										
Constipation										
Contusion										

9. Medical Care

Condition	October 1863					January 1864				
	A	B	C	D	E	A	B	C	D	E
Debility, General										
Diarrhea, Acute	75	34	7	45	11.8					
Diarrhea, Chronic	61	31	5	51	10.8	7	3	1	43	1.0
Diptheria	14	1	1	7	0.3					
Dysentery, Acute	31	11	3	35	3.8					
Erysipelas	79	14	7	18	4.9	4	0	0	0	0.0
Fever	12	0	1	0	0.0					
Jaundice	11	1	1	9	0.3					
Malaria	239	14	21	6	4.9	11	2	1	18	0.7
Mumps	9	1	1	11	0.3					
Neuralgia	15	1	1	7	0.3					
Other	35	9	3	26	3.1	12	2	1	17	0.7
Ottorrhea										
Pneumonia	39	17	3	44	5.9	17	9	1	53	3.1
Rheumatism, Acute	42	13	4	31	4.5	5	0	0	0	0.0
Rheumatism, Chronic										
Scurvy	118	25	10	21	8.7	16	0	1	0	0.0
Smallpox & Variola	230	99	20	43	34.5	37	2	3	5	0.7
Tonsilitis	47	1	4	2	0.3					
Typhoid Fever	49	12	4	24	4.2	3	1	0	33	0.3
Unknown	10	0	1	0	0.0	1	0	0	0	0.0
Wound	11	1	1	9	0.3	0	0	0	0	0
Total	1147	287				136	24			

Condition	July 1864					January 1865					Overall				
	A	B	C	D	E	A	B	C	D	E	A	B	C	D	E
Anemia	35	6	4	17	5.7						54	8	1.8	14.8	1.7
Bronchitis, Acute	27	3	3	11	2.9	37	0	5	0	0.0	77	6	2.6	7.8	1.3
Bronchitis, Chronic						36	2	4	6	4.7	36	2	1.2	5.6	0.4
Catarrh & Cough	16	1	2	6	1.0	48	0	6	0	0.0	75	3	2.6	4.0	0.7
Cholera Morbus	41	0	5	0	0.0						41	0	1.4	0.0	0.0
Colic	17	1	2	6	1.0						17	1	0.6	5.9	0.2
Constipation						11	0	1	0	0.0	11	0	0.4	0.0	0.0
Contusion						14	0	2	0	0.0	14	0	0.5	0.0	0.0
Debility, General						17	0	2	0	0.0	17	0	0.6	0.0	0.0
Diarrhea, Acute	163	15	20	9	14.3	81	4	10	5	9.3	319	53	10.9	16.6	11.5
Diarrhea, Chronic	12	1	1	8	1.0	39	5	5	13	11.6	119	40	4.1	33.6	8.7
Diptheria											14	1	0.5	7.1	0.2
Dysentery, Acute	53	7	6	13	6.7	15	2	2	13	4.7	99	20	3.4	20.2	4.4
Erysipelas	12	0	1	0	0.0	18	5	2	28	11.6	113	19	3.9	16.8	4.1
Fever											12	0	0.4	0.0	0.0
Jaundice											11	1	0.4	9.1	0.2
Malaria	115	19	14	17	18.1	78	0	9	0	0.0	443	35	15.1	7.9	7.6
Mumps											9	1	0.3	11.1	0.2
Neuralgia	13	0	2	0	0.0	30	0	4	0	0.0	58	1	2.0	1.7	0.2
Other	63	8	8	13	7.6	71	4	9	6	9.3	181	23	6.2	12.7	5.0
Ottorrhea						12	0	1	0	0.0	12	0	0.4	0.0	0.0
Pneumonia	27	4	3	15	3.8	38	10	5	26	23.3	121	40	4.1	33.1	8.7
Rheumatism, Acute	20	0	2	0	0.0	27	2	3	7	4.7	94	15	3.2	16.0	3.3
Rheumatism, Chronic						25	0	3	0	0.0	25	0	0.9	0.0	0.0
Scurvy	97	9	12	9	8.6	64	1	8	2	2.3	295	35	10.1	11.9	7.6
Smallpox & Variola	87	25	11	29	23.8	94	6	11	6	14.0	448	132	15.3	29.5	28.8
Tonsilitis	8	1	1	13	1.0	11	0	1	0	0.0	66	2	2.3	3.0	0.4
Typhoid Fever	6	3	1	50	2.9	1	1	0	100	2.3	59	17	2.0	28.8	3.7

Condition	July 1864					January 1865					Overall				
	A	B	C	D	E	A	B	C	D	E	A	B	C	D	E
Unknown	4	0	0	0	0.0	7	1	1	14	2.3	22	1	0.8	4.5	0.2
Wound	10	2	1	20	1.9	48	0	6	0	0.0	69	3	2.4	4.3	0.7
Total	826	105				822	43				2931	459			

Keys to Tables 9-4 and 9-5: A—Total Hospitalizations for that month for that condition. B—Total deaths that month for that condition. C—Percent of total hospital admissions for that condition. D—Percent of hospital admissions for that condition which resulted in death. E—Percent of all deaths resulting from that condition.

The seasonal patterns of hospital admissions shown in these months are similar to those shown in Table 9-4. Common winter illnesses such as catarrh and pneumonia are proportionately increased in winter months compared to the summer, while conditions related to organisms growing in food or water such as dysentery or diarrhea are proportionately reduced in winter months. Malaria is also greatly reduced in the winter months. The top diseases for hospitalizations were 1—smallpox, 2—malaria, 3—acute diarrhea, 4—scurvy, and 5—pneumonia. The highest number of deaths were 1—smallpox, 2—acute diarrhea, 3—pneumonia, 4—chronic diarrhea, 5 and 6—(tied) malaria and scurvy. The conditions which had the highest mortality rates were 1—chronic diarrhea, 2—pneumonia, 3—smallpox, 4—typhoid fever, and 5—acute dysentery.

A summary of Union troop hospitalizations is shown in Table 9-5. See above for the column keys to this table.

Table 9-5. Union Troop Hospitalizations for Selected Months

Condition	November 1863		January 1864		July 1864		January 1865		Overall				
	A	B	A	B	A	B	A	B	A	B	C	D	E
Bronchitis	1	0	2	0	3	0	5	0	11	0	4.0	0.0	0.0
Catarrh & Cough	1	0	4	0	0	0	7	0	12	0	4.4	0.0	0.0
Cholera Morbus	0	0	2	0	5	0	0	0	7	0	2.6	0.0	0.0
Colic	3	0	1	0	3	0	0	0	7	0	2.6	0.0	0.0
Diarrhea & Dysentery	0	0	5	0	25	0	2	1	32	1	11.7	3.1	9.1
Erysipelas	4	0	2	0	1	0	3	0	10	0	3.6	0.0	0.0
Malaria	7	0	1	0	19	0	9	0	36	0	13.1	0.0	0.0
Other	6	0	9	0	10	0	14	0	39	0	14.2	0.0	0.0
Pneumonia	1	0	6	0	0	0	8	2	15	2	5.5	13.3	18.2
Rheumatism	6	0	4	0	1	0	5	0	16	0	5.8	0.0	0.0
Scurvy	0	0	0	0	0	0	2	0	2	0	0.7	0.0	0.0
Smallpox & Variola	5	1	5	2	3	1	1	0	14	4	5.1	28.6	36.4
Tonsillitis	7	0	3	0	0	0	3	0	13	0	4.7	0.0	0.0
Typhoid Fever	1	1	0	0	2	2	1	0	4	3	1.5	75.0	27.3
Unknown	3	0	1	0	0	0	3	0	7	0	2.6	0.0	0.0
Wound	1	0	1	0	3	1	1	0	6	1	2.2	16.7	9.1
Syphilis	5	0	0	0	0	0	0	0	5	0	1.8	0.0	0.0
Eye, Inflammation of	0	0	3	0	0	0	0	0	3	0	1.1	0.0	0.0
Measles	0	0	0	0	29	0	6	0	35	0	12.8	0.0	0.0
Total	51	2	49	2	104	4	70	3	274	11			

Since there are relatively few hospitalizations for any particular condition in any particular month, no statistical data for individual months are given. The most common causes for hospitalization were: 1. malaria, 2. measles, and 3. diarrhea and dysentery. The conditions with the highest number of deaths were 1. smallpox, 2. typhoid fever, and 3. pneumonia. The highest mortality rates were from 1. smallpox, 2. typhoid fever, and 3.

pneumonia. These numbers and rankings have to be taken with large amount of skepticism, since the sample sizes are so small. Also, these would undoubtedly change based on the months chosen. For instance, measles was known to be an episodic disease, so the choice of July 1864 probably overemphasizes its occurrence among Union troops.

The mortality rate among Union troops admitted to the hospital for these four months was 4.0 percent, while the mortality rate for POWs for the four months in Table 9-4 was 15.7 percent. This percentage is skewed somewhat by the high number of cases of smallpox and its high mortality rate in the month of October 1863. Excluding that month, the mortality rate for hospitalized POWs was 9.6 percent. It is also interesting that while the monthly mortality rate for Union soldiers (again based on very few cases) remained about constant, the mortality rate for POWs consistently decreased with time, being 25.0 percent in October 1863, 17.6 percent in January 1864, 12.7 percent in July 1864, and 5.2 percent in January 1865. These are not overall death rates, since they don't take into account the total number of POWs present during those months.

Treatment of Specific Diseases[29]

In order to better understand how various diseases were treated it is important to know what physicians of the mid-nineteenth century thought about the origins of disease. At that time diseases were classified into broad categories, and the category of chief interest to this work is Zymotic Diseases, which were defined as "Diseases which are either epidemic, endemic or communicable, induced by some specific body, or by the want or bad quality of the food." In turn, Zymotic diseases were divided into four subclasses: 1. Miasmatic diseases, 2. Enthetic diseases, 3. Dietetic diseases, and 4. Parasitic diseases. None of the diseases considered by the U.S. Army were considered parasitic diseases.

On the other hand, Miasmatic diseases were those not parasitic and not caused by inoculation only or by errors of diet. They are the most important "class" of diseases we will consider, and they arose from "miasmas" such as those produced by vegetable decomposition, or by matter derived from decomposition of the human or other bodies. These miasmas were broadly understood to be any unknown atmospheric influences arising from these sources. In the U.S., this to some extent was interpreted more narrowly to cover, especially, malaria and malaria-like diseases (see Glossary above). However, the Army used it in its broader sense, and in various medical reports it included typhoid fever, typhus, typho-malarial fever, yellow fever, remittent fever, intermittent fever, diarrhea, dysentery, cholera, erysipelas, hospital gangrene, pyaemia, smallpox, varioloid, measles, scarlet fever, diphtheria, mumps and epidemic catarrh. Enthetic diseases include syphilis and gonorrhea, the only two of this type reported at Fort Delaware. The only dietic diseases reported at Fort Delaware were scurvy and inebriation.

In a sense the classification of enthetic and dietic diseases and their cause, was, in large part, correct, although the causative agents (or lack thereof) of these types of diseases were often not understood. On the other hand, the origin of miasmatic diseases was completely wrong, it being thought these diseases were caused by emanations from decaying vegetation (as in a marsh or swamp) or from decay of the animal bodies. This was not completely illogical. For example, malaria, the prototypical miasmatic disease, occurred near marshes and swamps in warmer climates where a great deal of vegetative decay occurred. This was why in many medical inspections, the inspectors commented that Pea Patch Island was a very poor place for a hospital, or prison camp for that matter. It was swampy. It was also why the U.S. Army Medical Department specified minimum required interior volumes for hospitals and barracks, and specified that such buildings should be well ventilated. This would reduce the concentrations of the miasmas inside these buildings.

For the most part treatment of most diseases relied more on ameliorating the symptoms than treating the actual disease itself. There were some effective drugs for doing this for some diseases, but such treatment relied on trial and error, and the predilections of the individual surgeons. Also considered important in treatment of disease was the diet supplied to the patient. Unfortunately, the only records that survive on how individual penitents were treated for various diseases are the drugs prescribed for officer POWs during sick call. Thus the discussion below will mention these (if known), and/or draw from Woodward and others on the general treatment of the individual disease. There is no way of knowing, other than Dr. Lee's prescriptions, whether surgeons at Fort Delaware followed the recommendations of Woodward or others for any particular disease.

Catarrh (common "cold") and Cough: These were very common in the wintertime, less so in the summertime, but still relatively plentiful as judged by Sick Calls, Tables 9-2 and 9-3. Hospitalizations were relatively a small percentage of total cases from sick calls, and Tables 9-4 and 9-5 indicate that the death rate of those admitted to the hospital for catarrh and/or cough was also relatively low. Then, as now, catarrh was mostly a relatively mild disease during which the sufferer was at times very uncomfortable, but the disease was and is usually not life threatening.

Woodward attributes the main cause of catarrh to exposure to damp and cold. Overcrowding, imperfect ventilation, want of cleanliness, and debility from the monotonous diets of camps are other contributing causes. For simple cases he recommends a mild cathartic (increases speed of defecation), followed by the use of quinine and iron or bitter tonics. An alternative treatment is bitters with a cough mixture. Other treatments are suggested for more serious cases. If a fever is involved, Woodward recommends a low diet for the first few days, mostly liquids. As the fever subsides a more substantial diet is introduced (more substantial liquids and then solids), and after the fever is gone a full diet should be given.

We now know that the use of quinine, cathartics, and iron and bitter tonics probably did nothing to cure the catarrh symptoms, but in some instances could have relieved some of the symptoms. Even today we have no "cure" for catarrh, and the old saying, "If you treat a cold or not, it will take about two weeks to go away," is still true. Today we use medicines to alleviate the symptoms, and that for the most part is what Dr. Lee did in his prescriptions for catarrh.

A random sampling of Lee's prescription book yielded 52 total diagnoses of cough and/or catarrh (6 of these were cough, one cough and catarrh, the remainder catarrh). Many diagnoses of catarrh were combined with other ailments, particularly in December 1864 and January 1865. These other ailments were typically scurvy, constipation and/or general debility. Only diagnoses which were cough and or catarrh alone are included so as not to complicate the results with prescription items that may not have been meant for the catarrh. In 12 of the cases "cough mixture" was prescribed, while in 37 cases "expectorant" was prescribed. Unfortunately, what these may have been is not specifically given. However, one prescription for cold and cough was for ipecac and capscium fruit, and another for cough was for a syrup made with *scilla* bulbs. Ipecac was used as an expectorant, especially for catarrh, while *scilla* was used as an expectorant in chronic bronchitis. Whether one or both of these was used in "expectorant" is not known. One catarrh prescription was for licorice, another was for licorice and expectorant, another was for camphor and opium, another for potassium iodide solution, and another for potassium iodide and quinine sulfate. However, the great majority of prescriptions were for expectorant (71 percent) or cough mixture (23 percent), items recommended by Woodward, and are still used today to treat the symptoms of colds (catarrh).

Diarrhea and Dysentery: Diarrhea is loose or watery stools, sometimes caused by a bacterial infection. Dysentery is a more serious infection of the digestive tract caused by bacteria, or parasites or protozoans. In both instances dehydration, usually with loss of electrolytes, is the most immediate problem, so the patient should be kept hydrated and electrolytes replaced if needed. Presently, if the underlying cause such as a bacterial infection can be identified, appropriate treatments such as antibiotics are used.

Diarrhea, Acute. This was among the top cause of sick calls, hospitalizations and deaths, see Tables 9-2 through 9-4. For the most part it is probably related to the purity of water and food, and also to general sanitary conditions, and seems to be more prevalent during the warmer months.

Woodward on page 209 confirms the partial seasonality of this condition. He blames changes in diet, especially to sudden ingestion of richer foods (fresh beef, fruits and vegetables), and also a change in water supply. This change in water supply is especially true if the "new" water contains minerals and/or possible traces of decaying organic matter. In more severe cases it may also be caused by saline drinking water, exposure to heat or cold, and fatiguing exercise during the heat of the day. In acute cases it may accompanied by fever. It can result in a chronic disease and/or be fatal. Treatment is a very limited diet (low diet) of liquids such as barley water, and toast and tea if desired, and initially a cathartic (laxative) to remove irritating food and secretions. This cathartic can be castor oil, magnesium sulfate, oxide of magnesia, rhubarb, etc. The use of warm "fomentations" (warm damp towels) or "dry cups" for relief of pain is recommended. Opiates such as laudanum are very desirable from the beginnings of the disease. As the patient improves the diet may be enriched. Woodward admonishes against the use of mercurials (mercury containing compounds). Note that Woodward's initial treatment of using a cathartic is opposite to that of modern treatment, since it would result in further dehydration of the patient.

Diarrhea, Chronic: Woodward describes this as a serious disease, which often can lead to death. The death may not be directly from this disease, but may make men prone to other diseases that can kill them. Typically, the disease starts as a mild diarrhea and progresses to a more severe chronic form, and the patient gradually becomes weaker and emaciated. It is said that camp diet, especially change in diet, can lead to the disease. Overcrowding, poor sanitation, exposure to inclement weather, and fatigue may also contribute. As indicated in Tables 9-3 and 9-4 warmer weather seems to favor development of the disease.

The most important "treatment" according to Woodward are good hygienic practices. Diet is important, and should be nutritious and supporting. Food in liquid and semiliquid form is more easily digested, and milk and rice are said to be especially efficacious. The recommended use of medicines is all over the place; materials such as copper sulfate, silver nitrate, bismuth subnitrate, aromatic sulfuric acid, a camphor mixture, opiates, and ipecac, to name some, were recommended according to Woodward, by various parties. Clearly there was no consensus on how to treat chronic diarrhea.

Dysentery, Acute: According to Woodward this disease was common in the army, but did not result in many deaths. However Table 9-4 shows that approximately 20 percent of those sent to the hospital with this disease died, a fairly high death rate. The disease often started with a chill followed by fever, and then perhaps by gripping pains in the abdomen. The patient often feels the needs to defecate, but is only sometimes successful, and the attempts are often painful. The stools are often bloody and usually contain mucous. Usually the patient starts getting better in 7–10 days, but in some instances the patient does not got better, becomes emaciated, and sometimes dies.

Woodward states the best treatment is a mild cathartic, such as castor oil or magnesium sulfate. If the patient does not get better after a few days, a mineral astringent such as lead acetate or copper sulfate is recommended. Opium is used to relieve pain and/or induce sleep. As a side effect it helps control the diarrhea, but this is said not to help cure the disease. By modern standards the use of a cathartic would only increase dehydration, but it could help rid the digestive tract of whatever organism is causing the disease. Not having drugs such as antibiotics, it may have been the most efficient way of ridding the body of the disease-causing organism.

Dr. Lee's Prescriptions: During sick call Dr. Lee would have sent the more serious cases of these diseases to the hospital. For acute diarrhea this was about 2 percent of the cases from sick call, for chronic diarrhea 0 percent during July 1864 and 35 percent in January 1865 to the hospital, and for acute dysentery 20 percent during the summer and 0 percent in the winter. Table 9-3 shows that acute diarrhea had a mortality rate of 16.6 percent of those hospitalized, chronic diarrhea 33.6 percent, and acute dysentery 20.2 percent. All of these were relatively dangerous diseases.

Dr. Lee himself has very detailed information about what he described for these diseases. On 6/26/64 Dr. Lee gives in his sick call register[30] a prescription for a powder. A dose of each powder contains [drug names converted to modern terms and amount in grams (g) and milliliters (mL)]: magnesium oxide, 27.4 g; dried rhubarb root, 0.65 g; and dried fruit of capsicum, 1.30 g. All of these are stimulants or purgatives designed to cause defecation, presumably, according to Woodward, to clean out the digestive system. On this same page it is listed as being given to 15 men with acute diarrhea, 1 man with chronic diarrhea, and 2 men with acute dysentery. Each man got two doses of the powder to be taken 4 hours apart. No other medication is listed as being given to them.

On the same date, on the next page is given another prescription as follows: nitric acid, 3.6 mL; tincture of opium, 1.9 mL; tincture of capsicum fruit, 2.5 mL; and camphor water, 237 mL. One tablespoon full (15 mL) was to be taken every 3 hours. The total number of doses to each man was not given. On this same page it lists 11 men with acute diarrhea, 3 men with chronic diarrhea, 6 men with acute dysentery, and 3 men with chronic dysentery who were to be given this medicine in liquid form. The concentrations of the various ingredients are not given, but presumably the nitric acid was dilute. A typical concentration for tincture of opium (laudanum) was about 0.7 percent (w/v) in ethyl alcohol. It still contains small amount of a "stimulant," the capsicum fruit. It is known that opiates will stop or at least alleviate diarrhea, so it did at least diminish the loss of fluids and/or electrolytes from the body. However, if there was an underlying infection, it did not relieve that.

Apparently Dr. Lee experimented with several variants of these prescriptions, and the details are shown in Table 9-6. Amounts shown in Table 9-6 are per dose. ADi is acute diarrhea, CDi is chronic diarrhea, and ADy is acute dysentery.

Table 9-6. Dr. Lee's Prescriptions for Diarrhea and Dysentery

Type	Ingredients	Dosage	Disease(s) Treated
Powder	Calcined magnesium oxide, 13.7 g Pulverized rhubarb root, 0.3 g	one night and morning	CDi, ADi, ADy,
Powder	Opium powder, 0.05 g Ipecac, 0.035 g ? Powder, 0.07 g	one every 6 hours	ADi
Liquid	Nitric acid, 0.59 mL Tincture of opium, 0.3 mL Camphor water, 39.5 mL	One or two doses or a tablespoon full every 3 hours	ADy, ADi
Powder	Dried capsicum fruit, 0.03 g Opium powder, 0.022 g Ipecac, 0.008 g Gum acacia, 0.03 g	one every 6 hours until ?	ADy, ADi, Cody, CDi
Powder	Opium powder, 0.03 g Tannin, 0.11 g Gum camphor, 0.04 g Gum acacia, 0.04 g	one every 3 hours	ADi, CDi, ADy,
Liquid	Tincture of opium, 219 g Tincture of capsicum fruit, 164 g Morphine solution, 56.6 g Oil of turpentine, 54.8 g Alcohol, 1 pint[?] Water, 2 pints[?]	One tablespoon full every 3 hours	ADy, ADi, CDi
Powder	Opium powder, 0.022 g Dried capsicum fruit, 0.03 g Ipecac, 0.011 g Gum acacia, 0.033 g	every 6 hours	ADi, ADy, CDi

All of the above prescriptions were tried during the first month of Dr. Lee's tenure doing sick calls for the officer POWs. Why he made these up is not known. During this period and later he also prescribed more conventional drugs for these conditions. Perusing his prescriptions at random, we found during July he prescribed ferric sulfate several times (9 for ADi, and 1 for ADy). He then switched to camphor and opium pills (24 for ADi, 2 for ADy, and 11 for CDi), and lead and opium pills (10 for ADi, 2 for ADy, and 3 for CDi). Most of the lead and opium pills were dispensed in August and September 1864, while after that mostly camphor and opium pills were prescribed. Thus in the end it would appear that Dr. Lee believed the best medicine for these diseases was something containing opium, and he apparently abandoned the use of purgatives. The opium at least ameliorated the diarrhea caused by these diseases.

Malaria: As noted above in the Glossary, malaria was often diagnosed as many other conditions, and actually was rarely called malaria. Some of the diagnoses of these other diseases may not have been malaria itself, but there is no way of telling in what percentage of these cases this was true. This apparently could have been especially true of typho-malarial fever, some of which may have been typhoid fever. Thus cases of malaria may be overstated and cases of typhoid fever understated.

Nevertheless, from Tables 9-3 and 9-4 it is clear that malaria was a widespread disease, especially in the warmer months. Although the hospitalization and mortality rates were not particularly high, the large number of cases made it a significant cause of death. The fact that we did not eliminate duplicate entries (in the sense that a single man may have more than one entry) in either sick calls or hospital admissions could have made these totals higher.

In his book J.J. Woodward in Chapter II, Section 1, discusses "malarial Influence," which he states is the chief cause of camp fevers. At the same time, he states, "*Malaria, or marsh miasm*, is a cause of disease concerning the nature of which much has been written, but in connection with which very few facts are actually susceptible of demonstration" (emphasis in original). In other words, they had no idea what caused these diseases or how they were transmitted, except through the notion of miasmatic air. Areas such as swamps or other damp areas where much vegetative decay took place were especially notorious for having miasmatic air, and hence caused a lot of fevers.

Chapter II of Woodward then deals with "Camp Fevers," which includes typho-malarial fever, and Chapter IV deals with intermittent fevers. In both cases he deals also with those diseases in which a "scorbutic taint" (scurvy) is also present. Since these diseases are so intertwined, we will outline here only the chief recommended treatments, and the reader is referred to Woodward for further details.

For typho-malarial fever Woodward states that it is very important to locate hospitals away from sites where malarial influences are present. Of course this was not the case with the hospital on Pea Patch Island. Secondly, heating, ventilation and sanitary condition of the hospital must be good. An air disinfectant of chlorine gas (very dilute) is recommended. The chlorine was (is) made by mixing NaCl, MnO_2, and dilute sulfuric acid (chlorine could also be used to disinfect water such as that in cesspools). The third element in treatment is diet, and the item to be especially taken into account is the amount of scorbutic influence in the disease. Most of the time a full diet should be prescribed, as long as the patient can tolerate it. Woodward also describes in great detail food items which can be prescribed if a full diet cannot be tolerated. As for medicines to be used, Woodward says this varies with the particular case. However, he says that if a malarial element is present (periodic fevers, and possibly chills), quinine sulfate should be used.

Woodward divides intermittent fevers into "simple intermittent fever," "congestive or pernicious intermittent fever," and "chronic malarial poisoning." Simple intermittent fever is well treated by quinine sulfate. In "obstinate" cases the quinine may be combined with opium. Congestive intermittent fever is a more serious malarial disease and usually characterized by more intense chills. Initially stimulants (for example alcohol) are administered to bring about some improvement, followed by quinine sulfate. A recommended pill has half a grain of opium, a quarter grain capsicum, and two grains of quinine sulfate. Prompt treatment usually results in eventual recovery. For chronic malarial poisoning the best treatment is to remove the patient from the malarial area. This was not an option for POWs at Fort Delaware. Again, quinine sulfate is the preferred treatment, 2 or 3 grains, 2 or 3 times a day. If the quinine is not effective, arsenic ("Fowler's solution") may be administered. Thus all intermittent fevers are treated effectively with quinine. It is well known now that quinine was the first effective treatment for malaria, but is not effective now in most areas because the malaria parasite has become resistant to quinine.

A random sampling of Dr. Lee's sick call register shows the following treatments for "malaria" as defined above in the Glossary. For intermittent fever, remittent fever, intermittent tertian, and similar fevers, quinine was prescribed in 48 out of 51 cases. In some instances, the quinine was combined with other medications, but in the great majority of cases it was quinine only. However for typho-malarial fever the treatment was different. In 25 out of 35 the treatment prescribed was a pill of "mercury" (probably calomel, Hg_2Cl_2) and colocynth pulp (dried fruit of *citrullis colocynthisdis*). Calomel is described as a cathartic among other things, and colocynth pulp is described as a "powerful drastic hydragogue [causes watery stools] cathartic." Why this was chosen as the medication is not known, because malaria and typhoid fever both are now known to cause diarrhea. However, Woodward reports that in typho-malarial fever with malarial influences, sometimes obstinate constipation is found, and he later writes that if constipation occurs in the early stages of the disease, a *mild* cathartic may be desirable. Of the other 10 cases of typho-malarial fever treated by Dr. Lee, 5 were given mercury pills and the other 5 were treated with other medication, mostly containing quinine. In some instances, where mercury in one form or another was given, quinine or other medications were also given.

Pneumonia (inflammation of the lungs): This was an often serious disease, and was common in the colder months. While the 5 cases diagnosed by Dr. Lee in July 1864 were not sent to the hospital, all 4 cases diagnosed in January 1865 were sent to the hospital (Table 9-3). The overall death rate for those admitted to the hospital with pneumonia, as shown in Table 9-4, was 33 percent, quite high, so that while there was a moderate number of cases reported in this Table, the number of deaths was high.

Woodward's description of the symptoms of pneumonia seems very similar to a present-day description. He states that the treatments used by civilian doctors such as bloodletting and mercurial have been found by Army surgeons to do more harm than good, and so he suggests the use of saline diaphoretics (induce perspiration) and perhaps also digitalis to reduce heart rate in the early stages, together with local remedies such as dry cups to relieve chest tenderness. These early remedies, if successful, give way to Dover's [powder to relieve cough] and also wine or spirits (considered stimulants). If, however the pneumonia progresses, spirits would be given, perhaps together with an anodyne (medication that relieves pain). Other medications are also mentioned. Diet should be supporting and nutritious, starting with a light diet, becoming more supporting as the disease lessens. Of course modern treatments differ. In bacterial pneumonia the primary treatment is antibiotics, while viral pneumonia is treated with antivirals. During the Civil War, bacteria and viruses were not known.

Dr. Lee did not treat many pneumonia cases, so a pattern of treatment cannot be discerned.

Scurvy: This pernicious disease was common among soldiers in the Civil War and in preceding and followings wars. It was well known that fruits and vegetables, especially fresh fruits and vegetables, could prevent (some believed) and cure scurvy, but except for potatoes, there were no fruits or vegetables in the U.S. Army ration, and potatoes were eliminated from the ration for Union soldiers in June 1864 (see Chapter 4), and for POWs in February 1865. It is now known that lack of Vitamin C (ascorbic acid) causes scurvy, but Vitamin C, much less the idea of vitamins as essential nutrients, was not known during the Civil War. The irony of this is that even many enlisted soldiers knew of the value of fresh fruits and vegetables in preventing scurvy. In answer to this, Congress made "desiccated vegetables" part of the army ration. They were compact and easy to transport, but the men detested and rarely ate them (they called them "desecrated vegetables"), and due to their preparation process and the long cooking time needed, they probably contained little Vitamin C. Some Army surgeons urged the addition of fresh fruits and vegetables to the Army ration, but this was not done because of the bulk of such materials and the fact that many spoil relatively easily.

As Bollet[31] relates, soldiers (not prisoners) had other ways of obtaining fresh vegetables and fruits. Soldiers were of course paid, so they could have used some of their pay to buy them. If they were out in the field or on the march they could forage (some would say steal) them from nearby orchards and fields. Another source of fruits and vegetables, especially for those soldiers in permanent garrisons, was the Company Fund, whose source of money was a tax on the local Sutler and credit for any uneaten rations. On June 9 and 16 Hamilton noted in his diary that they had strawberries and milk for supper, and on 8/9/64 the "Capt. Bo[ugh]t 25 baskets of peaches out of the Com[pany] fund."

However, prisoners could not forage, and while there was a Prison Fund it was not used to purchase foods outside of the regular ration, except for some desiccated vegetables which was authorized by the CGP. If POWs had money they could buy certain fruits and perhaps vegetables from the Sutler. Spoilage usually prevented fresh fruits and vegetables from being sent to the POWs. Thus the POWs had a limited supply of Vitamin C available to them, in the form of potatoes, and/or if they had money to buy from the Sutler.

Among the POW officers scurvy was apparently not too common in the summertime, but very common in the wintertime, see Table 9-3. This is not surprising since fruits and vegetables would have been more available from the Sutler during the warm months. It did not have a high hospitalization rate among the officers. Among the enlisted men its occurrence seems to be much higher compared to other diseases, and its death rate is moderate; see Table 9-4, which reflects mostly enlisted men. It was particularly bad in October 1863 and July 1864. This may reflect the fact that some enlisted men came to Fort Delaware in a rather poor nutritional state, which contributed to getting, and some succumbing to, scurvy.

As reported by Bollet, fatigue, lassitude, debility, "depression of spirit" etc., were symptoms of scurvy. They probably manifested themselves somewhat even before a mild case of scurvy could be diagnosed. They may account for remarks about at least some of the POWs being lazy, inactive or fatigued. For example, Surgeon Clark in his inspection of 11/13/63 stated, "Habit of men [prisoners]—indolent, can hardly be roused to take necessary exercise." While some of it was probably due to boredom and depression about being imprisoned, it is likely at least some of it was due to scurvy, which was prevalent at that time.

It was apparently a quirk of the U.S. Army system that fruits and vegetables, which were not part of the regular ration, could not be given to soldiers or prisoners unless they were in the hospital. Thus in Dr. Lee's treatment of scurvy at sick call, no such food was listed as issued. Instead Dr. Lee gave a variety of medications, presumably to relieve the symptoms of scurvy. Of course none of them actually helped cure the disease, but some of them may have helped relieve the obvious symptoms. Out of 50 scurvy cases found at random in Dr. Lee's sick call book, 26 were prescribed mercurial ointment, 15 were treated with sulfur ointment, five with potassium iodide solution, and five with other medications. There is no clear indication why any of these medications were used, but the fact that many of them were ointments points to treatment of external features, or perhaps even gums, which are known to be affected by scurvy.

Union soldiers were not immune to getting scurvy. On 4/3/65 Hamilton noted in his diary, "Many of our Boys are getting scurvy our supply of vegetables has been exceedingly limited this winter." Apparently most of these cases were not serious, as only 4 Union soldiers with scurvy were admitted to the hospital from February through April 1865.

Smallpox and Variola: Smallpox, and its less virulent form variola, were highly contagious and feared diseases. This fear was justified, since Table 9-4 shows it was the disease that caused the most hospitalizations and deaths, and had the highest overall death rate, at least in the months shown in that Table. On the other hand, it was also the only disease which could be avoided by vaccination, although vaccination was not reliable.[32]

Generally speaking most Union soldiers were vaccinated against smallpox when they joined the Army. However, the vaccination itself could be dangerous, because it involved cutting the arm and placing into the cut "lymph" from soldiers who had been vaccinated or had smallpox. The two problems were lack of sterile conditions which could cause infections, including blood poisoning which could lead to death, and sometimes the "lymph" even contained active smallpox virus so that the man actually contracted the disease from the vaccination. For these reasons, and because sometimes the POWs felt they were being deliberately poisoned, some of them tried to avoid being vaccinated. Table 9-3 shows that during sick call 21 officers were treated in July 1864 for vaccine complications.

Cox's experience illustrates this type of problem. He arrived on the island on 7/24/64 and it may be assumed he was vaccinated shortly thereafter. In his diary he reports on 8/3/64 that his arm is very sore, a surgeon (Dr. Lee?) examined it, and Cox was alarmed about the condition. His arm was still very sore the next day, but on 8/9/64 he reported it was improving. On August 13th he reported it was very sore again, but that is the last mention of it in his diary.

Others commented on smallpox vaccination. On 7/25/64 McCrorey was refusing to be vaccinated because the vaccine was said to be impure. The Rev. Handy reported on 8/8/64 that many men were suffering from "spurious" vaccine that caused gangrene. However, several times in 1863 Handy reported on vaccinations, including himself, which seemed to go well. Clearly some men were disinclined to be vaccinated for fear of the potential complications.

The uncertainty and dangers of smallpox are illustrated by what Union Surgeon Washington George Nugent did to protect himself from smallpox, which was chronicled in his letters home to his wife. On 1/10/64 he reports that vaccine matter "arrived safely" (not said from where), but most were failures. He had already been vaccinated twice, but unsuccessfully, and he was going to try again. On 1/15/64 he reports he requested from his wife some "crust" for vaccinations, but that may not be needed now since he obtained good crust from a child who had smallpox. He will see if it is successful. Months later on 11/6/64 he writes he wishes he had some good matter for vaccination, and he would try it on himself. Also suggests that his wife and "Minnie" (his daughter) get vaccinated. On 1/129/65 he reports that he received the crust his wife sent him, and he will be using it on various officers and their families, as there has been a sudden demand for vaccination.

It is clear from the above that getting good matter for smallpox vaccinations was hit or miss, and there was no way of telling whether any particular matter would be effective. Apparently it was an advantage if the vaccination matter was fresh. A vaccination was considered successful if the proper type of scar formed. Even materials prepared by the surgeons themselves were sometimes not effective. On 1/10/64 Nugent reported that

Surgeon Curtis had a very bad case of smallpox; presumably his vaccination had not worked.

We have no idea how smallpox was treated on the island, since men diagnosed with it were sent immediately to the contagious hospital where they were isolated from the rest of the population. No records exist from this hospital as to how these men were treated.

Typhoid Fever: Although the number of hospital admissions for typhoid fever was relatively low (but they may be understated because they were included as typho-malarial fever), the mortality rate was very high among those hospitalized. Woodward explains that the origin of typhoid fever is a subject of controversy, and that it has a high mortality rate. He also states it is also often confounded with scorbutic and/or malarial traits. Woodward's only specific recommendation for a drug for typhoid fever is potassium chlorate. Dr. Lee treated four cases of typhoid fever in June and July 1864. For three of these he prescribed quinine, while for the other opium. We don't know how it was treated in the hospital, where most cases were sent.

Effectiveness of Medical Treatment

It would be foolhardy to compare the death rates from various diseases to modern day treatments. Instead one should compare death rates from various diseases with other similar facilities during the Civil War. Gillispie[33] has previously pointed out that overall recovery rates at Fort Delaware for hospitalized patients were very good compared to various Union POW camps and Chimborazo Hospital in Richmond, Virginia. A variation of the data presented by Gillispie is in Table 9-7, where hospital death rates for specific (types of) diseases are shown.[34]

Table 9-7. Death Rates for Various Diseases of Hospitalized Patients

Disease	Chimborazo Hospital			Fort Delaware Hospital			All Union Camps
	Cases	Deaths	DR, %*	Cases	Deaths	DR, %*	DR, %*
Continued Fevers	2153	885	41.1	432	156	36.1	43.3
Malarial Fevers	1988	125	6.3	4725	175	3.7	2.7
Eruptive Fevers	760	166	21.8	2593	472	18.2	20.7
Diarrhea and Dysentery	4644	455	9.8	9659	644	6.7	9.1
Debility and Anemia	5780	117	2.0	792	38	4.8	4.9
Consumption	189	52	27.5	32	11	34.4	61.9
Rheumatism	1984	80	4.0	1494	19	1.3	1.1
Scurvy	119	8	6.7	6351	94	1.5	2.2
Bronchitis & Catarrh	1099	89	8.1	965	34	3.5	3.0
Pneumonia & Pleurisy	1568	583	37.2	1128	401	35.5	35.2
Total	20284	2560	12.6	28171	2044	7.3	10.4†

Overall death rate, %   †Total for listed diseases.

As can be seen from Table 9-7, the overall death rate of hospitalized prisoners for the listed diseases at Fort Delaware is about 30 percent lower than the overall Union prison camp rate, and about 42 percent lower than Chimborazo Hospital. The latter had the reputation of being among the best military hospitals in the Confederacy. However,

Chimborazo may have been hampered by severe shortages of some medicines in the South, such as quinine, caused by the Union blockade. This could be the reason why the death rate from "Malarial Fevers" was much higher at Chimborazo. Nevertheless, the overall death rate of hospitalized prisoners at Fort Delaware indicates that it was a superior medical facility, compared to similar hospitals North and South.

10

Death Rates: The Final Arbiter

The death rates of POWs, North and South, are a testament to how well or poorly those prisoners were treated, since the sum of those treatments affected not only their physical wellbeing, but also their mental state. They are the only unbiased (assuming they were correctly reported) quantitative measure of how well or poorly these men were treated. Mistreatment such as poor diet, starvation, physical torture, poor housing and/or clothing, etc., should reasonably lead to higher death rates. Discussions in this chapter deal with how to measure death rates, death rates at various prison camps, especially Fort Delaware, and analysis of those death rates. There is also a section on why death rates at prison camps in general, even well run camps, may have been higher than for soldiers who were not prisoners.

Measurement of Death Rates

Currently, the most common method of measuring death rates for Civil War prison camps is to take the total number of prisoners who died there, and divide it by the total number of individuals who were incarcerated there and multiply by 100. This of course gives the percentage of those who died there. However, this method has two important weaknesses.

First, the exact number of individual prisoners who were held at a given prison is not known with accuracy. For example, the Fort Delaware Society's list of prisoners is about 39,000 "names" long, but it is thought that only about 32,000–33,000 men were held there throughout the war. Some errors are obvious, such as a single letter for a last name, or a misspelling of a prisoner's name that is counted twice. However, others are more difficult to detect, for instance, prisoners that changed their names once or more while at the prison.[1] Differences such as these clearly would make a difference in a reported death rate.

The second weakness is more subtle. Even if the exact number of individuals held in a prison was known, it does not take into account how long those individuals were held at that prison. It counts a man held for two years the same as a man who was at a particular prison for a few days before being exchanged or transferred to another camp. The Army Medical Department recognized this and in the Medical and Surgical History gave sickness or mortality rates as annual per thousand of strength.[2] Under this system if the mortality rate is 100 annually per 1000 average annual strength, the annual mortality rate as a percentage would be 10 percent. To do this calculation the compilers of the Medical and Surgical History would calculate the average number of men involved over a year and do the calculation on that. If the period involved was less than or greater than a year, the result would be adjusted accordingly.

A variation of this Medical and Surgical History system is used in this book. A general form of the Death Rate (DR), it is calculated using the formula

$$DR = [(\text{number of deaths per period})/(\text{number of prisoner months})] \times 100 \quad (1)$$

In equation (1) the number of prisoner months are those in the period the number of deaths are taken from. Thus if there were 1000 deaths in a 12-month period, and the (average) number of prisoners was 10,000, the Death Rate would be 10 per 12-month period (year). This may also be expressed as a percentage of 10 percent of the prisoners dying during that 12-month period. For this form of Death Rate the time period (length) should be specified.

Herein, however, Death Rates are often calculated on a monthly basis (abbreviated DRM) using the formula:

$$DRM = [(\text{number of deaths in month})/(\text{number of prisoners that month})] \times 100 \quad (2)$$

Usually herein the number of prisoners that month is usually taken arbitrarily as the number of prisoners present at the end of the month. This can lead to some anomalies; for example, if the number of prisoners increases markedly through the month the DRM will be artificially low, and vice versa if the number of prisoners decreases markedly. However, these anomalies will average out over time. The data on the number of prisoners at the end of each month and how many died each month are known with much greater certainty.

The DRM can also be expressed as a percentage, and for any given month it is the percentage of prisoners present (at the end of the month) who died that month. It can also be converted to "annual rates of death per 1000 strength," the commonly used metric in the Medical and Surgical History, by multiplying the DRM by 120.

Overall Death Rates

Using the calculations described above, one can calculate the DRMs for Fort Delaware, and any prison camp or group of prison camps. Table 10-1 gives the data for various Union prison camps from which such calculations may be done.[3] Table 10-1 does not include convicts, who were still considered Union soldiers.

There now follows a series of tables and a graph, which will be further analyzed and discussed.

Using the data in Table 10-1, one can calculate the DRM for Fort Delaware and all Union prison camps (including Fort Delaware), and this is shown in Table 10-2 and graphically in Graph 10-1.

Table 10-1. Data for

Prison	Alton, IL				Camp Chase				Camp Douglas				Camp Morton				Elmira, NY			
End of	A	B	C	D	A	B	C	D	A	B	C	D	A	B	C	D	A	B	C	D
Jun-62	638	14	63	0	1430	7	29	550	7847	146	589	0	4018	21	120	0				
Jul-62	730	18	41	0	1669	4	22	605	7653	117	558	0	4190	26	103	0				
Aug-62	1256	9	158	0	861	5	29	699	7335	5	1	0	103	3	0	0				
Sep-62	850	22	204	0	701	6	37	738												
Oct-62	981	41	56	0	811	6	30	603												
Nov-62	535	35	126	0	442	3	49	28												
Dec-62	645	89	364	0	293	2	83	279												
Jan-63	1294	132	348	0	732	11	61	200	0	51	623	0								
Feb-63	1309	68	43	0	997	8	22	90												
Mar-63	123	15	41	132	534	3	30	117	332	33	0	0								
Apr-63	458	13	82	190	434	6	23	174	339	42	38	0								
May-63	1351	27	58	215	562	14	22	200	52	1	17	0								
Jun-63	402	24	82	231	380	9	17	159	49	1	18	0	111	16	39	3				
Jul-63	1292	38	222	190	2386	19	34	57	47	3	50	0	1252	26	98	13				
Aug-63	1106	75	120	202	1213	21	39	124	3196	17	102	0	1550	23	111	24				
Sep-63	1156	35	130	210	2073	26	31	167	5112	80	252	0	1487	36	261	37				
Oct-63	1428	37	134	210	2152	19	25	157	5973	100	207	4	2448	68	328	29				
Nov-63	1539	70	145	201	2585	14	29	123	5871	57	218	5	3075	91	244	33				
Dec-63	1577	84	300	187	2763	15	60	123	5661	53	231	1	3273	104	251	33				
Jan-64	1547	54	102	165	1968	18	74	112	5569	54	236	4	3158	69	326	32				
Feb-64	1064	51	72	136	1128	8	64	96	5517	66	259	1	3121	49	271	29				
Mar-64	1010	15	45	131	811	20	42	106	5460	50	254	1	2570	19	235	26				
Apr-64	647	6	59	183	1156	26	42	113	5379	54	256	1	2600	17	248	40				
May-64	1274	13	70	197	1501	10	45	134	5277	35	176	1	3186	34	324	38				
Jun-64	1188	13	68	200	1640	10	41	130	5234	49	245	0	4431	81	350	35		11	177	48
Jul-64	1245	8	55	206	1881	36	65	156	6748	98	288	0	4906	91	341	33	4411	115	394	47
Aug-64	764	9	96	228	4377	46	160	145	7554	123	310	0	4839	33	293	32	9480	385	563	47
Sep-64	884	9	75	235	5140	113	221	153	7420	109	362	0	4778	21	217	31	9082	276	640	46
Oct-64	942	40	173	246	5448	146	257	138	7399	217	505	4	4747	18	205	29	7878	207	666	78
Nov-64					5410	153	270	131	8741	323	407	7	4678	53	354	26	8027	269	758	75
Dec-64	1305	122	172	286	5289	293	535	130	11702	308	511	7	4737	117	355	24	8100	285	1015	69
Jan-65	1721	89	187	265	9045	499	495	121	11239	243	401	5	4199	133	272	19	8295	426	1398	71
Feb-65	899	45	161	307	7290	309	384	116	9266	147	230	4	2866	70	218	6	7046	491	823	56
Mar-65	916	6	104	270	4989	132	376	52	7165	86	249	2	1408	10	190	2	5054	267	647	35
Apr-65	581	8	58	208	4995	80	307	51	6107	63	280	2	1343	10	46	16	4754	131	509	34
May-65	391	4	0	138	3353	45	48	40	4136	16	30	1	319	2	0	13	3610	54	218	34
Jun-65	62	0	0	50	48	2	0	1	30	4	0	0	7	0	0	0	1047	16	0	0

Table 10-2. DRMs for Fort Delaware

Month	Fort Delaware	All Union Prisons
Jul-63	3.02	3.08
Aug-63	1.88	1.65
Sep-63	3.71	2.50
Oct-63	5.81	2.64
Nov-63	5.22	2.12
Dec-63	2.91	2.15
Jan-64	2.82	2.22
Feb-64	1.58	2.26
Mar-64	2.38	1.97
Apr-64	1.30	1.19
May-64	1.01	0.89
Jun-64	0.82	0.91

Calculation of DRM

Prison	Fort Delaware				Johnson's Island				Point Outlook				Rock Island, IL			
End of	A	B	C	D	A	B	C	D	A	B	C	D	A	B	C	D
Jun-62	1260	20	0	0	1141	4	21	0								
Jul-62	355	13	0	0	1149	2	21	26								
Aug-62	68	7	0	59	1462	1	32	31								
Sep-62	2532	14	23	45	822	9	34	33								
Oct-62	84	0	0	24	893	12	42	98								
Nov-62	106	3	0	1	205	6	32	119								
Dec-62	5	0	2	0	260	4	42	105								
Jan-63	17	0	0	0	308	11	33	98								
Feb-63	36	0	0	0	347	3	5	90								
Mar-63	30	4	57	27	106	1	3	40								
Apr-63	46	5	0	33	59	2	0	38								
May-63	51	66	248	44	40	3	14	44								
Jun-63	3673	111	300	52	806	6	35	40								
Jul-63	8982	169	350	77	1668	0	46	39	136	5	19	0				
Aug-63	8822	327	400	111	1817	11	47	31	1819	14	50	0				
Sep-63	6490	377	625	49	2155	3	104	29	3909	33	150	0				
Oct-63	2987	156	600	54	2156	16	69	28	7110	119	886	8				
Nov-63	2822	82	596	51	2381	18	78	46	8867	158	660	12	0	94		
Dec-63	2765	78	419	48	2623	20	62	41	8384	138	534	18	5498	231	635	0
Jan-64	2655	42	439	44	2603	17	55	39	7739	128	539	27	7009	346	708	19
Feb-64	2600	62	567	43	2206	10	50	38	8147	82	582	103	7233	283	843	17
Mar-64	5712	74	723	39	2192	4	51	37	6146	43	469	150	6946	141	469	17
Apr-64	6149	62	603	99	2088	4	55	36	5741	24	977	208	6679	78	441	16
May-64	8126	67	638	111	2134	1	62	34	12027	105	1400	252	6947	102	383	27
Jun-64	9174	110	686	111	2309	1	59	33	14489	204	1194	256	8287	71	421	90
Jul-64	9095	88	548	73	2441	1	62	32	9993	211	1174	185	8398	114	506	24
Aug-64	8585	48	355	99	2556	5	54	32	7088	110	611	175	8273	70	449	24
Sep-64	7979	10	640	46	2663	2	51	30	7828	111	955	201	8181	52	612	23
Oct-64	7630	19	399	421	2621	26	64	48	10387	52	973	240	5826	41	575	26
Nov-64	7625	28	562	71	2747	9	43	29	10377	86	1046	240				
Dec-64	7622	55	641	86	3209	7	57	29	10588	161	545	237	6633	108	611	24
Jan-65	7732	60	468	92	3017	6	26	10	10704	223	776	288	6187	56	28	6
Feb-65	6842	93	637	105	2444	2	26	9	7595	175	580	301	5089	34	240	75
Mar-65	7676	106	528	73	1817	4	51	9	7835	203	185		2772	20	242	20
Apr-65	8261	60	544	70	2778	5	44	10	19786	324	1818	177	2664	7	106	20
May-65	7126	41	26	55	2587	0	0	6	17890	256	0	134	1110	12	2	12
Jun-65	109	3	0	14	119	0	0	4					2	0	0	0

and All Union Prison Camps

Month	Fort Delaware	All Union Prisons
Jul-64	1.20	1.18
Aug-64	0.97	1.55
Sep-64	0.56	1.55
Oct-64	0.13	1.30
Nov-64	0.25	1.45
Dec-64	0.37	1.93
Jan-65	0.72	2.46
Feb-65	0.78	2.79
Mar-65	1.36	2.77
Apr-65	1.38	2.10
May-65	0.73	1.34
Jun-65	0.58	1.06

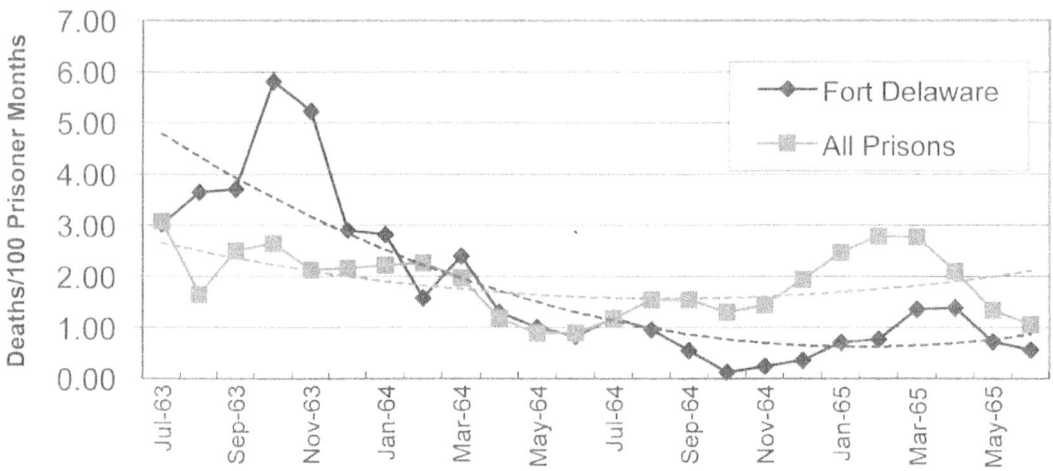

Graph 10-1. DRM for Fort Delaware and All Union Prison Camps

Similarly, the data in Table 10-3 show the overall DRM for each Union prison camp, as well as for Andersonville prison[4] for 6 months (the only time period for which accurate records are available), as well as the overall death rate for Union prison camps. The last column of Table 10-3 extrapolates the deaths that would have occurred if the death rate at Fort Delaware had been that listed in the middle column (DRM). Table 10-3 covers May 1863–June 1865.

Table 10-3. Overall Death Rates for Union Prisons

Prison	DRM	Deaths at Fort Delaware Extrapolated to this rate
Johnson's Island, OH	0.38	615
Point Lookout, MD	1.45	2347
Fort Delaware	1.52	2460
Camp Morton	1.56	2525
Camp Douglas	1.62	2622
Rock Island, IL	1.79	2897
Camp Chase	2.42	3916
Alton, IL	3.81	6166
Elmira, NY	3.82	6182
Union Average	1.825	2953
Andersonville (6 mos.)	6.61	10698

Using Army medical records as the basis,[5] by similar calculations, the data in Table 10-4 gives a slightly different result for overall death rates at various prison camps. The difference between Table 10-3 and 10-4 is the more limited time range considered for some of the prison camps, since complete medical records were not recorded and/or available for all camps in the time period covered by Table 10-3. However, as can be seen, the overall results are not significantly changed.

Table 10-4. Overall Death Rates for Union Prisons from Medical Records

Prison	Prisoner Months	Deaths	Overall DRM	Months
Johnson's Island, OH	52850	161	0.30	25

Prison	Prisoner Months	Deaths	Overall DRM	Months
Fort Delaware, DE	147338	2218	1.51	23
Rock Island, IL	102510	1604	1.56	17
Camp Morton, IN	71625	1187	1.66	25
Point Lookout, MD	211420	3704	1.75	22
Camp Douglas, IL	219801	4009	1.82	41
Camp Chase, OH	60690	1771	2.92	17
Elmira, NY	79092	2931	3.71	12
Alton, IL	34272	1475	4.30	34

In the original table from which Table 10-4 is taken, there is a typographical error in the number of deaths for Fort Delaware. The number for Elmira is repeated in the original table, and the correct number is 2218, which is the number obtained from the addition of the two following rows.

Turning to Table 10-2 and Graph 10-1, it is obvious that for July and August 1863 Fort Delaware was at about the Union average. However, for September through November of 1863, the DRM for Fort Delaware is horrendous, approaching the levels found at Andersonville. A bit of it can be explained by the fact that POW numbers were dropping rapidly those months, which as explained above will give artificially high DRMs. If we use the Commissary records to calculate the average number of men per day in those months, we can recalculate the DRM for Fort Delaware.[6] This is shown in Table 10-5 and Graph 10-2. The DRM numbers for all Union prison camps are also included. They are the same as shown in Table 10-2 and Graph 10-1.

Table 10-5. Corrected DRMs of All Union Prisons and Fort Delaware

Month	Fort Delaware		All Union Prisons
	Avg. No. Prisoners	DRM	DRM
Jul-63	8190	2.06	3.08
Aug-63	8950	3.65	1.65
Sep-63	8354	4.51	2.50
Oct-63	5175	3.01	2.64
Nov-63	3031	2.71	2.12
Dec-63	2943	2.65	2.15
Jan-64	2823	1.49	2.22
Feb-64	2814	2.20	2.26
Mar-64	5377	1.38	1.97
Apr-64	6129	1.01	1.19
May-64	7464	0.90	0.89
Jun-64	8394	1.31	0.91
Jul-64	9193	0.96	1.18
Aug-64	9018	0.53	1.55
Sep-64	8531	0.12	1.55
Oct-64	8189	0.23	1.30
Nov-64	7378	0.38	1.45
Dec-64	7621	0.72	1.93
Jan-65	7938	0.76	2.46
Feb-65	7875	1.18	2.79
Mar-65	7442	1.42	2.77
Apr-65	8091	0.74	2.10
May-65	7601	0.54	1.34
Jun-65	4129	0.07	1.06

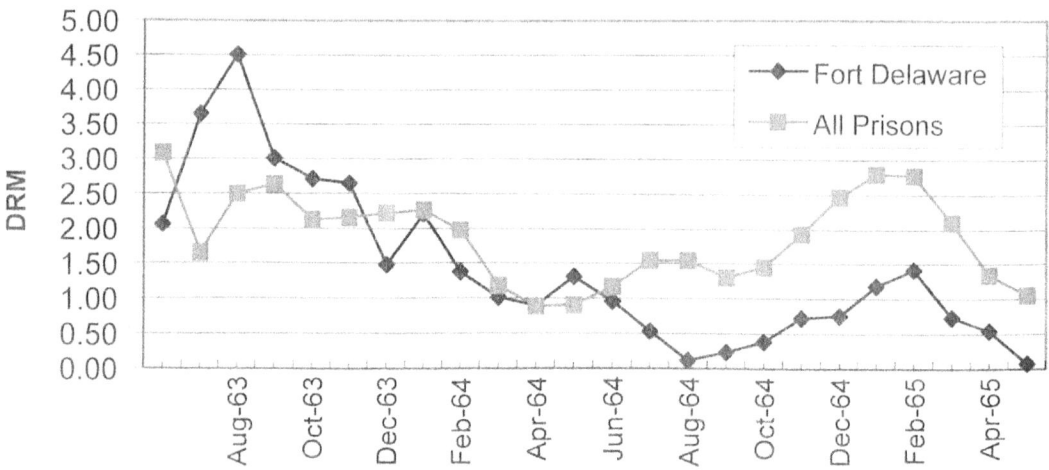

Graph 10-2. Corrected DRMs of All Union Prisons and Fort Delaware

The corrected DRMs from Fort Delaware differ mainly in being lower numerically for the late summer and fall of 1863, but for this period they are still very high. Later in this chapter we will discuss this further. From this peak in the late summer of 1863 the DRM at Fort Delaware decreases rather regularly, until in September 1864 the DRM is 0.12. This is quite remarkable when it is realized that the average DRM for the Union Army over the course of the Civil War is about 0.45.[7] In fact, it stays about 0.5 or less for four months in late summer and early fall of 1864.

In modern terms this is still a horrendous death rate, but we must put it in perspective. During the Civil War the overall strength of the Union Army (at least those present, for there were a lot of deserters) was roughly 600,000, about the strength of the active U.S. military in 2012. If the DRM is 0.5, it means 36,000 men would die of disease over the course of a year. Today that would be totally unacceptable, and is far more than the total battle deaths in the recent Iraq and Afghanistan wars. However, in the mid-nineteenth century this was considered fairly good for armies.[8]

After the late summer–fall 1864 the DRM starts rising again, peaks at about 1.5, and starts falling again after March 1865. These trends counter a commonly held view that with the reduction in POW rations in April–May 1864, and other "retaliations" for the perceived mistreatment of Union POWs by the Confederacy, conditions at prison camps in the North worsened considerably.

However, death rates at Fort Delaware and the whole Union prison camp system actually were down in the summer and fall of 1864, and while the Union prison camp system death rate as a whole was about the same as the previous winter, Fort Delaware's death rate was actually lower. We can test statistically how likely these lower death rates are for Fort Delaware by using the Student paired t-test, a standard statistical calculation.[9] We take the period July through December 1863 and compare it month by month with its corresponding month in the period July through December 1864, and do the same for the periods January through May 1864, and January through May 1865, using the DRMs for Fort Delaware given in Table 10-2. For Fort Delaware, for the period July through December 1863 and 1864, there is (statistically) more than a 99 percent chance that the DRMs for 1864 were lower than 1863's, while for the periods January through

May 1864 and 1865, there is greater than a 90 percent chance that the death rates were lower in 1865 than 1864. Similarly, for all Union prison camps, for the periods July through December 1863 and 1864 there is more than a 97 percent chance that the DRMs for 1864 were lower than in 1863. For all Union prison camps for the periods January 1864 through May 1864 and 1865, there is more than a 96 percent chance that in those months in 1865 the DRM was lower than in 1864. This result is not substantially changed if the camp at Elmira, New York, which started up in July 1864, is excluded. If one expects that the death rate would go up with prisoner mistreatment (retaliation), then that did not occur at Fort Delaware, which nominally was to serve the same rations as other prison camps. This may have been because rations served to the POWs at Fort Delaware were adequate as regards caloric content, and may have actually been somewhat more nutritious than Union soldier rations at least for a time (see Chapter 4). However, this so-called retaliation could have been a factor in the DRMs of the overall Northern prison camp system from late 1864 through early 1865.

Comparison of the overall death rates at Fort Delaware compared with other Union prison camps and Andersonville (Tables 10-3 and 10-4) shows that Fort Delaware has the second or third lowest DRM of any of the larger Union prison camps, and much lower than Andersonville. The only Union prison camp with a much lower death rate is Johnson's Island, which housed only Confederate officers (more about officer and enlisted POW death rates below).

Fort Delaware has sometimes been referred to as "The Andersonville of the North," presumably because of the supposed high death rate at Fort Delaware.[10] However, apparently other Union prison camps were also called that at times. Nevertheless, the above data clearly indicate that the death rate at Fort Delaware was actually lower than almost all other prison camps north or (possibly) south. The data also surprisingly show that the death rate at Fort Delaware actually decreased from late–1863 until the end of the war. Most books on prison camps at least imply or explicitly state that conditions at Union prison camps got progressively worse during this time, especially with the northern public anger over what was seen as mistreatment of Union soldier in Confederate prison camps, especially Andersonville. At Fort Delaware the exact opposite seems to have happened.

Finally, one aspect that does not directly involve Fort Delaware: The pervasive view is that Elmira, New York was by far the worst Union prison camp, at least in number of deaths. However, Tables 10-3 and 10-4 indicate that Alton, Illinois was just as bad or worse as Elmira as far as overall DRMs are concerned. Elmira had more deaths over a shorter period, but Alton was operated for a much longer time but housed fewer prisoners than Elmira, so that even though its death rate was very high, the absolute number of prisoners that died there was lower.

What Diseases Killed Prisoners?

Although the few deaths by shooting of prisoners at Fort Delaware have been well publicized, they actually amount to a very tiny percentage of the total. There are 7 deaths attributed to gunshot wounds, although it is unclear whether the shootings were on Pea Patch Island or these POWs had been wounded before they got to the island. At least some of them were shot on the island. There were also three POWs who died of drowning while trying to escape. This would not include men who were shot in the water while trying to escape but whose bodies were not recovered.

The vast majority of deaths were due to disease, and Table 10-6 lists these diseases.[11] Note that causes of death were not recorded consistently in the first half of September 1863, so these numbers are probably understated. Except for those explicitly stated, diseases causing less than 20 deaths are listed under "Miscellaneous."

Table 10-6. Diseases Causing Prisoner Deaths

Disease	Number	% of Total
Diarrhea and Dysentery	526	27.6
Inflammation of the Lungs	343	18.0
Smallpox	330	17.3
Malaria	139	7.3
Typhoid fever	133	7.0
Miscellaneous	122	6.4
Scurvy	90	4.7
Eryplesias	53	2.8
Measles	52	2.7
Bronchitis (all)	28	1.5
Rheumatism (all)	20	1.0
Inflammation of Brain	19	1.0
Dropsey	18	0.9
Inflammation of Bowels	17	0.9
Consumption	9	0.5
Catarrh	7	0.4
Total	1906	

A pleasant surprise in Table 10-6 is the low death rate from consumption (tuberculosis). However, for modern readers the number of deaths from Eryplesias (a bacterial skin infection) and measles may come as a surprise.

Of the 1906 known causes of death, not surprisingly, diarrhea and dysentery (D&D), combined are by far the most common cause of death. This includes acute and chronic diarrhea and dysentery, as well as those cases listed simply as diarrhea or dysentery. In most instances during the Civil War, these conditions were the leading cause of death in both armies. Graph 10-3 shows the DRMs for D&D at Fort Delaware.

The trends shown generally follow the overall DRMs for Fort Delaware shown in Graph 10-1. They are very high in the fall of 1863, perhaps indicating poor sanitation and/or that the POWs were in an especially weakened state. The numbers for late fall–early winter 1864–65 are also extraordinary low. In Chapter 9 it was stated the D&D decreased during the cooler months, and this is reflected in the DRMs during this period.

The second leading cause of death was "Inflammation of the Lungs," known then and today as pneumonia. Graph 10-4 shows the DRMs for this disease at Fort Delaware.

It is interesting that the peak DRMs for the fall–winter of 1864–65 do not coincide with the very high death rates in the fall of 1864, but are later. This seems to be a later winter to early spring disease, in the 1863–64 and 1864–65 periods, although the data are somewhat limited. Nevertheless, it was a very significant cause of death during those late winter–early spring periods.

Smallpox was a feared disease at that time, and that fear was well founded since it was the third leading cause of death at Fort Delaware. Its DRMs are shown in Graph 10-5.

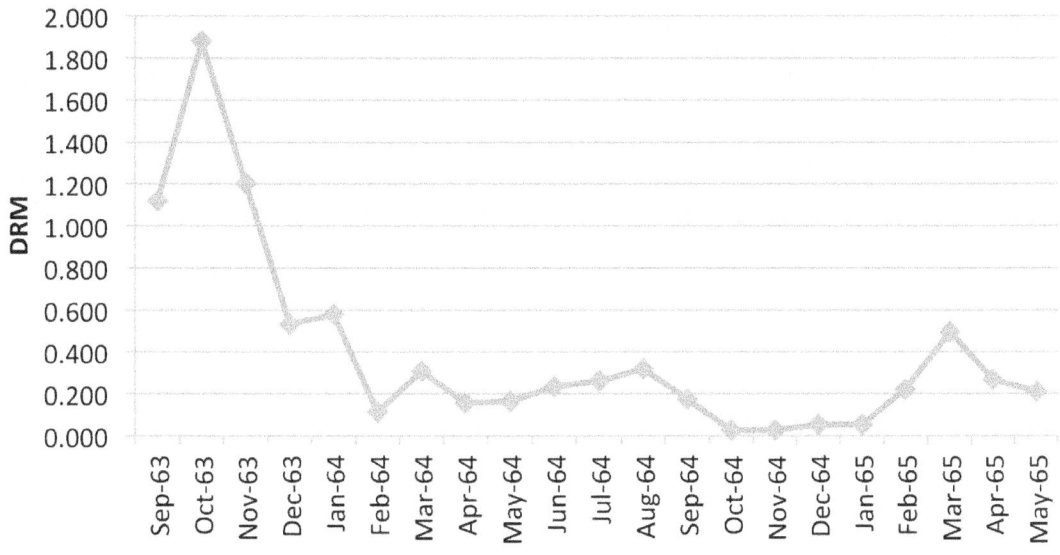

Graph 10-3. DRMs for Diarrhea and Dysentery

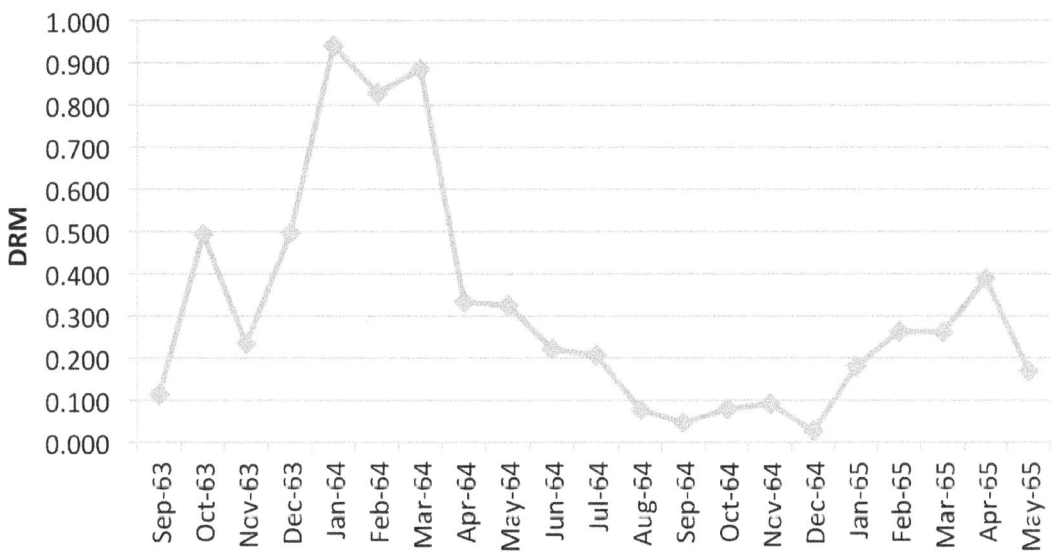

Graph 10-4. DRMs for Pneumonia

The DRMs for initial outbreak in the fall of 1863 peaked rapidly and declined relatively rapidly. This was almost certainly due, at least in part, to the vaccination program initiated on the island. There were three smaller outbreaks until the end of the war, likely resulting from new cases being introduced from the outside, and many of the newer POWs not being vaccinated against the disease. By comparison to the initial outbreak, these were relatively minor (but of course tragic for those who died and their families).

The fourth leading cause of death at Fort Delaware was malaria, and the DRMs for this disease are shown in Graph 10-6.

These relatively high DRMs are not surprising, since most of the island was below

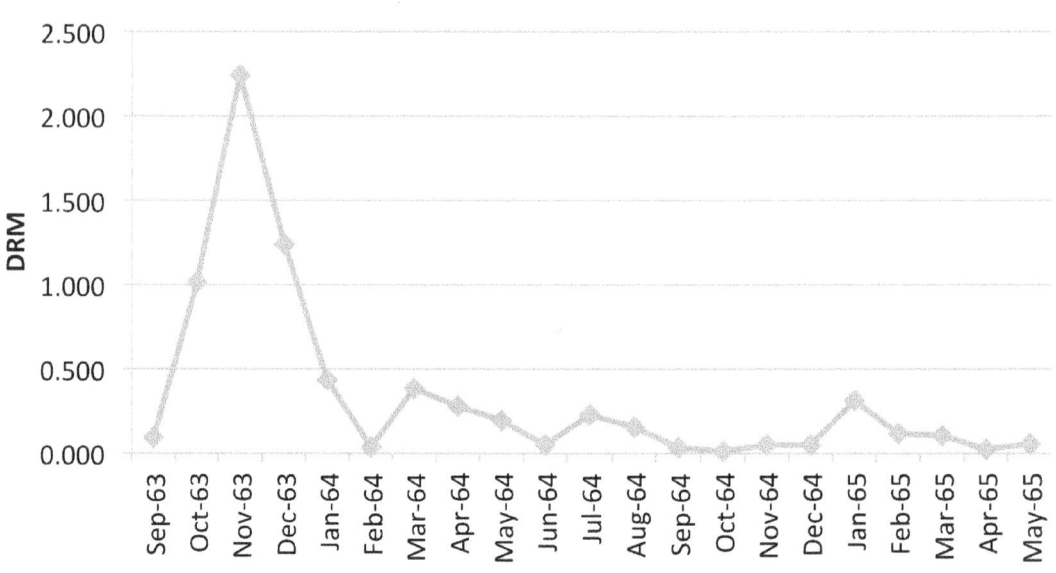

Graph 10-5. DRMs for Smallpox

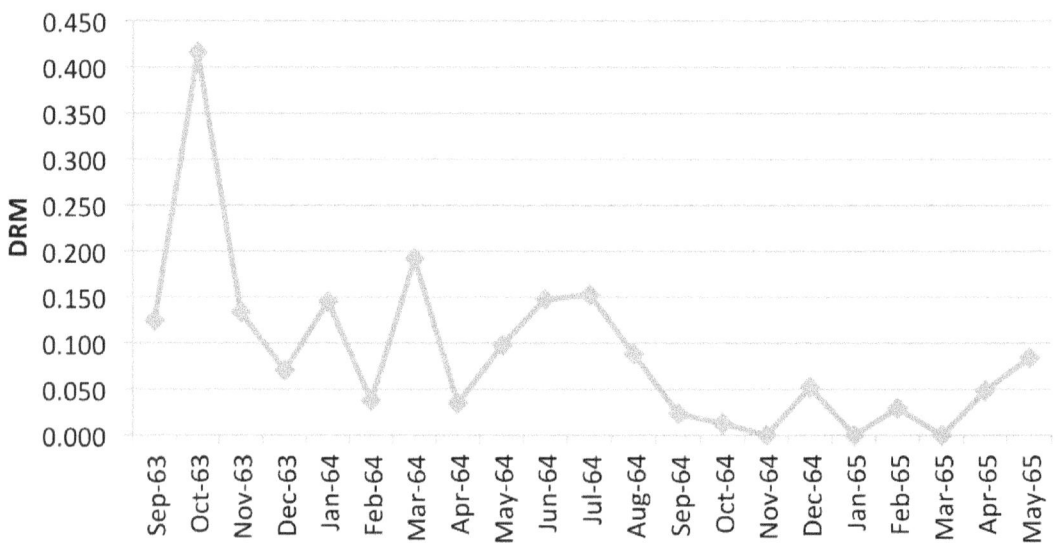

Graph 10-6. DRMs for Malaria

the high tide level, and there were permanent channels inside the seawalls. There were many remarks about the interior getting very muddy, especially after a rainy period, and there were boardwalks erected between many facilities so people's boots or shoes would not get excessively muddy when walking around the island. Medical Inspector A.M. Clark reported in part on his inspection of November 13, 1863[12]: "I have to report that in my opinion this post is an utterly unfit location for a prison, much more for a hospital. Lying so low, its level being some six feet below high tide, it is impossible to properly drain it or to prevent its surface being constantly marshy and wet. The island is traversed by ditches connecting with the main ditch encircling the island, and with the moat around the fort, and intended to be constantly full of water, changing with the tide. The moat is in process of repair, and during this the water is partially shut off, rendering the ditches partially dry. From the stagnant mud and partially stagnant water in these a constant, and in some cases a most offensive, effluvia is constantly given off, rendering the atmosphere in a high degree unhealthy. Some of these ditches run directly underneath the barracks. The influence of such an atmosphere on a large number of men congregated together, and whose vital powers are depressed, as those of prisoners naturally are, cannot but be most injurious." Although most physicians, apparently including Dr. Clark, believed in the miasmatic theory of disease, the conditions he describes are very good for mosquito breeding, and hence for the spread of malaria. Since mosquitos breed mostly in warm weather, from mid–1864 on the highest DRMs for malaria were in warmer weather. It is possible, however, that some POWs actually contracted the disease before they came to Fort Delaware, but it is impossible to determine from the records what proportion of men came to the island already having the disease.

Typhoid was another dreaded communicable disease, and it was the fifth leading cause of death for the POWs. Its DRMs are shown in Graph 10-7.

As can be seen from Graph 10-7, this disease was a serious cause of fatalities in late 1863, but by mid–1864 was removed as a serious cause of death. Typhoid fever is caused by consuming food, drink, or water contaminated with *S. typhi*.[13] The fact that it was a relatively unimportant cause of death in late 1864 and 1865 may indicate that sanitary conditions at Fort Delaware, while perhaps not good by modern standards, had improved greatly and perhaps by Civil War standards were good.

Finally, the sixth leading cause of death was scurvy, and its DRMs are shown in Graph 10-8.

The DRMs for scurvy were high in the fall of 1863, but decreased thereafter, and even got to 0.0 for several months in the fall of 1864. The increase in the summer of 1864 and the spring of 1865 may be due to an influx of "new" POWs who were already suffering from scurvy. However, especially in the spring of 1865, it could be due to a worse than

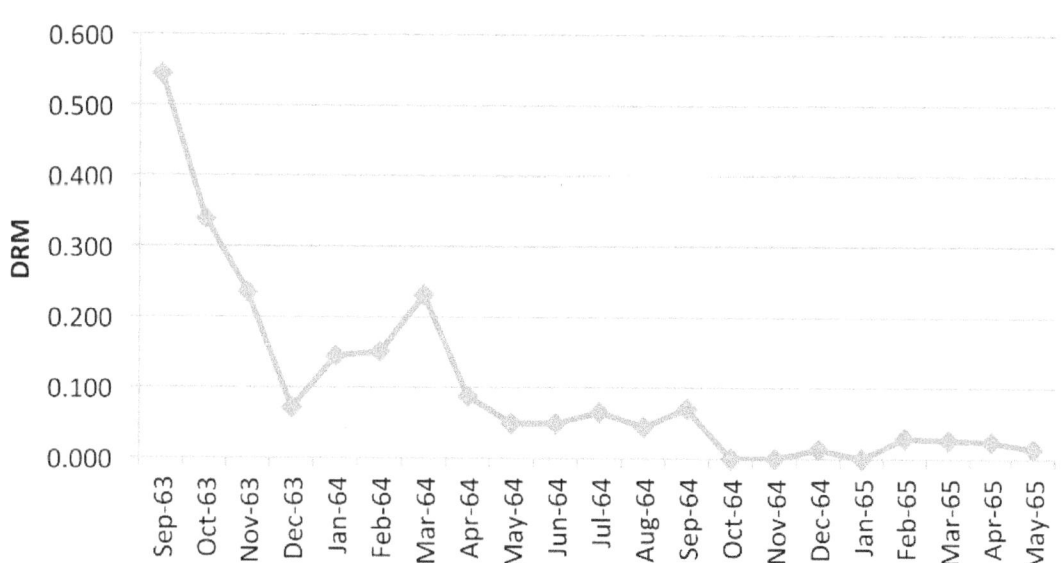

Graph 10-7. DRMs for Typhoid Fever

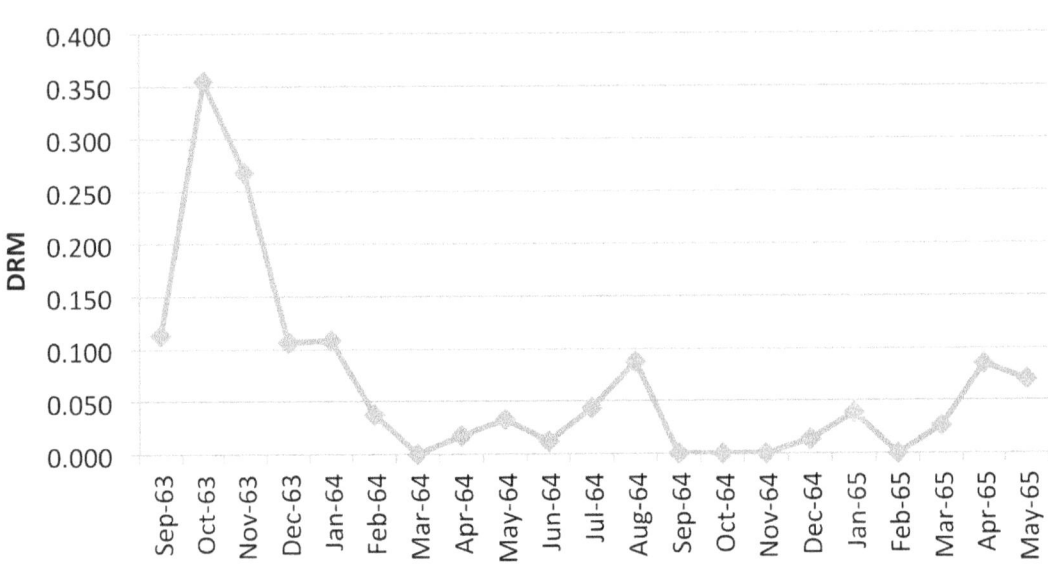

Graph 10-8. DRMs for Scurvy

usual lack of fruits and vegetables in the diet. Union Private Hamilton reported in his diary on 4/3/65 that Union soldiers were suffering from scurvy due to a lack of fruits and vegetables.

POW Officers vs. Enlisted Men

Looking at Table 10-3, one is immediately struck by the much lower overall DRM for Johnson's Island, 0.30, than any of the other Union prison camps, or the overall DRM of Union prison camps, 1.825. While the camps differed in many aspects, such as topography, efficiency of the camp administration, type of housing, etc., Johnson's Island was the only camp that housed only officers, and became a prison camp only after careful planning and construction. Did the fact that it housed only officer POWs account, at least in part, for its low overall DRM?

To help determine this, the overall DRMs for officer and enlisted POWs for the period June 1864 through to May 1865 were calculated using the data in Table 10-1 and the number of officer POWs present at the end of each month recorded in the POW Morning Reports.[14] The reason this period starts in June 1864 is that there were very few officer POWs before then. The overall DRM for this period for all prisoners was 0.75, the DRM for enlisted men 0.82, and the DRM for officers was 0.36. Thus the DRM for officers was less than half that for enlisted men. This overall DRM for officers is almost the same as the overall DRM at Johnson's Island, 0.38 (Table 10-3), and shows that officers had significantly lower DRMs than enlisted men.

Why this disparity between officer and enlisted death rates at Fort Delaware? Nominally at least, as far as can be determined, the prison conditions for officers and enlisted men were similar, such as the same rations, water supply, similar barracks, medical care, etc. The difference may lie in the outside help these two groups received. As noted in Chapter 8, per capita, officers got more money and packages containing clothing and perhaps other items than enlisted men. This probably happened because officers were on average wealthier and/or because of social connections had access to more outside resources, especially resources in the North. Money was an especially valuable resource since it would allow the recipient to buy supplies of various sorts, such as food and/or clothing from the sutler. For example, such a prisoner could supplement his food with items that provided nutrients that were absent or deficient in the official ration. It is also noted in Chapter 8 that "extra" food sent to or purchased by officers was often shared with other officers, so that the effect of these outside sources of help was magnified beyond the officer actually receiving the help.

Another possible reason officers had lower DRMs was that their condition upon arrival at Fort Delaware was on average better than that of the average arriving enlisted man. Although a bit snobbish, the average officer was from a higher social class than the average enlisted man, and may have had better sanitary habits. All of these reasons, or a combination of them, may or may not account, in whole or in part, for the lower DRMs of officers. Whatever the reason(s), the fact remains that the DRMs for officers were lower than those for enlisted men.

As an aside, one can contemplate about whether the (in)famous "Immortal 600" based what happened on their return to Fort Delaware in March 1865. On 8/8/64 the CGP sent a letter[15] to General Schoepf ordering him to prepare to transfer 600 Confederate officers to Hilton Head, South Carolina, to be held under fire of Confederate guns in retaliation for the Confederacy doing a similar thing to Union officers POWs in Charleston, South Carolina, which was under fire from Union artillery. The CGP also furnished a roll of officers to be sent. The officers were informed of this on 8/12, according to several diaries, and again according to several diaries these 600 officers left for Charleston on 8/20. Many of those sent were hopeful that they would be exchanged, as had an earlier group of 50 officers.

As it turned out, these officers were not exchanged and were held under fire, in what were described as very bad conditions, until March 1865. The story of the "Immortal 600" has been used for generations as an example of the bad treatment of Confederate prisoners by the Union. Are there any objective facts (not written by former prisoners, especially in postwar accounts) that support very bad treatment?

In March 1865 these officers were sent back to Fort Delaware, where they arrived on March 12th (several diaries). One returned prisoner, Mauck, one of the "600," wrote in his dairy on March 12th that "all seemed much relieved although in a Northern prison." Thus those coming back to Fort Delaware seemed relieved to be there.

An interesting thing happens to the number of officer deaths for the months of March and April. Although the median number of officer deaths per month for the period June 1864 to May 1865 was 4, in March 1865 it was 15 and in April 1865 it was 7. According to the Morning Reports of Prisoners for March 1865, the number of sick officers from March 10th through 19th was 46–53, and on March 20th jumped to 148, and decreased slowly after that through the remainder of March and April. Many of the officers' diaries for the middle of March 1865 note how sickly and skinny the officers returning from Charleston (Hilton Head) were, and how many of them were suffering from scurvy. There is therefore a strong possibility that the great increase in officers reported sick and in officers' deaths in March and April 1865 were due to the return of (most of) the "Immortal 600."

It would thus appear that the tales of the generally poor treatment of these POWs in South Carolina were true, although any specific incident described should be further checked.

Why Were Prison Camp Death Rates So High?

In the author's opinion there is no single smoking gun that one can point to and state with reasonable certainty that it was the cause of high death rates in prison camps, North and South. This to some greater or lesser extent is almost certainly dependent on the conditions at any given camp, but are there many general factors which may be common to a greater or lesser extent at most if not all camps, and to Fort Delaware in particular.

For Union prison camps we can use the overall DRM for the Union Army of about 0.45 as a baseline, in the sense that it was perhaps the best that medical science and the Army was capable of at that time. The overall DRM for all Union prison camps was about 4.1 times that, and Fort Delaware in particular was about 3.4 times that.

For Fort Delaware in particular, the evidence is fairly strong that in the first few months of holding large numbers of prisoners, conditions on the island were poor, with inadequate housing, medical care, sanitation, and most likely food preparation. This seems to have been improved, so that by November 1863 conditions were much better. The overall DRM for December 1863 through May 1865 was 0.93 (see Table 10-1 for data used to calculate this value). This is still about twice the "baseline" value of 0.45 for the Union Army.

Scurvy was found in every prison camp, North or South, and men had acute cases of scurvy, and it was sometimes fatal. Surgeons had realized that "Moreover, it seems probable that these rates greatly overestimate the extent of the pervasion of our white regiments by the scorbutic taint. It is usually considered that if one man in a command be affected with well-developed signs of scurvy many other men in that command, all of whom have been subject to the same dietary, will be more or less disabled, although they may not be borne on the sick-report."[16] Thus diagnosed cases of scurvy usually meant that many more men than those diagnosed probably had some subclinical level of the disease. Doctors also realized that scurvy was also often associated with other diseases, and this was sometimes described as a certain disease having a "scorbutic taint." Woodward discusses this in his book,[17] and specifically mentions diarrhea, dysentery, malaria, typhoid fever, typhus, chronic diarrhea, and pneumonia as sometimes having a scorbutic taint. Note that except for typhus, all of these diseases were quite deadly at Fort Delaware. Woodward states on p. 58 that "the scorbutic influence shows itself as a modifying agent in the diarrheas, dysenteries, and other camp diseases from which the army may suffer; and in truth large numbers of cases show only the preliminary symptoms of the early stages of scorbutic disease thus variously complicated, the further progress of the disorder being arrested by the resisting power of the individual, or by the opportune arrival of hygienic and therapeutic aid." Thus it was recognized that a complication of these diseases was scurvy, or vice versa. We now know that even subclinical scurvy can "increase the severity of other diseases and the mortality rate from treated gunshot wounds."[18]

It has been stated[19] that scurvy was more prevalent among Confederate soldiers and prisoners on both sides than in soldiers in the U.S. Army. Given the fact that Confederate POWs in Union prison camps got the same ration as Union soldiers before April 20, 1864, and the POWs got a ration that had the same amount or more Vitamin C in it than Union soldiers after that date, why did the prisoners suffer more from scurvy?

Union and Confederate soldiers had a number of ways of obtaining food containing vitamin C and other nutrients outside of their regular ration.[20] While in the field on campaign, troops could forage and/or buy (from the sutler or local farmers or grocers) all manner of food. If, however, the troops became bogged down and exhausted all the local sources of forage, they were then subject to getting scurvy. On Pea Patch Island the main sources of "forage" for the Union troops were "special rations" bought from the Company Fund by the company commander (see Hamilton 8/9/64), buying from the sutler, or buying meals or food while off the island while on leave or official duties (see Hamilton 9/9/63, 9/22/63, 9/25/63). The latter two required the Union soldier to have some money, which could have come from his pay. Thus the Union soldiers on Pea Patch Island did have access to foods which could alleviate nutritional deficiencies in the Army ration. Another factor for Union soldiers on Pea Patch Island is that many of them were only assigned to the island for relatively short periods, a week to 2 or 3 months. These were troops who were part of the infantry regiment assigned to help guard prisoners on the island. Usually scurvy does not develop in time periods this short.

POWs at any prison camp could not forage in the countryside, nor did they have company funds, nor, except in rare instances, did they leave the island for any reason. If they had friends or relatives nearby, perhaps they could have been sent food packages, but these would have frozen in cold weather, when they were most needed. In a few instances small amounts of fruits and vegetables were distributed by persons such as Miss Julia Jefferson (see Chapter 9). For most of the POWs the only practical way of obtaining food not in the ration was to buy it from the sutler. This of course required money, and this is one of the important reasons why outside help was so important. Money put into the POW "economy" was important not only to the men who received it, but it probably got spread around to some extent as these richer men used that money to buy services or items from the other prisoners (see Chapter 8). This may explain, at least in part, why officers had a lower DRM than enlisted men (see above).

It is thus the author's belief that one of the major reasons for higher death rates in prison camps in general, outside of any deliberate mistreatment or mistreatment due to administrative deficiencies, were dietary deficiencies in the Army (Union and Confederate) rations, especially lack of food containing vitamin C. As noted above there were probably other causes also, but their importance in any particular prison camp was dependent on many local factors, such as quality of prison camp administration, physical layout, local weather, etc. In a well-run, well-designed prison camp (for the period), the nutritional quality of the prisoner ration was most likely a major contributor to a higher than baseline DRM.

11

Life on Pea Patch Island

We do not have a great deal of information about the everyday life of Union enlisted men simply on the island because there is only one diary extant—that of Hamilton, a member of Independent Battery G, Pennsylvania Heavy Artillery—and several series of letters from a few more men.

Hamilton's diary[1] gives one the general impression that an enlisted man's life on the island was very dull and repetitive, interspersed with periods of more interesting and new events, mostly off the island. When on the island, his time mostly consisted of one of two types of activities, guard duty or off duty.

Although an infantry regiment, if present, was primarily responsible for prison guard duties, apparently, when infantrymen were available, the Fort garrison (artillerymen) would guard inside the fort, while the infantry would be the majority of guards, who were outside the fort.[2] Guard duty appears to have been mostly boring, except when sometimes, against orders,[3] Hamilton would occasionally talk to the prisoners if he was on a guard post where he could do so and not get caught (9/24/64). Typically Hamilton would be on guard duty from 0900 to 0930 (9:00 a.m. to 9:30 a.m.) the next day. Often when he came off guard duty, he would sleep and then perhaps spend some time cleaning his equipment. Guards had loaded weapons while on duty, and did not unload them by firing them, but by drawing the loads from them.[4]

Although Army Regulations stated that guards would usually be relieved after 2 hours on Post,[5] it is believed that at Fort Delaware they were relieved at 4 hour intervals. Although Hamilton does not state this specifically, on 1/2/64 he states that he stood guard for only 2 hour intervals, and on 2/18/64 he stood guard for only 1 hour intervals, as if these were unusual. In both instances the weather was very cold. Thus it is *believed* that guards were usually on duty for 4 hours and then relieved. Since they were part of the guard detail for about 24 hours, it is not known how many shifts they actually were on guard, but it seems that twice is likely. When not on post they were part of the relief guard, which could be called out in emergencies to help back up the guards which were on Post. How "pleasant" guard duty was, was highly weather dependent, and Hamilton reports many times on how the weather was quite pleasant and so the duty was fine, or at times with foul weather standing guard was awful; see Figure 18. Indeed one guard was apparently frozen to death on 1/24/65. When no or very little infantry was present to help guard the prisoners, the artillerymen appear to have been on Guard every other day (see 1/22/64 to 1/27/64, for instance).

Off guard duty, Hamilton mentions a variety of activities. He cleaned his equipment, slept, occasionally drilled (from the context it appeared this was company or battalion drill, not drilling on the artillery pieces), read, 'played ball" (7/5/64), and went out drinking (on the island) and sometimes got drunk. Hamilton spent a lot of time reading, since he was able to get books from the Post Library, which he mentions at least 6 times between 5/19/64 and 3/17/65. On 4/3/63 he was reading *Les Miserables,* which he enjoyed and finished on 4/9/63, on 4/27/63 was reading the Bible, on 10/3/63 *The Countess of Amheim* (an English novel), on 7/27/64 McCauley's *History of England,* which he finished on 9/18/64 and which he laments the author did not complete, on 12/6/64 reading *Brice Bridger,* on 12/20/64 was reading Bancroft's *History of the United States* which he finished on 1/17/65, a murder mystery on 2/28/65 (on a boat), a poetry book ("Moor's poems") on 3/17/65, *Harpers,* and *Police Gazette* on 6/23/65, and on many days various newspapers. In fact, when Hamilton had spare time on the island it appears he mostly did a lot of reading or "played" (cards?).

On the island there were some places he could go to relax. There was a beer shop (9/16/63), and an oyster saloon (1/25/65). Drunkenness was a problem on the island among the troops, and Hamilton reports he got drunk on 7/14/63, 8/21/63, and 9/1/63. He makes many other reports of officers and enlisted men being drunk, for example Schoepf was drunk on 5/12/63 (only report of his being drunk), and the officer of the guard, Bill Hall, was drunk as usual on 3/19/65. Hamilton also states, unsurprisingly, that drunkenness was the cause of many fights and disturbances.

Figure 18. Shower in the Night of 9/9/64, from the sketchbook of Pvt. Baldwin Coolidge, 6th MA VV. Apparently a man on guard duty (courtesy Delaware Historical Society).

It seems his best times, or perhaps his most interesting times, were when he got off the island, usually on furlough or as part of a guard escorting prisoners to another location. On 7/16/63 he had permission to go to Philadelphia, and arrived in Wilmington (Delaware) at 7 p.m. He then got a supper of 6 oysters and a griller, "went to a house or two," and then to the Music Hall. Then he took the cars (railroad) to Philadelphia, got a room and went to sleep. Next morning he got breakfast, then rode the street cars, saw several fine parks, went to Camden, and in the evening to the theater at Chestnut and

13th Streets, and then slept in a room in the United States Hotel. After breakfast the next morning, at noon he started by foot to New Castle. He was picked up, went to the Delaware House and had a good supper. Next morning he rose early and went back to the fort.

On 8/19/63 he had a brief excursion to New Jersey, where he stayed overnight in Salem at the Nelson House. Next morning after breakfast he returned to the Fort. He had a similar day on 9/9/63. On 8/28/63 he went to Wilmington by boat and had a 9 a.m. breakfast. There was a celebration because of the surrender of Forts Sumter (this was not true) and Wagner, and they called on the Ladies, first at Bradies, then at Gettys, Boyds, Ayers and Catlers[?], then went back to the Fort.

On 9/18/63 Hamilton was assigned to guard some prisoners being taken to Columbus, Ohio. They departed at 4 p.m. and left Delaware City at 8:30 p.m., after having a good time stealing and eating peaches. Next day in Philadelphia after standing guard from 3 to 5 a.m. he got breakfast and went to Independence Hall. They got on a westbound train, where he almost got into a fight with some Copperheads (southern sympathizers). On 9/20/63 they arrived at Pittsburgh at 1:30 a.m., and left the prisoners in charge of the provost marshal. After some sleep and breakfast, he saw many friends (Hamilton was from Pittsburgh). He got some champagne, cigars and tobacco and was back at the depot at 11 p.m., and headed west. After delivering the prisoners in Columbus, he took the cars for Pittsburgh at 4:40 p.m., arriving there at 3 a.m. and going to sleep. After awakening at 1 p.m. he got dinner and spent the evening with a friend[?], Davitts. The next day he went to East Liberty, arriving at 5 p.m. On 9/25/63 he got on the 2:30 p.m. train back to Pittsburgh and arrived at 4:30 p.m. He then went to Davitts' house again, had supper downtown and "John" gave him a box of cigars, 3 bottles of whiskey and some tobacco; he left Pittsburgh at 8:35 p.m. He got to Philadelphia at 1:30 p.m., had dinner at the Arch Street House, and took the boat for Fort Delaware, arriving at about 6 p.m.

There were other times off the island, such as 10/27/63 to Delaware City, 1/18/64 to 1/21/64 to Washington, D.C., 4/30/64 to Delaware City, and 7/1/64 to Wilmington. However, Hamilton's longest trip was to Charleston South Carolina, when he was a guard for the "Immortal 600" (600 prisoner officers being transported there as "hostages"). This trip lasted from 8/20/64 to 9/3/64. They left the island about 5 p.m. on 8/20/64 on the steamer *Crescent*. The trip appears to have been mostly routine, although Hamilton wished they had better food and water. They delivered their prisoners on 8/26/64 and immediately got on another boat, the *Truxton*, headed for New York. After stopping at Fort Monroe the *Truxton* went to Washington, D.C., and then continued on to New York, arriving there on 9/2/64. From there he went by train to Philadelphia, getting there sometime after 11 p.m. After having breakfast, and visiting the Navy Yard, he got on board the steamer *Major Reybold* going to the Fort, and arrived there at 6:30 p.m.

The detailed descriptions of these trips, and other trips, show that Hamilton, on his time off the island, whether on a furlough or on a trip guarding prisoners, when he had the time engaged in a variety of activities, such as getting meals (not restricted to the Army ration), "seeing the ladies," visiting places of interest (in Washington, D.C., visited the Capitol on 1/19/64), going to theaters and music halls, and visiting friends (in Pittsburgh). This presumably broke up some of the monotony while on the island.

The attitude of Union troops who were not permanently attached to the Fort towards being on the island seemed much different. On 8/27/64, Pvt. William I Fletcher of the 6th MA Veteran Volunteers, who had been there almost two weeks, noted the Post is usually quiet, that he will have guard duty every three days, and he found everything quite pleasant compared to their previous service in V. He states their barracks are very good, being 2 stories high and water tight with a large number of windows, the upper stories being for bunks and the lower for cooking and a mess room. The next day he notes in his letter that they have ice water in abundance, a nice little chapel, in which the men are welcome any time to play the small organ. The street on which the chapel stands is described as having a very neat appearance with two neat officer's cottages with flower and vegetable gardens, the other side being pasture for 4 or 5 cows. Sometimes the General's children are seen at play with 2 black goats pulling a wagon up and down the street. Fletcher also mentions that the officers of the Post "seem inclined to do the best they can for the men, who in turn are well satisfied with their officers." In a 9/15/64 letter Fletcher mentions one of their number has died of chronic diarrhea and many of the men are sick. On 9/17/64 he writes home that he and his bunk mate have rigged up their old tent cloths into a "tick" which they stuffed with straw to make an "elegant warm bed." Punishment of Union soldiers for minor offenses consisted of walking a beat near the barracks with a log on the shoulder, the amount of time being determined by the gravity of the offense (see Figure 11). He describes in a letter of 10/1/64 an inspection on 9/30/64, and in a letter of 10/3/64 described going to church the previous day (Sunday). He also states that the flies and mosquitoes are still troublesome, even in October. On 10/10/64 Fletcher reports it is getting colder, especially on guard. Fletcher made no complaints generally about his life on the island.

In the only letter we have written by Pvt. Charles N. Clark of the 6th MA VV, penned on 9/7/64, he seems quite satisfied with his life on the island, and he had been assigned to the prisoners' clothing room (see Figure 2, item 25). There all he had to do was to take charge of the clothing, and with 5 other men clean the lanterns used in the prisoners' quarters. He did have guard duty once in a while. In his letter he *seems* quite contented with his lot.

Pvt. William D. Lank of the 9th DE Volunteers writes on 10/26/64 that they are fixing up their quarters. He writes that he likes Fort Delaware very well so far, and has to go on guard duty every third day, but does not have to drill much. On 10/31/64 he states he doesn't mind guarding the rebels because "we have got such a nice place to live." Apparently his regiment had gone home and returned (to vote in the election?) shortly before he wrote a letter stating that their quarters had been torn up by the men who took their place, but they got it cleaned up. Through his last letter, of 1/18/65, Lank does not complain about the conditions at Fort Delaware, except to state he is looking forward to leaving and getting home.

The Union ration was invariable, and was cooked by men (who were untrained cooks) chosen from their unit for that duty. The monotony was relieved occasionally by special food bought using the company funds, such as Hamilton reporting on 6/11/64 that they had strawberries and cream for dinner, on 8/9/64 the Captain bought 25 baskets of peaches from the Company Fund, and had a large bushel of apples and peaches for dinner on 5/28/65. There were also sometimes holiday meals, for which the men *apparently* chipped in and/or which partially came from the Company fund. The two holidays celebrated in this way were Thanksgiving and Christmas. On Thanksgiving Day, 11/26/63, Hamilton's battery had a dinner of oysters, turkey, ciders, cranberry, butter and celery and their officers ate with them. On Christmas Day 1863 the men apparently celebrated by drinking beer, while on Christmas 1864 the men drank again but the next day on 12/26/64 had a good turkey dinner.

Except for Hamilton, there are no comments like the one he made on 12/22/64, "Thank Heaven only 8 months more to serve we feel bully over it." Union soldiers who were there only a few months *apparently* felt it was a good place to be stationed, while *perhaps* soldiers who were there a long time such as Hamilton felt almost " imprisoned" on the island. The routine of all the Union enlisted men was to be on guard duty every second or third day, keep their equipment and quarters clean, drill, pass inspections, etc., but this allowed for much free time. Diversions on the island were few, and so the men read, played cards, wrote and received letters, and sometimes got drunk.

Union Officers

We know very little about the everyday life of Union officers, since we are unaware of any diaries written by them. The only specific sources we have are two series of letters by two different Union surgeons, William M Eames, Assistant Surgeon of the 157th OH Infantry, and Washington George Nugent, an Assistant Surgeon in the island Medical Department.

Some officers of the permanent garrison lived in the Fort in Officers' quarters, and some lived in cottages or houses on the east side of the island.[6] At least some of these cottages or houses had flower and/or vegetable gardens.[7] Officers who were temporarily on the island, usually those attached to an infantry regiment, lived in officers' barracks outside the fort, except for occasionally one or two of the higher ranking officers who *may* have lived in the fort. These temporary officers *apparently* did not have their families with them, since there is no mention of their families. For these temporarily assigned officers, this was just another place where their regiment was stationed, although it was probably better than being in the field. As previously described, some officers ate at boarding houses on the island. Some surgeons lived in quarters near the hospital.

From general descriptions, especially those provided by Nugent, at least some of the permanently assigned officers lived with their families. Since officers had to supply their own food, they could have a variety of foods and *probably* some of them had cooks (who may also have carried out other chores, such as cleaning).

From Nugent's letters it is obvious that at least some of the garrison Union officers, and their wives where applicable, enjoyed an active social life on the island. This apparently was true of Nugent, even though his family was not living on the island. On 9/22/64, Nugent visits Miss Arrott (sister of another surgeon) and Mrs. Muhlenbrock (the engineer's wife), visits the Arrotts on 9/30/64, visited Mrs. Muhlenbrock on 10/14/64, reports that Mrs. DeHaven, Mrs. Woolsey and other ladies are meeting in a room next to his on 10/30/64, visited Mrs. Muhlenbrock again on 11/6/64, entertained by Lt. Lewis and Capt. Warren on 5/22/655, and reports also on that date he has frequently seen the Schoepfs, etc. Officers also could have visitors on the island, for example Nugent reports that on 9/19/64 Surgeon Stovall had 12 ladies and 4 gentlemen visit him on the island, the main problem being how they were going to feed these visitors.

Since officers were allowed to have their families present if they chose, events connected to normal family life also occurred. For example, on 10/4/64, Nugent reports Dr. Goddard's wife had a baby the previous day, and the mother and daughter, Marie Mary, were doing fine. On 10/20/64 Nugent attended to this baby, which had colic, Dr. Goddard being away at the time. On 12/2/64 he also reports the Muhlenbrock's daughter took ill with the croup and the parents were very worried.

Thus it would seem that most Union officers on the island, but especially those whose families were also present, led lives somewhat similar to how they lived in civilian life. While they were in the Army, and to some extent "stuck" on the island, their prerogatives and privileges as officers allowed them much more freedom in how they lived their lives, including choosing their own food, having their families with them, and having more freedom of movement on the island, than Union enlisted men. In some instances, officers who had been lower middle class or lower class economically before the war actually *may* have had a better standard of living in the Army.

Prisoners of War

We have much more information on how the prisoners lived thanks to about 20 surviving prisoner diaries, and some other miscellaneous sources.[8] Most of these diaries were written by officers, but for the most part it *appears* that officers and enlisted men were treated similarly, although a bit more deference may have been shown to officer prisoners.

The most sweeping single description of prison life was given in the diary of Lt. Col. John A. Gibson (see below). There may be pages missing and some words are illegible, but Gibson covers ordinary life in the prison, some of these details having been covered in earlier chapters.[9]

> The court yard is traversable [?] By walks & ditches the walks are about 4 feet wide and run all around three sides [?] front of the officers Barracks [?] one through the center and several leading from this to the center. The ditches all but one are about 6 feet wide by 3 feet deep the outer ditch is about 20 wide by 6 deep when the tide comes in these ditches fill up and empty again when the tide goes down. The Barracks are laid off in Divisions 40 or 50 feet long by 25 wide and 15 feet high constructed of frame work (planks laid?) up and down inside there are [?] in of bunks the first bunk only about 2 feet from the [g]round it is the coldest in winter [missing] next is about 4 feet above that fixed with uprights of [scan]tling 3 by 4 inches from [missing] [r]oof down and about 7 [missing] from the outer wall and two scantling of about the same size reaching from the outer wall to 3 uprights and inch planks nailed to the cross ties the next [missing] & top bunk is about 4 feet above the middle one and is the warmest in the cold weather There is one stove in each Division to heat and warm all hands but it is hardly sufficient in very cold weather although it has been very pleasant up to this time, (Nov. 29, 1864) There are cross pieces about 12 or 15 inches long nailed to the uprights to enable the men of the upper [illegible] to get up to roost. In front of the Barracks on the opposite side of the court yard there is a plank fence 12 feet high in three of the corners[?] there is a very large tank which furnish water for the Barracks they are filled up with rain In wet weather in dry weather the water is brought from Brandywine Creek in boats and pumped into the tanks by steam through leather hose in the left hand corner and on a line with the Barracks on that side is the dining room, about 80 feet long by 40 wide in which there are some 8 or 10 tables about a foot wide on which are placed the rations of the officers in the morning it is a little piece of bread and bacon or beef and in the evening [?] same quantity of bread and bacon [?] beef as the case may be & a pint [?] soup sometimes corn rice or bean [so]up & occasionally a potato or two. [?] rear of the Barracks on the left hand side is another yard in which is the sutlers shop &c there is a passage or gangway leading to this yard between the officers Barracks and the dining room which also leads to the back yard on the edge of the bay it is in this passage next to the back yard that the washing & cooking is done in the rear of this area is a pen called the galvanized into which all men applying to take the oath are place and left 12 months on probation and then if they are willing the oath is administered to them only 2 officers that I have heard of availed themselves of this [?] privilege. There are now some 100 of 150 in this pen they are treated about the same as the other prisoners that 3 times a day they have a great deal of work to do in the rear of our Barracks. in the Fort in the front is the privates Barracks

and between our Barracks there is a platform elevated about 6 or 8 feet from the ground on which is posted sentinels There is 2 sentinels inside of the court yard for the purpose I suppose of keeping everything straight inside. The officers & privates communicate occasionally by writing on a piece of paper and wrapping it around a rock and throwing it over into each other pen sometimes the sentries get hold of the letters and destroy them on the inside of the Barracks [the]re is a continual confusion a[l]most carried on there are shoemakers & carvers all the time at work those that do not work are engaged in talking playing cards chess and drafts. The first thing in the morning is a general rush for the stove to get breakfast the favorite dish is hash & coffee around the stove is a large rim and on that bricks or rocks are laid and on this the coffee & hash pots are set & soon nicely cooked and they are continually following who has a place not engaged. We also have a barber in our division. Have a bible class Law class & other studies. We have prayers every night have one or two preachers in our division We get papers nearly every d[ay] have mail every evening. Have a fight or 2 occasionally that tends to remove the monotony of every day life. Out in the yard when the weather permits there are tables of vantom[?] & Faro shooting marbles pro[?]ing & speculating on the war exchange &c. There is generally a grape comes in every day as the boys call it. What is a tale of some kind. There is a flag (the stars & stripes) hangs over the fort from sunup to sundown for all rebels to gase it and admire. At sun down there is a piece of artillery fired and the flag is lowered [?] [?] yanks that are guarding us are a very civil & generous cast of fellows. If a man has plenty of money he can do fine the Sutler is allowed to sell coffee sugar potatoes (sweet & Irish) cheese and everything of the kind great many men here are faring as well as they could anywhere have plenty of friends north. There is a hospital out side somewhere to which the sick are removed when they take sick.

(This is at the end of diary—probably written November or December 1864. Seems to be a continuation of material earlier) The divisions are lighted by a globe lamp hung to a wire in the center of the division an[d] is kept burning all night all other lights are put out at the sound of the Bugle which is precisely at 9 o'clock and if all of the private lights are not extinguish at once some of the Yanks will be after you as a general thing they have very little to say but some of them are very insolent and do what they can to put you to inconvenience There are a great many scoundrels in the Division it is nothing unusual for rations of bread coffee & meat to be stolen and very often rations are taken off the table I[?]went[?] with Division 34 & slept in Division 34 The divisions are [l]aid off in groups from 8 to 10 men each & numbered every man knows his place and goes to it. Every division has its chief who superintends the dining room making details appoints meetings draws soap vinegar & such things as are necessary & allowed. Capt. Berry 25th VA Regiment is the chief of our Division we have also a Post Master who goes to mail call every evening and gets the letters belonging to the Division. There is a hole in the North corner of the pen at which place the PM of each division goes and a Yankee sergt who calls over the names and the PM of each Division takes them and distributes [?] the different officers. [?] [?] Capt Springs is the P.M. of our Div[ision] we have also a money clerk who collects our money the Letters are all examiner in the Provost Marshalls office and if any man is fortunate enough to get money it is taken out of the letters and kept by the Yankees and an endorsement put on the letter so much deposition at such a date that envelope is handed to the money clerk who takes it out to money call which takes place every day or two. Who does not get the green backs but puts sutler checks which we can buy anything we want [?][?] money clerk [?] the sutler that he has [?] have been allowed [?] receive boxes of clothing by first getting a permit from the authorities here and sending it to the person whom you are to get the articles from They are boxed up and the permit posted on the box and you are allowed to receive nothing that is in the box except what is on the permit. Everything else will be confiscated and a Sergt will come in for you and you have to leave what you have on they will not let you have but one suit do not allow us to receive anything to eat but will let us receive anything that comes from Dixie They allow us to wri[te] as many letter as we want and receive as many on[?] we are not allowed to wri[te] but one side of a half sheet at a time but can receive as long a one as we please We have also an Adjt to our Division whose duty it is to act as secretary to all musterings and make them [?] as many detail to police the house which is 2 men and an officer of the day whose duty it is to sweep the house out. Twice a day and keep the Division bucket full of water The house is all the time wet great deal of spitting on the floor &c Sutler keeps open from 8 [unt]il 12 & from 1 until [?] sell things very high Coffee 1 dollar & 20 cents sugar 6 cents bread 10 cents [?] loaf small [?] [?] very light cheese 50 cents butter 1 dollar onions 23 cents a pound meal 10 cents a pound and every thing very high sausage for 40 cents per pound If a man has plenty of

money in this pen he can live finely we are allowed to get a paper every day of the Yankees own selection the Philadelphia Enquirer is dealt out to us daily now at 10 cents per paper we have inspection every Sabbath morning when we have to take down our clothes clear & scrub out our house The inspection is gene[rally] AA Genl of the island Geo Ahl Gen Schoeff comm[?] here.

Governance of POWs

The long passage above describes things related to many items covered in earlier chapters—rations, clothing, shelter (barracks), water and sanitation, and others—but it also gives details about daily life in the prison. For example, Gibson mentions Division chiefs. From other prisoner diaries we know that these chiefs (in the officers' barracks) were elected by the men of each division, as related by Handy 8/12/63 and 10/7/64; Gibson 10/2/64 and 3/31/64; and Park 2/21/65. Apparently chiefs were elected by the officers without regard to the Chief's rank, since those chiefs mentioned by name were lieutenants to colonels. A listing of chiefs in the officers' barracks in April 1865[10] indicated that of the 16 chiefs, 4 were lieutenants, 7 were captains, 2 were majors and 3 were colonels. By all accounts those elected were popular with the men in their division.

Cox reported on 7/26/64 that the chief was responsible to attend to the men's letters and Table, keep order in the Division, and to see that the rules are not violated. On 9/26/64 Handy reported that wood for cooking was very scarce, so some of the men had been taking wood from the boardwalks. This endangered the privilege of the men doing their own cooking, so the Chiefs of the barracks posted a sign demanding a stop to it or those responsible would "wear the barrels" (a form of punishment in which a man would be paraded around wearing a barrel with arm holes, and perhaps a sign such a "thief" or "idiot," a form of humiliation; see Figure 10). Handy also reported that the Christian Association asked the Chiefs to take votes in their divisions regarding regular evening prayers in each division, and reports on 10/11/64 that votes were held in all the (officers) divisions approving evening prayers. Chiefs were also involved in discipline and maintaining good order. On 1/11/65 Cox reports a fight between an officer POW and a Union Sergeant in the dining hall. Union Lt. Wolf, in charge of the officers' prison, ordered the Chief of the Division to make out written charges against the *Sargent* which Wolf would present to Schoepf personally. On 2/6/65 Park states the duties of the Chief are to keep a roll of prisoners, make all [working] details, look after the cleaning and sweeping of the room, report names of the sick, preserve order, preside over meetings, etc. On 4/24/65 PAMcMichael was appointed "director of public worship" by his Division Chief, Col. Hinton.

The more routine duties of the chiefs in the officer barracks were to make sure the POWs quarters were clean, the men got their mail and rations, etc. Thus on 6/11/64 Mauck reports that he is "on detail sweeping." On 7/26/64 Cox states that "the duty of the detail is to sweep room bring water and any thing else that may be required for the comfort of the members of the Division." There are no complaints noted in any of the officer diary writers about having to do these chores, as one *supposes* they knew these things were necessary and someone had to do them.

On 3/12/65, on his arrival on the island, Private Henry Robinson Berkeley noted that "Frank Kinckle was made a sgt of our company. His duties are to lead us into breakfast and dinner, to have barracks cleaned up every morning, the sick sent to the hospital, get our mail and to make a report every morning to Lt. Di[e]tz,[11] the officer in charge." He was apparently First Sgt. Frank A. Kinckle of Kirkpatrick's Battery, Berkeley's unit. This sounds very much like the duties of a Chief of Division for the officers. However, it is unclear whether he was appointed to this post by the Union administration or whether he was elected by the prisoners, as Chiefs were in the officers' barracks. Apparently Kinckle was still "sgt" on 4/22/65, since he was informed that the prisoners' mail would be distributed as before (Lincoln's assassination). On 6/8/65 Kinckle received a special release, according to Berkeley, who the next day reported it had been obtained by some of Kinckle's friends in Lynchburg, and apparently not because he was a division leader. Berkeley describes Kinckle as a very fine fellow, so *maybe* he was elected. There are no other mentions of division leaders in the enlisted men's barracks.

Thus it seems that within each of the Divisions in the POW camp, the men were, to some extent, self-governing. Their leaders (Chiefs) were at least in the officers' quarters elected by the men, and in the enlisted men's quarters either appointed by the camp administration or elected by the men. Routine activities such as cleaning the barracks, getting and distributing the mail, taking roll, keeping order, etc., were carried out by these barracks leaders who were themselves prisoners. These leaders, to some extent at least, may have also participated in the punishment of men who had committed minor offenses. Of course, the Union camp administration always had the prerogative to overrule or change Chiefs if it desired.

Everyday Life in Prison

To some extent at least, life in the prison camp revolved around certain events that happened during the day. Among these were mealtimes and roll calls, which occurred daily. As noted in Chapter 4, breakfast was usually at about 9 a.m., and dinner about 3 p.m. Roll calls were usually daily occurrences. On 5/12/65 Allen noted there was roll call twice a day, on 5/14/64 Mckey states these are at reveille and retreat, Allen notes roll call on 6/13/64 is at 5 p.m., McCrorey on 7/7/64 states there was roll call at "dinner," while on 7/10/64 Handy states there was no roll call today or last night, but the next day roll call has been resumed. From other entries after July 1864 it is unclear whether the officers had roll call once or twice a day. Roll call was apparently done by Divisions (Allen, 7/16/64). Roll call was also taken at least sometime in the enlisted POW barracks (Alburtis, 9/16/64), while on 3/13/65 Alburtis reported that orders were posted by Lt. Dietz that roll call would be done every day at 12:30 p.m. On 4/1/65 Berkeley reports that they received orders for roll call at 1:00 p.m. that day. Mauck noted on 7/6/64 and 7/7/64 that they were kept in the hot sun for a long time during roll call.

As noted in Chapter 8, some officers (and perhaps enlisted men) could afford to buy some or all of their food, and/or got some food in packages, rather than depending partly or completely on the ration furnished by the Federal Government. Much of this food or drink (mostly coffee) had to be cooked or at least heated. In the warmer months the officers who cooked did so outside "on the bank," using a variety of cooking apparatuses. Some bought small stoves or "patent lamps" that they used to cook with, and there were many varieties of homemade stove (Handy, 9/6/64 and 10/12/64). Handy describes one "cooking furnace" made of two long preserve cans joined laterally with a miniature grate and a smoke pipe made of a smaller can, the whole kept in a small square box. Other stoves are described by Handy as being made from fruit cans on top of tin plates with a square hole for the insertion of sticks and splinters. During the colder months the stoves in the barracks were also used for cooking, since in the morning there was a general rush to cook breakfast there (Gibson, 11/29/64). POWs arriving at the Fort sometimes had frying pans with them (Handy 10/3/63), and McCrorey reports (7/20/64) he had a frying pan to cook in. Tin plates and cups would also have been useful for cooking food or making coffee or tea.

At the beginning of September 1864 the guards prevented cooking in the officers pen by dispersing the men who had gathered to cook (Cox, 9/2/64, confirmed by Cox on 9/12/64 and 9/15/64, Mckey on 9/2/64, and Handy on 9/6/64). On 9/12/64 Cox additionally reports that no additional wood for cooking was allowed. Cox confirms this on 9/25/64 and 11/17/64, and states that if they want wood they have to buy used barrels or boxes at 25 cents ($0.25) each (it is not stated who supplied the wood). Thus, at least for those who could afford getting food outside the ration, cooking became somewhat more difficult.

Activities concerning personal cleanliness were also routinely reported by the POWs, especially washing themselves and their clothing. For instance, on 3/7/65 Park reports that "We have to wash our hands, faces and feet in the sluggish ditch water which runs through the campus, and a good many strip to their waists and bathe themselves.... The water is brackish and covered with green scum. Men stand in a row along the banks, and all wash at one time. The dirty off-scouring from each man flows to his neighbor, and is used again. Some throw back the water with their hands and seek a cleaner supply." Although this is a relatively more detailed description than most, many other diaries confirm personal washing in the ditches. Washing of prisoners' clothes was also done in the ditches (Handy, 9/10/64). Prisoners washed their own clothing (Handy, 11/1/63, 8/24/63, 3/4/64, 3/12/64, and 9/10/64; Purvis 7/9/64; Mauck 5/4/65) or got others to wash their clothes for them (Berkeley, 3/25/65). In some instances, men took in wash for payment, as Park reported on 4/16/65 that officers "'Take in washing,' calling for clothes every Monday morning, or as their customers may direct. Five cents per garment is the charge, and the washermen pull off their coats, roll up their sleeves, and work with a vim, using water from the ditch." Purvis reports on 7/9/64 that he hired out his clothes washing. On 5/11/65, Park reports that a second edition of the *Prison Times* was published, and in it had an advertisement for washing and ironing by J.G. Davenport of the 10th GA Regiment and J.D. Boswell of the 33rd GA Regiment.[12] When considering the conditions of the prisoners washing themselves and/or their clothes, it should be kept in mind that according to Clark's Commissary records (see Chapter 4) soap was issued to all prisoners throughout this period.

As previously described in Chapter 6, the POWs lived in large barracks with three "shelves" running the length of both sides of the buildings, on or near which the POWs slept and kept their belongings. Most prisoners apparently paired up into "bunkmates," these two men sleeping together (Park, 2/5/65; Mauck, 3/13/65 and 3/18/65). Since each man had one blanket after November 1864, in cooler weather this had the advantage of each man being covered by two blankets, as well as sharing their body heat. As noted by Park on 2/5/65, of the men who did not have bunkmates, "Several poor fellows, who have no bunk mates and a scarcity of covering, sit up around the stoves and nod all night." The men arranged their belongings in such a way that although there was not much privacy, and limited space, their space was comfortable (Boyle, 7/1/64, 1/10/65 and 1/18/65; Cox 9/12/64). As described by Boyle on 7/1/64, "These 'cuddies' can be arranged so as to be quite comfortable. The lower ones, however, labor under the disadvantage of having to take all the dust, sweepings &c from those above." Gibson reports on 11/17/64 that in cold weather the lowest shelf is the coldest and the top shelf is the warmest. Thus the top shelves were considered the best, even though one would have to climb up to them.

As noted in Chapter 7, inspections of the barracks were frequent, especially after 8/14/64, when the CGP ordered a weekly inspection report be submitted to him. The POWs themselves were responsible for keeping their barracks clean, and such inspections are reported by many of the men [Mckey 10/31/64; Cox, 11/1/64, 1/8/65 and 3/29/65 (inspection every day); Gibson 11/30/64 (every Sunday); Berkeley 3/18/65, 3/19/65 (did not pass inspection), 4/1/65 (inspection every day at 1 p.m.), 4/16/65 (did not pass inspection); and Alburtis, 3/31/65 (inspection every day)]. This was a simple fact of life and none of these men reported it with apparent animus, just that it was done. One *supposes* that they believed that inspections were something that happened in the military.

Of course, there were the petty incidents that happen in a prison. These were sometimes particularly noted by the officers, seemingly because they offended the dignity of being an officer. For instance, on 7/30/64 McCrorey reported, "A sentinel made an officer mark time this evening. The officer was reading a paper and gave some thing the d-m lie which offended the sentinel." On 3/7/65 PAMcMichael noted, "Witnessed a disgraceful exhibition. Three officers tossed up from blankets by the Yankees. All very indignant." (This was in retaliation for harassing men who wanted to take the oath.) There were *undoubtedly* other indignities and happenings associated with being a prisoner.

One type of these indignities were "raids," as they were sometimes called by the prisoners, which were a thorough inspection of the barracks for contraband.[13] Generally the men had to leave the barracks when these inspections happened, and the prisoners often reported their belongings remaining in the barracks were tossed about. Some of the items confiscated were canteens, wood, "excess" (more than the allowable) clothing and blankets, etc. Sometimes the men were ordered outside for a barracks whitewashing and a "raid" took place then. Sometimes the POWs were ordered outside and to take everything they had, since anything left behind would be confiscated.

Not surprisingly, the sending and receiving of letters from family and friends is often mentioned in POW diaries. Often it is just a mention, such as "Received a letter from my stepmother, also one from Susan Godlove of California, MO" (Peters, 7/6/63), and "Wrote two letters, one to my wife" (Mauck, 7/20/64). Occasionally there is more of an explanation of the letter's contents, such as, "It [a letter] told me of the reception of one of my letters by brother James, the latest and only one since October 27th, and pained and saddened me by news of my dearest of mothers having had her arm broken in December" (Park, 4/20/65).

The sending and receiving of letters by POWs was a privilege granted in the CGP's circular of 4/20/64,[14] which stated, "XVII. Prisoners will be permitted to write and receive letters, not to exceed one page of common length paper each, provided the matter is strictly of a private nature. Such letters must be examined by a reliable noncommissioned officer, appointed for that purpose by the commanding officer, before they are forwarded or delivered to the prisoners." This was generally followed at the Fort, with one exception. In early August 1864 several prisoners (Alburtis, 8/9/64; JRMcMichael, 8/10/64; Allen, 8/10/64 and Handy 8/17/64) complained that letter writing has been much restricted. Apparently the CGP got wind of this, for on 9/9/64 he wrote to Schoepf inquiring whether such restrictions had been put in place and why, given the wording of paragraph VII of the circular of 4/20/64. Schoepf replied on 9/12/64[15] with a copy of the orders he had issued and the explanation that the 4 clerks reading the POWs letters were overloaded with over 2000 letters a day, many of them from prisoners to rebel sympathizers asking for assistance.[16] In turn the CGP forwarded this on to the Sec. War on 9/15/64. There does not seem to be any further correspondence on this matter. However, on 9/26/64 Boyle reports that the restraints on writing letters have gone back to those prevailing before the newer batches of restrictions went into effect. Apparently Schoepf started employing more clerks to read letters, since in May 1865 there were a total of 14 full time clerks working for the prison, a large number of which were *probably* reading letters (see Table 5-6).

Prisoners' "Free" Time

For the POWs, except as noted above, most time they were not sleeping was free or leisure time to spend as they wished. Actually this was most of their waking hours. Enlisted men could volunteer to work at various chores on the island, it *apparently* being beneath the dignity of officers to do this. Employment of POWs was specifically sanctioned in the CGP's Circular No. 3 of 6/13/64,[17] which stated that POWs, if employed, were to be paid 10 cents per day for mechanics and 5 cents per day for laborers. In addition, Clark's commissary records (see Table 5-4) show that POWs who worked also got a full Union ration. From these records, from July 1864 through May 1865 an average of about 179 POWs were employed at various jobs each day. These tasks included cooking in the POW kitchens, baking bread in the bakery, laborers moving food about the island, moving construction materials when construction was in progress and sometimes also helping with the construction, and other miscellaneous tasks.[18]

Schoepf also had POWs employed in tasks not necessarily requiring physical labor but that required clerical and other skills, and this got Schoepf into a bit of trouble. On 7/22/64 the CGP wrote to Schoepf that employment of a POW as a deckhand was "unauthorized and improper" and that no POW should be employed at any public work except as a prisoner under guard.[19] The CGP further wrote to Schoepf that M.B. Dorr, a POW, was employed as an ordnance clerk,[20] and it appeared that at least two prisoners had been employed as clerks by Mr. Welch, the sutler, and that the employment of any POW in private or public works in a confidential position had not been authorized.[21] On 10/1/64 Capt. Ahl wrote to CG Goddard, the Chief Surgeon, that the CGP had directed that no prisoners could be employed as clerks, and thus the two POWs acting as hospital clerks should be returned to their barracks.[22] Thus Schoepf was willing to employ POWs in varied positions, the most surprising (to me) being that of ordnance clerk, who *presumably* had access to all of the information about the armament of the Fort!

There is no mention of a lack of POW volunteers for working. This is understandable for two reasons. Some pocket change could be earned so that a man could write home. Also, since he got a full ration, some of the extra food could be traded for cash, or needed items such as postage stamps or an item of clothing. *Perhaps* an important reason for volunteering was that working provided relief from the boring daily routine of prison life, and gave the POW a purpose in life. Another reason for working, given by Peters on 6/29/63, was that he could get fresh air and exercise.

As noted above, Peters volunteered to work because he believed he needed exercise.

Exercise, or the need for exercise, is also mentioned by some: Purvis (7/12/63, walked by river), Mckey (8/8/64, and 5/3/64, the latter needed to keep warm), Barringer (4/12/165, 7/10/65 to 7/14/65, walked along river), McCrorey (7/22/64, deliberately walking in "bull pen" for exercise), Boyle (1/10/65, walks each day between 4 and 5PM), and Park (2/10/65, POWs exercise by walking, running, jumping, pitching quoits, etc.). On 6/10/64, Union Surgeon Eames reports in a letter home that the rebel officers may exercise for about half an hour outdoors (this seems to be at odds with prisoners' accounts). Finally, on 10/10/64, Fletcher, a Union guard, reports in a letter that "They were more active than in warmer weather, and played football with great zest." Although not stated, he was *probably* observing the enlisted POWs. Thus if they desired, the POWs could, and some did, exercise.

Drinking alcoholic beverages was also done by the prisoners, sometimes to excess. On 10/31/64 Handy reports that whiskey bottles were finding their way into their quarters in the Fort. On 6/27/64, Handy reports the sutler selling beer for $1.25 a keg, and Division 34 bought a barrel, while on 6/30/64 he also reports that some stands in the pen were selling corn beer, while on 8/4/64 Cox reports the sale of beer from stands. On 8/10/64 Handy states there are 16 beer stands in the officers' prison selling home brew. On 8/17/64 JRMcMichael reports beer is plentiful, while on 8/31/64 Handy reports the "beer barrels are empty." On 5/7/65 Park reports beer is sold at stands and made from corn or molasses. This of course led to at least some drunkenness. On 5/10/64 Mckey reported many officers drunk but on 5/12/64 further reports that drunkenness has been stopped. On 6/11/64 Alburtis apparently reports himself "drunk as usual." Although fights between POWs were not uncommon (see Mckey 4/9/64, which involved a stabbing; Handy 5/2/64, McCrorey 7/6/64, Mckey 12/4/64 and Cox 1/8/65), and Gibson on 11/29/64 states one or two fights happen occasionally, only the fight reported by Handy on 4/16/64 was attributed to alcohol.

The POWs apparently had access to alcoholic beverages such as beer. For instance, as previously noted, the Sutler at least sometimes beer, and at the end of Barringer's diary on an undated page is a recipe for beer—2 [gallons] of molasses to 40 of water with proportion of [corn] meal, bread crumb [?]. Lt George H.[23]

One fight among POWs apparently ended in a homicide. On 1/23/65 Schoepf wrote to the CGP[24] that Pvt. Tho[mas] R. Manchester, Co. A, 2nd NC,[25] had been killed by Pvt. Fred L. Adams, Falconetts Battery, AL Cav. (in Soldiers and Sailors Database, National Park Service, in Co. A), and inquired what action should be taken. On 3/23/65[26] Schoepf wrote again, reminding the CGP of his previous letter concerning this matter. On 4/4/65 the CGP replied[27] that by order of the Sec. War, Pvt. Adams should be sent with the next group of POWs for exchange, together with any POW witnesses to the incident. Also to be sent with these men were the full statements of witnesses, who were to be delivered to the "rebel agents of Exchange." Thus it appears that Sec. War Stanton did not want to deal with the incident, but rather foist it off on the Southern authorities. Given the state of the Confederacy at the time, one wonders whether any action could have been, or was, taken.

At least in the officers' barracks, men also tried to better themselves by studying various subjects. Courses were offered in mathematics, languages (French, Greek, Latin), medicine, and law.[28] Some of these officers took their studies seriously and noted that they were keeping up in "class."[29]

Reading was also an important pastime for many of the POWs. Religious reading, such as reading the Bible and various tracts, was important. These books were usually supplied by the Christian Association (Boyle 1/26/65; see below for information on this group), and by various individuals and organizations not on the island, such as Mrs. Emley of Philadelphia, the Pennsylvania Bible Society, and a bible society in New York. Handy noted many of these gifts on 5/30/64, 6/16/64, 6/20/64, 8/23/64 and 9/23/64. There were other donations of religious publications, for on 6/21/63 Peters states there was a large distribution of religious publications, including bibles. However, at least the officers read other types of published material. On 4/9/64 Allen wrote that the officer POWs had established a library, while Mckey borrowed a book from that library on 6/21/64, and Cox noted on 7/30/64 that the library had good and useful books, and on 11/7/64 that a large number of new and interesting volumes were contributed.

Handy, throughout his diary, mentions many times that the men are reading, particularly when they are reading religious materials. Of course he also mentions when he reads religious materials. However, he mentions four books which are not religious tracts (although they had some religious connection) that he read: *Dairyman's Daughter* (11/16/63), *David Copperfield* (3/24/64), *Parson of the Islands* (4/8/64), and *Beyond the Lines* (4/26/64). There are many other notations of reading in many other diaries, early notations being by Peters on 6/26/63 and by Purvis on 7/8/63 when he is reading his Bible. Boyle mentions several books he read, including *History of the Reformation of the 16th Century* by JHM D'Aubigne (9/26/64), *Gibbon & Pope* (10/21/64), JL Motley's *The Rise of the Dutch Republic* (1/10/65), and W. Cobbett's *A History of the Protestant Reformation in England and Ireland* (3/8/65). Evidently a great number of more serious books were available to the officers. On the other hand, books of a not strictly religious nature *probably* were not readily available to enlisted men, since Berkeley noted on 3/28/655 that he reads "when I can get anything to read."

The POWs could also receive newspapers, most especially the *Philadelphia Inquirer*. As noted by Park on 3/29/65, the *Inquirer* could be gotten for 10¢ an issue, while he also stated that guards could get it for 5¢ an issue. Whether it was sold by the Sutler was not mentioned. As the prisoners noted, they could not get papers that had Southern sympathies, since the *Inquirer* was strongly pro–Union and Republican. It is *likely* that the *Inquirer* was received on the day it was published, since there was daily steamboat service from Philadelphia to the island. Newspapers to the Confederates were occasionally interrupted when there was some serious news; for example, when Early's army menaced Washington and Baltimore no newspapers were allowed from 7/8/64 to 7/29/64.[30] Similarly, after the Lincoln assassination newspapers were stopped for a while.[31]

Another "pastime" of many of the POWs was performing services for others or making items for others for barter or sale. For example, the *Prison Times* No. 1 has a number of advertisements for various products and services, including Lt. W.S. White for engraving, B.F. Curtright & Co. for plain and Gutta-percha rings, chains, breastpins, etc., tailoring by Griggs and Church, washing and ironing by Davenport and Boswell. Broughton and Walker had a barber shop, Lt. R.F. Taylor performed dental work, while T. Gordon Blandon gave guitar lessons, and the Variety Works was prepared to do sawing, turning and drilling. There was another barber shop in Division 31 charging 10¢ for a haircut, 5¢ for a shave, and 15¢ for a shampoo, and cobblers Atkins and Beall made and repaired footwear.

There is much mention of men making jewelry and trinkets for sale to other POWs, the guards and visitors (see Figures 18 and 19); for instance, Handy wrote on 8/27/63, "The manufacture of rings and breast-pins, from gutta-percha buttons, is one of the means resorted to by the prisoners to raise money. The number of these trinkets made is no less astonishing, than the variety of patterns. Some are set in gold; others in pearl; but most of them are inlaid with silver, ingeniously fastened with rivets, bringing prices ranging from 10 cts. to $1. I have procured a number of them as prison relics, for my children, and friends." On 9/28/63 he observed others working on gutta-percha and sawing bones, while on 2/27/64 spent about $20 hunting for such items for others, and on 4/12/64 he stated Generals Vance and Thompson were making gutta-percha chains as mementos. On 5/27/64 Allen and on 7/29/64 Alburtis sent two rings each to friends, while on 5/3/65 Berkeley observed that tourists who came from other places to see the prison camp came down among the POWS looking for "rings, toothpicks and other trinkets" which the POWs made in great number. This is all summed up in an article from an unknown newspaper of unknown date which is pasted in the sketchbook[32] of a Union guard which reads, "Rebel Prisoners and their Work.—A chief employment of the rebel prisoners at Fort Delaware is the manufacture of rings, pins, studs, and buttons of gutta-percha, inlaid with gold and silver, some of which are really very elegant. The rings are sold at from $1 50 to $3 50 apiece, and other articles at proportionate prices. The material is obtained by special permission at the sutler's, and the tools with which the work is done are made by the prisoners themselves of pins, needles and knife blades of which they in some way obtain possession.... Formerly bone was much used in the manufacture of the articles above referred to, but this has fallen into disuse since they have been able to purchase gutta-percha, which is so much more easily wrought."

One can fairly ask the question of how the POWs were able to carry on their businesses of making rings and other trinkets, and selling them, when presumably they could not possess much in the way of manufacturing equipment (although the sutler was allowed to sell pen knives and pocket knives), and were to have no direct personal contact with guards or visitors, except under very limited circumstances.

The answer may lie in a letter sent from Julia Schoepf (Schoepf's wife) to Joseph Holt, on 8/19/64.[33] At that time, Holt, who was a family friend and who had used his influence to get Schoepf appointed as a

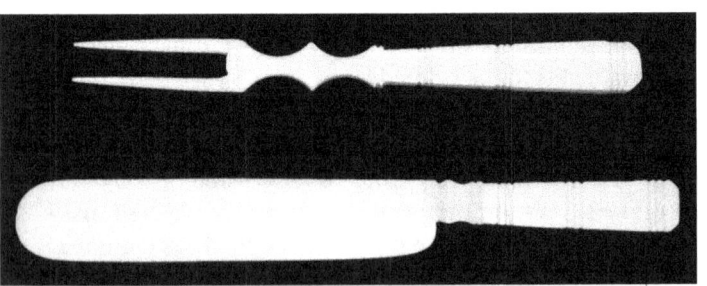

Top: Figure 19. Bone Ring, carved by Col. O.M. Butler, 1st LA Cav., and presented to Capt. George W. Ahl as a token of appreciation by Butler towards Ahl, while Butler was a POW at Fort Delaware. We don't know what Butler was appreciative of. The incised letters and some of the incised stars are colored dark blue, while the other incised stars are red.

Bottom: Figure 20. Bone Knife and Fork, belonging to Capt. George W. Ahl (Union). The knife is 6-⅛ inches (15.0 cm) long, and the fork is 5-¼ inches (12.9 cm) long. No details are known who made the set, or how Ahl acquired it (courtesy Delaware Historical Society).

General, was the Judge Advocate General of the Federal Army. The letter read, in part, "As my husband, (Genl Schoepf) is so fully occupied with the complicated cares of his office, I use the privilege conferred by your friendship to send for your inspection and acceptance two pair of [?] and rings as specimens of the handy work wrought out of very simple material by the prisoners of this island. It is a principle with my husband to encourage all practicable modes of industry as a source of comfort and greater contentment to the prisoners and you perceive altogether contradictory of the many false representations of his course towards the unfortunate committed to his Supervision."

If this statement is at all true, Schoepf realized the prisoners would be more "contented" if they had something useful to do, and while this action was somewhat altruistic, he also probably realized that it had the side effects of lessening discontent among the prisoners, which in turn would improve prison discipline, and lessen the number of escapes attempted.

The POWs also engaged in many other activities. The *Prison Times* No. 1 on pages three and four also lists 2 debating clubs, a "Musical Association" (complete with President, Secretary, Manager and Musical Director), and 2 chess clubs. However, the most often mentioned activity, especially by some of the more religious men, was gambling in various forms. Among these were faro, various card games such as poker, euchre, vingt et un, seven up, marbles (for money?), chuck-a-luck (a dice game), and others.

Prisoner Religious Activity

In a sense opposed to the "wicked sin" of gambling, there appears to have been a great deal of religious fervor and interest.[34] From about the beginning of August 1863 to spring 1864, most of the information about religion is found in Handy's diary. He was a Presbyterian minister who was imprisoned as a political prisoner, and his diary covers the period 7/21/63 to 10/12/64. Handy, during this entire time period, tried to minister to all those who would listen, including giving sermons, speaking individually to various prisoners, describing in his diary his attempts to fight evil tendencies such as gambling and swearing, and doing his best to bring the light of Christian belief to the prisoners. Much of his diary is devoted to these endeavors. He often mentions gambling or more commonly "cards" as a problem, in a sense perhaps competing with more moral activities.

Handy's diary discusses activities in places all over the island, since he had a "parole of the island" during the periods 8/25/63 to 10/13/63, 11/14/63 to 2/28/64 and 3/25/64 to 5/17/64.[35] This allowed Handy access to most of the island during daylight hours, so he could visit at will places such as the hospital and the enlisted and officer (after they opened) POW quarters. Handy thus describes in his diary for this period sermons and other religious activities he was involved in, personal counseling he gave, his interactions with Union chaplains Way and Paddock, and interactions with POWs who were ordained or unordained ministers and preachers. According to Handy, he had many requests to preach to the enlisted and officer POWs, and at times also to Union soldiers. These sessions happened not only on the Sabbath (Sunday) but also on other days of the week. He also, sometimes with the help of Chaplains Paddock or Way, distributed bibles and other religious tracts that were sent to the island for the prisoners by the U.S. Christian Commission and also by individuals such as Mrs. Emley of Philadelphia (Handy, 11/20/63 and

5/30/64). While Handy's diary is sometimes very personal and his view is colored by his desire to save souls, it nonetheless does give an account of one view of religion on the island, when we have few other sources.

Reports of religious activities by the enlisted men are not very numerous, perhaps because we do not have as many diaries from them as from officers. Peters reports on 6/23/63 that preachers came down and preached and distributed (religious?) books, but on 7/5/63 that there were no divine services on the Sabbath, and is clearly disappointed by that. On 7/30/63 he heard preaching by "Stonewall's old preacher." Purvis reports on 7/26/63 that they had preaching on that Sabbath by one of their own Chaplains, who was also a prisoner, and had preaching on the evenings of 8/2/63 and 8/16/63. On 8/30/63 there was no preaching but they had a prayer meeting. Franklin reports on 7/23/63 that they heard from preachers from Philadelphia. *Apparently* by 5/8/63 things had become a little more organized in the enlisted men's barracks, because Purvis stated that a "Christian society" or a "union prayer meeting" was in their barracks, and that these prayer meetings "grow in interest daily." The last mention of religious activities in an enlisted man's diary is by Berkeley on 5/21/65, who states that he heard a fine sermon.

On 6/27/64 Handy wrote a note to Schoepf asking if an awning or rough shed could be erected in the officers' pen for the purpose of "public worship during the summer."[36] He offered to have the POWs erect it and asked if they could be provided with old boards for the construction. This would allow them to hold services outside the crowded, noisy divisions, in the shady, cooler, breezy outdoors. Handy heard nothing in writing from Schoepf, but on 7/8/64 Schoepf visited the POW officers' barracks and there Handy spoke to Schoepf, who expressed "a perfect willingness to comply with the request." At the same time Mrs. Emley informed Handy that some lady had contributed $10—for the benefit of the POWs—and Handy suggested it be put into a fund for an awning. After the Christian Association had been formed, on 8/3/64 $25 was appropriated to be sent to Mrs. Emley for an awning.

On 8/22/64 Handy found out that a relatively large sum of money had been collected from civilian individuals by Mrs. Emley, and had heard that a large sail donated by someone from New York was now on the island. When Handy asked Schoepf about the sail, Schoepf replied he would send it into the barracks, but that was not done. However the next day Handy met with (Union) Lt. Wolf, who asked where the carpenters should erect the sail. The next day, 8/23/64, Handy was informed the POWs would have to erect the sail, and had to improvise the poles and rope needed to secure the awning. Although the structure was somewhat flimsy, the 40 by 100 foot sail was at least up! This was celebrated by a grand gathering of 400–500 officers. The awning was used for services and religious classes, but by 10/9/64 it was getting too cold to hold these out-of-doors. On 10/10/64 the awning (sail) was taken down and transferred to (the Rev.?) Mr. Harris, who used it as a mattress. There is no further mention of the awning.

In the officers' barracks, there was much reported religious activity, spurred on by Handy. On 7/29/64 Handy reports that a Christian Association has been formed, and the minutes book of this association is available.[37] The organization, originally called (in its first Constitution) Christian Association of Confederate Prisoners at Fort Delaware (although it included no enlisted men), had during its existence from July 1864 to June 1865 approximately 210 members, although it is *likely* that nonmembers participated in one or more of its activities, such as worship services. Its importance in prison life may be somewhat overstated in extent in officer diaries, since at least 7 officers who wrote diaries appear to have been members: Mckey, Handy, PAMcMichael, Boyle, McCrorey, Hawes and Allen. Nevertheless, for at least a substantial number of prisoners, this association played an important part in their lives. There are many mentions of association activities, especially in these officers' diaries.

The standing committees of the Association were Divine Worship, Sick and Destitute, and Procuring and Distribution Religious Reading. On 8/1/64 a committee on Contributions was formed to raise money by voluntary subscriptions, and on 8/2/64 $25 of this money was to be forwarded to Mrs. Emley of Philadelphia for purchase of an awning to conduct services outdoors out of the sun. Other committees were created as needed. Interestingly enough, at the 10/1/64 meeting it was decided to combine the efforts of the Committee of the Sick with the "Masonic fraternity" efforts to help the sick and destitute. On his release on 10/15/64, a resolution was passed thanking Handy for helping found and being the first president of the Association. General Vance became acting President for that meeting. Later the Rev. Harris was elected president.

A meeting on 10/25/64 changed the constitution of the Association, so it was now called The Confederate States Christian Association for the Relief of Prisoners. At a meeting on 10/26/64, a resolution was passed that LCol & Mrs. Edgar send letters to various religious newspapers in the South with a statement of the aims of the Association, so that various member churches could help the Association achieve its objectives. At the next meeting on 10/28/64, a committee of 3 was appointed to send a circular to other Northern prisons, the "aims and objects" of the Association, to obtain their cooperation in its work. At this same meeting, another committee was set up for these officers to visit the enlisted men's barracks so that the objectives of the Association could be accomplished. Another result was to form a committee to make an appeal to the people of the Confederate States about the existence and objectives of the Association, so that people could help the Association achieve its objectives. The next few meetings were chiefly concerned with carrying out these items. A now more prominent aim was to improve conditions for sick and destitute prisoners (officer and enlisted) through the use of charity and money raising on a wider scale. Religious items also continued on. There was much correspondence with Mrs. Emley of Philadelphia over items that she was buying for, or furnishing herself, to the Association.

On 12/2/64 the Committee on the sick and destitute was directed to inquire of the Federal authorities whether or not they would be able to receive medical supplies by contribution or by purchasing abroad. On 12/17/64 it was reported that this question had been asked of Capt. Ahl, but no reply received. In addition, it was reported on 12/23/64 that "Capt. Shaw received letters from Parties at Point Lookout [a prison camp in Maryland] in want of clothing & which were on motion referred to Committee on Sick and Destitute." Apparently word had reached at least one other prison camp that the officers at Fort Delaware were organizing some kind or organization that could (would?) assist them.

More mundane items were also reported. On 12/30/64, General Vance was elected President of the Association. On 1/27/65 the death in the hospital of Lt. Mackey, an association member, was announced. Through the first four months of 1865 other routine business was conducted, including fundraising for the sick and destitute. It is unknown whether this was for the benefit of prisoners only at Fort Delaware, or some money or other items were sent to other prisons.

In the minutes of 4/7/65 meeting, a copy of an article in a newspaper, *The Central Presbyterian*, appears.[38] This document lays out an ambitious undertaking for the relief of Confederate POWs, nothing less than a large, perhaps national (Confederate) organization for sending relief supplies to Confederate POWs in northern prisons, with the hope that Union authorities would cooperate in this endeavor, and that many, if not all, of the northern prisons would have similar organizations. It also appeals to the Southern people to provide similar help to Union POWs in Southern prisons, perhaps, at least in part, to make the enterprise more palatable to Union authorities.

As noted in this section, the Christian Association was apparently able to send messages concerning their activities to the South, and perhaps other northern prison camps. It is not known exactly how this was accomplished.

Letters sent by POWs were subject to restrictions, enforced by censorship. Who letters could be sent to was not restricted, but the subjects mentioned in the letters were restricted to "strictly personal" items, and limited to one handwritten page. Obviously the appeal to persons and organizations in the South appearing in at least *The Central Presbyterian*, and perhaps correspondence with other prison camps, did not fit the category of items of a strictly personal nature. Nevertheless, these types of messages obviously got to their destinations. We have no inkling of how this was accomplished, and there is nothing in the records to indicate how or why this occurred. Perhaps messages were smuggled out, or the Union authorities above Schoepf allowed it, or Schoepf on his own initiative allowed it. It is also possible that censorship at Fort Delaware was careless and these letters simply slipped through. However, the item appearing in *The Central Presbyterian* would have been multiple written pages, which would have been quite noticeable.

By 5/5/65, in its regular meeting the Association members were considering what to do with the funds they had on hand if there were a general release of POWs and the Association dissolved. The meeting on 5/13/65 also considered what to do with the books in the Association Library when the POWs were released (it is believed these were mostly or all of a religious nature). Much of the meetings in May and June was taken up with what to do with the Association assets when the POWs were released and how the Association would continue. For example, on 6/2/65 it was resolved that new officers be elected for 1865, and Handy was elected President, Adjt. Boyle Recording Secretary (which explains how the minutes of the Association ended up in the Boyle family papers). The last meeting of the Association was on 6/10/65, during which the Constitution was amended to provide for "Branch Associations," presumably to be formed after the release of the POWs. We have no evidence that in fact after the POWs were released that any part of the Association remained or became active.

The Association was apparently not the only group in the officers' barracks concerned with "sick and destitute" men. On 3/21/65 Mauck, PAMcMichael and Cox reported that a minstrel show was held for the benefit of these men, and PAMcMichael reports a second show was held on 3/28/65. On 4/1/65 Boyle indicates that this was not a Christian Association activity, since he states it was done by an "organization of officers" and that about $100 was raised by the first concert. A program and songs for the show exist.[39]

The "Bull Pen"

Figure 21 is a somewhat remarkable, very detailed, drawing by Max Neugas of the "Bull Pen" and the activities taking place in it. If the date on the drawing is taken at face

11. Life on Pea Patch Island

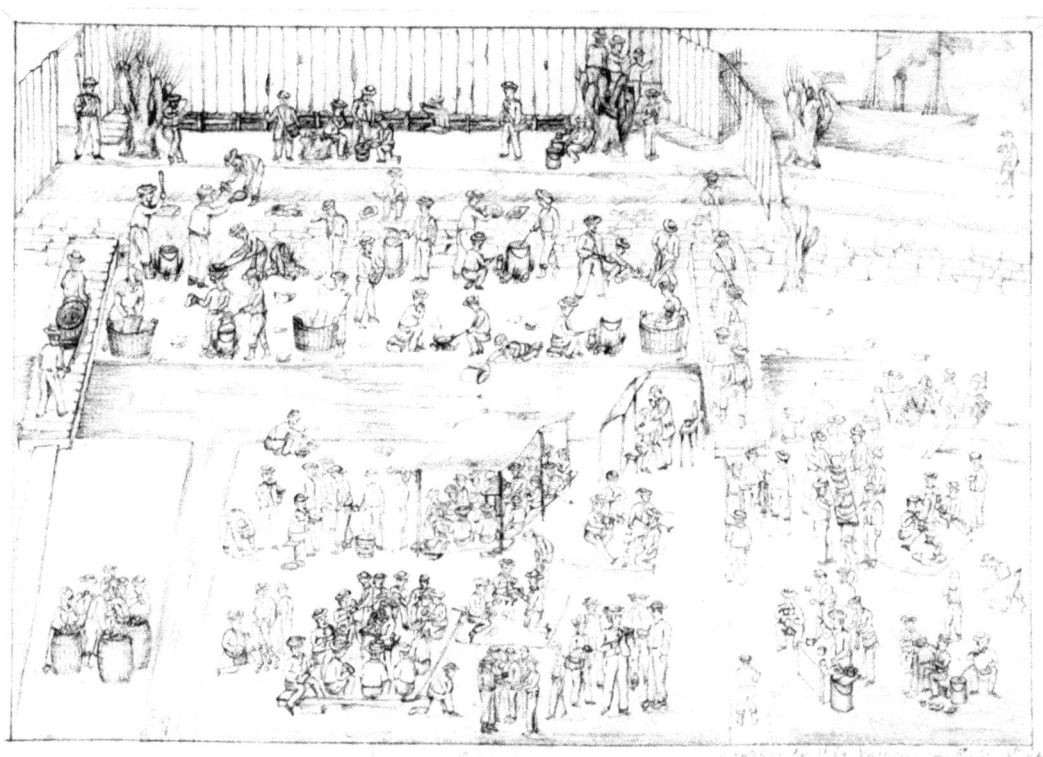

Figure 21. The "Bull Pen," drawn by Max Neugas, 1st SC Inf, and dated 2/18/65. See text for details (courtesy Delaware Historical Society.

value, it was drawn before there were any appreciable number of officer POWs on the island, so the men shown are enlisted men. Many activities discussed or described in this or previous chapters are shown. Among them are:

- Many men apparently cooking, some of them perhaps cooking and then selling the cooked food.
- At least three men apparently doing laundry along the bank of the ditch using large wash tubs. One of them clearly has a wash board. Whether they are washing their own or other's clothes is not known.
- A man sitting in a partial enclosure apparently getting a shave or haircut.
- At least one dice game (probably gambling), chuck-a-luck, taking place, right center, just below the man getting the shave or haircut, at the ground cover which has the number 1 through 6 on it.[40]
- Men playing cards (for money?), just to the left and below the chuck a luck game and on the right just below the ditch.
- Two guards patrolling with muskets and fixed bayonets, top left and top right.
- Men fishing in the ditch on right and one fisherman walking to the ditch (bottom right) and one fisherman walking over the right hand bridge. A fisherman is apparently showing off his catch just below the right hand bridge.
- Possibly the men standing at a long narrow table just below the ditch near the

right bridge are eating rations they got from the dining hall, since there is no cooking apparatus next to them. However, this is a bit speculative.

There are other men doing a great number of things but it is difficult to say exactly what they are doing. Clearly there is a lot of activity.

The date on the drawing, however, is probably not the date on which Neugas actually made it. The weather was very cold on 2/18/64, with a high temperature of 21°F (-6°C), although it was fair with light winds.[41] It is likely that the men would not be out there in such cold weather, and some of the water shown would probably freeze, for instance in the laundry tubs.

12

FREEDOM!

> ...though the desire for freedom grows as time passes. Though Man is naturally bound to disappointment, and I should be resigned to my fate, notwithstanding it may seem to frown on me.—Lt. E.L. Cox, 68th NC Infantry, POW at Fort Delaware.

Lt. Cox's lament about his being in prison—at that point he had already been at Fort Delaware for over 8 months—was undoubtedly being felt by many of the prisoners there. Although there had been some limited exchanges, mostly of sick and invalided men, many of the POW diaries from this period exhibit a sense of hopelessness and/or longing to be free. Even gazing out their windows (when they could) to the outside world, their situation must have seemed forlorn (see Figure 22).

Earlier Releases

Meanwhile, long before April 1865, and unbeknownst to the POWs, some plans were underway for exchanges and/or paroles of POWs. On 9/10/64 the CGP informed Schoepf[1] that by order of the Sec. War, 500 invalid prisoners, preferably those who could not actively serve soon, were to be prepared to be sent for parole, and on 9/15/64 Schoepf received the order to send these men.[2] On 9/18/64 20 officers and 496 enlisted men were in fact sent.[3] On 10/7/64 another 123 invalided rebel officers were sent to Point Lookout.[4] This was followed by an exchange of letters, 10/26/64 to 1/4/65, concerning the parole of invalid prisoners who would not be fit for duty for 30 days, officers captured at Fort Butler, Louisiana, and all chaplains and medical officers, but this does not appear to have actually resulted in any releases.[5]

Then on 2/4/65 Schoepf was ordered to prepare rolls of 3000 POWs for exchange, which was to include all enlisted men from Missouri, Kentucky, Tennessee, Arkansas, Kansas and Louisiana and all invalids, to be sent in parties of 500.[6] This was apparently "amended" 2/7/65 to state 6 percent of officers will be included.[7] This was followed on 2/8/65 by the sending off of 655 POWs.[8]

On 2/17/65 Schoepf received the startling news that a general release had been arranged.[9] This was then followed by a series of letters and orders concerning such a release, that lasted until 3/18/65.[10] These communications concerned arranging transportation, starting and stopping the process, details about how many were to be sent at one time, preferably not to send those who had received clothing through Gen Beall, etc. However, the net result of all of this was the sending off of about 1000 POWs on

Figure 22. From Our Window, drawn by Lt. R(andolph) A(bbott) Shotwell, 8th VA Inf., and dated 6/12/65, in the autograph book of 2nd Lt. Andrew J. Leftwich, 22nd Battalion, VA Inf. A perhaps almost wistful look outside the prison through a window in the officer POW barracks. The Fort can be seen in the background. By this date the men expected to be released any day (courtesy Mr. John T. Frawner and Mrs. Jean Leftwich Frawner).

3/7/65.[11] There were no other large groups of men sent off the island for release or under parole. It appears that with the impending collapse of the Confederate government in early April 1865, no more such exchanges or paroles took place.

The POWs were also aware of the situation outside the Fort, with Confederate fortunes steadily declining in the first three months of 1865. In January Fort Fisher at

Wilmington North Carolina, the last major seaport held by the Confederacy, falls and the prisoners are sent to Fort Delaware.[12] Charleston, South Carolina, had been abandoned to the Federals, and Gen. Sherman's army was, by early March, in North Carolina where he defeated Gen Johnston at Bentonville, which threated to cut off supplies from the south to Lee's Army. Capture of Goldsboro, North Carolina, a railroad hub, allowed Sherman to rest and resupply his troops. It looked like only a matter of time until Sherman's Army would be able to join Grant's Army in the siege of Petersburg and Richmond. On 3/2/65 Gen Sheridan had defeated Gen. Early in the Battle of Waynesboro, giving the Union complete control of the Shenandoah Valley (Confederates captured were sent to Fort Delaware).

As noted above, the POWs were very well aware of this critical situation for the Confederacy. On 1/18/65 to 1/25/65 Gibson, Boyle and Cox mention that Fort Fisher has fallen. On 2/25/65 Boyle wrote, "We are anxiously waiting, too, for news from the South. So far as we know the aspect of things looks badly for our cause. The *only hope* that any entertain is that Beauregard may turn upon and drive back Sherman. Many have not even this hope. Disasters have come so thick upon us that before the mind has well received *one*, another comes to shock and stupefy." Cox writes on 2/28/65 that "The prisoners generally are low spirited over the affairs of late." Perhaps the most straightforward assessment came from an enlisted man, Berkeley, who wrote on 3/27/65, "The end of this long and bloody war is certainly drawing to a close and that very rapidly. And what an awful close it is going to be. A great many of our people have seen it, since ill-fated Gettysburg; but they would not acknowledge it, even to themselves. Maybe I ought not write it down even in this little diary."

With this background, the capture of Petersburg and Richmond by Grant on 4/3/65, and the surrender of Lee's Army of Northern Virginia on 4/9/65, as one would expect, greatly disheartened the POWs, and made them wonder what was going to happen to them and the Confederacy in general. The assassination of Abraham Lincoln, who died the morning of 4/15/65, immediately became known to the POWs, and added to their anxiety about their fate. Their diaries reflect these concerns.

The effects of the Lincoln killing were immediate, but for the most part temporary. On 4/15/65 Mauck reported the POWs were being treated "very insultingly," and men on parole on the island were returned to their barracks. Many of the prisoners were crushed with fear and alarm (Barringer, 4/15/65). Cox reported the same thing about the paroles. Berkeley reported (4/15/65) Lt. Dietz came in drunk with a club and hit some of the men.

Other things happened in the days that followed. Gibson reported on 4/16/65 that minute guns were firing. On the same day Cox reported that "there seems a settled sadness upon the countenance of almost every man tis deemed a most unfortunate thing." Park states also on 4/16/65 that the "guards are very harsh and preemptory in their orders." Also on the 16th Boyle reports the mail has been stopped, and he reports on the previous day that orders were issued to fire on anyone expressing satisfaction about the assassination, but that the prevailing opinion is that things will gradually return to normal. Mauck also reports no mail since Friday. Mauck reports on 4/17/65 that mail will not be resumed until the burial of Lincoln. On the same day PAMcMichael reports no mail or newspapers. Alburtis and Cox on the 17th state all mail stopped and "All business has stopped." On 4/20/65 conditions appeared to be eased, as Mauck reports newspapers were available, but still no mail. On the 22nd Berkeley states that he was told mail will be resumed. Finally on 4/23/65 the mail was resumed (Berkeley, Boyle and Mauck). Boyle also reports "other privileges" restored.

Aside from the general anxiety of what will happen to them, especially in view of the Lincoln assassination, there were two overriding concerns of the POWs. The first, as one would imagine, was when they would be released, assuming they would be released, and the second, especially for the officers, was violating their oaths as officers by taking the oath of allegiance to the U.S. Government.

The Oath

There was much discussion and introspection about the taking of the oath of allegiance to the U.S. Government by the officers, and sometimes the enlisted men, and some of these are illustrated below.

- Berkeley, 4/26/65. Today I have to decide for myself one of the most important questions of my life. God only knows what mental anxiety I have suffered. I have tried to act as I think for best interest of my country and my family. We surrendered to these people as prisoners of war, and now they wish and are trying to thrust their vile oath of allegiance down our throats on bayonets. It is a vile piece of tyranny of which they ought to be ashamed. Yet these people cannot take from us our liberty without destroying their own. They pretend to have made war on us to save the Union; but is a Union pinned together by bayonets worth saving? I think certainly not. We are very near hopeless, and it is not wise for the US government to render us desperate. It can certainly afford to [be] liberal and magnanimous; but the question is, will it be liberal and magnanimous? I hope so, but very much doubt [it]. There are here some 6000 prisoners of "enlisted men of war," as the Yanks call us, and some 1500 officers. Of these nearly all have agreed to take the oath on condition of being permitted to go home. When first approached on this subject, they all refused with 1 or 2 exceptions.
- JRMcMichael, 6/5/65. It appears from what we hear that our government has ceased to exist. Our armies have all been forced to surrender and disarmed. Most all the prisoners are taking the oath and being released. I am at a loss to know what to do. I want to know what action my state has taken. I have taken the oath of allegiance to the C.S. Government and I must be convinced beyond a doubt that it has failed before I can abandon it. We are told that those who refuse to take the oath will be kept in prison and put to hard labor. I am determined not to act hastily or unthoughtedly.
- JRMcMichael, 5/7/65. I have now made up my mind to take the oath of allegiance to the U.S. government and return (with a consciousness of having done my duty) to share the fate of my country and parents. We all consider our Confederacy a failure and it is for me to say whether I will take the oath and become a citizen of the U.S. or remain in prison or be banished. I hope my course will not be condemned by my friends at home for it is love for them that actuates me.
- Gibson, 4/26/65. Still taking the oath I did not know what to do at first was very much disturbed but after m[?]t[?]ify thinking over the thing I came to the conclusion to take the oath and go home. My reasons were these 1st a government can claim allegiance from its subjects only as long as it can afford

12. FREEDOM!   179

them protection which I think now has lost its powers 2nd I do not expect to leave the United States and therefore expect to have taken the oath before I can do anything 3rd Gen Jos E Johnston conditions of surrender which I have no doubt that he had the sanction of higher officials his terms over that all leaders should take the oath and we cannot be expected[?] to get better terms. [?] be ashamed[?]. It may be an unfortunate thing & it may be a fortunate [?][?] responsibility and believed that I have acted pro[?]ly if I have not I have no one to blame but myself I expect to observe my [?][?] as long as I can not [?][?] and hope I never will have to regret taking it.

- Park, 4/24/65. Captain Ahl came into the pen, arranged the officers in three sides of a hollow square, and had the roll called alphabetically, offering the oath of allegiance to all, with a promise of early release, if accepted. Nearly 900 out of 2,300 agreed to take it. It was a trying and exciting time as each name was called and the response "Yes" or "No" was announced. I answered "No" with emphasis and bitterness. Born on Southern soil, reared under its institutions, nurtured upon its traditions, I cannot consent to take the hated oath. The very thought is repulsive in the extreme.

There were a number of oaths that were offered to POWs over the war years. Below are three of them.

A proclamation of 12/8/63 from Lincoln[13]:

I, ____ ____, do solemnly swear, in the presence of Almighty God, that I will henceforth faithfully support, protect, and defend the Constitution of the United States and the union of the States thereunder, and that I will, in like manner, abide by and faithfully support all acts of Congress passed during the existing rebellion with reference to slaves, so long and so far as not repealed, modified, or held void by Congress, or by decision of the Supreme Court, and that I will, in like manner abide by and faithfully support all proclamations of the President made during the existing rebellion having reference to slaves, so long and so far as not modified or declared void by decision of the Supreme Court. So help me God.

A proclamation of Andrew Johnson on 5/29/65 (also sometimes called an amnesty oath).[14]

I, ____ ____, do solemnly swear (or affirm) in the presence of Almighty God, that I will henceforth faithfully support, protect, and defend the Constitution of the United States, and the Union of the States thereunder; and that I will, in like manner, abide by and faithfully support all laws and proclamations which have been made during the existing rebellion with reference to the emancipation of slaves; So help me God.

An actual oath used at Fort Delaware during the major part of the POW releases (signed by POW Richard D Adams on 6/12/65, and countersigned by Capt. George W. Ahl).[15]

I, ____ ____ of the County of _____, State of _____ do solemnly swear that I will support, protect and defend the Constitution of Government of the United States against all enemies, whether domestic or foreign, that I will bear true faith, allegiance and loyalty to the same, any ordinance, resolution of laws of any State Convention or Legislature, to the contrary notwithstanding; and further that I will faithfully perform all the duties which may be required of me by the laws of the United States; and I take this oath freely and voluntarily; without any internal reservation [sic] or evasion whatever.

It is interesting that in the oath actually used at Fort Delaware, anything specifically related to slavery is not mentioned, even though the 13th Amendment abolishing slavery had not yet been ratified. The previous oaths were likely alluding to Lincoln's Emancipation Proclamation, which took effect on 1/1/63.

Starting about mid–April 1865 the oath is mentioned many times in POW's diaries. For instance, Cox alone mentions on 4/12/65 that many applications to take the oath have been made, on 4/20/65 that many officers have made application, on 4/22/65 that the oath is talked about and many men intend to take it, and on 4/24/65 many applications are being made to take the oath. Many enlisted men also wanted to take the oath, as reported by Berkeley on 4/14/65. On 4/26/65 Mauck and PAMcMichael stated that the Union officers such as Ahl called the roll to determine who would take the oath. At first about half the men offered to take the oath, but it was offered again and again after 4/26/65. But although the number agreeing to take the oath increased there were still many holdouts by 4/30/65. On 4/30/65 Mauck describes a meeting of VA officers debating whether to take the oath, and in the end most of them agreed to take it. On 4/30/65 Boyle reports only about a dozen enlisted men refusing to take the oath, while 1680 officers agree to take it. On the same day Park states only 165 officers were refusing to take the oath. Offers were made again on 5/1/65, and on 5/2/65 Mauck, PAMcMichael and JRMcMichael state that only 159 officers out of 2252 men refusing to take the oath. More offers to take the oath were made on 5/3/65 and 5/4/65.

There was a campaign of sorts to encourage men to take the oath. About 4/30/65 POW Gen Barringer urged the men to take the oath. Whether Barringer made this plea at the suggestion of Schoepf we don't know. Cleverly, Schoepf apparently arranged for the *Richmond Whig* newspaper to be distributed around the prison camp. This southern paper described many important and prominent men in the south taking the oath, and Berkeley states that this convinced many men to offer to take the oath. By 6/1/65 Park reports almost all men agreeing to take the oath, especially since the last Confederate Army in the field, that of Kirby Smith, had surrendered, and there was no longer any existing Confederate military force.

Of course, one consideration in deciding whether or not to sign the oath was what would happen to someone who did not sign the oath. Among the possibilities discussed were "banishment" from the U.S. (Park, 4/30/65) and being imprisoned at least an extra 6 months (Barringer, 5/16/65). None of this happened, and nothing official was ever announced to the prisoners about what would happen to someone who actually refused to take the oath. Actually, those few who refused to take the oath were released anyway.

Freedom

The paramount thing on most prisoners' minds was when they would actually be free. Since the middle of April 1865 rumors had swirled through the camp about when the releases would start, and newspapers were carefully studied for any clues to orders for release that may be issued (many diaries in this period). In actuality, while there were 8192 POWs present at the beginning of May 1865, during that month 134 officers and 944 enlisted men were released, about 13 percent of those present on May 1st. Many of these were so-called special releases in which the prisoners themselves or somebody else who knew them applied to the war Department for release. Almost every day in May there is correspondence between Schoepf and either the war Department or the CGP, orders being given to Schoepf to release certain individuals or groups of prisoners, Schoepf reporting back on the names of the men released, or inquiries from the CGP or the war Department whether certain men had been released.[16] However, by the end of May there was still no order issued for a general release.

In June 1865, almost all the other POWs were released. Table 12-1 lists the number of POWs and those released each day (numbers may not add up because of transcription errors and/or deaths of POWs).

Table 12-1. Release of POWs in June 1865

June	Present					Released		
	Field Off.	Com. Off.	Surgeons	Enlisted	Total	Com. Off.	Enlisted	Total
1	92	2018	5	4950	7065	9	3	12
2	92	2018	5	4943	7058	1	1	2
3	92	2017	5	4941	7055	0	0	0
4	92	2006	5	4940	7043	23	7	30
5	89	1986	5	4931	7011	9	8	17
6	89	1980	5	4920	6994	3	2	5
7	88	1978	4	4918	6988	14	483	497
8	86	1961	4	4485	6536	31	9	40
9	84	1932	4	4475	6495	11	285	296
10	84	1921	4	4189	6198	128	468	596
11	84	1794	4	3720	5602	6	505	511
12	84	1788	4	3214	5090	501	50	551
13	84	1287	4	3162	4537	21	7	28
14	81	1269	4	3162	4516	74	483	557
15	79	1197	4	2570	3850	23	291	314
16	79	1173	4	2179	3435	419	252	671
17	78	754	2	2126	2960	744	0	744
18	78	10	2	2126	2216	3	1	4
19	78	7	2	2123	2210	1	707	708
20	78	6	2	1316	1402	1	683	684
21	78	5	2	624	709	8	429	437
22	74	1	2	200	277	4	135	139
23	74	1	2	64	141	0	21	21
24	74	1	2	41	118	0	0	0
25	74	1	2	40	117	3	0	3
26	72	0	2	35	109	0	3	3
27	72	0	2	35	109	0	0	0
28	72	0	2	25	99	1	0	1
29	71	0	2	25	98	0	7	7
30	71	0	2	17	90	0	0	0

In Table 12-1, as is the usual convention, Field officers are Major and above in rank, Com. Off., Captain or below in rank, and enlisted include privates and noncommissioned officers. By the end of June, the Field Officers were still being held because Schoepf had not yet received permission to release them. The remaining enlisted POWs were all in the Hospital, and too sick to move.

The actual release process was simple but large in scale. Rolls of those being released had to be prepared, copies of oaths taken and signed had to be prepared, transportation for each POW arranged (see below), and rations for each man released prepared (see below). Each document, as was normal Army practice, probably was filled out in triplicate, with one copy of the rolls being sent to the CGP, and two copies being retained at the Fort. As far as copies of the oaths, one copy was given to the released POW, one copy retained at the Fort, and one copy sent to the CGP (and now in the National Archives).

It appears from one copy of a such an oath that it was printed especially for Fort Delaware, since the title of the Union official signing is preprinted ("Capt. & A.A.A.G."), and Capt. Ahl's signature was applied with a rubber stamp. Not too complicated for a single POW, but it was done almost 7,000 times in June 1865.

The preparation of rolls of the prisoners may have started as far back 4/21/65, for on 4/26/65, Schoepf acknowledged receipt of the CGP's letter of 4/21/65 ordering rolls of all POWs in alphabetical order.[17] These rolls were transmitted on 5/1/65.[18] Also, Schoepf was having the rolls of those agreed to take the oath perfected during late April and May 1865 (see "The Oath" section above). There were other minor details to take care of; for example, on 6/9/65 Schoepf telegraphed the CGP stating, "Please send immediately 1000 blank rolls & oath of allegiance forms."[19]

Going Home

As for transportation home, on 6/3/65 Schoepf received a telegram[20] stating, "By order of LGen Grant transportation to the nearest point to his home by rail or water will be furnished to released prisoners." Schoepf telegraphed the CGP on 6/7/65 that all of the prisoners released between May 26th and June 2nd were not provided with transportation.[21] On 6/11/65 the CGP telegraphed Schoepf stating, "If you require sea transportation for released prisoners please report by telegraph."[22] There was no reply found to this telegram.

Apparently Schoepf on his own initiative decided to provide the released POWs with a few days rations, the amount of rations depending on the estimated time to get home. Schoepf possibly had second thoughts about this, because on 6/8/65 he telegraphed the CGP stating, "Am I right in furnished released prisoners with rations according to their length of travel, not exceeding 5 days?" The CGP replied also on 6/8/65 that "Bread may be furnished."[23] Presumably this was hard bread (hardtack). Schoepf apparently ignored the limitation to bread, because on 6/20/65 Berkeley reported that when he left Fort Delaware they were given 3 days' rations of hardtack and "mess pork."

Finally a first order for "general" releases is issued on 6/6/65, when LGen Grant orders that all enlisted POWs in a hospital who are well enough to travel, and who take the oath of allegiance, be released.[24] Strangely enough, this does not appear to have been done until June 21st–22nd. On the same day another order for a "general" release was issued by the War Department as General Orders 109, ordering, with a few exceptions, the release of almost all POWs.[25] Exceptions to this order included West Point graduates, officers with a rank higher than captain (or equivalent in the Navy), and officers who held a commission in the U.S. Army or the U.S. Navy at the beginning of the war. Releases were to be as fast as possible, consistent with being able to complete rolls, sign oaths, etc., and that the first to be freed were those that have been imprisoned the longest and/or live the furthest distance from the prison. The POWs could alternatively take the amnesty oath instead of the oath of allegiance. The order also stated that the released prisoners would be furnished transportation to the nearest accessible point by steamboat or rail. This order of course "opened the floodgates" to releases, and as can be seen in Table 12-1, large numbers pf prisoners were released in the approximate period June 7th to June 21st.

Several of the diaries continue with a description of the trip home, and a few representative journeys are described below.

Berkeley signed the oath on 6/19/65, and at about dark the next day, 6/20/65, was given (verbally?) the oath, transportation to Richmond, and three days' rations of hardtack and mess pork. He got on the boat to Baltimore, going through the (Chesapeake and Delaware) Canal, where he was not allowed to go to the dining room, and reached Baltimore about 7 a.m. The boat ride was very pleasant. As he had been directed, he went to the quartermaster's office in Baltimore to get transportation to Richmond, and was told to go to a steamboat at a certain wharf. He went on board the *SS Eagle*, an older boat, which had about 1000 other released POWs from all parts of the South. At about 5 p.m. on 6/21/65 they got under way, and at sunrise passed Point Lookout, and at about 4 p.m. passed Fort Monroe. At least half the men on the boat, North Carolinians, got off at the boat City Point to take the train to Petersburg. When the *Eagle* reached Richmond they were met by some U.S. Cavalry, who started them to Chimborazo Hospital. When Berkeley inquired why the cavalry was there he was told that they were going to give the ex–POWs something to eat and a place to sleep. Berkeley said he could take care of himself, so he was told, "Then you can go." He spent the night at the Powhatten Hotel, and he paid $1 for supper, which included a glass of milk. On 6/24/65 he went to the Richmond Customs House to find the quartermaster to get transportation to Staunton, but the line was so long that he briefly walked about the damaged and destroyed part of Richmond and then went to the Central Depot. He got on the train, where there were about 20 other released prisoners on their way home. Even though Berkeley did not have a ticket he was allowed to stay on the train. He got off at the Noel stop (station no longer there, but railroad now part of Piedmont Division of the Chesapeake and Ohio Railroad) about 30 miles north of Richmond, immediately met some neighbors, and then walked home to *White House Farm.*

JRMcMichael took the oath on 6/16/65, and the next day was on the steamer *Meteor* (this steamer had regular daily commercial service to Fort Delaware) bound for Philadelphia. After landing at Philadelphia at 12:30 p.m. he went to the Merchant's Hotel and had a good dinner. At midnight he left by train for Pittsburg, Pennsylvania, via Harrisburg, arriving there at 11 a.m. At 3 p.m. on 6/19/65 he left Pittsburg for Indianapolis, arriving at 1 p.m. the next day. At 10 p.m. on the 20th he (and other ex–POWs) got in box cars for the ride to Jeffersonville, Indiana, across the Ohio River from Louisville, Kentucky, arriving there at 10 a.m. on the 21st, and they crossed the river to Louisville on a ferry. They were greeted warmly by the ladies of Louisville, and waited for a train. They arrived in Nashville at 7 a.m. the next day and got on a freight train for Chattanooga at 2 p.m. They arrived at Cartersville at 4 p.m., drew hard tack and bacon and marched for 5 miles before camping for the night. They marched another 27 miles the next day, passing many negroes who were working repairing the railroad. On 6/25/64 he crossed the Chattahoochee River on a pontoon bridge, and got onto a boxcar going to Atlanta. At this point, the end of the diary, he says he is completely broken down.

On 6/4/65 Mauck took the oath. He left Fort Delaware at 10 a.m. the next day, traveling by boat to Wilmington, where he took the train to Baltimore. After staying overnight with a friend[?], he went to get transportation to Harper's Ferry, Virginia, but found he could not leave until later, so he went around Baltimore and met some friends and had a pleasant time. He arrived in Harper's Ferry at 3 a.m. on the 7th, and then at 9 a.m. took a train to Winchester, Virginia, where he arrived at 3 p.m. "We" hired a hack and started up the (Shenandoah) Valley and got to Wood Stock at dark, staying with Mr. Melborns overnight. On the 8th he started for Harrisonburg (Virginia) and after a long, tiresome ride reached New Market, had dinner, got to Melrose, walked home, and met loved ones.

13

Conclusions[1]

Article 56. A prisoner of war is subject to no punishment for being a public enemy, nor is any revenge wreaked upon him by the intentional infliction of any suffering, or disgrace, by cruel imprisonment, want of food, by mutilation, death, or any other barbarity.—General Orders 100,[2] Issued April 24, 1863

General Living Conditions of Prisoners

At Fort Delaware, the living conditions of POWs and other prisoners generally conformed to Article 56. Prisoners were not tortured or wantonly killed, had adequate rations so they did not starve, lived in barracks similar to those of Union soldiers which were heated in winter, when necessary provided with other needed items such as clothing, and they were also provided with excellent medical care. These are all outlined in previous chapters.

They were also provided with privileges that today are not usually afforded to POWs. They were able to send and receive letters freely, although the content of letters they sent was censored and limited to "personal items." They could also receive money and, at least to a limited extent, packages containing items such as clothing or food.

However, at the beginning of the period during which POWs were being held in large numbers, May to about September 1863, living conditions for POWs were bad. This probably resulted mainly from two factors: lack of facilities and personnel to adequately provide for the large POW population, and the inexperience of the Union personnel at Fort Delaware in running a prison camp. There was no Army "Field Manual" or other instructions on the details of running a prison camp. These poor living conditions are manifested by a high death rate during this period (Graph 10-2).

An example of this is medical care during this early period. When large numbers of POWs started arriving in May 1863, the medical care system on the island was overwhelmed. During May to September 1863 there were 5 small hospitals on the island, none of them particularly sanitary or well stocked with medicines. There was also a shortage of surgeons (medical doctors). Schoepf urgently asked for more doctors and better hospital facilities. He knew that he had more sick and wounded POWs than he could handle and tried to send some of them to nearby Army General Hospitals. Almost desperate attempts were made to procure medical supplies such as drugs. For example, on 7/11/63 Union Lt. J.J. McConnell wrote to Julia Jefferson[3] asking her to send as many pillow cases for the Hospital as she could provide. In the same letter he wrote he was going to Philadelphia that day to get "beds, blankets, and other necessary articles" for wounded POWs (probably from Gettysburg) that had arrived, who were at that time lying on the hard boards in the barracks. Eventually the medical care improved. By about 9/10/63 a 600 bed general hospital and a 250 bed contagious (isolation) hospital had opened, and by November 1863 there were 8 surgeons on the island.

The improvements in medical care during this period were paralleled by improvements in general in the living conditions of the POWs. This may be best illustrated by comparison of the inspection reports of Surgeon Alden on 7/11/63[4] and Surgeon Clark on 11/13/63.[5] These reports not only described the Medical Department, but also general conditions on the island. Perhaps the great improvement in conditions on the island is best summed up by a sentence from Clark's report: "With the exception of the want of drainage and of occupation for the prisoners (spoken of hereafter), everything connected with this prison reflects credit on the officers in charge of it."

Clark's inspection report also dealt with the location of the prison camp on Pea Patch Island, and he wrote:

> I have to report that in my opinion this post is an utterly unfit location for a prison, much more for a hospital. Lying so low, its level being some six feet below high tide, it is impossible to properly drain it or to prevent its surface being constantly marshy and wet. The island is traversed by ditches connecting with the main ditch encircling the island, and with the moat around the fort, and intended to be constantly full of water, changing with the tide. The moat is in process of repair, and during this the water is partially shut off, rendering the ditches partially dry. From the stagnant mud and partially stagnant water in these a constant, and in some cases a most offensive, effluvia is constantly given off, rendering the atmosphere in a high degree unhealthy. Some of these ditches run directly underneath the barracks. The influence of such an atmosphere on a large number of men congregated together, and whose vital powers are depressed, as those of prisoners naturally are, cannot but be most injurious.

Surgeon Clark was referring to the causes of diseases, namely, miasmas in the air (see Chapter 9). While Clark was wrong about what caused most diseases, it is true the stagnant water on the island was a source of mosquitos that spread malaria, and malaria was a serious disease on the island.

However, the increased occurrence of malaria may have been more than made up for by a decrease in diarrhea and dysentery, which were leading causes of mortality in prison camps and the armies in general. For instance, at Camp Douglas in Chicago, Medical Inspector Surgeon A.M. Clark (same as above) reported that in an inspection on 10/9/63[6] that

> Water—there are at present but three hydrants provided to supply water for the whole camp. These are utterly inadequate, but the post quartermaster informs me that he intends to furnish ten additional, which I think will suffice. Drainage—a sewer is being laid, communicating with the lake; this—a plan of which I have been shown by the quartermaster—will very much improve the present condition of the camp, but still is not sufficient, as it only runs around two sides of the camp, leaving the third side (the fourth side being higher ground does not need it), on which are the quarters of the [invalid] Corps detachment, unprovided for. Here are located the three hydrants now in use, and the ground being low the water accumulates in pools. In addition to this a ditch runs along this side of the camp just inside of the fence in which, no proper outlet being provided, stagnant water collects. A branch of the sewer should be run down this side of the camp; it might readily be done.

Thus Clark reports that sewage is not being handled properly, and there is a shortage of water supply (hydrants) in the camp. This combination was deadly at other camps, such as Andersonville and Elmira, and led to many deaths from diarrhea and dysentery in those places.[7]

By contrast, the prison camp at Fort Delaware was on an island surrounded by saltwater, and since the only source of drinking water was rainwater, more potable water had to be imported from a relatively unpolluted source, the Brandywine River, which was an important water source for Wilmington, Delaware. In addition, no sewers were built on the island since all of the sinks (privies) were out over the Delaware river, which carried away the human waste (except for toilets in the Fort, which flushed into the moat which in turn was, in theory, flushed out by the tides). Thus some of the conditions on the island which were a product of its topography, and mentioned by Surgeon Clark as making the island unfit for a prison, much less a hospital, may have actually helped decrease death rates.

Of course exactly what the conditions were for the prisoners on the island was determined mainly by two factors, the local military establishment on the island and the authorities in Washington, D.C. The former was commanded by BGen Albin F. Schoepf, and the latter is represented best by Col. (later Bvt. BGen and then Bvt. MGen) William Hoffman, who was the Commissary General of Prisoners for almost the entire War.

BGen Albin F. Schoepf

Unlike most volunteer officers (including generals) in the Union Army, Schoepf had received professional military training from an early age and had been a military officer until about 10 years before the war started. As such, he was probably more like a volunteer officer who had graduated from West Point and had retired or resigned from the U.S. Army before the Civil War.

As large numbers of POWs were beginning to be received at Fort Delaware (Schoepf had been warned that the number may be much higher and these POWs would stay), he started reorganizing the island into a prison camp. Although others may have started or authorized the expansion of the prisoner barracks, the general hospital, and other needed facilities, these were built on the island in relatively short periods of time, and this can be at least partially credited to Schoepf. From the awarding of the contract to construct the General Hospital to patients actually being treated there was less than 2 months, and the Hospital was probably the best constructed building on the island, after the Fort.

Before the General Hospital was in operation, however, Schoepf showed genuine concern for the welfare of the many sick and wounded POWs that had recently been received. On 7/16/63 Schoepf telegraphed the CGP that 175 sick POWs had been sent to Chester Army Hospital. The Sec. War then asked by what authority they had been sent. Schoepf answered by telegram that the Surgeon General had ordered the transfer of 500 sick prisoners to the Chester Hospital, but they had returned about 350 of them because they had no room for them. Schoepf also stated he had a total of about 1,500 sick and wounded POWs and had inadequate resources to deal with them, and inquired of the Sec. War, "What shall I do?"—a remarkable question for a general to be directly asking the Secretary of War. Schoepf and his staff also made almost desperate attempts to find medical supplies and equipment.

There are many other such instances of Schoepf showing concern for the welfare of the POWs there, and these span the entire period of interest to us, about April 1863 to June 1865. On 9/24/64 he informed the CGP that when POWs were transferred in disagreeable weather he usually sent them with blankets; on 11/28/64 Schoepf wrote a letter to Capt. Craig (his quartermaster officer) reminding him that 2000 tons of coal were needed to heat the prisoner's barracks, and since cold weather was fast approaching to buy it on the open market rather than putting it on bids; on 6/19/65, apparently against orders, Schoepf provided three days rations of hard tack and pork to released prisoners; around November 1863 he asks for permission to build a contagious hospital on the New Jersey shore, because their existing contagious hospital is overcrowded (permission was granted but this hospital was never built because smallpox cases subsided); and on 8/21/64 Schoepf requested a supply of antiscourbetics for the POWs, from the CGS.

Schoepf was also clever about the way he handled the prisoners' living conditions, and showed a good understanding of human nature (see Chapter 11). The Divisions within the POW prison were, to some extent, self-governing. In the officer's barracks Division Chiefs were elected, while in the enlisted POWs barracks it is not certain if they were appointed or elected. These Chiefs of Division were POWs, and were in charge of routine everyday life in the barracks, such as going for meals, mail delivery, keeping the barracks clean, and to some extent discipline. Of course, while the prison administration could always overrule these Chiefs, it probably gave most of the POWs some satisfaction that routine things in their lives were controlled by their compatriots.

Along the same lines, Schoepf also encouraged small crafts among the POWs, such as making trinkets of various kinds that they could sell as souvenirs to other prisoners, guards (although it was forbidden for the guards to speak to the prisoners), and civilian visitors. According to Mrs. Schoepf, he did this deliberately to keep the POWs busy and not thinking about their overall situation, and apparently many prisoners availed themselves of this opportunity, even one or more generals. It is not known if this idea originated with Schoepf or with Surgeon A.M. Clark, who inspected the island on 11/13/63 and in whose inspection report it stated, "At every post I think that by some judiciously devised plan sufficient work could be found for all the prisoners to answer this purpose, if enforced by the commanding officer. At present I am convinced that idleness and ennui are more pregnant sources of disease than any other to be found in our various prisons." This suggestion was never implemented, and there is nothing in the record to indicate that Schoepf ever saw Clark's full report, but Schoepf did implement a sort of voluntary work program.

Around the end of April 1865, when Schoepf was trying to convince the POWs to sign the oath of allegiance before being released, he circulated copies of the *Richmond Whig* in the camp, which was reporting on the large number of people in the South, including prominent people, who were taking the oath (Chapter 12). This clever idea apparently convinced many of those who were skeptical of taking the oath to agree to sign it.

Concerning escapes and punishment, Schoepf sometimes used tough talk about what could happen to those who tried to escape,[8] but actually there was no penalty if a POW was recaptured actually trying to escape. In fact, as related in Chapter 3, there were no dead lines on the island over which a sentry could automatically shoot a prisoner, and a sentry had to warn a prisoner at least three times before shooting at him. As noted in Chapter 3, there were very few shootings on the island, especially of men who were not trying to escape. If a man was caught simply trying to escape, usually the worst that happened was detention in the guard house for a day or two.

As related in Chapter 3 Schoepf made every effort to try to get certain POWs released, and in the cases of men petitioning for release for various reasons, he usually made a recommendation which supported the petition. He actively tried to get some men released because he believed they could help the Union war effort, such as men who were skilled in shipbuilding.

Severe punishments of POWs are rare, at least if one relies on extant written reports (Chapter 3). There are two or three reports of POWs being hung by the thumbs. However, most punishment may have been meted out by the Division Chiefs, such as "wearing the barrel," which was probably more humiliating than painful.

The only things apparently initiated by Schoepf that negatively affected living conditions for the POWs apparently were temporary closing of the sutler, or restriction of the items the sutler could sell, and a restriction on the sending of letters. These closings and restrictions were always temporary, and lasted no more than a week or two. Against this must be balanced the fact that the sutler was selling items that were not on the CGP's approved list. Presumably Schoepf knew about these unapproved items. Probably the unapproved item that caused the most excitement was ice cream, which caused a great commotion when it went on sale on 6/11/64. The next day the sale of ice cream was stopped by Schoepf's order, but resumed on 6/17/64 and was on sale at least through 7/8/64. After that date there is no further mention of ice cream.

As for the limiting of the privilege of writing letters, on 8/26/64 Mckey records that letters will be limited to 10 lines. Schoepf on 9/14/64 wrote to the CGP explaining why he had limited letter writing by the POWs to 10 lines, limited to family matters, and written only to a father, mother, sister, brother, wife, son or daughter.[9] The reason was that his 4 mail clerks could not possibly read the 2000 letters per day that were being sent, and that many of the letters were being sent to "notorious rebel sympathizers" asking for assistance (see Figure 23). Handy reports on 9/21/64 that Schoepf had revoked these orders.

Schoepf had an advantage not shared by many other prison camp commandants: that is, through the last 2 years of the war the commandant and officers connected to the prison camp did not change appreciably. Schoepf and his staff who ran the camp learned how to manage the prisoners and care for their needs, all the while securing the camp against escapes and other misadventures. This took a while; for example, the major security measures did not take a final form until early summer 1864, about a year after large numbers of POWs were present. Schoepf's staff, such as the Commissary General of Prisoners Capt. Ahl, the Commissary of Subsistence Officer Capt. Clark, the Provost Marshall (usually) Lt. Hawkins, Assistant Commissary General of Prisoners Lt. Wolf, and the chief medical officers Surgeons Silliman and Goddard (at different times), all seem to have been competent and energetic men.[10] Thus Schoepf learned together with his chief assistants how to run a prison camp, and the fact that most of these men remained on the island for the entire period covered was of great value to the prisoners.

Despite the apparent efforts of Schoepf and his staff, within their orders, to make the prison camp a tolerably good and healthy place to live, of course the POWs did not want to be there. They wanted their freedom, and were greatly bothered by the fact that in the end, they had little control over their own lives. The food provided, while sufficient, was monotonous, and was prepared and "served" in a poor manner. For at least some of the POWs, the island was also unsanitary, the barracks crowded and sometimes noisy, and while there were diversions such as religion, the making of trinkets, and reading and studying, many of the men were probably bored and felt their time in the prison was

13. Conclusions

Figure 23. Interior of Prison Office, drawn by Max Neugas, 1st SC Inf, and dated 7/30/64. This office is Figure 2, Item 26. Probably censoring of the POW mail was done here. Note Bill the Cat on the chair in the center back, and apparent rugs on the floor. Someone wrote "Office of Maj. Wolf" in the margin, but Lt. Wolf was just one of the officers of the prison, and Capt. Ahl was in charge. Wolf later became a lighthouse keeper, and lighthouse keepers were often referred to by the title of "Major" (courtesy Fort Delaware Society).

wasted and unproductive. They also worried about what was happening to their country (the Confederacy) and their comrades still in the Confederate Army and in Union prisons. Most of all perhaps, they were concerned with what was happening to their families, friends and hometowns. For those whose loved ones were near the fighting this must have been especially true, but these prisoners were also aware that as time went on, general conditions for civilians in the South were gradually getting worse because of the combat, not to mention the destruction of the South's transportation system. The POWs were generally quite aware of what was happening in the war, both from Northern newspapers and newly arrived POWs.

Perhaps the best summary of Schoepf's treatment of the POWs is found in Handy's diary entry of 5/13/64, which states:

> These officers of opposing armies [including Confederates Gen Thompson and Col. Duke with Schoepf] spent an hour together this morning, as they have done several times before, and they seem to be mutually well pleased. It is the opinion of the Confederates that Gen. Schoepf is disposed to make them comfortable, just as far as he may be allowed. I can add my own testimony here. But the General has many eyes upon him, and a number around who are ready to report at Washington any new leniency. Hence he is obliged to be cautious, and sometimes has the appearance of severity, when he does not mean it. Schoepf says, he had to sit up all night not long since, to 'prevent the guards

from shooting Rebels, who were trying to make their escape!' There is a report now circulating, that the General is shortly to be removed. Some of his brother officers may desire a change; but the prisoners generally would be averse to the measure.[11]

Col. William Hoffman, Jr., CGP[12]

As noted in the previous paragraph, the POWs realized that Schoepf was liable to orders from higher authorities in Washington, D.C., such as the Sec. War and the CGP. Most communications for the running of the prison camps were passed through the CGP, whether they originated with Hoffman or from someone else. For Fort Delaware, occasionally Schoepf heard directly, and answered directly the Sec. War, Edwin M. Stanton. It is evident that Hoffman had influence in determining not only routine orders to the camps, but almost certainly also the overall policy towards POWs and political prisoners. As such Hoffman has been blamed through the years, including today, for many of the (supposed) ills of the Union prison camp system.

Hoffman was the CGP from the time of the inception of the "office" in 1862 until 11/11/64, when he was made CGP only of camps west of the Mississippi River. BGen Wessells was CGP of all camps east of the Mississippi River from 11/11/64 to 1/31/65, when Hoffman was again made CGP of all prisoners.[13] During his tenure, Hoffman issued several principal Circulars, which governed the overall running of the camps.[14] One of Hoffman's problems was that he was not the person that prison commandants primarily reported to. For the most part, these commandants reported through the chain of command up to their department or area commanders, although they were supposed to take directions for running the prison camps from Hoffman. This sometimes caused problems when Hoffman's orders conflicted with the local commander's orders.

The Federal prison camp system became more and more organized as the war went on, and the CGP gained more and more influence over the camps. This was especially true when Hoffman was promoted to BGen in late 1864 and then MGen in 1865. By early 1865 prison camp commanders were reporting regularly, usually monthly, on things such as accounting for the prison fund and prisoner's hospital fund, inspection reports on the prisoner's conditions, prisoner rolls, and other routine items. The CGP's office had devised special forms for reporting on expenditures from the prison fund, for prisoner morning reports, and the like.

The Union, however, had a major weakness in planning for new prison camps. While Johnson's Island, a camp for Confederate officers, was planned out carefully in advance, other Union prison camps, including Fort Delaware and Elmira, were designated as such just before they started receiving large numbers of prisoners. This meant for the first 4–8 months the prison camp was holding large numbers of men; facilities such as barracks, hospitals, cooking facilities, etc., were being built; and enough necessary personnel to take care of the prisoners, such as surgeons, were not present. This often resulted in high death rates during these periods. The other "source" of Union prisons was existing facilities such as Federal or State army posts or training camps, state or local prisons, etc. Some of these too were initially unprepared to take care of large numbers of POWs. In most cases the reason a location was chosen for a camp was that it seemed secure (Fort Delaware was an Island, for instance), and/or there already was an existing facility which could be enlarged and used. Apparently little thought went into whether the site was useful as a prison camp, for example, was there a good water supply, could human waste be disposed of reasonably well, etc. At Fort Delaware there was little time to prepare before large numbers of POWs started arriving, but perhaps this was somewhat excusable, since these POWs starting arriving as the exchange cartel broke down in the spring of 1863.

Reading orders issued by Hoffman and correspondence between (mostly) Schoepf and Hoffman, one gets the impression that Hoffman was an old line professional officer who was used to a system in which officers were held strictly accountable for their actions, including authorizing anything that would cost money. In the peacetime army between 1849 and 1860, this was probably a strong factor in deciding which officers to promote. Therefore, in his famously mentioned penny-pinching ways, when he could, he would ask for some authorization or request from another (usually subordinate) officer to make the expenditure, or save some money by not doing (spending) something. For example, on 7/3/64 the CGP authorized the buying of antiscourbetics for the POWs on a surgeon's certificate, and also stated that tea and sugar could be issued to sick POWs, also on a surgeon's certificate.

He was also loath to withhold something that had already been authorized, but sometimes gave a subordinate the option to not spend money, if the subordinate felt it useful or beneficial. Probably the most well-known of these authorizations was the withholding of some of the food authorized for the prisoners' rations. The Circular of 7/7/62 stated, "A general fund for the benefit of the prisoners will be made by withholding from their rations all that can be spared without inconvenience to them, and selling this surplus under existing regulations to the commissary, …," and the Circular of 4/20/64 similarly stated, "A fund, to be called "the prison fund" and to be applied in procuring such articles as may be necessary for the health and convenience of the prisoners, not expressly provided for by General Army Regulations, 1863, will be made by withholding from their rations such parts thereof as can be conveniently dispensed with." Note that these two orders do not actually order a reduction in ration to the prisoners from what is authorized, but allows the commandant at each prison camp to make the determination as to whether these reductions would take place.

However, Hoffman rarely if ever turned down a request by Schoepf that would aid the prisoners. For example, when Schoepf requested antiscourbetics be ordered in August 1864, the CGP authorized the purchase of desiccated vegetables, and when Schoepf requested the building of a contagious hospital in New Jersey gave permission to build it.[15]

Hoffman also issued orders or provided "advice" to Schoepf that made life better or more tolerable for the prisoners. Hoffman suggested that Schoepf try "Ridgewood Disinfecting Powder" and report back on its efficacy,[16] and told Schoepf that there was no penalty for attempting an escape.[17]

Hoffman also showed concern for the POWs in other ways. In 1864 a series of POW officers was ordered held in close confinement in retaliation for Union officer POWs of a similar rank being held in close confinement in Confederate prison camps.[18] On 6/27/64 the CGP wrote that if any of the officers to be held in close confinement were too sick, then Schoepf was to choose another officer of equal rank.[19] When Schoepf told the CGP that an officer held in close confinement, Maj. Elliott, was sick in the hospital, the CGP ordered another major be chosen.[20] The CGP also routinely ordered that when POWs were "sent South" (repatriated), no POW was to be forced to go South.[21]

The CGP may have also expressed concern about deaths from smallpox in the fall of 1863, for on 11/7/63 Schoepf sent a letter to the CGP with an enclosure from Surgeon Silliman about the number of deaths and control of the diease.[22] The CGP also had concerns about the shooting of prisoners by guards, since on 3/17/64 he ordered[23] that all shootings of prisoners by guards in all prison camps were to be investigated by a board of officers, with a report forwarded to the CGP's office.

The relationship between Schoepf and Hoffman was at least correct, and they perhaps even respected each other. Hoffman's letters to Schoepf, even when Hoffman was stating a problem with reports sent by Schoepf, were always respectful, and to this author's mind never disparaging, and vice versa. This could have been because for most of this period Schoepf was a superior officer, and/or Hoffman knew that Schoepf had a powerful political backer in Washington (Judge Advocate General Holt), and/or that Schoepf had been a successful field commander and was apparently respected by both Sec. War Stanton and other Army officers.

However, there were a series of actions by the authorities in Washington, starting in May 1864, that have been seen by many as highly detrimental to the prisoners, and these are discussed in the next section.

The "Retaliation"

In early 1864 it gradually became known to the public in the North that there were reports that Northern soldiers who were in Southern POW camps were being treated in a horrendous manner [it does not matter for this discussion if this was true or not or what the reason(s) were]. Apparently to stoke patriotic fervor in the North, the Federal government encouraged the spread of this information, and this climaxed in the publication of the book by the United States Sanitary Commission[24] which essentially compared treatment of POWs in the North and South. This produced two reactions in the Northern public: a demand for retaliation against Confederate POWs being held in the North (what Hesseltine called "war psychosis," see the Preface), and a demand that the Federal government negotiate with the Confederate government to resume prisoner exchanges. As time went on considerable political pressure was brought by the public on politicians in Washington, and these demands could not be completely ignored.

This retaliation program is generally agreed to have started with the reduction on the POW's rations on 6/1/64 (see Table 4-1). While there had been some reduction in the prisoner's ration on 4/20/64, the reason(s) for this first reduction are unclear. There was consideration being given to reducing the Union soldier's ration, which was done on 6/1/64, and perhaps this influenced the 4/20/64 reduction for prisoners.

However, the prisoner ration reduction of 6/1/64 seems to initially have been set in motion by a 5/4/64 letter from Hoffman to Sec. War Stanton,[25] which stated in part:

> The enlisted men who had endured so many privations at Belle Isle and other places were, with few exceptions, in a very sad plight, mentally and physically, having for months been exposed to all the changes of the weather with no other protection than a very insufficient supply of worthless tents, and with an allowance of food scarcely sufficient to prevent starvation, even if of wholesome quality, but as it was made of coarsely ground corn, including the husks, and probably at times the cobs, if it did not kill by starvation it was sure to do it by the disease it created.

After more descriptions of the sad plight of these returned POWs, Hoffman states, "… and while a practice so shocking to humanity is persisted in by the rebel authorities I would very respectfully urge that retaliatory measures be at once instituted by subjecting the officers we now hold as prisoners of war to a similar treatment." Hoffman's letter was passed on to B.F. Wade, the Chairman of the Joint Committee on the Conduct of the war, a very powerful congressional committee.

On 5/19/64 Hoffman followed up the above letter with a letter to the Sec. War suggesting a reduced ration for prisoners.[26] In turn Stanton sent this proposed ration for comment to Gen. Halleck, Army Chief of Staff, and J.K. Barnes, the Surgeon General. Halleck suggested making the ration issued to Confederate POWs be the same as the ration issued to Confederate soldiers by *their government*, which was supposedly what was also issued to Union soldiers who were POWs, and Barnes asked for a modification of what could be given to those prisoners in the hospital. With these changes the ration reduction was approved by Stanton on 5/28/64, and went into effect on 6/1/64.

However, most of the charges of starving the POWs in Union prison camps from 6/1/64 stem not just from the reduction in rations but on the supposed fact that prison camp commanders, as they were permitted but not required to do, further reduced the POWs rations, which is shown by the huge amounts of money in the Prison Funds "returned" to the Commissary general of Subsistence by Hoffman after the end of the war. However, as shown Chapter 5, "The Prison Fund," the large amounts of money remaining in the Funds was readily accounted for by the difference in cost of the rations for Union soldiers and the prisoners. No "extra" reductions in the authorized rations were necessary for these monies to accumulate.

Actually at Fort Delaware no food at all was withheld from the reduced ration of 6/1/64 (Chapter 5). A definitive answer as to whether food was withheld from the reduced ration, especially significant amounts of food, at other prison camps will have to await an evaluation of the Commissary reports from those camps, which are probably in the National Archives. However, one can roughly estimate how much should have been added to the Prison Funds for those camps just by the number of Prisoners in those camps and the approximate difference in price between a prisoner ration and Union soldier ration. Table 13-1 shows the major prison camps, and the amount in the "$ to Prison Fund" column estimates how much money was added to the Prison Fund by calculating the number of prisoner months from June 1864 through June 1865 (except for Elmira, which is from July 1864 through June 1865), and multiplying that by 30.5 (the number of days in an average month, see Table) and then 0.135 (the estimated difference in the daily cost between a Union soldier's ration and a prisoner's ration, in dollars). The "$ Returned" column is the amount of money returned by the Prison Fund of each camp,[27] and "% Dollars Returned" is the percentage of money in "$ to Prison Fund" that was unused and "returned." Just for comparison, the overall DRM for this period for each prison camp is given in the last column.

Table 13-1. Return of Prison Fund Monies

Prison Camp	$ to Prison Fund	$ Returned	% Dollars Returned	DRM
Alton	44578	33583	75	3.2
Camp Chase	240951	126534	53	3.2
Camp Douglas	379357	181739	48	1.9
Camp Morton	179947	155815	87	1.5
Elmira	314085	58151	19	3.8
Fort Delaware	390463	316674	81	0.8
Johnson's Island	128065	109126	85	0.2

Prison Camp	$ to Prison Fund	$ Returned	% Dollars Returned	DRM
Point Lookout	550418	570410	104	1.6
Rock Island	259428	182046	70	0.9
Totals	2487292	1734078	70	

Two camps stand out in Table 13-1. Elmira returned a relatively small percentage of its Prison Fund money. Perhaps that was because Elmira was started in June 1864 and probably required the building of many facilities, such as barracks, a hospital, mess hall, kitchen, privies, sewage system[?], and other things. This would have required a lot of money, which probably came out of the Prison Fund. It is unknown why or how Point Lookout could have returned more than the calculated amount from Prison Fund. Perhaps part of the reduced ration was withheld at Point Lookout, or there was a source of income for the Prison Fund we are unaware of, or there was a difference or mistake in bookkeeping. Just as a check on the calculations, the actual Commissary Records from Fort Delaware indicate the income for the Prison Fund during this period totaled $419,250 (from Table 5-4). Although not exactly in agreement with the $390,463, it is reasonably close, within 10 percent. There is no sure way of knowing whether food was withheld from the reduced ration at any particular prison camp without examining the Commissary returns from that camp.

Actually, having the difference in cost between the prisoner ration and a Union soldier's ration be the main source of the Prison Fund was a canny move by Hoffman for several reasons. If the Prison Fund at a particular camp was in need of funds, it took pressure off the Commandant for reducing rations to add to the prison fund, since ample money was available from the difference in cost of the two rations. It also perhaps allowed Hoffman to give permission for smaller projects or expenditures at a prison camp without consulting the Sec. War, since money was readily available from the prison fund. Any expenditures of a few thousand dollars or more, as judged by Fort Delaware, for example repair or expansion of barracks, required the approval of the Sec. War, at least before 6/1/64. Finally, if Hoffman was looking ahead when he issued the order, after the end of the war it made him look good for saving money (this was really illusory, since no actual money changed hands).

No evidence of significant changes at Fort Delaware in the medical treatment of prisoners, or of their housing, was found after 6/1/64. Their access to outside help (see Chapter 8) was somewhat changed, which did affect their ability to receive money to buy things from the sutler, and to receive packages containing items such as clothing. There were also temporary interruptions in the sutler being able to sell items to the prisoners. However, most of these restrictions did not last long and did not materially affect the prisoners. For example, Handy on 12/19/63 (before the retaliation) reported that boxes could only be sent by "immediate relatives." This was easily gotten around by the prisoners and donors by simply addressing letters to "Dear Cousin" or "Dear Sister." As Boyle described this type of restriction on 8/22/64 in regard to sending and received letters, it was easily evaded by using this subterfuge. The only meaningful restriction was on the sending of clothing. Starting in September 1864 a prisoner had to obtain a permit for someone to send him clothing. This permit was mailed to the intended donor, who in turn attached it to the package of clothing to be sent. The exact reason for the permit system is unknown, but it may have been to enforce Section XV of the Circular of 4/20/64, which stated "Any excess of clothing over what is required for immediate use is contraband." Prisoners basically were to have only one set of clothes.

13. Conclusions

In November 1864 several prisoners reported that a search had been made and "excess" blankets were confiscated. Each prisoner was allowed to have only one blanket. There is no specific reason for this found in the records, but perhaps it was also part of enforcing Section XV of the circular of 4/20/63. On the other hand, newly arrived prisoners were still receiving blankets, since Schoepf requested that his requisition for blankets be filled so he could supply them with blankets.[28]

The above are the only new or more rigidly enforced restrictions instituted after 5/4/64 mentioned in prisoners' diaries or the official records which affected the prisoner's ability to receive outside help. Some of them were easily evaded by the POWs, or were enforced for such short periods that they really did not affect the prisoners' situation significantly. Perhaps the blanket restriction and clothing restriction did affect the prisoner's comfort in the especially cold winter of 1864–65, and could have led to a somewhat increased incidence of catarrh (common cold) and even pneumonia. These could also have caused some additional suffering and maybe even a few additional deaths.

As mentioned at the beginning of Chapter 10, Death Rates, this is "the only unbiased (assuming they were correctly reported) quantitative measure of how well or poorly these men [prisoners] were treated." Graph 10-2 shows death rates (DRM) for Fort Delaware and all prison camps (including Fort Delaware) by month. It shows that during the period of retaliation, from June 1864 through June 1865, the death rates at Fort Delaware had actually decreased dramatically from the previous 12 months. Indeed, in the late summer and fall of 1864 they were very low. For all Union prison camps as a whole the DRM was a bit lower than the previous summer and early fall, but increased during the winter to greater than the previous winter. However, these DRM figures in Graph 10-2 include Elmira, which is well known to have a high death rate, and was not in operation until July 1864. If we eliminate Elmira and choose only prison camps in operation the winter of 1863–1864 (all except Elmira), Graph 13-1 shows the results. Graph 13-1 now shows that the DRMs for all prison camps during the winter of 1864–1865 were approximately the same as for the winter of 1863–1864, even though the winter of 1864–1865 was the coldest winter in about 30 years (Chapter 1).

It is likely that because of the severe winter of 1864–1865 the POWs suffered more in their barracks, and perhaps from more illness, because of the weather. One would expect illnesses such as catarrh (common cold) and inflammation of the lungs (pneumonia) to have increased in such weather, and Graph 10-4 (for Fort Delaware only) shows that indeed pneumonia deaths did increase appreciably in the winter of 1864–65. As discussed in Chapter 10, the incidence of scurvy may have been connected to higher death rates from diseases in general, and on 4/3/65 Hamilton reported Union soldiers were getting scurvy because the supply of vegetables had been "exceedingly limited" that winter. This combination may have contributed to the significant increase in DRMs for both Fort Delaware and all Union prison camps over the fall and winter 1864. It is noted that as soon as the winter conditions started abating in March 1865, the DRMs started falling to values similar to those in the spring of 1864 (or even below at Fort Delaware), before the retaliation started.

Thus there is no evidence that the retaliation greatly affected the lives of POWs at Fort Delaware, and it is very unlikely that it increased the death rates there. As for the Union prison camp system in general, it is more difficult to make such sweeping conclusions. As for death rates in all prison Union camps, the data in Graph 13-1 show that death rates during the retaliation period were about equal to or less than those for the

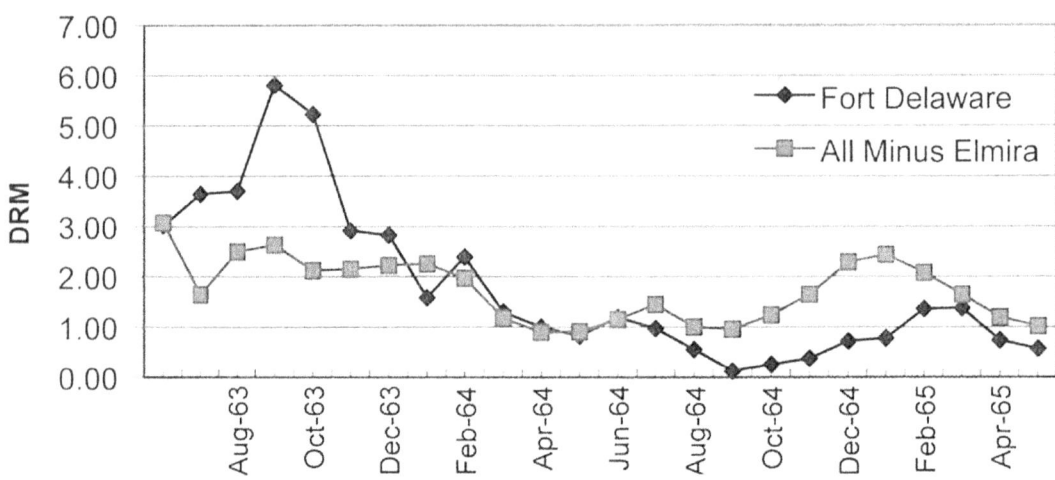

Graph 13-1. Union Prison Camp DRMs Minus Elmira

same period a year earlier. This would indicate that DRMs were not increased by the retaliation, but does not preclude the possibility that they may have been even somewhat lower without the retaliation. The question of whether this possibility happened probably can't be answered. It is very likely, however, that the retaliation did not cause a significant increase in death rates in the Union prison camp system as a whole.

As for causing additional suffering for the POWs in other particular Union prison camps, this book cannot directly address that. As suggested above, Commissary records for different prisons would have to be reviewed, and in the present author's opinion the detailed official correspondence and other contemporaneous documents such as diaries would have to be studied and compared with periods before the retaliation started.

Summing Up

In the Preface to this book, it was mentioned that two relatively recent books about Fort Delaware have been published: Brian Temple, *The Union Prison at Fort Delaware, A Perfect Hell on Earth,* McFarland & Co., Inc., Jefferson, North Carolina (2003), and Dale Fetzer and Bruce Mowday, *Unlikely Allies, Fort Delaware's Prison Community in the Civil War,* Stackpole Books, Mechanicsburg, Pennsylvania (2000). Their principal interpretations of what happened at the prison camp lay at opposite ends from each other, the Temple book arguing that the prison camp was a hellhole, while the Fetzer and Mowday book presented an interpretation of the prison as a place where the treatment of prisoners was relatively benevolent. This study has shown that what happened at the Fort Delaware prison camp was, for the most part, closer to the Fetzer and Mowday version of events.

For the first five months or so of operation, May to about October 1863, conditions at Fort Delaware were poor, despite the camp authorities' vigorous efforts to improve them. Death rates were high, and to some extent the prisoners were living in squalor. This was mainly because within a month of choosing Fort Delaware as a major POW prison, thousands of POWs had arrived and facilities for their care were just being built and established. By November 1863 the prison camp facilities were good.

General Schoepf, the commandant throughout the last two years of the war, was an efficient administrator who treated the prisoners as humanely as he could within the orders he received from higher authorities in Washington, D.C. Not surprisingly, Schoepf's leadership of this army post was of paramount importance in the treatment of the prisoners.

The authorities in Washington, especially the Commissary General of Prisoners and the Sec. War, were not hostile to the humane treatment of the prisoners; in fact, by modern standards of POW treatment were relatively lenient. This changed somewhat in mid–1864 when some Union soldiers who were POWs in Confederate prison camps were found to be in very bad, emaciated condition.[29] The publicity surrounding these returned POWs and the attendant public backlash, and the Washington authorities' anger at their bad condition, led to a less benevolent attitude ("the retaliation") towards those POWs held in Union prison camps. However, there is no evidence that at Fort Delaware this caused "excess" suffering among the POWs or an elevated death rate. Whether this "retaliation" resulted in excess suffering and/or deaths in other Union prison camps is not as clear, although overall death rates in these prison camps during the retaliation period did not increase over a similar period in the previous 12 months. However, the "propaganda" issued by both the Federal and Confederate governments during the war about prisoner treatment, and subsequent postwar writings perpetuating this point of view, has led to a general belief that POW treatment on both sides was horrible, and this appears to be generally accepted American lore.

Overall, it may be fairly stated that the Union authorities at Fort Delaware and in Washington, D.C. (at least judged by their actions towards Fort Delaware) did adhere to the letter, and for most part the spirit, of Article 56 of General Orders 100.[30]

Epilogue[1]

At the beginning of July 1865 there were still POWs at Fort Delaware: officers above the rank of Captain (68), a few citizens (13) Surgeons (2), and enlisted men in the Hospital too sick to move (16 plus two citizens).[2] Eleven of the citizens were released on July 2nd. None of the enlisted men appears on the reports after July 13, and perhaps they were well enough to travel and/or be transferred to another hospital (on 7/15/65 PAMcMichael reports "Miss Tarring" came with ladies to take the sick prisoners to Baltimore.). On July 24th all except two of the staff and field officers (above Captain) were released, as was the remaining citizen.[3]

During the time most of these prisoners remained, restrictions on them were greatly eased. On 6/20/65 PAMcMichael reported that the gates to the officers' prison had been thrown open and the Field and Staff officers were free to walk about the island. The next day they were moved to better quarters near the Hospital, again free to move about the island. On 6/23/65 he reported they were receiving rations "in abundance." On 7/7/65 he reports they had a "grand collation" with ladies from Philadelphia, and enjoyed ham, mutton, brandy, peaches, wines, and especially ice water, it being very hot at the time. On 7/9/65 more ladies visited the island and obtained a recommendation for release of the officers from Gen. Schoepf, and the ladies were to take this to the authorities in Washington.

PAMcMichael's conditions took a small turn for the worse on 7/11/65 when some ladies were turned away and the POWs could not go to the Sutler's shop. This may have been occasioned by an exchange of telegrams on 7/11/65 in which the Sec. War (through the CGP) inquired what persons had been allowed to see the remaining POWs except for those men who had been captured with Jefferson Davis.[4] PAMcMichael had no other negative news before his release a few days later.

Union troops who had been at the Fort for a long time were also being mustered out, starting in June 1865. On 6/12/65 Hamilton reported in his diary that Independent Battery G, Pennsylvania Heavy Raillery (Capt. J.J. Young Commanding), his unit, got ready to leave the Fort, and had a dance that night. The next day they left the Fort and were mustered out on 6/18/65, having lost 9 men dying by disease during the war. Independent Battery A, Pennsylvania Heavy Artillery (Capt. Stanislaus Mlotkowski Commanding) was mustered out on 6/30/65, having lost 17 men from disease during the war. Both of these Pennsylvania batteries had been at Fort Delaware since early 1862. The 1st Delaware Heavy Artillery Regiment (consisting of only Ahl's Battery, and commanded by Capt. G.W. Ahl) was mustered out on 7/27/63, after suffering 11 deaths from disease.[5] The enlisted men of this Battery had been recruited from Confederate POWs during

July 1863, and these men had served faithfully for two years (except for at least one man known to have deserted).

For those who had been on the island more than a couple of months, by mid–August 1865 it must have seemed like a ghost town. Capt. Clark's commissary records[6] show that while there were 869 U.S. Volunteers (not including officers) at the Fort on 8/1/65, on 8/11/65 there were 262 and on 8/23/65 there were 4. The pattern was the same for September 1865, with 269 on 9/1/65, 263 on 9/11/65 and 4 on 9/26/65. In October there were 327 on 10/1/65, 358 on 10/21/65 and 205 on 10/26/65. There were of course other people on the island, such as the sutler and his workers, men working on finishing construction of the Fort, and civilian dependents, but after the thousands of people on the island in the first half of the year, it must have seemed empty, especially with the empty prisoners' barracks and related buildings.

There were also three prisoners still listed on Capt. Clark's reports through October 1865. The three remaining prisoners were men who had been captured with Jefferson Davis: Col. Preston Johnston, Col. Francis R Lubbock, both Aides-de-camp to Jefferson Davis, and Col. Burton Harrison, Davis' secretary. They were held in solitary confinement, not being allowed to have any contact with each other or the outside world, although sometimes exceptions were made for sending and receiving letters. They were allowed to walk the ramparts for exercise for half an hour each day.

Johnston (who was the son of Confederate General Albert Sidney Johnston, army commander killed at the battle of Shiloh) and Lubbock were at first put in the general prisoner (officers) population. They apparently arrived on 5/22/65. The next day Schoepf received a Telegram from the Sec. War stating, "I have ordered General Wheeler and officers captured with Jefferson Davis to be taken to Fort Delaware. You will take measures for their secure confinement and prevent all communications between or with them verbally or in writing. Report whether the guard force is adequate for securely guarding them." Schoepf replied the same day that this had been done.[7] The release of Johnston was reported in the *Baltimore American and Commercial Advertiser* on 8/5/65, and presumably happened a short time before then. Lubbock was released on 11/23/65,[8] and in a memoir Lubbock briefly described his imprisonment at Fort Delaware.[9]

However, through at least October Capt. Clark's records indicated there were still three prisoners at the Fort. One of them may have been Col. Henry Kyd Douglas, who was a prisoner at the Fort, having been convicted at (union) court martial of a crime and serving a brief sentence at Fort Delaware.[10] He was released on 8/23/65. On 9/16/65 the CGP wrote to Schoepf that Schoepf was authorized to gives the *two* POWs still present full Union soldiers' rations.[11]

This meant the only POW left at the Fort at the beginning of December 1865 was Burton Harrison, Davis' private secretary. The reason he was held so long was apparently that some Union officials believed he was involved, or at least knew about, the plot to kill Lincoln.[12] This letter by Holt to Stanton may have been prompted by a letter written by Harrison to the Sec. War, which stated:

> Fort Delaware, Del.
> December 8, 1865
> Hon. Secretary of War

Sir:

I am now the last prisoner of war remaining in custody at this post and have the honor to apply for an order releasing me.

I was private Secretary to Mr. Davis. All the other men of his staff have been released and allowed to proceed to their homes—all the members of his Cabinet have, I believe, been sent upon their parole.

I have been a prisoner in solitary & close confinement for seven months. There have never been any charges preferred against me, nor am I aware of the existence of accusations upon which any could have been based. Whatever may have been the object of the Government in retaining me in captivity it has probably been attained before this time.

The people of my State, Mississippi, have shown a readiness to conform themselves to the views and policy of the Government, and it is to be expected that they will submit to the results of the war in good faith.

I am willing to take an oath of allegiance to the U.S. Government.

very respectfully
your obt sevt
\s\ Burton N. Harrison[13]

This and efforts by his fiancée, family, and friends to have him released apparently were successful, for he was released on 1/16/66. Gen. Schoepf was so impressed by Harrison that he named a son born later "Benjamin Harrison Schoepf."

There were still a few Union officers on the island in late 1865 that were there for much of the war. Capt. Clark's records show that Lt. Charles Hawkins, who was Provost Marshall through most of the last two years of the war, was still on the island at the end of October 1865. Clark's records hint he may still have been in charge of the Union convicts present.

Clark himself was promoted to Bvt. Maj. on 10/20/65[14] and mustered out on 10/25/65. He had married Lizzie Brown of Salem, New Jersey, on 10/7/65,[15] since his first wife, Seraphine, had died about 10/29/62[16] while he was on duty at the Fort. He then apparently moved to or near Salem NJ, where he went into the glass bottle making industry as a partner in the firm of Holtz, Clark, & Taylor. By 1870 he had moved back to New York City (only Manhattan then) where he was born, and was back at his old occupation of making pen and pencil cases.[17] He died on 10/23/82 of Bright's (kidney) diease,[18] and is buried in Bayview–New York Bay Cemetery, Jersey City, New Jersey.

Since Capt. Clark was a Commissary Officer he was required to post a bond, and was responsible for making certain his accounts were properly closed out after he left the Army.

His accounts for 1863 and 1864 were successfully closed out before he was mustered out.[19] However, his accounts for 1865 (#6548) were not closed out[20] The contents of Clark's record bundle consist of a large number of papers—such as forms submitted by Clark to justify his expenses, some of these having been lost and been resubmitted, and a few corrected, and a couple of sworn affidavits by Clark attesting to certain expenditures. On the back of one of these affidavits is a note written on 2/2/67 by Schoepf which reads: " I do hereby certify to the credibility of Capt. G. S. Clark's statement herein concerning the amount of fifty four dollars discrepancy and believe that the same has been properly expended and that no loss has been sustained by the Government. Captain Clark has always sustained an excellent reputation and would not in my opinion do or say anything for or account of being benefitted by a few dollars herein."

Capt. Clark was so vexed by this situation, which lasted over a year, that he apparently hired Isaac Hackett, a self-described attorney and claim advocate who was located at 221 Pennsylvania Ave. in Washington, D.C.

Finally, a receipt dated 12/29/66 certifies that Capt. Clark deposited to the credit of the Treasurer of the United States $1.50, which apparently helped to effect closing of his account. It seems ironic that a volunteer who served three and a half years in the Army, and spent over one and one-half million dollars of Government money, had to pay $1.50 in order to close out his accounts..

Gen. Schoepf was mustered out of service on 1/15/66, at which time he turned over the command of Fort Delaware to another officer.[21] Finally settling in Hyattsville, Maryland, he went back to work for the Patent Office, where he rose in rank to a "principal" or perhaps "chief" Examiner. He died of cancer on 5/10/86, and was interred in Congressional Cemetery in Washington, D.C.[22]

As mentioned above, Capt. Clark was promoted to Bvt. Major just before being mustered out. Lt. Charles Hawkins was also brevetted, from 1st Lt. to Capt., effective 3/13/66.[23] This was apparently for meritorious service during the war. These two officers may have been chosen by Schoepf because they may have volunteered to stay several extra months on the island.

Part of the reason the island seemed like a ghost town by mid–August 1865 was that all of the buildings outside the fort, comprising the POW barracks, POW kitchens and bakery, offices, Union barracks, water tanks, etc., were still standing, and there was much equipment, clothing, blankets, etc., present. Schoepf and the CGP started to work on this. On 8/18/65 Schoepf apparently sent a letter, part of which concerned whether the blankets left behind should be washed so that they could be sold. On 8/23/65 the CGP replied that he did not think it worth the cost of washing, considering what the blankets would probably bring when sold.[24]

A bigger question was what to do with all the buildings that had been built to accommodate and serve the POWs. On 8/18/65 the CGP wrote to Schoepf that he should turn all such buildings over to the Quartermaster Department.[25] Previously, on 7/24/65 the CGP requested a list of buildings erected and paid for by the Prison Fund.[26] On 8/2/65 Capt. Craig, the Quartermaster Officer, sent a letter to the CGP reporting all buildings paid for by the Prison Fund, and their dimensions.[27] Sometime after 8/18/65, the CGP (Hoffman) visited Fort Delaware and on 8/24/65 wrote to the Assistant Adjutant General that all the wooden buildings associated with the prison camp outside the Fort should be scrapped with the exception of the surgeon's quarters near the hospital, which should be used as the post hospital.[28] He also suggested the existing Post Hospital could remain. He states the remaining buildings are not worth much, and should be taken down by the convicts and the scrap burned. He also states the barracks are infested with rats, and the rats are eating anything available on the island, including some corn being grown in the gardens.

This apparently percolated around the chain of command, and ended in a decision to auction off the buildings as scrap lumber.[29] This reference also describes each of the lots in detail, such as specific buildings, fences, etc. There were 39 lots originally, plus 32 water tanks that could each hold from 2000 to 6000 gallons. Schoepf ordered removal of two of the lots. A newspaper advertisement for the sale at auction is also pasted to one page. The auction on 12/2/65 yielded $6120 for the government, and the successful bidders had 120 days to remove the items they bought. Almost all the buildings associated primarily with the prison camp were sold, except for the surgeon's quarters and hospital.

By the time General Schoepf left, the post had become a backwater part of the Army. The Army suspected that the weapons in the Fort were obsolete, due to the development of ironclad, and later armored ship, and it was also suspected that masonry forts were easily penetrated by shells fired from rifled guns. In 1868 the Army conducted a test at Fort Delaware to determine if brick and masonry forts could withstand modern weaponry.[30] They could not.

In the 1870's some of the gun platforms were modified to fit 15-inch Rodman guns.[31] By the 1880's the Fort had been virtually abandoned by the Army, with only three families living on the island, the caretaker being an ordnance sergeant.[32]

By 1890 plans were afoot to modernize the Fort.[33] During the 1890's part of the Fort was demolished and a new reinforced concrete section (the Endicott section) was constructed, on which were mounted three 12 inch disappearing guns. A torpedo (mine) station and two batteries of rapid-fire guns were also added to the island. These, in combination with Fort Mott (New Jersey shore) and Fort DuPont (Delaware shore), now constituted the main defense for Delaware Bay.

Approximately from 1904 to 1908 the Delaware River was dredged to increase the depth of the shipping channel from 35 to 45 feet. At least some of the dredge spoils were put on Pea Patch Island inside the seawall, raising the height of the island above the high tide level.[34] Also, cribbing was built north of the existing Island to hold dredge spoils in that location, and the entire size of the island, including the marshes that formed, expanded from about 75 acres to about 375 acres.[35]

In World War I the fort was briefly manned to protect the Delaware River. Not much happened at the Fort between World Wars I and II, and by 1940 a new defensive scheme had been decided on, and fortifications for Delaware Bay were erected at Cape May, New Jersey, and Fort Miles, Delaware, at the mouth of the bay. This rendered Fort Delaware, which was then being used only as a searchlight station, totally obsolete, and it was declared surplus on 10/1/1944, and reverted back to the State of Delaware.[36] Interestingly, there was a German POW camp at Fort DuPont, and before Fort Delaware was closed, occasionally (according to former German POWs who revisited long after WWII) groups of POWs were brought to Fort Delaware to help maintain it. When the Army abandoned the Fort, apparently they removed some metal present for use in World War II scrap drives.[37]

Nothing "official" happened on the island between 1944 and 1951. Unofficially, vandals raided the island periodically to remove metal and other valuables (one cannot tell the difference between what the vandals and what the Army removed when they abandoned the Post). Unofficially, in 1950 the Fort Delaware Society was formed with the objective of preserving the Fort and its historical heritage. They succeeded on June 21, 1951, in lobbying the Delaware State Government to establish a State Park there.

The state early on provided only a caretaker, and up until the early 1990's the Society actually did most of the cleanup work and restoration..[38] For example, in the early 1980's security on the island during nonworking hours was provided by guard dogs roaming about.[39] In the early 1990's the State began a program to restore some of the rooms of the Fort and provide historical interpretation. During the park season in the summer usually about 6 to 15 costumed interpreters present programs and interpret the history of the fort and what life was like during the Civil War. About 12 rooms have been restored and are interpreted. An authentic 8-inch Civil War period Columbiad cannon is mounted on the Northeast parapet, and is fired many days using a reduced charge of gunpowder.

In 2001 a reproduction POW barracks was built, which is open to the visitors during the season. It is an accurate reproduction of the Civil War barracks, except to help preserve it, it is built on pilings.[40] The island was eroding badly on the eastern (New Jersey) side, partly because the very active main shipping channel passes very close to the island. In the winter of 2005–2006 the Corps of Engineers returned to the island and built a new 3500-foot seawall along the eastern side of the island in the place where the original seawall of the 1850's was located. Large areas of erosion were filled in. Some artifacts were recovered from the eroded areas when they were pumped out. Among these is what appears to be the iron head for a pile driver, which may have been used in the 1850's to drive the piles that support the Fort. It is still on the island.[41]

Appendix:
The Shotwell Fort Delaware "Diary"

The Fort Delaware Diary of 2nd Lt. Randolph Abbott Shotwell, 8th Virginia Infantry, is a well-known one, having been published in 1931 by the North Carolina Historical Commision.[1] It is the most widely quoted diary of all the Fort Delaware journals in various works about the prison camp at Fort Delaware, and indeed probably one of the most quoted prisoner diaries dealing with Northern prison camps in general.[2]

The Shotwell diary is actually part of a set of three volumes which include a "war diary" before Shotwell was captured, a section on his imprisonment at Point Lookout and then Fort Delaware, and about the last half of the set is taken up with his diary on Reconstruction. In a "Prefatory Note" presumably written by Shotwell and published in Volume 1,[3] he states, "Much of the narrative, especially of Camp and Prison experiences, will be taken *verbatim* from the daily jotting in my notebook, save when supplemented or corrected by later information." The journal about Fort Delaware is found in Chapters 44 and 45 of Volume 2, while a more general undated description (not covered here) appears in Chapter 43.

There are a relatively large number of (contemporaneous) diaries written by prisoners at Fort Delaware, and the great majority are by officers. Besides Shotwell, the most famous are probably the diary of the Rev. Handy, the diary of Capt. Robert Emory Park, and the diary of Col. William Walker Ward. All three were published. More generally the Fort Delaware diaries may cover a few weeks to more than a year, and how often the diarists wrote and what they recorded and commented on varies widely.

Randolph Abbott Shotwell (1844–1885) was born in West Liberty, Virginia (now West Virginia). In 1856 he attended Tuscarora Academy in Mifflin, Pennsylvania, and while he was in Mifflin, in 1858 the remainder of his family moved to Rutherfordton, North Carolina. In 1860 he attended Media College in Media, Pennsylvania. When the Civil War broke out he crossed the lines and enlisted in the 8th Virginia Infantry, with which he participated in a number of battles. He was promoted to lieutenant for gallantry at Gettysburg. Just before the Battle of Cold Harbor he was captured, sent to Point Lookout, and then to Fort Delaware, where his first diary entry was July 12, 1864. He was released from Fort Delaware on June 19, 1865, after taking the oath of allegiance to the United States.[4]

When reading the Shotwell diary, and comparing it to the other Fort Delaware prisoners' diaries, one is struck by the rather constant negative tone of the diary towards the Union prison camp and its personnel, and often towards his own prisoner compatriots.

He never mentions any friends or comrades whom he assists or who assist him, something very unusual in these diaries. This is in contrast to almost all of the other diaries, which are not as negative, and many also mention fellow prisoners, usually in a more favorable light.[5] One also notices some glaring errors in dates and/or happenings he reported, especially when compared to other diaries. A detailed comparison was therefore made of the entries in Shotwell's diary with entries in other diaries from Fort Delaware, and also in some instances with other contemporaneous records. Table A shows the results of these comparisons. The first column is the entry date in Shotwell's diary, the second column is a synopsis of Shotwell's entry, and the last column gives comparisons to other diaries, and in some instances other records. There are about 60 entries (days) in the Shotwell diary, and all are included, except those of a personal nature such as a notation of a letter received, or general comments about the war.

Something very striking characterizes the entries as a whole. Between July 12, 1864, and October 9, 1864, there are numerous entries, and from then until about early February 1865 very few entries appear. Starting in early February there are more entries in the Shotwell diary until he is freed. On comparing this chronological pattern with other diaries, one finds that the Handy diary runs until October 12, 1864, when Handy was released, and the Park diary starts at Fort Delaware on February 3, 1865, and runs until June 15, 1865, when Park was released. Both of these diaries were published in the 1870's, and presumably were available to anyone, including Shotwell, interested in what happened to prisoners at Fort Delaware.

The individual entries also form an interesting pattern. From the beginning of Shotwell's dairy at Fort Delaware (July 12, 1864) until October 12, 1864, virtually all of the events mentioned by Shotwell also appear in Handy, although sometimes on different dates. The relatively few items not reported by Handy are mostly unconfirmed or appear to have happened at very different times. After reading about 20 diaries from Fort Delaware, one finds it incredible that Shotwell and Handy mention the same things on so many similar or identical dates. This is not to say that prisoners' diaries do not contain similar items, but they tend to vary greatly from prisoner to prisoner, even if most include important events such as the assassination of Lincoln (April 15, 1865), or the leaving (August 20, 1864) and return of the "Immortal 600" (March 12, 1865). A particularly striking instance of parallel entries in Shotwell and Handy is the entry about rat hunting (the "rats" were probably muskrats, today still considered a delicacy by some) by Shotwell on October 4, 1864. There is no other mention of this activity in any of the other diaries.

For the period between the Handy and Park diaries, October 12, 1864, to February 3, 1865, there are only 5 entries. While most of them appear to have happened, the dates appear to be wrong, sometimes by a few days, sometimes longer.

Finally, there is a time period from the start of the Park diary until Shotwell was released. Although not every entry during this period is mentioned by Park, a great many of them are. Park made entries in his diary usually every few days and covers those days in that entry. When Shotwell has a similar entry it is often different by a day or two from diaries other than Park, but within the range given by Park.

Besides these coincidences of entries with the Handy and Park diaries, the dates in Shotwell for some of the events are in error, sometimes by a day or two, sometimes by months. The following are some of the more egregious errors (the dates are Shotwell's entry dates):

- The "mark time" incident on July 12, 1864.
- The blanket incident on July 22, 1864, where Shotwell seems to have gotten two different events mixed together.
- Blankets being "stolen" on November 24, 1864, actually occurred about 3 weeks earlier.
- Gen'l Vance went to New York February 10, 1865.
- The date of return of the Immortal 600 as March 15, 1865.
- The information about capture of Jefferson Davis on May 10, 1865.
- Prisoners learn of assassination of President Lincoln on May 17, 1865, followed up by the entry on May 18, 1865.

The most shocking of these errors is probably that of May 17–18, 1865, when the prisoners are supposed to have learned of Lincoln's murder. All prisoner diaries, including Park's, state that they found out on April 15, 1865, and thereafter describe measures taken on the island over the next few weeks because of this event. Even the Editor of the Shotwell papers, Hamilton, was somewhat incredulous, stating in a footnote that "It seems incredible that no news of Lincoln's assassination had reached the prisoners before this."

All of this evidence, although circumstantial, strongly suggests that Shotwell did not have a systematic "journal" in which he recorded dates and events. Indeed, it seems most likely that he paraphrased events reported by Handy, and possibly Park, and entered them in this "journal," in some instances deliberately changing dates slightly so that these did not appear copied. Given that not all the events described by Shotwell were in the Handy and Park diaries, it is quite possible that Shotwell supplemented these entries from his own memory and/or from scattered notes or letters in his possession, and/or possibly dates of other widely known historical events, such as the date of capture of Jefferson Davis. The Editor's Foreword in Volume 1 states that this is part of Shotwell's autobiography. The Randolph Abbott Shotwell papers from which these three volumes were apparently drawn are in the North Carolina State Archives,[6] and the online description of this collection states, "Manuscript drafts about the war include drawings, sketch maps, and quotations from his wartime diary, which is not included in the collection." This description also states that some of these documents were typescript. Thus it is not known if Shotwell or someone else actually wrote the journal entries concerning Fort Delaware, or if they actually were in a contemporaneous diary. The weight of the circumstantial evidence is that it is not a contemporaneous diary, and it is not used or quoted in this volume. In addition, while we make no judgment here on the veracity of the other parts of the Shotwell Papers, it does perhaps cast some doubt on all three volumes of this work.

The Shotwell diary has had a great impact on the modern perception of Union prisoner of war camps, and of course especially Fort Delaware. Whether it is a contemporaneous diary or a postwar document is vital to the understanding of how much weight it should be given in studying prison camp conditions, and the conclusions described above indicate the Shotwell Diary probably should be given little weight.[7]

Table A. Comparison of Shotwell "Diary" with Other Documents

Shotwell Date	Shotwell General Description	Other Diaries, etc.
7/12/64	Capt. Gordon pulling wagon with convicts. Officer, Capt. Lewis of 38th VA,	Lewis incident noted by Handy on July 30. Gordon sentenced to hard labor 7/9/64

Shotwell Date	Shotwell General Description	Other Diaries, etc.
	ordered by sentinel to mark time on exclaiming "Hurray for Jubal Early."	according to Mckey & Handy. On 7/11/64 Mckey & Handy report Gordon seen pulling a wagon. Also reported by Handy on 7/13.
7/16/64	Philosophical description of Sabbath, but it is Saturday! Reports Handy sent note to Schoepf about guards making Roll Call during services.	Handy was sick this day, may have to go to hospital. No mention of note by Handy. Only letter to Schoepf in July mentioned by Handy is a request for a temporary parole.
7/22/64	Blanket tossing of Major Shearer for abusing a so-called spy or abolitionist in barracks, who reported incident. Done by galvanized Yankees.	Maj. Geo. Shearer reported by Handy to be removed to the fort & is with Co. Q, on 7/25/64. Three officers reported tossed in blanket on 3/7/65 reported by PAMcMichael & Boyle, after they tossed a Conf. Officer who refused to return South.
8/03/64	Reports large commotion last night with guards yelling "Shoot em," Kill em" etc., during apparent escape attempt. Sounded like whole guard of 250 men called out. Musketry heard. However it was only a few men trying to escape.	Escape attempt confirmed by McCrorey & Handy, Handy also confirms gunfire.
8/04/64	Describes "Fox," a Sergeant of "Police Squad." He is "Dutchman" from Vermont.	"Old Fox" mentioned by Mckey on 9/5 & 9/6/64 He is apparently a Union man, perhaps a Sergeant. Mentioned by Mckey on 9/5 & 9/6/64.
8/07/64	Reports gunfire last night during attempted escape. Note tossed from enlisted men says one or more shot.	Handy reports same on 8/8/64.
8/08/64	Reports Lt. Woolf detected in pen spying, disguised as Confederate.	Nothing reported on this day by others at this time. Handy reports Woolf in disguise on 9/26.
8/10/64	Speaks of bad rations & no meat for 5 days. Reports mostly "rusty bacon." Also bad water. Says day is very hot.	Mckey & Morton report it is "very warm." On 8/11 Handy reports "Heat intolerable." On 8/8 Handy reported no meat for several meals. On 8/8 McCrorey reports no meat that day. High temperature 96°F.
8/11/64	"Shocking report of Pestilence" Vaccination going on.	Nothing reported by others that day. Such reports by Handy on 8/8, McCrorey on 7/25 & Cox on 8/15.
8/12/64	Reports Gen. Schoepf et al. came into pen and announced some would be sent South to Hilton Head SC for exchange. Names for exchange called.	McCrorey reports it is just rumors. JRMcMichael, Mckey, & Bingham report Schoepf says some will be sent to Charleston. Handy also states it's rumors. Handy, JRMcMichael, McCrorey, Cox & Mckey state names called on 8/13.
8/14/64	Reports those to be sent South preparing baggage.	Handy reports all in readiness for move on 8/15–16. On 8/20 Handy states officers took their baggage with them. Cox confirms.

The Shotwell Fort Delaware "Diary"

Shotwell Date	Shotwell General Description	Other Diaries, etc.
8/17/64	Two large transports at wharf. No movement yet.	Reported by Handy on 8/14 as being anchored nearby.
8/19/64	Talks of suspense of those chosen.	Reported by Handy on 8/14, 8/15, 8/16, 8/18 & 8/19. Cox confirms 8/18.
8/20/64	Reports leaving of officers to South.	Confirmed by Alburtis, JRMcMichael, Handy, Mckey & Mauck.
8/21/64	Talks of services, then of bribes, etc., from those who wanted to go South.	Services were held as usual on Sabbath–Handy.
8/22/64	Complains of Sutler's prices. Reports it was learned Friday Schoepf recd orders to close Sutler shop. Says it is rumored Schoepf gets bribes from Sutler.	Handy reports on 8/21 that Sutler will be closed after today. Boyle also reports Sutler closed today. Confirmed by Cox on 8/25 & Morton on 8/25, 8/26.
8/26/64	WH Mowry killed by guards for no reason. Seen 9 men shot since then, reports a sergeant in a note, so informed by Capt White. Reports Col. Baker of 41st NC denounces South & fight breaks out.	Handy reports on this date that Mowry previously reported drowned was shot. No other shootings reported.
8/27/64	Reports food restrictions & letters restricted to 2 per week, 10 lines each.	Restrictions on letters confirmed by Handy. Reported on 8/25 by Morton.
8/29/64	Reports arrival of 119 officers & moans about deterioration of quality of officers.	Arrival of 119 officers confirmed by Handy & Cox.
9/01/64	Reports Capt WH Stewart, 5th SC, placed in dungeon in retaliation.	Confirmed by Handy on 8/31.
9/05/64	Woolf came in, "drunk as usual," and ordered the sentry to allow no more than 4 men at a time to go to privy. Reports terrible storm of rain & sleet in evening.	Confirmed by Handy as 5 men at first, later changed to 1 man. Handy reports it is rainy.
9/10/64	Reports officer who took some water to wash out eyes stopped by guard.	Sort of confirmed by Handy. Says officer drew basin full & was taken to guardhouse.
9/17/64	Reports 7 officers ordered to Fort for retaliation.	Confirmed by Mckey & Handy, & Cox on 9/18.
9/24/64	Reports guns fired in salute of Sheridan victory in Valley.	Confirmed by Morton, & by Handy as having been done at night.
9/30/64	*Philadelphia Inquirer* reports immediate exchange of 10,000 prisoners. Reports arrival of Early's officers captured in Valley.	Newspaper report confirmed by Handy. Mckey reports on 9/28 that about 180 of Early's officers arrived. Handy reports 119 officers arrived on 9/29, and some of them are from Petersburg.
10/04/64	Comments on catching rats & rat hunt that day.	No confirmation. Rat hunting described generally by Handy on 10/11/64.
10/06/64	Reports 126 wounded/sick officers on way South. Comments on bribing of doctor.	Confirmed by Handy. Reported as leaving on 10/7 by Mckey. Both report paroles signed on 10/6.
10/9/64	Very cold. General comments.	Confirmed by Handy & Morton.

Shotwell Date	Shotwell General Description	Other Diaries, etc.
11/24/64	Comments on being cold. Complains about blankets being "stolen," 3 biscuits each for breakfast & dinner & morsel of rusty meat.	Boyle reports on 12/10 prisoners allowed only one blanket and excess taken about month ago. Cox & Mckey report it happening on 11/2. 11/4 or 11/5. High temperature 39°F, low 26°F.(*a*).
1/1/65	High winds overnight, then calming, and when he looked out about a foot of snow. The Rev. Kinsolving conducted services at noon. Two men died of small pox in this pen.	McMichael reports it to be cold but sunny on 1/1. On 12/31 McMichael reports it snowed heavily at night and snowing heavily during the day. Weather reports, snow fell night of Dec. 30–31, no high winds Dec. 29–Jan. 3.8(*a*) Cox confirms snow on ground & very cold. There were no officer deaths from smallpox reported from July 11, 1864 to Jan. 19, 1865.(*b*).
1/6/65	For a week hasn't slept at night because of the cold, but slept during day. Reports Delaware River frozen. Have to melt water for drinking and washing.	PAMcMichael reports it raining but pleasant indoors and snow melting rapidly. Very cold Jan. 1–Jan. 5 (weather reports), but warm on Jan. 6, high 54F at 9 p.m. and some rain that day.(*a*) Mckey states weather moderating on 1/5. Cox reports weather very pleasant.
1/16/65	Reports arrival of 80 officers from western armies & civilians from GA arrested by Sherman. Many of officers decrepit.	No confirmation. Morning Reports of Prisoners indicate 18 civilians arrived on 1/13 and 107 officers on 1/17.(*c*).
1/24/65	Gen'l Vance & others moved to fort. States they have a lot of baggage. Mentions Mrs. Emley of Phila. as sending items for general distribution.	Genl Vance move confirmed by Cox on 1/22.
2/9/65	Wild rumors about exchanges.	Confirmed by Park.
2/10/65	Gen'l Vance gone to New York on parole to assist Gen'l Beale buying blankets.	Reported by Cox on 1/26.
1/22/65	Salutes fired for Washington's Birthday.	No confirmation.
2/27/65	100 officers & 1200 men, "sick and wounded," left for exchange.	Confirmed by Boyle, Cox, Park & PAMcMichael.
3/2/65	Reports weather abysmal, much dysentery. Says it is 700 yards to sinks.	No confirmation. Nowhere is the island 700 yards wide.
3/12/65	Gen'l RL Page arrived together with 50 officers from Mobile.	Confirmed by Park on 3/13–15, says 50 officers were from (Shenandoah) Valley.
3/15/65	Survivors of "Immortal 600" returned.	Actually happened on 3/12, Alburtis, PAMcMichael, Mauck (one of "600"). Park records it on 3/13–15.
4/28/65	Reports 900 Confederate officers taking oath right now.	PAMcMichael confirms, but says it was over two days, 4/26–4/27. Mauck states this was a process over 3 days, 4/26 to 4/28, with oaths being taken each day.

The Shotwell Fort Delaware "Diary"

Shotwell Date	Shotwell General Description	Other Diaries, etc.
		Park confirms 4/26–27. Cox says oath offered 4/26.
4/29/65	Out of 10,000 privates only 100 refused to take oath.	Alburtis confirms officers busy making out rolls of those who will take oath.
5/1/65	Reports Gen'l Johnston has surrendered.	Confirmed by JRMcMichael on 5/2. Page reports on 4/26–29.
5/10/65	Prisoners informed Pres. Davis captured.	Reported by Mauck on 5/14 when a prisoner saw a dispatch. Rumor reported by Cox on 5/14. Reported by Page 5/19–31. Davis actually captured on this date.
5/17/65	Lincoln assassination becomes known. Great anger by guards. Names John Wilkes Booth.	Assassination became known to prisoners on 4/15. Mauck, PAMcMichael, Barringer, Alburtis & Cox.
5/18/65	More about assassination as if it is new news.	See 5/17.
5/25/65	Talks about officers cursing over delay in release.	Mentioned by others in this general period.
6/12/65	All POWs except field officers, etc., to be released.	Not confirmed. Cox mentions reports on 6/6.
6/13/65	Reports a number of prisoners were called out yesterday.	Confirmed by PAMcMichael & Cox. Also by Park who is released.
6/14/65	600 officers departed yesterday.	Not confirmed. Morning reports—501 officers released 1/12, 21 on 1/14 and 419 on 1/17.(c).
6/16/65	Still in suspense. Woolf says they will be released tomorrow.	Not confirmed.
6/19/65	All line officers taken out & given oath. All, including Shotwell, released.	Confirmed by Cox, who is released. Also confirmed by PAMcMichael.

Notes to Table A: (a) RG27. E59, Vol. 126. (b) M598, Roll 47, "Register of Deaths of Rebel Prisoners." (c) M598, Roll 48, "Morning Reports of Prisoners."

Chapter Notes

Preface

1. See for instance W. B. Hesseltine, *Civil War Prisons: A Study in War Psychology*, Frederick Ungar Publishing Co., New York, 1964 (republication of original published by the Ohio State University Press, 1930), p. 172-176, for opinions in the North; and B. G. Cloyd, *Haunted by Atrocity: Civil War Prisons in American Memory*, Louisiana State University Press, Baton Rouge, 2010, p. 20-23, for opinions on both the North and South.

2. U.S. Sanitary Commission, *Narrative of the Privations and Sufferings of United States Officers and Enlisted Soldiers While Prisoners of War in the Hands of the Rebel Authorities*, King & Baird, Philadelphia, 1864.

3. SHSP, Vol. I, March 1876, No. 3, entitled *The Treatment of Prisoners During the War Between the States*.

4. Hesseltine 172-176.

5. C. W. Sanders, *While in the Hands of the Enemy: Military Prisons of the Civil War*, Louisiana State University Press, Baton Rouge, 2005.

6. J. M. Gillespie, *Andersonvilles of the North: The Myths and Realities of Northern Treatment of Civil War Confederate Prisoners*, University of North Texas Press, Denton, 2008.

7. Hesseltine supports this position in footnote 9 on his page 116 which states "It is almost impossible to determine the exact ration issued to prisoners of war at any one time. Official reports of rations are lacking and the accounts of prisoners are open to suspicion of exaggeration. It is difficult to imagine that a prisoner writing from three to twenty years after his release from captivity is able to remember the rations issued in any given month. Prisoners' narratives place the amount of meat anywhere from one ounce to a one-half pound. Bread is usually not mentioned by weight but some accounts state that the prisoners received a half pound of cornbread."

8. See OR, Ser. II, Vol. VII, p. 150-151.

9. Gillespie, p. 57-58; Sanders, paragraph bridging p. 310-311, which describes the results of, in effect, the "retaliation program." No specific data or references related to these results are given.

10. While doing research for this study, many documents were found in the National Archives which had been stamped "Official Records" with a circular rubber stamp. Not all were included in the printed publication, and apparently a second round of selection was applied after the first survey of things to be included. In the case of items concerning POWs, for example, correspondence to and from the Commissary General of Prisoners, most of the unpublished items do not seem to be biased for or against good Northern treatment of POWs.

11. The key word here is "contemporaneous." Memoirs or recollections written after the War are remarkably different in tone from what is reported in contemporaneous writings. The entries for specific dates in the various diaries were checked against each other to confirm that the documents were indeed contemporaneous. It was found that one diary that claimed to be contemporaneous, the famous "diary" of Randolph Abbott Shotwell, was in fact most likely fabricated after mid-1877 (see Appendix). This "diary" is the most anti–Northern of the diaries, and since it was published, is often quoted to show how bad conditions were in Northern prison camps. Since it is not a contemporaneous diary, it is not referred to herein.

12. For a description of what happened at the Fort before then, see D. Fetzer and B. Mowday, *Unlikely Allies: Fort Delaware Prison Community in the Civil War*, Stackpole Books, Mechanicsburg, PA, p. 16-91.

13. OR, Ser. II, Vol. VIII, p. 989.

Chapter 1

1. D. Tvaryanas, HAER No. DE-56, National Park Service, available from the Library of Congress, and also (in 2014) website http://lcweb2.loc.gov/master/pnp/habshaer/de/de0400/de0497/data/de0497data.pdf

2. *Ibid.*

3. RG249, E3, Vol. 9, #2864; Handy, 10/5/64.

4. Handy 2/1/64, 4/13/64, 5/20/64, 5/26/64, 6/6/64, 8/27/64/ 9/5/64, 10/2/64 and 10/6/64; McKey, 10/2/64, 12/11/64; Morton, 10/4/64; Cox 11/29/64 12-17-19/64; Park 2/4/65; Alburtis 3/23/65; Mauck 3/31/65; and Berkeley 5/2/65.

5. Tvaryanas.

6. *Ibid.*

7. *Ibid.*

8. RG27, E59, Vol. 126.

9. National Oceanic and Atmospheric Administration, 30-year climate averages, 1981-2010.

10. *Regulations for the Medical Department of The Army*, Washington, A.O.P. Nicholson, Public Printer, 1856, p. 42-45.

11. *Ibid.*, p. 25-31; A good description of the evolution of Medical Deportment meteorological data is found in G.K. Grice and p. Boulay, *History of Weather Observation, Fort Snelling, Minnesota, 1819-1892*, December 2005, which was found online (2014) at http://mrcc.sws.uiuc.edu/FORTS/histories/MN_Fort_Snelling_Grice_Boulay.pdf. This also discusses the shortcomings of these measurements.

Chapter 2

1. William Kesley Boynton (born Kesley Schoepf Boynton), *Albin F. Schoepf: A Family Biography*, unpublished manuscript, 1990, copy in FDS. Contains a complete biography of Schoepf from birth to death, including his Civil War activities.
2. RG194, E159, Schoepf. Military records relating to Schoepf.
3. Most of this information from GW Ahl service record, NARA.
4. GS Clark service record, NARA, and obituary, *New York Times*, July 28, 1882.
5. Letter from GS Clark to William Rowe (a friend), 9/23/61, author's collection.
6. RG393, Pt. 4, E352, p. 81.
7. Charles Hawkins' service record, NARA.
8. RG94, Entries 561, 570, 572, 575 and 584.
9. *Ibid.*
10. Claim for pension No. 1204473, dated March 10, 1898 (Department of the Interior, Bureau of Pensions), and Declaration for Pension by Abraham G. Wolf, dated December 5, 1910.
11. RG77-10-44-1.1, 1862 vol. 2, p. 581, 1863, vol. 2, p. 581, 1864 vol. 3, p. 114, and 1865, vol. 3, p. 331. These volumes also have many letters concerning construction at the Fort. They are located in NARA Philadelphia.
12. RG393, Pt. 4, E350, OB532, #150.
13. RG393, Pt. 4, E352, p. 43.
14. *Ibid.*, p. 46.
15. *Ibid.*, p. 59.
16. *Ibid.*, p. 60.
17. *Ibid.*, p. 62.
18. *Ibid.*, p. 64.
19. *Ibid.*, p. 79.
20. *Ibid.*, p. 81.
21. *Ibid.*, p. 86
22. *Ibid.*, p. 88.
23. *Ibid.*, p. 50.
24. *Ibid.*, p. 61.
25. RG393, Pt. 4, E350, OB352, #29.
26. *Ibid.*, #32.
27. RG393, Pt. 4, E346, OB522, p. 34.
28. RG393, Pt. 4, E346, OB522, p. 89.
29. RG323, Pt. 1, E238, Vol. 4, #778.
30. M504, R196, #151.

Chapter 3

1. On 3/16/64 Schoepf sent a telegram to the CGP stating he could accommodate 1500 rebel officers separate from the enlisted men, RG249, E21, vol. 3, #19.
2. On 5/9/64 Handy recorded in his diary that the political prisoners were being moved to the barracks. On 5/1/64 Handy also wrote that the political prisoners were about to be moved into the convicts' former quarters, so the convicts had evidently been transferred to their quarters outside the Fort.
3. RG393, Pt. 4, E346, OB522, p. 86.
4. These persons were sent to Washington City about 6/30/64 for exchange, RG393, Pt. 4, E350, OB532, #94.
5. On 2/25/65 a telegram from the CGP ordered these persons to be released on taking the oath of allegiance, RG393, Pt. 4, E350, OB533 #2(?).
6. a. M504, R196, #15.
7. M711, R63, #955.
8. RG393, Pt. 1, vol. 5, #82.
9. RG393, Pt. 4, OB522, p. 98.
10. M711, R64, #489.
11. RG393, Pt. 4, E346, OB522, p. 110.
12. M504, R196, #123.
13. M221, R248, #S542.
14. RG393, Pt. 4, E346, OB552, p. 99.
15. M221, R248, #S542.
16. RG393, Pt. 4, E346, OB522, p. 123.
17. RG393, Pt. 4, E350, OB532, #105.
18. RG249, E21, vol. 3, #114.
19. See for example OR. Ser. II, Vol. VIII, p. 986–1003.
20. RG249, E10., vol., 3, #315.
21. RG393, Pt.4, E352, p. 59.
22. RG393, pt. 4, E346, OB522, p. 9/
23. RG393, pt. 1, E2322, vol. 4, p. 360.
24. RG393, Part 1, E2327, vol. 4, p. 503.
25. RG249, E10, vol. 12, #161.
26. RG249, E10, vol. 3, #393.
27. RG249, E10, vol. 3, #391.
28. RG249, E10, vol. 3, #564.
29. RG249, E3, vol. 10, #537.
30. RG249, E3, vol. 11, #2195.
31. RG249, E3, vol. 11, #2234.
32. RG249, E10, vol. 5, #847 and also RG393, Part 4, E346, OB522, p. 45 (both entries record the same letter).
33. RG249, E10, vol. 3, #648, #649, #654, #654, #655, #656, #660, and RG393, Pt. 4, E346, OB522, p. 17 (note names may be misspelled in transcription to typed script and some of these could be political prisoners).
34. RG249, E3, vol. 3, #3357, #3365.
35. RG393, Pt. 4, E350, OB532, #24.
36. RG393, Pt. 4, E352, p. 80.
37. M504, R196, #147.
38. RG393, Pt. 4, E350, OB532, #68.
39. RG393, Pt. 4, E346, OB522, p. 30.
40. RG393, Pt. 4, E350, OB532, #69.
41. RG393, Part 4, E346, OB522, p. 36.
42. M504, R196, #181.
43. RG393, Pt. 4, E350, OB532, #70; M473, R83, p. 358.
44. RG393, Pt. 4, E350, OB523, #74; M473, R83, p. 69.
45. RG393, Pt. 4, E346, OB522, p. 51; M504, R196, #180.
46. RG49, E3, vol. 6, #43.
47. RG393, Pt. 4, E346, OB522, p. 103.
48. On 14034, M504, R300, #407.
49. RG249, E10, vol. 12, #333.
50. RG249, E10, vol. 12, #320.
51. RG249, E10, vol. 12, #397.
52. RG393, Pt. 4, E352, p. 64.
53. RGRG249, E3, vol. 11, #2731 and #2737.
54. *Philadelphia Inquirer*, May 26, 1864; and *Philadelphia Press*, May 27, 1864.
55. RG249, E3, vol. 9, #3313.
56. RG249, E3, vol. 9, #3489.
57. M598, Rolls 49, 50 and 52.
58. For a few years in the early 2000s there was a triathlon (a competition involving swimming, bicycle riding and running) which started on the Island, the first part being a swim to Delaware City, about a mile away. Typically, about one-third of the participants, trained athletes, failed to get to Delaware City and had to be rescued. Under poor conditions (high winds), about 70 percent had to be rescued. For untrained swimmers, such as most POWs, it would have been even more difficult (author's knowledge).
59. RG393, Pt. 4, E352, p. 66.
60. *Ibid.*, p. 86.
61. OR, Series II, Vol. VII, p. 1256.

62. Kevin p. Mackie, done while at the University of Delaware, *Fort Delaware Prison Escapes, 1862–1865,* copy at Fort Delaware State Park.

63. Also found in *Fort Delaware Society Notes,* vol. XXXI (April 1981), p. 2.

64. OR, Series II, Vol. VIII, p. 986–1003.

65. RG393, Pt. 4, E346, OB522, p. 120.

66. RG249, E3, vol. 9, #2919; OR Ser. II., Vol. VII, p. 461–462.

67. Handy reports on 8/18/64 an escapee was held in the guardhouse for 17 days.

68. R. H. Simmons article, *Union Volunteers at Fort Delaware,* FDS website.

69. RG393, Pt. 4, E346, OB522, p. 97.

70. RG393, E3, vol. 6, #1127.

71. RG92, E2212, p. 35–159.

72. See the following: Webpages at http://www1.chem.leeds.ac.uk/delights/texts/Demonstration_19.htm (anonymous) and P. Lauginie, *Drummond Light, Limelight: a Device in Its Time,* at http://archive.ihpst.net/2013/Procs/Lauginie.pdf, and E. Thompson, *Searchlight Development,* in *General Electric Review,* Vol. XXII, Sept. 1919, p. 722–724 (available on Google Books®).

73. RG393, Pt. 4, E346, OB522 (no page).

74. Information from *Dictionary of American Fighting Ships,* Anonymous, Department of the Navy, Navy Historical Center (online).

75. RG393, Pt. 4, E346, OB522, p. 86.

76. RG393, Part 4, E346, OB522 (no page).

77. RG249, E10, vol. 12, #243.

78. RG393, Pt. 4, E350, OB532, #133.

79. *Revised United States Army Regulation of 1861,* Government Printing Office, Washington, 1863, Articles 25, 38 and 45.

Chapter 4

1. *Revised Regulation for the Army of the United States,* 1861. War Department. Philadelphia, J.G.L Brown, Printer, 1863

2. OR, Series II, Vol. VII, p. 72.

3. OR, Series II, Vol. VII, p. 183; U.S. Army General Orders 226, July 8, 1864.

4. OR, Series II, Vol. VII, p. 151.

5. A table similar to this one appears in MSH, Part III, Vol. I, p. 69.

6. F. L. Byrne in *Civil War Album Complete Photographic History of the Civil War,* Edited by W.C. Davis and B. L. Wiley, Tess Press, New York, 2000, p. 596; J.I. Robertson, Jr., *Soldiers in Blue and Gray,* University of South Carolina press, 1988, p. 199; R. H. Simmons, *The Fort Delaware Prison Fund,* Fort Delaware Notes, Vol. LI, February 2001, p. 11–18.

7. *United States Army Regulations of 1861.* Government Printing Office, Washington, D.C., 1863 (revised up until June 25, 1863). Forms are on pages 250–300.

8. W. C. Davis, *A Taste for War,* Stackpole Books, Mechanicsburg, PA, 2003, p. 43.

9. *Narrative of the Privations and Sufferings of United States Officers and Soldiers,* U.S. Sanitary Commission, printed by King & Baird, Philadelphia, 1864, p. 203.

10. RG192, E10, Box 197, #1596.

11. RG192, E 10, Box 197, #1597.

12. OR, Series II, Vol. VIII, p. 62.

13. RG192, E10, Box 211, #304.

14. RG192, E1, Vol. 53, #647.

15. J. D. Citron, *The Great Fresh Beef Scandal,* Fort Delaware Notes, February 2007. Original documents in RG92, E225, Box 491.

16. The supplies from Philadelphia are accounted for on "Invoice for Subsistence Stores" forms in Capt. Clark's records. This form does not have a form number.

17. For instance, advertisements for bids for fresh beef appear in the *Philadelphia Press* on April 11, 13, 15, 18, 22 and 25, May 24, 30 and 31, December 3 and 22, 1864, and March 22 and June 26 and 27 1865. Not all local newspapers could be searched, and in some instances newspaper files are not complete.

18. Handy, 7/29/63 and 8/3/63.

19. RG249, E10, Vol. 5, #884.

20. RG249, E3, Vol. 11, #2531.

21. RG93, E2212, p. 135 et seq.

22. Mauck 3/22/65; JAG 11/29/14; Mckey 6/17/64, 6/21/64, 9/15/64; Handy 6/22/64, 9/10/64.

23. Handy, 7/25/63, 4/14/64, 5/16/64 and 6/22/64; Alburtis, 6/2/64; Cox 7/21/64; Park, 2/5/65 and 3/7/65.

24. W. C. Davis, *A Taste for War,* Stackpole Books, Mechanicsburg, PA, 2003, p. 4, 22, 23.

25. *United States Army Regulations of 1861.* Government Printing Office, Washington, D.C., 1863 (revised up until June 25, 1863). Forms are on p. 23.

26. RG93, E2212, p. 135 et seq.

27. W. C. Davis, *A Taste for War,* Stackpole Books, Mechanicsburg, PA, 2003, p. 130.

28. M598, Roll 47, *List of Clothing Issued to Bakers, Sept. 1864.* Lists 18 names of prisoners (some illegible) along with their regiments and clothing issued, including shirts and pants.

29. Letter of Pvt. William I. Fletcher, 6th MA VV, 27084.

30. *United States Army Regulations of 1861.* Government Printing Office, Washington, D.C., 1863 (revised up until June 25, 1863). Section 1229, p. 252.

31. *Ibid.,* p. 358–363.

32. Based on a man weighing 146 lbs (65 kg) and 5 feet 8 inches (1.76 m) tall, and 18–30 years old. Calculated using the method described in Chapter 5 of *Human Energy Requirements,* Report of a Joint FAO/WHO/UNU Expert Consultation, Rome 17–24 October 2001 (published 2004), ISBN 9251065123.

33. J. Bollet, *Civil War Medicine, Challenges and Triumphs,* Galen Press, Ltd., Tucson, AZ, 2002, Chapter 13.

34. *Joint FAO/WHU Expert Consultation on Human Vitamin and Mineral Requirements 1998,* Bangkok Thailand, published 2004, ISBN 9241546123, p. 35.

35. *Ibid.,* p. 138.

36. J. Bollet, *Civil War Medicine, Challenges and Triumphs,* Galen Press, Ltd., Tucson, AZ, 2002, p. 344; J. J. Woodward, *Outlines of the Chief Camp Diseases of the U.S. Armies,* J.P. Lippincott & Co., Philadelphia, 1863, pp. 5–73, especially p. 65. The discussion in Woodward also lists other possible causes for scurvy besides diet, such as fatigue, cold, moisture, bad ventilation, dirt and nostalgia (depression).

37. OR, Series II, Vol. VIII, p. 62.

38. U.S. Department of Agriculture, Food and Nutrition Information Center, *Food Composition* (online 2009).

39. RG393, Pt. 4, E359, OB522, #95.

40. RG249, E3, Vol. 9, #2707. This also authorized Schoepf to purchase additional antiscorbutics on a surgeon's certificate of need.

41. U.S. Bureau of the Census, *Historical Statistics of the United States, Colonial Times to 1970,* Bicentennial Edition, Part 1, U.S. Government Printing Office, Washington, D.C., 1975, p. 201.

42. *Ibid.,* p. 197–214.

43. N. James, *The Federal Prison Population Buildup: Overview, Policy Changes, Issues and Options*, Congressional Research Service, Report No. R42937, 2014, p. 16.

Chapter 5

1. Frank L. Byrne, *Prison Pens of Suffering*, in William C. Davis and Bell L. Wiley, Ed., *Civil War Album*, Tess Press, New York, 2000, p. 596.
2. The Commissary Records are in RG 217, UD1001, Boxes 593 (1863), 909 (1864) and 1739 (1865).
3. *Revised Regulations for the Army of the United States, 1861*, War Department, 1861, Articles 205–208 and 1195–1197.
4. OR., Series II, Vol. IV, p. 151.
5. Data abstracted from Capt. Clark's records RG217, UD1001, Boxes 594 and 909.
6. Calculated from Table 5-1 and from Ref. 5.
7. Calculated from Ref. 5.
8. Taken from Capt. Clark's records, RG217 UD1001, boxes 909 and 1739.
9. OR., Series II, Vol. VII, p. 72.
10. OR., Series II, Vol. VII, p. 183.
11. L.R. Speer, *Portals to Hell*, Stackpole Books, Mechanicsburg, PA, 1997, p. 317.
12. *Revised Regulations for the Army of the United States, 1861*, Government Printing Office, 1863, p. 262–263.
13. RG249, E3, vol. 13, #1479.
14. RG249, E3, vol. 14, #2658.
15. RG249, E3, vol. 19, #2894.
16. RG249, E3, vol. 14, #3009.
17. OR., Vol. VIII, p. 767; RG249, E3, Vol. 14, #3035.
18. See Capt. Clark's records, RG217, UD1001, Box 1739.
19. *Webster's 7th New Collegiate Dictionary*, G&C Merriam Co., Springfield, MA, 1963, p. 256.
20. OR, Ser. II. Vol. VIII, p. 62–63. These General Orders No. 1 essentially recodified the Circulars of April 20th and June 1st 1864, but made a few changes, eliminating potatoes from the prisoner ration, and giving prison commandants the option of increasing the amounts of soap, salt or vinegar in the U.S. Army ration. It also allowed compressed potatoes and desiccated vegetables to be issued. The main source of the Prison Fund did not change.
21. RG249, E3, vol. 4, #2190.
22. RG249, E3, Vol. 11, #2531.
23. RG249, E3, vol. 3 #3641.
24. RG249, E3, vol. 3, #3723.
25. RG249, E3, vol. 3, #3748.
26. RG249, E3, vol. 6, #1127.
27. RG393, Pt. 4, E350, OB 532, #95.
28. RG249, E3, vol. 9, #2707.
29. RG249, E10, vol.19, #738.
30. RG249, E3, vol. 13, #1340.
31. *The National Police Gazette* (1854–1906), Sep. 27 1879, Vol. XXXV, No. 105, p. 5 (available from APS Online); *Juniata Sentinel and Republican*, Nov. 5, 1879, p. 1 (available from Library of Congress).
32. RG249, E3, vol. 14, #3008.
33. RG249, E3, vol. 12, #956
34. RG249, E10, vol. 19, #647.
35. RG249, E3, vol. 12 #1198.
36. RG249, E10, vol. 19, #1194.

Chapter 6

1. OR, Series II, Vol. V, p. 457.
2. D. Fetzer and B. Mowday, *Unlikely Allies*, Stackpole Books, Mechanicsburg, PA, 1999, p. 62–63.
3. *Ibid.*
4. OR, Series II, Vol. III, p. 471.
5. *Ibid.*, Vol. IV, p. 291–292.
6. *Ibid.*, Vol. V, p. 467.
7. *Ibid.*, p. 484.
8. *Ibid.*, p. 492.
9. *Ibid.*, p. 501.
10. *Ibid.*, p. 538.
11. RG249, E10, vol. 3, #343.
12. *Ibid.*, #321.
13. *Ibid.*, #326.
14. RG393, Part 4, E346, OB522, p. 3.
15. The data about the barracks are taken from RG92, E2212 p. 35–159, which was the sale of most of the wooden outbuildings on Pea Patch Island in December 1865. The building dimensions and descriptions were given in detail, and there is also a detailed map.
16. This request was sent approximately 7/2/63 to QM General Meigs, RG393, Part 4, E346, OB522, p. 12 (letter undated).
17. Letter Pvt. William Fletcher, 6th MA VV, 9/1/64. In a letter on 8/24/64 Fletcher reported that they would not occupy the barracks occupied by the 157th OH, building K and L, but moved into new two story barracks, M-P.
18. On 7/6/64 Schoepf sent an estimate of costs for these barracks to the CGP RG393, Part 4, E346, OB522, p. 117), the CGP replied on 7/9/64 (RG249, E3, vol. 9, #2864), on 7/16/63 there was some back and forth about the cost of the barracks [RG393, Pt. 4, E350, OB532 #97; RG249, E21, vol. 3, #95; and RG393, Pt. 4, E346, OB522 (no page)]; and on 7/22/64 the CGP gave permission to go ahead with the barracks and stated that lumber from demolished barracks should be reused (RG249, E3, vol. 9, #3109).
19. RG393, Pt. 4, E346, OB522, no page.
20. United States Sanitary Commission, *Narrative of the Privations and Sufferings of United States Officers and Soldiers*, King & Baird, Philadelphia, 1864, p. 211–212.
21. RG393, Part 4, E346, OB522 (no page).
22. M598, R47, Morning Reports of Prisoners.
23. Handy states that on 5/1/64 the political prisoners were told to prepare to move into the convicts' former quarters.
24. *United States Army Regulations, 1861, Revisions to June 25, 1863*, Government Printing Office, 1863, p. 159, article 1068.
25. The records of a number of Civil War QM officers have survived and been collected under the officers' names in the National Archives (in RG92). However, these tended to be QM officers in charge of large areas or commands, such as the Army of the Potomac.
26. *Narrative of the Privations and Sufferings of United States Officers and Soldiers While Prisoners of War*, Printed for the U.S. Sanitary Commission by King & Baird, Printers, Philadelphia, 1864, p. 211.
27. See Table 10-1.
28. OR, Series 2, Vol. VI, p. 516 and 653.
29. See Chapter 3 for the reasons for this.
30. Clark stated all he and 4 others had to do was to take charge of the clothing and clean and fill the "lanterns" which were used to light the prisoners' quarters.
31. RG249, E10, vol. 7, #1019.
32. RG393, Pt. 4, E350, OB532, #15.
33. *Ibid.*, #2531.
34. RG393, Pt. 4, E346, OB522, no page.
35. *Ibid.*, no number.
36. RG349, E3, vol. 14, #3077.

Chapter 7

1. Jonathan Letterman, *Medical Recollections of the Army of the Potomac*, D. Appleton & Co., New York, 1866, p. 98.
2. See for instance A.J. Bollet, *Civil War Medicine*, Galen Press Ltd., Tucson, AZ, 2002, p. 380 (Andersonville), and p. 391 (Elmira).
3. The water is probably not potable at any time of the year now, since the runoff from the upper drainage of the Delaware River watershed was greatly reduced when New York City built reservoirs for municipal water supply between 1937 and 1964 in the west Catskill mountains.
4. M22, R107, #S986.
5. RG393, Pt. 4, E346, OB522, p. 31.
6. OR, Ser. II, Vol. VI, p. 516.
7. MSH, Part III, Vol. 1, p. 57.
8. RG92, E2212, p. 135–159 (in Philadelphia).
9. Papers of United States Sanitary Commission, New York Public Library (42nd Street Branch)., Box 613, Documents 2364 and 2388. When these letters were written sanitary conditions on the Island were probably at their worst.
10. *Revised Regulations for the Army of the United States, 1861*, War Department, J.G.L. Brown, Philadelphia, 1861, p. 24.
11. M221, R261, #S1983.
12. J. M. Hyson, Jr., et al., *A History of Dentistry in the U.S. Army to World War II*, Office of the Surgeon General United States Army, Falls Church, VA and Borden Institute, Walter Reed Army Medical Center, Washington, D.C., 2008, Chap. 2.
13. RG249, E3, Vol. 9, #3494.
14. OR, Series II, Vol. VII, p. 664, 695, 766, 836, 909, 956, 1003, 1064, 1102, 1187, 1244, 1285; Vol. VIII, p. 40, 80, 112, and 143.
15. MSH, Part III, Vol. 1, p. 57. OR, Series II, Vol. VI, p. 235, 281, 516, 517, and Vol. VII, p. 421.
16. OR, Part II, Vol. VI, p. 651.
17. RG249, E3, vol. 3, #3641.
18. I Hays, Ed., *The American Journal of Medical Sciences*, Vol. 47, Blanchard and Lee, Philadelphia, 1864, p. 287.
19. Forks and knives were confiscated, according to a letter quoted by Handy, on August 25, 1864, which states, "We are not even allowed a knife, or spoon, because one of our officers got drunk, and threatened that he could take the Fort with knives." Another reason for the confiscation may have been described by Schoepf on August 10, 1864 when he wrote to the CGP describing an escape in which Schoepf stated, "They made saws out of case knives and used canteens for buoys. Since then I have had all their knives and canteens taken from them." (RG393, Part 4, E346, OB 522, no page number.)
20. M598, R47, approximately pages 6–9.
21. OR, Part II, Vol. VII, p. 1252–1256. This text is the report of the Court of Inquiry into the shooting of Pvt. Bibb.
22. W. A. Hammond, Ed., *Military Medical and Surgical Essays*, J. B. Lippincott & Co., Philadelphia, 1864, Chap. 1 and 2, and J.J. Woodward, *Outlines of the Chief Camp Diseases of the United Sates Armies*, J.B. Lippincott & Co., Philadelphia, 1863, Chap. 1.
23. Papers of United States Sanitary Commission, New York Public Library (42nd Street Branch), Box 613, Documents 2364 and 2388.
24. J.J. Woodward, p. 118–119.
25. As specific instances, Gibson stated in an undated entry in his diary that "The house is all the time wet [illegible—because?] of spitting on the floor &c." Also in a microfilm record (M598, Roll 47), on what is apparently the back cover of a notebook or record book, it states that John Conch (12th SC), John Rodes (7th LA), Charles Jacob (38th AL) and John Long (6th AL) were "urinating in yard." There is no notation of what, if anything, happened to them for doing this.

Chapter 8

1. A copy of the list of things authorized to be sold by the sutler, sent to Schoepf by the CGP, was sent to Assistant Sec. War Dana on 8/5/64, RG393, Pt. 4, E346, OB522, the list actually appears in M221, Roll 262, #S1983, which includes all of the enclosures. On the sheet with the list, it notes in handwriting, "signed Wm Hoffman, Comy Genl of Prisoners."
2. OR, Ser. II, Vol. VI, p. 625.
3. This was a time when there were many escape attempts, and apparently taking of greenbacks from the prisoners was to lessen the chances of guards being bribed and/or depriving escaping prisoners who successfully made it ashore of money to aid in their escape.
4. OR, Ser. II, Vol. VII, p. 72.
5. M598, Rolls 49 and 50, "Ledgers of Prisoner's Accounts."
6. RG249, E3, Vol. 2, #1147.
7. RG249, E10, vol. 19, #784.
8. These numbers are very approximate. They were counted as officers' and citizens' contribution only when the account book explicitly identified them as officers (usually by their rank) or citizens. If they were not identified as officers or citizens, they were credited in these totals to the enlisted men's accounts. Therefore the enlisted men's accounts may be artificially inflated at the expense of the officers' accounts. There were also a very few accounts in which not even a name could be made out and these were not counted.
9. See for instance Boyle 7/15/64, 8/29/64, 1/10/65, Barringer 6/18/65, Mauck 6/7/64, McCrorey 7/11/64, 7/29/64, and 7/16/64, JRMcMichael 8/1/64 and Cox 12/6/64, which all mention sharing food or being in messes (a mess being a group of people, usually soldiers, who eat together) with other men.
10. See for instance Alburtis and his compatriots 5/7/64, 5/24/64, 6/25/64, 7/10/64, and 8/15/64; Allen 5/27/64, 7/4/64, and 7/7/64; Boyle 7/16/63 (3 packages, one of which was partially pilfered), and 8/8/64 (contained boots, hat, carpet bag, and vegetables); and McCrorey, 7/10/64 and 8/5/64.
11. RG393, Part 4, E346, OB522, no page, and also M221, R261, #S1983.
12. B.G. Cloyd, *Haunted by Atrocity, Civil War Prisons in American Memory*, Louisiana State University Press, Baton Rouge, 2010, pp. 20–24.
13. RG249, E3, vol. 9, #3313; The actual accounts are found in M598, Roll 52.
14. RG249, E3, Vol. 9, #3489.
15. Letter for sale described on the internet July 29, 2014 on the site of Cohasco., Inc. Document Preservation Center, www.cohascodpc.com/cat63/cat63_auction.html.
16. OR, Series II, Vol. IV, p. 309.
17. Delaware Historical Society Library, Wilmington, DE.
18. References for "Cotton for Clothing" are OR, Ser. 2, Vol. VII, pages 1101, 1107–8, 1109, 117, 1131, 1164, 1192, 1206–7, 1226–7, 1260, 1276–80; Ser. 2, Vol. VIII, pages

13–15, 25, 56, 73–4, 79, 82, 114, 131–2, 154, 180, 215, 227, 228, 257, 389, 502, 713, and 748–50. The last mentioned pages are Gen. Beall's summary of his involvement, written after the war was over, and meant for publication. Also, Gen. Beall's personal papers concerning this episode are in the Elenor S. Brockenbrough Library of the Museum of the Confederacy, Richmond, VA, and in particular have more detail concerning what happened at Fort Delaware.

19. RG393, Pt. 4, E350, OB532, #192.
20. RG249, E3, vol. 12, #1060.
21. OR, Ser. 2, Vol. VIII, p. 114.

Chapter 9

1. Letter written by Pvt. Inslee Deaderick, Pvt. 2nd TN Cav. to Ch. McClung, Macon, GA on 2/4/65. The letter quoted was written in invisible ink (onion juice) so was not subject to censorship. Also written on the same paper was a letter written with regular ink, which probably served as a "cover" for hidden letter. The typescript copy and a copy of the original letter are in the files of the Fort Delaware Society.
2. This is an estimate based on the fact that Clark's Commissary records show that there was an average of about 1100 Union soldiers, convicts, and laundresses on the Island in March 1863, plus an unknown number of civilians.
3. M598, Roll 47.
4. RG112, E570 and E584.
5. M598, Roll 47.
6. RG112, E570.
7. *Ibid.*
8. MSH, Part III, Vol. 1, p. 57–59.
9. New York Public Library Man Branch (42nd Street), Files of the United States Sanitary Commission, Box 613, Documents Nos. 2364 and 2388 (from New York Register Box 903).
10. OR, Part II, Vol. VI, p. 215–216.
11. RG249, E10, Vol. 3, #321.
12. RG393, Pt. 4, E350, OB532, #216. M504, R196, #163.
13. M504, R196, #166.
14. RG393, Pt. 4, E346, OB522, p. 14.
15. RG393, Pt. 4, E350, OB532, #52.
16. M504, R196, #183; RG393, Pt. 4, E350, OB522, #215.
17. RG393, Pt. 4, E346, OB522, p. 31.
18. OR, Part II, Vol. VI, p. 281.
19. RG393, Pt. 4, E346, OB522, p. 73.20.
20. OR. Part II, Vol. VI, p. 516–518.
21. Letter written by Pvt. Inslee Deaderick, Pvt. 2nd TN Cav. to Ch. McClung, Macon, GA on 2/4/65.The typescript copy and a copy of the original letter are in the files of the Fort Delaware Society.
22. Adapted in part from M. Beck, et al, *The Sharper End: Military Images*, Volume 19, July/August 1999. See also RG95, E561, Medical Officer's files.
23. R. Dunglison, *A Dictionary of Medical Science, 2nd Ed.*, Blanchard & Lea, Philadelphia, 1858, see pages 296–300.
24. S. Smith, Ed., *The American Medical Times*, Vol. V, Dec. 6, 1862, Bailliere Brothers, New York, p. 321–322. (Available on Google Books); J.J. Woodward, *Outlines of the Chief Camp Diseases of the United States Armies*, J.B. Lippincott & Co., Philadelphia, 1863, p. 133, 231 and 254. (Available on Google Books).
25. Extracted from RG94, E544, Registers 36 and 47.
26. RG112, E544, Register 54.
27. RG94, E544, Registers 36 and 49.
28. RG94, E544, Registers 26 and 35 (covers 1861 to Sept. 1865 with exception of Sept. and Oct. 1863).
29. Most of this discussion concerning specific illnesses and their treatment is taken from J.J. Woodward, *Outlines of the Chief Camp Diseases of the United States Armies*, J.B. Lippincott & Co., Philadelphia, 1863, p. 133, 231 and 254. The medicines mentioned in this discussion may mostly be found in G.H. Beasley, *The Book of Prescriptions*, 6th Ed., J&A Churchill, London, 1883.
30. RG112, E544, Reg. 54.
31. See A.J. Bollet, *Civil War Medicine, Challenges and Triumphs*, Galen Press, Ltd. Tucson, AZ, 2002, p. 343–361 for an excellent discussion about scurvy and its general history and effects during the Civil War.
32. A.J. Bollet p. 290–296 has a discussion about smallpox, particularly about the vaccination and the prisons.
33. J.M. Gillispie, *North and South*, April 2003, vol. 6, p. 40–49, at p. 45.
34. MSH, Part III, Vol. 1, Chapter 1, Tables XII, XVIII, and XIX.

Chapter 10

1. RG249, E10, vol. 5, #847 and also RG393, Part 4, E346, OB522, p. 45 (both entries record the same letter).
2. See for instance Medical and Surgical History, Part III, Vol. I, Chapter 1, Tables XV and XVI.
3. Number of prisoners at the end of each month by prison camp, as well as the number that died, is found in OR, Series II, Vol. VIII, p. 986–1003.
4. Data for Andersonville are from the Medical and Surgical History, Part III, Vol. 1, the last paragraph on p. 36. There is a long discussion about the conditions at Andersonville on p. 34–43. This discussion does raise the specter of the controversy over treatment of POWs.
5. Medical and Surgical History, Part III, Vol. I, Chapter 1, Table XVIII.
6. RG217, UD1001, new Box Numbers 594, 909 and 1739.
7. Calculated from MSH, Part I, Vol. I, p. XL to XLI.
8. As an example of the horrendous death rates from diseases in armies in the 19th century before the Civil War, see H. Martineau, *England and Her Soldiers*, Smith, Elder & Co., London, 1859, especially pages 40–42, 195, 234, 257 and 259, which chronicles losses in the British Army during this time.
9. "Student," *The Probable Error of a Mean*, Biometrika, Vol. 6, p. 1–26 (1908). "Student" was a pseudonym for William S, Gosset, who developed it as part of his job to improve beer quality. The use of the t-test and its actual application can be found on many websites, simply by searching for the "Student t-test."
10. See for instance D. Fetzer and B. Mowday, *Unlikely Allies*, Stackpole Books, Mechanicsburg, PA, 2000, p. xiv.
11. See M598, R47, Register of Deaths at Fort DE, April, 1862 to July 1865, and the hospital lists in RG94, E544, Registers 36 and 49.
12. OR, Series II, Vol. VI, p. 516–518.
13. A.D.A.M. Medical Encyclopedia of Medline Plus (online) from the U.S. National Library of Medicine.
14. M598, Roll 47, Morning Reports of Prisoners, May 1863 through July 1865.
15. RG249, E3, Vol. 9, #3367.
16. MSH, Pt. III, Vol. I Chapter VIII, p. 684.
17. J.J. Woodward, *Outlines of the Chief Camp Diseases*

of the United States Armies, J.B. Lippincott & Co., Philadelphia, 1863, p. 57–73, 152, 234, and 317. (Available on Google™ Books).
  18. A.J. Bollet, *Civil War Medicine, Challenges and Triumphs*, Galen Press Ltd., Tucson, AZ (2002), p. 338.
  19. Medical and Surgical History, Part III, Vol. I, Chapter VIII, p. 696.
  20. See A.J. Bollet, p. 349–353, for a further discussion of this topic, and from which this writing is partially abstracted.

Chapter 11

  1. W. Emerson Wilson ed., *A Fort Delaware Journal: The Diary of a Yankee Private A.J. Hamilton 1862–1865*, Wilmington, Fort Delaware Society, 1981. However, this version of the diary is highly edited and incomplete, with many entries omitted or changed. The original diary is in the Delaware Historical Society archives, Wilmington, DE.
  2. RG393, Pt. 4, E352, p. 82 (8/7/63)
  3. Hamilton reports sentinels arrested on 6/19/63 for talking with prisoners.
  4. RG393, Pt. 4, E352, p. 63, Special Order 90, 6/15/63.
  5. *Revised United States Army Regulations of 1861*, Government Printing Office, Washington, D.C., 1863, §399, p. 61.
  6. Fletcher 8/28/64.
  7. Fletcher 8/28/64 and Nugent 3/27/64.
  8. Most of the information we have before about March 1864 is from Handy's diary, although there are a few enlisted men's diaries from before this time. Handy was living an atypical prisoner's life on the Island before he was transferred to the officers' barracks in May 1864. He lived in the Fort before his transfer with other political prisoners to the officers' barracks. During that time Handy and the others appear to have more privileges than the ordinary POWs, so much of what Handy reports before March 1864 has not been included in this section.
  9. A slightly different transcription is available online (as of 4/15/2014) at http://freepages.genealogy.rootsweb.ancestry.com.
  10. *Prison Times*, J.W. Hibbs (13th VA Cav.), editor, Vol. 1, No. 1, April 1865. A newspaper written by hand and published by officer POWs at Fort Delaware. A copy may be viewed online by searching http://memory.loc.gov, and the original copy is in the collection of the New York Historical Society.
  11. Probably 2nd Lt. Louis Dietz of Independent Battery A, PA Heavy Artillery.
  12. Apparently no copy of this issue of *Prison Times* has survived.
  13. See Mckey, 7/3/64 and 7/5/64; Mauck 7/6/64, 7/18/64 and 3/28/65; Handy 8/24/64; and Boyle 1/18/65.
  14. OR, Ser. II, Vol. VII, p. 72–75.
  15. RG249, E3, vol. 8, p. 224.
  16. RG393, Part 4, E346, OB522, no page. OR, Ser. II. Vol. VII, p. 809.
  17. OR, Ser. II, Vol. VII, p. 366–367.
  18. Some of this information is given by Handy in his diary on 7/22/63, 7/29/63, 8/3/63, 9/14/63 and 11/14/63.
  19. RG249, E3, vol. 9, #3136.
  20. RG249, E21, vol. 3, #97.
  21. RG249, E3, vol. 9, #3176.
  22. RG393, Part 4, E346, OB522, no page.
  23. This is a basic recipe for a "molasses beer," popular in the United States for home brewing, *ca.* 1730 to 1840. Nothing in this recipe acts to preserve the beer, so it must be drunk almost immediately. Typically when home brewed it also included flavorings or spices. The bread was added to provide yeast for fermentation. Pers. Com., Frank Clark, Master, Historic Foodways, Colonial Williamsburg Foundation, Williamsburg, VA.
  24. RG249, E10, vol. 19, #268.
  25. According to Roger H. Harrell, *2nd North Carolina Cavalry,* MacFarland & Co., Publishers, Jefferson, NC, p. 400. Pvt. Thomas R. Manchester was captured in Cherokee County, NC on 2/18/64, and died at Fort Delaware of a "punctured wound" on 1/22/65.
  26. RG249, E10, vol. 19, #1142.
  27. RG249, E3, vol. 13, #1854.
  28. See for example Cox, 7/29/64, 10/8/64, and 11/7/64; Boyle, 1/25/65; and Mckey, 6/21/64, 7/25/64, and 9/8/64.
  29. See Mckey, 7/25/64, 9/8/64, and 9/15/64.
  30. See Handy, 7/8/64; Allen 7/8/64 and 7/29/64; Boyle 7/15/64; McCrorey 7/15/64; and Mckey 7/16/64.
  31. See for instance Boyle 4/16/65 and Cox and PAMcMichael, 4/17/65. Also stopped for a time were mail and the sending of money or packages to the POWs.
  32. Sketchbook of Pvt. Baldwin Coolidge, 6th MA Veteran Volunteers, at the Library of the Delaware Historical Society, Wilmington, DE.
  33. Joseph Holt Papers, 1817–1895, Library of Congress, MSS26385, Document No. 5856.
  34. There are many references to gambling in the POW diaries; see for instance Handy 6/30/64, Gibson 11/29/64, Park 2/8/65, Mckey 4/1/64, and Cox 8/11/64 and 3/29/65.
  35. Handy's diary explains that the ostensible reason for Schoepf granting this privilege was the fact that Handy's health was delicate.
  36. All of this awning information taken from Handy's diary.
  37. SHC, Francis A. Boyle Books, Collection No. 01555-z.
  38. The *Central Presbyterian* was published in Richmond, VA starting in 1856 and continued to 1908. Collections of this newspaper in various libraries are quite incomplete, so the date that this was published is unknown. However, given the dates provided, it was probably sometime between November 1864 through March 1865.
  39. SHC, So. Pam. 3279, T.F. Roche, *Songs written by R.F. Roche while a prisoner of war at Fort Delaware*, Enterprise Printing Co., Winchester, VA, 18??.
  40. "Trumps" (a pseudonym), *The American Hoyle*, Dick Fitzgerald Publishers, New York, 1864, p. 480 (available on Google Books).
  41. RG27. E59, Vol. 126.

Chapter 12

  1. RG249, E3, Vol. 8. p. 234.
  2. RG393, Pt. 4, E350, OB532, #130.
  3. M598, R47, Morning Reports of Prisoners. RG393, Pt. 4, E346, OB522, no page;RG249, E21, vol. 3, #124; RG393, Pt. 4, E346, OB522, no page.
  4. M598, R47, Morning Reports of Prisoners,
  5. RG393, Pt. 4, E350, OB532, #147; RG249, E 21, Vol. 3, #156; RG393, Pt. 4, E350, OB522, #164; RG393, Pot. 4, E350, OB532, #164 and #165.
  6. RG393, Pt. 4, E350, OB532, #191.
  7. RG393, Pt. 4, E350, OB532, #195.
  8. M598, R47, Morning Reports of Prisoners.

9. RG249, E3, Vol. 12, #951.
10. RG393, Pt. 4, E350, OB532, #202; RG249, E3, Vol. 12, #1060; RG393, Pt. 4, E350, OB532, #206; RG393, Pt, 4, E350, OB533, #1; RG393, Pt. 4, E350, #9, RG393, Pt. 4, E350, OB533, #11; RG393, Pt. 4, E350, OB533, #16; and RG249, E21, Vol. 4, #118.
11. M598, R47, Morning Reports of Prisoners.
12. RG393, Pt. 4, E350, OB522, #177.
13. OR, Ser. II, vol. VI, p. 680–682.
14. OR, Ser. II, Vol. VIII, p. 579–580.
15. From the website (accessed Aug. 19, 2014) http://digitalcollections.vmi.edu/cdm/ref/cooolection/p15821coll11/id/273.
16. Much of this correspondence is found in RG393, Pt. 4, E350, OB 533; RG249, E10, Vol. 15; and RG249, E21, Vol. 4. See for instance RG393, Pt. 4, E350, OB 533, #68 (5/11/65), #59 (5/15/65), and #69 (5/17/65); RG249, E10, Vol. 15, #1998 (5/11/65), #2049 (5/15/65), #2094 (5/17/65), and #2274 (5/27/65); and RG249, E21, Vol. 4, #171 (5/11/65) and #194 (5/17/65).
17. RG249, E10, Vol. 15, #1771.
18. RG249, E 10, Vol. 15, #1854.
19. RG393, Pt, 4, E348.
20. RG393, Pt. 4, E350, OB533, #91.
21. RG393, Pt. 4, E348.
22. RG393, Pt. 4, E350, OB533, #100.
23. RG249, E21, Vol. 4, #219.
24. RG393, Pt. 4, E348 and RG393, Pt. 4, E350, OB 533, #92.
25. OR, Series II, Vol. VIII, p. 641.

Conclusions

1. Unlike previous chapters, which presented "evidence" in the form of contemporaneous documents concerning Fort DE during the last two years of the Civil War, much of this chapter deals with conclusions reached by the author based on the evidence given in previous chapters.
2. General Orders 100 was written by Professor Francis Lieber, LL.D., a law professor at Columbia College (New York) at the request of General Halleck, U.S. Army Chief of Staff. After review by a board of military officers, with very few changes, it was ordered to be issued by Abraham Lincoln. Within a few years similar orders were issued by a number of European nations, and it led eventually about a decade later to the first Geneva Convention on the laws of war.
3. Papers of Julia Jefferson, Delaware Historical Society Library, Wilmington, DE (letter of 7/11/63 from Union Lt. J.J. MacConnell).
4. MSH, Part III, Vol. 1, p. 57–59.
5. OR. Part II, Vol. VI, p. 516–518.
6. OR, Ser. II, Vol. VI, p. 371. Compared to the inspection report by Surgeon Clark done about a month later at Fort DE, Camp Douglas was very poor by comparison.
7. Details about the sanitary situation in Camp Douglas, especially the sewers, can be found in G. Levy, *To Die in Chicago*, Pelican Publishing Co., Gretna, LA, 1999, Chapters 8 and 9.
8. For instance, on 7/8/64 Schoepf told Handy that "They shall shoot down any man who tries to get away." This was after a series of incidents, including attempted escapes.
9. OR, Ser. II, Vol. VII, p. 809–811.
10. This is not to say that other officers, such as Chaplains Way and Paddock, Quartermaster Craig, Lt. Dietz, and others, were not competent, but we simply don't know that much about them.
11. An article in SHSP, Vol. XXII, p. 127–146, written by (former) Col. A. Fulkerson, 63rd TN Inf. tends to confirm Handy's conclusion. This memoir, written 27 years after the fact, states, on pages 130–131, in part: "General Schoepf, a foreigner by birth, was in command at Fort Delaware. He was a humane officer and did all that he dared to alleviate the sufferings of the prisoners and to supply their wants. He married a Virginia lady who was said to be a Southern sympathizer, and on this account, possibly, the General's actions were closely watched, and it is said Captain Ahl, one of his aids [sic] was sent there and forced upon him, for the special purpose of spying upon his actions and reporting his conduct to the authorities at Washington. However this may be, it was known that many of the harsh prison rules were adopted and enforced by the General at the instance of Captain Ahl, who was a cold-blooded, heartless, cruel, and cowardly South-hater. But, still, I believe that Fort Delaware was one of the best Northern prisons." Much of the supposition in this paragraph is not supported by the facts. There is no evidence that Schoepf's wife Julia was a strong Southern sympathizer, Captain Ahl had arrived with one of the early artillery batteries present long before April 1863, and Schoepf had himself promoted him to Captain and appointed him the AAAG of his command. Although perhaps complimentary of Fort Delaware as a whole, it does show some signs of "Lost Cause" thinking.
12. Hoffman was a regular Army officer and commanded the Third Infantry (regulars). He was the son of a career army officer and a West Point graduate. While he was a colonel he was a superior officer to any U.S. Volunteer officer who was an officer of the same or lesser rank. He was brevetted a BGen on 10/7/64 but was still inferior to a volunteer BGen. He was brevetted a MGen on 3/13/65 and was now superior to all Army officers except for those with the rank of (not brevetted) MGen and LGen (Grant). See *Revised Regulations for the Army of the United States*, 1861. War Department. Philadelphia, J.G.L Brown, Printer, 1863, Articles 5 and 9.
13. OR, Ser. II, Vol. VII, p. 1117; OR, Ser. I, Vol. XLVI, Part 2, p. 314; *Ibid.*, p. 343. Wessells largely continued Hoffman's policies issuing one major general order, on 1/13/65. (OR, Ser. II, Vol. VIII, p. 61–63). The only major change in this order from Hoffman's previous orders was the elimination of potatoes from the ration, and the addition of hominy (or rice).
14. OR, Ser. II, Vol. IV, p. 151 (7/7/62); OR, Ser. II, Vol. VII, p. 72 (4/20/64); OR, Ser. II, Vol. VII, p. 183 (6/1/64). The last one deals mostly with the ration.
15. RG249, E3, Vol., 3, #3723 (this hospital was not built because the smallpox epidemic had abated).
16. RG249, E3, Vol. 3, #3641.
17. RG249, E3, Vol. 9, #2919.
18. This reciprocal close confining of POWs on both sides when the other side placed a POW in close confinement apparently started sometime in the Spring or Summer of 1864. Stopping this practice was discussed between the two sides; see OR, Ser. II, Vol. VII, p. 683 and 833. On 9/3/64 the CGP ordered all POWs held in close confinement released, but this apparently broke down and on 9/17/64 they were ordered to be reconfined (RG393, Pt. 4, E350, OB532, #126). This apparently continued until 2/18/65, when LGen Grant ordered all POWs in close confinement released (RG393, Pt. 4, E350, OB532, #202).
19. RG249, E3, Vol. 9, #2644.
20. RG393, Pt. 4, E350, OB532, #108.
21. Many instances, especially for men who applied

to take the oath of allegiance; see for instance RG249, E3, Vol. 12, #362.

22. OR, Ser. II, Vol. VI, p. 476–477.

23. OR, Ser. II, Vol. VI, p. 1073 (sent to all prison camps).

24. *Narrative of the Privations and Sufferings of United States Officers and Soldiers,* U.S. Sanitary Commission, King & Baird, Philadelphia, 1864.

25. OR, Ser. II, Vol. VII, p. 110–111.

26. OR, Ser. II. Vol. VII, p. 150–152. This includes all the endorsements mentioned.

27. OR, Ser. II, Vol. VIII, p. 767–768,

28. RG393, Pt. 4, E346, OB522, no page (11/15/64).

29. These men appeared very emaciated to the CGP who saw them on their return, and assumed they had been deliberately starved. It is possible that they were suffering from advanced scurvy and/or chronic diarrhea or dysentery, which can cause a victim to appear the same way.

30. It is the author's personal opinion that this was true for both the higher Union and Confederate authorities, and probably for the most part in most prison camps, North and South. In many respects the backbone and mores of the Confederate and Union armies was based on the U.S. Army (pre Civil War) and what its officer Corps had been taught at West Point. However, the officers actually in command of individual prison camps, who were almost always Volunteers, not professional officers, varied greatly in their competence and in their attitude towards the prisoners they had charge of. This probably accounted for much of the variance in treatment between different prison camps, North and South. Especially as the War went on, the South had more problems than the North supplying its troops and prisoners with things such as food. By the end of the War it is also generally conceded that the Northern prison camp system was better organized than its Southern counterpart.

Epilogue

1. Unlike most of the references in preceding chapters, many of those cited in this chapter are not primary references.

2. M598, Roll 47, Morning Reports of Prisoners.

3. This was done on orders from President Johnson; see OR, Ser. II, Vol. VIII, p. 709–710.

4. RG393, Pt. 4, E350, OB533, #126. RG249. E21, Vol. 4, #251.

5. F.H. Dyer, *A Compendium of the War of the Rebellion,* The Dyer Publishing Co., Des Moines, Iowa, 1908, Part 3. W.F. Fox, *Regimental Losses in the American Civil War,* Albany Publishing Co., Albany, New York, 1889, p. 489. Both Dyer and Fox list Batteries A and G as Light Artillery Batteries.

6. RG217, UD1001, Box 1739.

7. RG393, Pt. 4, E350, OB533, #71, #72. M473, R89, p. 457.

8. OR, Ser. II, Vol. VIII, p. 816.

9. C.W. Raines, Ed., *Six Decades in Texas or Memoirs of Francis Richard Lubbock,* Austin, Texas, Ben C. Jones & Co., Printers, 1900, p. 577–590 (available from Google Books).

10. See Mrs. Burton Harrison, *Recollections Grave and Gay,* Charles Scribner's Sons, 1911, p. 240–242.

11. RG249, E3, vol. 14, #3191.

12. OR, Ser. II, Vol. VIII, p. 838–840, letter from Adj. Gen. Holt to Sec War Stanton.

13. Mrs. Burton Harrison, *Recollections Grave and Gay,* Charles Scribner's Sons, 1911, p. 240–244. Burton Harrison's imprisonment is briefly described.

14. RG192, E87, Vol. 1, p. 34. The FDS has the original paper commission as Bvt. Major.

15. Pers. Com. From NJ State Archives.

16. *New York Times,* Oct. 29, 1862, obituary.

17. 1880 U.S. Census, New York State, Roll TG9-0896, page 128B.

18. *New York Times,* July 30, 1882, obituary.

19. RG217, E563. Vol. 5 and Vol. 7.

20. RG217, UD1002, Box 254, Account No. 6548.

21. This paragraph, except where noted, was derived mostly from William Kesley Boynton (born Kesley Schoepf Boynton), *Albin F. Schoepf, A Family Biography,* unpublished manuscript, 1990, copy in FDS. Contains a complete biography of Schoepf from birth to death, including his Civil War activities.

22. *National Tribune* (Washington DC), May 20, 1886, p. 8. There was also a piece in the *Washington Evening Star* on May 12, 1886, describing a meeting at the Patent Office which passed appropriate resolutions about Gen. Schoepf. One of the men attending this meeting was Assistant Commissioner of Patents R.B. Vance, who as a BGen was a POW at Fort Delaware for a little more than a year, and eventually became Schoepf's boss in the postwar Patent Office!

23. *Journal of the Executive Proceedings of the Senate of the United States of America,* Vol. 15, 1866, p. 439 and 636.

24. RG249, E3, vol. 14, #3077.

25. RG249, E3, vol. 14, #3063.

26. RG393, Pt. 4, E350, OB533, #129.

27. RG249, E10, vol. 9, #1077.

28. OR, Ser. II, Vol. VIII, p. 727.

29. RG92, E2212 p. 35–159 (in NARA Philadelphia).

30. Fort Delaware Notes, Vol. XXVII, Fort Delaware Society, Delaware City, DE, January 1878, p. 6–7.

31. D. Tvaryanas, *Historic American Engineering Record, Fort Delaware,* HAER No. DE-56, National Park Service, Philadelphia, PA, Fort Delaware Notes, Vol. Vol. XXX, Fort Delaware Society, Delaware City, DE, April, 1980, p. 10. At the time 15 inch Rodmans were thought useful against ironclad ships, but fully armored ships soon made them obsolete.

32. Fort Delaware Notes,, Vol. VII, December 1957, p. 3–4; and Vol. VI, April, 1956, p. 1–3.

33. *Ibid.,* Vol. XX, No. 1, January 1970, p. 5; Vol. XXVIII, January 1978, p. 5, Vol. XXXIX, April 1989, p. 4.

34. Tvaryanas.

35. Author's personal observation.

36. Tvaryanas.

37. Author's personal observation.

38. Fort Delaware Notes, Vol. Vol. XXX, Fort Delaware Society, Delaware City, DE, Vol. X, January 1960, p. 1–2; and Vol. XX, p. 3–4; *Ibid.,* Vol. XXXIV, April 1984, p. 8.

39. Author's personal observation.

40. *Ibid.*

41. *Ibid.*

Appendix

1. J. G. de Rouhlac Hamilton, Ed., *The Papers of Randolph Abbott Shotwell,* Vol. 2, The North Carolina Historical Commission, Raleigh, 1931.

2. See for instance R. Pickenpaugh, *Captives in Gray: The Civil Prisons of the Union,* University of Alabama Press, Tuscaloosa, AL, 2009; F.H. Casstevens, *Out of the Mouth of Hell: Civil War Prisons and Escapes,* McFarland & Co., Jefferson, NC 2005; B. Temple, *The Union Prison*

at Fort Delaware: A Perfect Hell on Earth, McFarland & Co., Inc., Jefferson, NC, 2003; J. I. Robertson, Jr., *Soldiers in Blue and Gray*, University of South Carolina Press, Columbia, SC, 1998; Lonnie R. Speer, *Portals to Hell: Military Prisons of the Civil War*, Stackpole Books, Mechanicsville, PA, 1997; F. Dale, *Delaware Diary: Episodes in the Life of a River*, Rutgers University Press, New Brunswick, NJ, 1996; and W.C. Davis and R. A. Pritchard, *Fighting Men of the Civil War*, University of Oklahoma Press, Norman, OK, 1998, all make reference to the Fort Delaware Shotwell diary. There is also an excerpt of the Fort Delaware Shotwell diary in H. S. Commager and E. Brunn, *The Civil War Archive: The History of the Civil War in Documents*, Black Dog & Leventhal, New York, 2000, p. 466–469. Searching the internet for "Fort Delaware" and "Randolph (Abbott) Shotwell" will return many hits.

3. Hamilton, Ed., Vol. 1.

4. *Ibid.*

5. This is not to say that other diaries do not contain negative remarks about prisoner treatment. Such remarks are fairly common, but not with the consistency and venom exhibited by Shotwell. For instance, Cox on October 19, 1864 reports, matter of factly, that "The weather is pleasant to day every thing goes on Smoothly (very smoothly) fare is very hard and growing smaller almost daily we get about four ozs of meat and about nine oz's of bread per day and about ½ or ¾ of a pint of rice or bean supe those who have means of getting money here almost board themselves from the Sutler the health of the prisoners is very good." The Park Diary is similar to Shotwell in many respects, for example criticizing fellow prisoners, and making what would later become classic "Lost Cause" arguments. However, the Park diary agrees with many other diaries on at least approximately when events took place, so it is included in the present volume as a "valid" contemporaneous document.

6. The actual location of the original Shotwell papers is the North Carolina State Archives, Raleigh, NC, *Randolph Abbott Shotwell (1844–1885) Papers*, Call Number PC.243, Location 3B, MARS Id. 753 (Record Group).

7. It also, of course, points out the necessity of investigating, when possible, a claim or belief that a particular document is an authentic primary source. Fortunately, in this instance there were many other diaries from Fort Delaware to compare it to.

Bibliography

Abbreviations

number
ACWM Eleanor S. Brockenbrough Library, American Civil War Museum (formerly Museum of the Confederacy), Richmond, VA.
DHS Delaware Historical Society Library, Wilmington, DE
E entry (number) (NARA)
FDS Fort Delaware Society Library, Delaware City, DE
FDSP Records at Fort Delaware State Park, Delaware City, DE
M Microfilm (number) (NARA)
MSH *The Medical and Surgical History of the War of the Rebellion (1861-1865)*, Second Issue, Government Printing Office, Washington, 1875.
NARA National Archives and Records Administration
OB old book (NARA)
OR *The War of the Rebellion: A Compilation of the Official Records of the Union and Confederate Armies,* Government Printing Office, Washington, 1880 (this series has about 128 volumes and this is the date of the first volume).
p. page or pages
Pt. part (NARA)
QM quartermaster
R roll (NARA)
Reg. Register (NARA)
RG Record Group (NARA)
Ser. series
SHC Southern Historical Collection, University of North Carolina, Chapel Hill, NC
SHSP Southern Historical Society Papers, published by the Southern Historical Society, Richmond, VA, original series, Vol. 1-38, published 1876-1909.
VHS Virginia Historical Society, Richmond, VA
Vol. volume (NARA)
VV Veteran Volunteers

Diaries and Letters

In the text many items are referenced by giving a name and usually a date or time period. These are almost always references to diaries or letters written by either prisoners or Union personnel. The names are given below, together with the source(s) of the document(s), and in most instances date ranges at Fort DE. Alternate sources are also listed for some documents.

Alburtis—Diary of Pvt. William B. Alburtis, Richardson's Battery Cavalry (Confederate). 6/3/64 to 6/9/65. FDS.
Allen—Diary of 1st Lt. John C. Allen, 7th VA Cavalry. (Confederate) 3/28/64 to 8/30/64. VHS.

Bibliography

Barringer—Diary of BGen Rufus Barringer (Confederate). 4/8/65 to 8/8/65. SHC.

Berkeley—W.H. Runge (ed.), *Four Years in the Confederate Artillery, The Diary of Private Henry Robinson Berkeley,* Virginia Historical Society, Richmond, 1991. Berkeley was serving Kirkpatrick's Battery when captured.

Bingham—Diary of Capt. Robert Bingham, Co. G, 44th NC Regiment. (Confederate) 7/8/64 to 7/18/65. SHC.

Boyle—Diary of Ajt. (Lt.) Francis A. Boyle, 32nd NC Infantry. (Confederate) 6/28/64 to 5/12/65. SHC.

Cox—Diary of Lt. E. L. Cox, 68th NC Infantry. (Confederate) 7/24/65 to 6/19/65. VHS.

Crumrine—Letters of Sgt. Bishop Crumrine, Independent Battery G, 3rd PA Heavy Artillery (this is listed as a light artillery battery by Dyer). (Union) 8/28/62 to 5/26/65. FDSP (obtained from U. Grant Miller Library, Washington and Jefferson College, Washington, PA 15301)

Eames—Letters of Assistant Surgeon William M. Eames, 157th OH Militia. (Union) 6/10/64 to 8/12/64. FDS.

Fletcher—Letters of Pvt. William I. Fletcher, 6th MA Veteran Volunteers. (Union) 8/24/64 to 10/10/64. HSD (privately published book, contains line illustrations)

Franklin—Diary of Sgt. James H. Franklin, Co. A, 4th AL Infantry. (Confederate) 7/23/63 to 7/29/63. ACWM.

Gibson—Diary of LCol John Alexander Gibson, 14th VA Cavalry (Confederate) 11/29/64 to 6/8/65. VHS

Hamilton—Diary of Pvt. Alexander James Hamilton, Battery G, 3rd PA Heavy Artillery (Union). 8-22-62 to 6/13/65. DHS. There is a published version of this diary, *A FORT DELAWARE JOURNAL: The Diary of a Yankee Private, A. J. Hamilton, 1862-65*, Wilson, W. Emerson (edited by), Wilmington, DE: The Fort Delaware Society, 1981, but this version is highly edited and many items are left out.

Handy—Diary of Rev. Isaac W.K. Handy (southern political prisoner) 7/21/63 to 10/12/64. I.W.K. Handy, *United States Bonds,* Turnbull Brothers, Baltimore, 1874. Reprinted as *Imprisoned for Conscience Sake,* by Sprinkle Publications, P.O. Box 1094, Harrisonburg, VA 22803.

Hawes—Diary of Lt. Samuel Horace Hawes, Fry's Battery (Confederate). 3/12/65 to 6/1/65. VHS.

JRMcMichael—Diary of Capt. James Robert McMichael, Co. K 12th GA Infantry (Confederate) 5/12/64 to 8/21/64 and 3/12/65 to 6/17/65. SHC and FDS.

Lank—Letters of Pvt. William D. Lank. 9th DE Volunteers (Union). 10/19/64 to 1/18/65. FDSP.

Mauck—Diary of Lt. Joseph W. Mauck, 10th VA Infantry. (Confederate) 5/17/64 to 8/21/64 and 3/12/65 to 6/5/65. ACWM.

McCrory—Diary of 2nd Lt. James L. McCrorey, 4th SC Infantry. (Confederate) 6/26/64 to 8/15/64. FDS.

Mckey (or McKey)—Diary of Lt. James Taswell Mckey, 48th TN Infantry. (Confederate) 3/27/64 to 1/5/65 (died). ACWM.

Morton—Diary of Capt. John P. Morton, Co. K, 18th MS Cavalry. (Confederate) 7/18/64 to 10/27/64. Mississippi Department of Archives and History, Jackson, MS.

Nugent—Assistant Surgeon Washington George Nugent Letters (Union). 11/13/63 to 5/31/65. FDS

PAMcMichael—Diary of LCol. Paul Agalus McMichael, 20th SC Infantry. (Confederate) 10/24/64 to 7/24/65. South Carolina Historical Society, Charleston, SC. (original), and SHC.

Park—Diary of Capt. Ralph Emory Park, 12th AL Infantry. (Confederate) 2/3/65 to 6/13/65. SHSP, Richmond, VA, Vol. II, No. 6 and Vol. III Nos. 1-6, 1876-1877.

Peters—Diary of 1st Sgt. Scott Peters, 3rd MO Cavalry (Confederate). 6/18/63-9/2/63. SHC.

Purvis—Diary of Sgt. Joseph Edward Purvis, 19th VA Infantry. (Confederate) 7/7/63-8/31/63. FDS and FDSP.

Ward—Diary of Col. William Walker Ward, 9th TN Cavalry. (Confederate) 3/30/64 to 6/24/64. W. W. Ward, Edited by R. B. Rosenberg, *For the Sake of My Country,* Southern Heritage Press, P.O. Box 1615, Murfreesboro, TN 37133.

Index

Numbers in ***bold*** italics indicate pages with illustrations

Adams, Pvt. Fred L. (Confederate) 166
Ahl, Capt. George Washington (Union) 11, 13–14, 17, 26, 29, 78, 86–87, 161, 165, ***168***, 171, 179, 180, 182, 188–89, 198, 220*con.n*11
Ahl's Battery 11, 13, 15–16, 27, 198
Alburtis, Pvt. William B. (Confederate) 20, 32, 49, 86, 97, 101, 162, 164, 166, 168, 177, 209–11, 224
Alden, Surgeon C. H. (Union) 83, 87–88, 106–7, 109, 185
ale *see* beer
Alexander, [medical inspector] (Union) 87, 89
Allen, Lt. John C. (Confederate) 31, 36, 49–51, 96, 98–100, 162, 164, 167–68, 224
Alton, Illinois 140, 142, 145, 193–94
Andersonville 142, 145, 185, 218*ch*10*n*4
Arrott, Dr. Colin (Union) 78, 106, 158

bakers 44, 49, 90, 165
bakery 34, 44–46, 49, 201
Baltimore, Maryland 11, 18, 24, 32, 106, 109, 167, 183, 198
Baltimore American and Commercial Advertiser 199
Barnes, Surg. General Joseph K. (Union) 193
barrel, wearing the *see* punishment
Barringer, Brig. Gen. Rufus (Confederate) 50, 89, 98, 166, 177, 180, 211, 224
bathing 82–83, 85, 87–89, 92, 110, 113, 163, 210
Beall, Brig. Gen William N. R. (Confederate) 87, 103–4, 175, 218*ch*8*n*18
Beauregard, Gen. P.G.T. (Confederate) 177
beer 95, 99–100, 157, 166, 219*n*23
Berkeley, Pvt. Henry Robinson (Confederate) 50, 85–87, 89, 101, 104, 16–64, 167–68, 170, 177–78, 180, 182–83, 224
Beyond the Lines (book) 167
Bibb, John H. (Confederate) 91, 217*n*21
Bingham, Capt. Robert (Confederate) 49, 85, 208, 224
blankets 69, 79–81, 88, 102–4, 163–64, 184, 186, 195, 201, 207–8, 210
boardwalks 5, 86, 148
boiling *see* cooking
Bollet, Alfred J. 53, 134
Booth, John Wilkes 211
Boyle, Lt. Francis A. (Confederate) 31, 75, 80, 84, 89, 95–96, 101–102, 104, 112–13, ***114***, 115, 163, 165–67, 171–72, 177, 180, 194, 209–10, 224
bread 40–47, 49–51, 53–54, 57, 59–61, 89, 98–100, 114, 117, 159–60, 165–66, 182–83, 187, 213*pref.n*7, 219*n*23, 222*n*5
bribery 33, 36–37, 50–51, 96, 209, 217*ch*8*n*3
Buchanan, Col. Robert (Union) 3, 4
Buell, Maj. Gen. Don Carlos (Union) 13
"bull pen" 172–74, ***173***
Byrne, Frank L. 57

Camp Chase 140, 142–43, 193–94
Camp Douglas 112, 140, 142–43, 193–94, 220*n*6
Camp Morton 140, 142–43, 193–94
canteens 35, 164, 217*n*19
cards (playing) 155, 160, ***173***; *see also* gambling
catarrh 92, 121–26, 128–29, 195
cauldrons 47, 49, 67
The Central Presbyterian 171–72, 219*n*38
CGP (Commissary General of Prisoners) 11–13, 23–25, 27–29, 33–36, 41, 45, 47, 54, 57, 61–63, 65–66, 69–70, 72–73, 80, 86–87, 96, 101, 104, 164, 166, 180–82, 186, 188, 190–92, 194–95, 197–98, 201, 216*ch*6*n*18, 217*n*19, 217*ch*8*n*1, 220*con.n*12, 217*con.n*13, 221*con.n*29
Cheeseborough, Lt. Col. (Union) 18, 106, 109
Chimborazo Hospital 136–37, 183
cholera morbus 121–26
Christian Association 161, 167, 170–72
Christmas 95, 157
Clark, Surgeon A.M. (Union) 79, 83, 87–88, 110–11, 134, 148–49, 185–87, 220*n*6
Clark, Pvt. Charles N. (Union) 79, 157
Clark, Capt. Gilbert Smith (Union) 13, ***14***, 40–41, 45–47, 50, 52, 54–56, 58, 66, 76, 78, 115, 163, 165, 188, 199–201, 215*n*16
coffee 40, 49–50, 59–60, 63–65, 95, 100, 112, 116–18, 160, 162–63
Coleridge, Samuel Taylor 82
colic 121, 124–26, 158
Columbiad cannon 202
Commissary General of Prisoners *see* CGP
Commissary Generals of Subsistence and Prisoners 3, 39, 45–46, 56, 63–65
commissary inspection 218*ch*9*n*2
commissary medical records 110
commissary returns 62, 194
Company Q 19, 21–23, 37
Company Savings 51
convicts 6, 17, 19, ***21***, 21–23, ***23***, 24–25, 31–33, 37–38, 44, 46, 74, 77, 105, 112, 115, 139, 200–1, 207, 214*ch*3*n*2, 216*ch*6*n*23, 218*ch*9*n*2
cooking 44, 47, ***48***, 50, 52, 54–55, 90, 110, 120, 157, 159, 162–63, ***173***, 188
Coolidge, Pvt. Baldwin (Confederate), sketchbook ***21***, ***37***, ***38***, ***66***, ***80***, ***155***
Copperheads 19, 156
corn meal 44–45, 49–50, 52–54, 59, 61, 95

225

Index

court martial 17, 19–20, **21**, 22–23, 199; *see also* punishment
Cox, Lt. E.L. (Confederate) 32, 49, 75, 77, 84, 86, 89, 96, 101, 104, 135, 161, 163–64, 166–67, 172, 175, 177, 180, 208–11, 222*n*5, 224
Craig, Capt. Samuel R. (Union) 14, 65, 76–80, 187
Crane, Surgeon C.H. (Union) 87, 88, 109
Crescent (steamer) 156
Crossman, Col. George H. (Union) 72–73, 108
Crumrine, Sgt. Bishop (Union) 17, 22, 52, 94, 224
Cuyler, Surgeon John Meck (Union) 87–89, 91

Dairyman's Daughter (L. Richmond) 167
Dana, C.A. 101, 217*ch8n*1
David Copperfield (Dickens) 167
Davis, Jefferson 198–99, 207, 211
"dead boat" 65, **66**
dead lines 29, 187
Deaderick, Pvt. Inslee (Confederate) 105, 111
deserters, Union 17, 19–20, 21–22, 36–37, 144, 199; *see also* Company Q; convicts; punishment
detectives 36
Dietz, Lt. St. Louis (Union) 161–62, 177, 219*n*11, 220*con.n*10
diarrhea 82, 90, 92, 107, 120–27, 129–31, 133, 136, 146–47, 152, 157, 185, 221*con.n*29
disinfectant 69, 89–90, 132, 191
division chiefs 160–61, 187
Drummond Light 35,
Duke, Col. Basil (Confederate) 189
Dunglison, Robley 113, 115

SS *Eagle* 183
Eames, Surgeon William M. (Union) 22, 32, 51–52, 78, 158, 166, 224
Early, Gen. Jubal (Confederate) 167, 177, 208–9
11th MD Infantry 34
Elmira, New York 140, 142, 143, 145, 185, 190, 193–94, 195
Emancipation Proclamation 180
Emley, Ann W. 101, 102, 167, 169, 170, 171, 210
erysipelas 121, 125, 146
escapes 22, 29–36, 69, 91, 112, 146, 169, 187–91, 208, 215*n*67, 217*n*19, 217*ch8n*3, 220*n*8; *see also* punishment
exchanges 72, 105, 151, 160, 166, 175–76, 191, 192, 208, 210
executions 17–18, 26, 145, 146

fence 6, 34–35, 70, 77, 83, 111, 159, 185, 201
Fetzer, Dale 3, 194
5th DE Infantry 34
5th MD Infantry 34

Finley, Lt. G. W. (Confederate) 113, 115
1st DE Heavy Artillery *see* Ahl's Battery
1st Eastern Shore Regiment (MD) 34
Fletcher, Pvt. William I. (Union) 22, 32, 38, 74–75, 77–78, 156–57, 166, 224
folate 52–53
Form 1 47
Form 2 41, 55, 64, 65
Form 10 10
Form 16 65–66
Form 36 24
Fort DuPont 202
Fort Miles 202
Fort Monroe 156, 183
Fort Mott 202
Franklin, Sgt. James H. (Confederate) 30, 82–83, 89, 170, 224

"galvanized rebels" 26, 37, 77
gambling 169, **173**, 219*n*34
Geneva Convention 220*n*2
Gettysburg, Battle of 19, 88, 107–8, 177, 185, 205
Gibbon and Pope (book) 167
Gibson, Capt. Augustus A. (Union) 13, 72, 102
Gibson, Lt. Col. John Alexander (Confederate) 75, 80, 84, 89, 98, 159–61, 163–64, 177–79, 224
Gillespie, J.M. 2, 136
Goddard, Surgeon Charles E. (Union) 14, 70, 106, 112, 158, 165, 184
Grant, Lt. Gen. Ulysses S. (Union) 177, 182, 220*con.n*12, 220*con.n*18
guards *see* sentries

Halleck, Maj. Gen. Henry (Union) 45, 193, 220*n*2
Hamilton, Pvt. Alexander James (Union) 16, 20, 22, 30, 31, 37, 51, 54, 57, 78–80, 94, 134, 150, 154, **155**, 156–58, 195, 198, 207, 210*ch*11*n*3, 224
Hammond, Surgeon Gen. William A. (Union) 92, 112, 113
Handy, the Rev. Isaac W. K **6**, 20, 22, 23, 30–32, 35–38, 49–51, 77, 79, 82–90, 95–96, 98, 100–3, 107–8, 113, 135, 161–67, 169–72, 188–89, 194, 205–9, 219*ch*11*n*8, 219*n*35, 220*n*8, 224
hanging-by-thumbs *see* punishment
hard tack *see* bread
Harper's 155
Harrison, Burton (Confederate) 199–200, 221*n*13
Hawes, Lt. Samuel Horace (Confederate) 171, 224
Hawkins, 1st Lt. Charles (Union) 14, **15**, 21–22, 96, 188, 200
Hesseltine, W.B. 1–2, 192
The History of England (McCauley) 155

A History of the Protestant Reformation in England and Ireland (W. Cobbett) 167
History of the Reformation of the 16th Century (D'Aubigne) 167
History of the United States (Bancroft) 155
Hitchcock, Maj. Gen. Ethan A. (Union) 88–89
Hoffman, Col. William (Union) *see* CGP
Holt, Gen. Joseph (Union) 12–13, 168, 192, 199–200
hostages 20, 156

Immortal 600 151, 206–7, 210
inflammation of the lungs 121–26, 133–35, 146–47, 152, 195
inspections 44, 83, 86–89, 107, 110, 127, 134, 148, 157–58, 161, 164, 185, 187, 220*n*6
Irvine, Lt. Col. William (Union) 79, 88–89

Jefferson, Julia 102–3, 184
jewelry 35, 167, **168**, 187–88
Johnson, Andrew 179, 221*n*3
Johnson, [medical inspector] (Union) 87, 89
Johnson's Island Prison Camp 77, 103, 141–42, 150, 190, 193–94
Johnston, Gen. Albert Sidney (Confederate) 199
Johnston, Gen. Joseph E. (Confederate) 177, 179, 211
Johnston, Col. Preston (Confederate) 199

Kernstown, Battle of 72
Kinckle, Frank (Confederate) 161–62
knives 35, 49, 90, 95, 116–20, **168**, 217*n*19

Lank, Pvt. William D. (Union) 95, 157, 224
laundry 85–86, 88, 91, 97, 100, 120, 159, 163, **173**, 218*ch9n*2
Lebanon Advertiser 21
Lee, Gen. Robert E. (Confederate) 177
Lee, Surgeon William D. (Union) 112, 128–36
Leftwich, 2nd Lt. Andrew J. (Confederate) **8**, **76**, **176**
Lenny, William C. (Confederate) 103
Letterman, Dr. Jonathan 82
letters 68–69, 97, 160, 164, 172, 184, 188, 194, 199, 209; *see also* Union letters and diaries
Lincoln, Abraham 18–21, 29, 101, 162, 167, 177, 179–80, 206–7, 211, 220*n*2
"Lost Cause" 2, 220*con.n*11, 222*n*5

MacConnell, Lt. John G. (Union) 103
Mackie, Kevin P. 32–33

mail 2, 94, 160–62, 177, 187, **189**, 194, 219*n*31
SS *Major Reybold* 156
malaria 6, 92, 120–23, 125–27, 131–33, 136–37, 146–49, 152, 185
Manchester, Thomas R. (Confederate) 166, 219*n*25
Mauck, Lt. Joseph W. (Confederate) 35, 36, 80, 86, 89, 104, 151, 161–64, 172, 177, 180, 183, 209–11, 224
McConnell, Lt. J.J. (Union) 184
McCrory, 2nd Lt. James L. (Confederate) 31, 36, 49, 84, 86, 89, 98, 135, 162, 163–64, 166, 171, 208, 224
Mckey, Lt. James Taswell, (Confederate) 20, 30, 31–32, 35–36, 49, 50, 75, 79, 80, 84, 86, 89, 95–96, 162–64, 166, 167, 171, 208–10, 224
McMichael, Capt. James Robert (Confederate) 82, 85, 89, 96, 164, 166, 178, 180, 183, 208–11, 224
McMichael, Lt. Col. Paul Agalus (Confederate) 75, 161, 164, 171–72, 177, 180, 198, 210–11, 224
meat 40, 41–46, 47, **48**, 49–53, 56, 59–61, 63–64, 95, 182–83, 187, 208, 210
medical inspections 69, 79, 87–89, 127–28, 190
medical records 110–11
Meigs, QM Gen. Montgomery (Union) 72
miasma 92–93, 110, 127, 128, 149, 185; *see also* catarrh; cholera morbus; diarrhea; erysipelas; malaria; smallpox; yellow fever
Middle District 11, 21, 27, 109
Les Misérables (Hugo) 155
Mitchell, Dr. S. Weir 85, 107
Mlotkowski, Capt. Stanislaus (Union) 11, **15**, 198
U.S.S. *Moccasin* 36
Morton, Capt. John P. (Confederate) 80, 86, 89, 208–9, 224
Mowday, Bruce 3, 196
mud 5, 86, 185

Neugas, Pvt. Max Neugas (Confederate) **8**, **18**, 49, 172, **173**, **189**
newspapers 155, 160–61, 167, 180, 189; *see also Baltimore American and Commercial Advertiser*; *Lebanon Advertiser*; *Philadelphia Bulletin*; *Philadelphia Inquirer*; *Philadelphia Press*; *Philadelphia Times*; *Prison Times*; *Richmond Whig*; *Washington Evening Star*
niacin 52–53
9th DE Infantry 34
Nugent, Surgeon George Washington (Union) 31, 52, 106, 111, 115, 121, 135, 158, 224

oath of allegiance 24–26, 28, 74, 101, 159, 164, 178–80, 181–83, 187, 200, 205, 210–11, 221*con.n*21

157th Ohio Infantry 34, 158
165th NY Infantry 34
196th PA Infantry 34
SS *Osceola* **8**, 84
Ould, Mr. 89

Paddock, William H. (Union) 112, 169
Park, Capt. Ralph Emory (Confederate) 37, 75, 85, 90–91, 111, 161, 163–64, 166, 177, 180, 205–6, 210–11, 222*n*5, 224
Parker, C.H. **114**
Parson of the Islands (Adam Wallace) 167
Penrose, Capt. C. B. (Union) 44–47, 50–51
permits (clothing) 101–2, 160, 194
Peters, 1st Sgt. Scott (Confederate) 30, 83, 164–65, 167, 170, 224
petitions (for release) 26, 187–88
Philadelphia, Pennsylvania 3, 11, 36, 46, 76, 78, 155–56, 170, 183, 198
Philadelphia Bulletin 108
Philadelphia Inquirer 73, 161, 167, 209
Philadelphia Press 16–17, 19, 73, 215*n*17
Philadelphia Times 70
pneumonia *see* inflammation of lungs
Point Lookout Prison Camp 102–3, 141–42, 171, 175, 183, 193, 205
Police Gazette 155
political prisoners 19, 23–24, 77, 79, 94, 109, 214*ch*3*n*2; *see also* Handy, the Rev. Isaac W.K
potatoes 47, 49, 51, 53–54, 64, 95, 112, 115–16, 118–20, 122, 133–34, 159, 160, 216*ch*5*n*20, 220*con.n*13
POW diaries 224; *see also* Alburtis, Pvt. William B. (Confederate); Allen, Lt. John C. (Confederate); Barringer, Brig. Gen. Rufus (Confederate); Berkeley, Pvt. Henry Robinson (Confederate); Bingham, Capt. Robert (Confederate); Boyle, Lt. Francis A. (Confederate); Cox, Lt. E. L. (Confederate); Franklin, Sgt. James H. (Confederate); Gibson, Lt. Col. John Alexander (Confederate); Hawes, Lt. Samuel Horace (Confederate); Mauck, Lt. Joseph W. (Confederate); McCrory, 2nd Lt. James L. (Confederate); Mckey, Lt. James Taswell, (Confederate); McMichael, Capt. James Robert (Confederate); McMichael, Lt. Col. Paul Agalus (Confederate); Morton, Capt. John P. (Confederate); Park, Capt. Ralph Emory (Confederate); Peters, 1st Sgt. Scott (Confederate); Purvis, Sgt. Joseph Edward (Confederate); Shotwell, Lt. Randolph Abbott (Confederate); Ward, Col. William Walker (Confederate)
Prison Fund 57–71, 89, 115, 190–91, 193–95, 201, 216*ch*5*n*20
Prison Times 163, 167, 169, 219*n*10
punishment 21–23, 36–38, **37**, **38**, 157, 162, 187–88: hanging-by-thumbs **37**, 188; wearing the barrel 37, **38**, 161, 188; *see also* convicts; deserters; executions; political prisoners
Purnell Legion 34, 109
Purvis, Sgt. Joseph Edward (Confederate) 30, 39, 80, 82–83, 85, 163, 166–67, 170

rations 2, 39–56, 100, 115–20, 145, 150, 153, 157, 159, 161–62, 165, 174, 181, 184, 187, 191–94, 199, 208, 220*con.n*14, 224; *see also* Prison Fund
rats 70, 201, 206, 209
recruiting 17, 22, 26–27, 102, 198
recruits 13, 16–17
"retaliation" 2, 62, 144–45, 151, 164, 191, 192–96, 197
Richmond Whig 180, 187
The Rise of the Dutch Republic (J.L. Motley) 167
Rock Island, Illinois 141–43, 194
rolls (of POWs) 17, 24–25, 162, 175, 179, 181–82, 190

Sanders, C.W. 2
Schneck, Maj. Gen. Robert C. (Union) 11, 18, 109
Schoepf, Brig. Gen. Albin (Union) 10, 12–13, **13**, 155, 158, 186–90, 197, 201, 221*n*21; assessments and descriptions 107, 112, 186–90, 192, 197, 209, 219*n*35, 220*con.n*11, 221*Ep.n*22; correspondence with CGP (Hoffman) 11, 23–28, 31, 33–36, 45, 47, 54, 69–71, 73–74, 81, 86, 89, 95–96, 102, 108–9, 151, 164–66, 175, 180, 182, 186, 190–91, 199, 201, 216*ch*6*n*18, 217*n*19; correspondence with Secretary of War 23, 26–27, 83, 109, 180, 190, 199; duties of 11–12, 15, 20–21, 23, 28, 65, 86, 91, 107, 172, 180, 195; and orders 13, 16, 22–24, 27–29, 58, 86, 96, 112, 175, 180, 182, 201, 215*n*40, 220*n*8; other communications 14, 16–18, 22–24, 26–28, 30, 36, 76, 86–87, 101, 104, 106, 109, 112, 161, 170, 175, 180, 184, 186–87, 198, 208; and personnel 12, 14, 165–66, 168–69, 192, 200
Schoepf, Julia 12, 158, 168–69, 187, 220*con.n*11
scurvy 45, 53–54, 64, 92, 122–28, 132–36, 146, 149–51, 152–53, 191, 195, 215*n*36, 215*n*40, 218*n*31, 221*con.n*29
sentries 3, 12, **13**, 16–17, 22, 24, 29–38, 69–70, 74, 78, 91, 96, 154, **155**, 156–57, 160, 164, 167, **173**,

187, 189–90, 199, 208–9, 211, 217*ch*8*n*3
Sharp, Richard 109
Shearer, Maj. George (Confederate) 23, 208
Sheridan, Gen. Philip H. (Union) 177, 209
Sherman, Gen. William Tecumseh (Union) 177, 210
Shotwell, Lt. Randolph Abbott (Confederate) **76**, *176*; diary 205–11, 217*pref.n*11, 222*n*2, 222*n*3
Silliman, Asst. Surgeon Henry Ridgway (Union) 14, 86, 106–7, 109–10, 188, 192
sinks (privies) **8**, 29, 31, 34–35, 87–88, 90–91, 186, 194, 209
6th DE Infantry 34
6th MA Veteran Volunteers 34, 156
smallpox 69, 92, 110, 113, 122–23, 125–27, 135–36, 146, 148, 187, 191, 210, 218*n*32, 220*con.n*15
soap 40, 43, 45–47, 51, 60–62, 64, 85, 95, 116–20, 160, 163, 216*ch*5*n*20
Southern Historical Society Papers 1–2
Stanton, Edwin 12, 21, 23–24, 26–28, 34, 36, 70, 72–73, 83, 95, 101–2, 109, 165–66, 175, 186, 190, 192, 193–94, 197–99
steamboat to Philadelphia 28, 46, 167
sugar 40, 41–46, 59–60, 63–64, 70, 95, 99, 101, 114–16, 118, 119–20, 160, 191
surgeons (medical doctors) 78, 93, 105–6, 107–10, 152, 158, 184, 190, 198; *see also* Arrott, Dr. Colin;
Clark, Surgeon A.M.; Crane, Surgeon C.H.; Cuyler, Surgeon John Meck; Eames, Surgeon William M.; Goddard, Surgeon Charles E.; Lee, Surgeon William D.; medical inspections; medical records; Nugent, Surgeon George Washington; Silliman, Asst. Surgeon Henry Ridgway; Taylor, Surgeon A.C.
sutler **15**, 50, 79, 94–97, 100–1, 134, 151, 159–60, 165–68, 188, 194, 199, 209, 217*ch*8*n*1

C.S.S. *Tallahassee* 16
Taylor, Surgeon A.C. (Union) **114**
Temple, Brian 3, 196
Tevis, Charles C. (Union)
Thanksgiving 52, 157
3rd Maryland Cavalry 27
Thompson, Gen. M. Jeff (Confederate) 168, 189
thumbs, hung by *see* punishment
toothbrushes 86, 94
Trenton, New Jersey 3, 11
trinkets *see* jewelry
201st PA Infantry 34
215st PA Infantry 34

Union letters and diaries 224; *see also* Crumrine, Sgt. Bishop (Union); Eames, Surgeon William M. (Union); Fletcher, Pvt. William I. (Union); Hamilton, Pvt. Alexander James (Union); Lank, Pvt. William D. (Union); Nugent, Surgeon George Washington (Union)
United States Sanitary Commission 1

Vance, Gen. Robert B. (Confederate) 103, 168, 171, 207, 210, 221*Ep.n*22
Vandereedt, John 39–40,
vegetables, desiccated 45, 54–55, 191, 216*ch*5*n*20
visitors, civilian 28
vitamin A 52–54
vitamin C 52–55, 122, 134, 153

Wade, B.F. 193
The War of the Rebellion: A Compilation of the Official Records of the Union and Confederate Armies 3
"war psychosis" 2, 192
Ward, Col. William Walker (Confederate) 205, 224
washing (clothes) *see* laundry
washing (personal) *see* bathing
Washington Evening Star 221*Ep.n*22
Watson, P.H. 102
Way, the Rev. Elon J. (Union) 14, 220*con.n*10
wearing the barrel *see* punishment
Wessels, Brig. Gen. Henry W. (Union) 54, 190, 220*con.n*13
whiskey 65, 70, 116–20, 156, 166
whitewashing 87–89, 164
Wilmington, Delaware 3, 9, 11, 155–56, 183, 186
Wolf, 1st Lt. Abraham G. (Union) 14, **15**, 36, 80, 161, 170, 188–89, 208
Woodward, Joseph Janvier 92, 128–30, 132, 133, 136, 152, 215*n*36

yellow fever 6, 92
Young, Capt. John J. (Union) 11, 198

www.ingramcontent.com/pod-product-compliance
Lightning Source LLC
Chambersburg PA
CBHW081553300426
44116CB00015B/2862